Public Health Systems in the Age of Financialization

Studies in Critical Social Sciences Book Series

Haymarket Books is proud to be working with Brill Academic Publishers (www.brill.nl) to republish the *Studies in Critical Social Sciences* book series in paperback editions. This peer-reviewed book series offers insights into our current reality by exploring the content and consequences of power relationships under capitalism, and by considering the spaces of opposition and resistance to these changes that have been defining our new age. Our full catalog of *SCSS* volumes can be viewed at https://www.haymarketbooks .org/series_collections/4-studies-in-critical-social-sciences.

Public Health Systems in the Age of Financialization

Lessons from the Center and the Periphery

Ana Carolina Cordilha

Haymarket Books
Chicago, IL

Published in paperback in 2024 by
Haymarket Books
P.O. Box 180165
Chicago, IL 60618
773-583-7884
www.haymarketbooks.org

ISBN: 979-8-88890-243-1

Distributed to the trade in the US through Consortium Book Sales and
Distribution (www.cbsd.com) and internationally through Ingram Publisher
Services International (www.ingramcontent.com).

This book was published with the generous support of Lannan Foundation,
Wallace Action Fund, and the Marguerite Casey Foundation.

Special discounts are available for bulk purchases by organizations and
institutions. Please call 773-583-7884 or email info@haymarketbooks.org for more
information.

Cover design by Jamie Kerry and Ragina Johnson.

Printed in the United States.

Library of Congress Cataloging-in-Publication data is available.

Contents

PART 2
From Theory to Practice: How Financialization Reshapes Public Health Systems

3   The French System
Pioneering Financialized Strategies in PHS   121

Acknowledgments

This book is a revised version of my thesis entitled "Public Health Systems in the Age of Financialization: Lessons from France and Brazil", carried out at Sorbonne Paris Nord University from 2016 to 2022. Walking this life-changing path was only possible because of those who led the way and those who stood by my side during these years.

First, I am greatly indebted to Professor Lena Lavinas for the decade of continuous exchanges and collaboration that has taught me more than any book ever could. I am grateful for her generosity and unwavering support, and her guidance as the co-director of the thesis. I also thank Prof. David Flacher, the Ph.D. director, who trusted in my potential as a researcher and provided valuable feedback along the way.

I am grateful for the privilege of having some of the authors that sparked my interest in the topic as the members of my thesis committee, and who yielded invaluable insights for this and future research during my defense: Ben Fine, Ève Chiapello, Ewa Karwowski, Susan Murray, Cédric Durand, and Nathalie Coutinet. I extend these thanks to other brilliant minds I met during the elaboration of the thesis and who had a major influence on different parts of what later became this book. I am particularly thankful to Robert Guttmann, Benjamin Lemoine, Camila Arza, Kate Bayliss, Denise Gentil, Francisco Funcia, José Sestelo, and José Gomes Temporão for their time and generosity. The same goes for my colleagues in the research groups *Financeirização e Política Social* at the Federal University of Rio de Janeiro and *Capitalisme Sanitaire* at Sorbonne Paris Nord University.

I must also express my sincere appreciation to the members of the *Centre d'Économie de l'Université Paris Nord* (CEPN) research lab and the INSPIRE project, which provided the necessary funding for undertaking this endeavor.

Last but not least, I owe a special thanks to those who gave me the emotional support I needed for everything else to come about. My family and *parceros* were an incredible network of mutual support and encouragement throughout, for which I am forever grateful. Cecilia Rikap deserves a special mention for her close presence despite the physical distance, always showing up when I needed her most. The same goes for Robson Cruz, Robert Ross, and Arnaldo Neto, who helped me during difficult periods of the thesis with empathy and wisdom.

My acknowledgments would not be complete without a special mention to Jeffrey Althouse. I was lucky to share this journey with a person of great intelligence and a huge heart, who was there for me during the highs and lows of this process. I am thankful for his patience in reading my work and for his calm presence, holding me tight whenever the wind blew too hard.

Figures and Tables

Figures

Tables

Acronyms

ACOSS	Agence Centrale des Organismes de Sécurité Sociale (Central Agency of Social Security Organizations)
AMELI	Assurance Maladie
ANFIP	Associação Nacional dos Auditores Fiscais da Receita Federal (National Association of Fiscal Auditors of the Federal Internal Revenue Service)
AP-HP	Assistance Publique – Hôpitaux de Paris
CADES	Caisse d'Amortissement de la Dette Sociale (Social Debt Amortization Fund)
CCSS	Commission des Comptes de la Sécurité Sociale
CGU	Controladoria Geral da União (Office of the Comptroller General)
CRDS	Contribution au Remboursement de la Dette Sociale (Contribution for the Reimbursement of the Social Debt)
CSG	Contribution Sociale Generalisée (General Social Contribution)
DF	Distrito Federal (Federal District)
DREES	Direction de la Recherche, des Études, de l'Évaluation et des Statistiques
DRU	Desvinculação de Receitas da União (Unbinding of Union Revenues)
ECB	European Central Bank
ERJ	Estado do Rio de Janeiro (Estado do Rio de Janeiro)
FES	Fundo Estadual de Saúde (State Health Fund)
FMS	Fundo Municipal de Saúde (Municipal Health Fund)
FNAS	Fundo Nacional de Assistência Social (National Social Assistance Fund)
FNS	Fundo Nacional de Saúde (National Health Fund)
IBGE	Instituto Brasileiro de Geografia e Estatistica (Brazilian Institute of Geography and Statistics)
IMF	International Monetary Fund
IPC	Indice des Prix à la Consommation (Consumer Price Index)
IPCA	Índice de Preços ao Consumidor – Amplo (Consumer Price Index)
OF	Orçamento Fiscal (Fiscal Budget)
OSS	Orçamento da Seguridade Social (Social Security Budget)
PHS	Public Health Systems
PFI	Private Finance Initiatives
PPP	Public-Private Partnerships
SEF	Secretaria de Estado de Fazenda (State Department of Finance)
SES	Secretaria Estadual de Saúde (State Health Secretariat)
SFC	Secretaria Federal de Controle Interno (Federal Internal Control Secretariat)
SIB	Social Impact Bonds
SMS	Secretaria Municipal de Saúde (Municipal Health Secretariat)
SNA	Sistema Nacional de Auditoria (National Auditing System)

STN   Secretaria de Tesouro Nacional (National Treasury Secretariat)
SUS   Sistema Único de Saúde (Unified Health System)
TCU   Tribunal de Contas da União (Federal Court of Accounts)
UHC   Universal Health Coverage
WHO   World Health Organization

Introduction

Public health systems are undergoing a silent revolution with detrimental impacts on social justice and democracy. Historically, public health services and infrastructure were funded directly by public revenues from taxes and contributions. This model no longer holds entirely true. In the era of financialized capitalism, governments in general and health systems in particular are increasingly inclined to bring in money from the financial sector through ever-new channels, while taxpayer money pays for the costs of this intermediation. In the process, the interests of financial players can be placed above those of citizens, in ways that are often hidden from the public eye.

This book addresses crucial yet overlooked changes in public health financing in the neoliberal period that are steered by the growing power of finance over the economy and society. To do so, it deploys a concept that has been far removed from research on public health systems up to now: financialization. Within the heterodox economic literature, the concept of financialization is associated with the unprecedented expansion of the financial sector in scale, scope, and power over the past several decades. Drawing from this literature, I examine how financial actors, instruments, and interests have reshaped the trajectory of two universal health systems over the past three decades, one in a central and one in a peripheral economy.

This book offers thus an original approach to assess PHS reforms in the period of neoliberal, financialized capitalism. Reassessing the trajectory of public health systems through the lens of financialization can shed light on a series of profound changes in their funding strategies. By bringing financialization into the analysis, it demonstrates that PHS have been reshaped in ways that support the expansion of the financial sector and the accumulation of financial capital. Building on the case studies of a central and a peripheral economy, it is also possible to understand how a country's position in global hierarchies of power influences how financialization will reshape the national health systems in each case.

The evidence presented throughout this book dispels a common myth in the health care literature: that the accelerated expansion of the financial sector over the past decades has completely transformed private health care provision while public systems passively watch this process unfold. I seek to show that public, universal health care systems themselves have also witnessed an increasing participation and influence of financial instruments, actors, and interests in their activities and decision-making processes. I contextualize this movement within the longstanding process of transformation of health care systems in the neoliberal era, as the resort to finance seems to be one of the different ways through which PHS have been managing to cope with the continuous austerity and restriction of public funds.

Neoliberal reforms in public health systems appear to undermine their capacity to meet the health care needs of the population, a fact that became startlingly clear during the COVID-19 pandemic. Therefore, it is critically important to understand the forces driving and benefitting from these reforms. This book contributes to this task by revealing how financial actors, instruments, and interests have been involved in the trajectory of public health systems over the past decades. I show that the apparent benefits that PHS can reap from such a turn toward finance are mostly a smokescreen, obscuring the political, economic, and social drawbacks arising from the increased dependence on financial capital.

1   The Conventional Approach to Examining Health Care Systems Change

When referring to public health systems (PHS), I refer to health systems financed by the government or another collective entity on a solidary basis, open to all residents of the country, and providing equal standards of services to all members of the society. Systems operating under such principles have a unique capacity to promote the universal right to health care – meaning that all individuals of a country are entitled to receive the health care services they need, irrespective of their individual capacity to pay. In the countries in which they exist, these systems represent the main gateway of access to services by the population. Moreover, they can mitigate the high inequalities and exclusions from access typically observed in countries dependent on private financing, offering services according to medical needs rather than the ability to pay. By providing the same services to all citizens, PHS can foster social equity like few other institutions in a country.

Several countries today have publicly organized systems following principles of universality, equity, solidarity, and comprehensive health care provision, under different institutional arrangements and at varying degrees of consolidation. Examples include England (*National Health Service*), France (*Assurance Maladie*), Italy (*Servizio Sanitario Nationale*), Canada (*Medicare*), Israel (*National Health Insurance*), Brazil (*Sistema Único de Saúde*), Costa Rica (*Caja Costarricense de Seguro Social*), and Cuba (*Sistema Nacional de Salud*), to mention a few. The relevance of PHS also transcends national frontiers, as these systems may serve as blueprints for other countries still in the quest for expanding and universalizing health care access.

Most countries today face ever-increasing challenges to meet the health care needs of the population, including those with established public and universal health care systems. Global trends in health care have been a cause for concern: according to the World Health Organization (WHO), by the end of the 2010s, at least half of the world population still lacked access to essential health services, and almost 100 million people per year were being pushed into extreme poverty due to health expenses (WHO, 2017). And the quest for universal access to health care seems no longer an issue reserved for low-and middle-income countries. In the OECD region, a relatively wealthy area where most countries are committed to providing comprehensive public health assistance, approximately 14% of the population reported that they had given up seeking medical care in 2016 due to the lack of income to cover the costs of services. Naturally, this hit the most vulnerable the hardest: among low-income individuals (those living in households with income below 50% of the national average), the share of the population with unmet health care needs due to financial costs reached 25% (OECD, 2017).

The importance of having proper access to care became strikingly clear during 2021, a watershed moment in recent history marked by the coronavirus (COVID-19) pandemic. By mid-2022, official statistics counted more than 6.2 million deaths directly associated with the disease (WHO, 2022) – and the real numbers are likely to be much higher. Unlike other modern pandemics, the coronavirus pandemic had devastating effects across low-, middle-, and high-income countries, revealing the dangers of not prioritizing investments in health care access and infrastructure on an ongoing basis. It also exposed the perverse distortions of the global pharmaceutical system, whose discoveries were put at the service of profit maximization rather than population health.

Trends such as those presented above suggest that, despite not having necessarily diminished in size and importance, PHS seem to be falling short in their capacity to meet the needs of the population. Such challenges are often explained in light of dramatic changes in public governance under the neoliberal paradigm. Neoliberalism emerged in the 1970s as a political project advocating in favor of policies that were supposed to be necessary for individual entrepreneurship and freedom to flourish. These included, first, policies for protecting private property rights and profits, and second, for promoting free financial markets and trade. Such objectives were placed above virtually all other policy goals (Yilmaz, 2017). Today, the term neoliberalism can be used broadly to refer to a set of economic and political ideas, as well as the policies, institutions, and practices accompanying these ideas, which advocate for unregulated markets and favor private capital (Fine and Saad-Filho, 2017).

The idea of comprehensive public health care has been under immense pressure since the neoliberal paradigm started taking over economic ideology and practice. Public health policies, and PHS in particular, can absorb a significant share of the public budget – one of the main arenas of political dispute in the neoliberal era. From the neoliberal lens of austerity and private market efficiency, public health expenditures represent a high and increasing burden on government accounts. A large share of PHS expenditures is considered a waste of resources funding supposedly inefficient service provision (André and Hermann, 2009; Bayliss, 2016; Maarse, 2006). France offers a recent and sound illustration of this state of affairs: in October 2017, the newly-appointed Minister of Health drew attention from the media by claiming that nearly one third of public spending on the French universal health system was "not pertinent", with significant "room for maneuver" for a "smooth revolution" (Le Journal du Dimanche, 2017). The following year, almost €2 billion were cut off from the system's main fund (La Tribune, 2018), accompanied by further cuts later on.

It is no surprise, then, that successive waves of neoliberal reforms over the past four decades have managed to significantly reshape modes of public health provision and financing according to neoliberal principles. There is a vast international literature demonstrating that health policy reforms worldwide are similarly informed by the neoliberal paradigm, while following specific paths in each case. These paths usually pass through measures to compress the wages of health professionals, cap hospital budgets, downsize or outsource public service provision, and introduce or increase co-payments for patients, to cite a few.

While neoliberal reforms do not necessarily eliminate public systems, evidence shows that they contribute to turning these systems into platforms for income-extraction activities for private capital – a point that will be expanded in the course of this book. In the process, these reforms undermine these systems' capacity to guarantee and expand quality health services for the population. Among the detrimental consequences of such measures, evidence from single and cross-country studies identifies that neoliberal reforms tend to deepen inequalities in access to health care, once the burden of health expenses is increasingly passed onto individuals and private insurers. They also find that, in most cases, these measures do not bring superior outcomes in terms of saving costs or improving efficiency for the public sector, deteriorating the quality and quantity of public services available to the population

(André et al., 2015; Böhm, 2017; Hassenteufel and Palier, 2007; Ortiz et al., 2015; Whitfield, 2015; Yilmaz, 2017).

The devastation caused by the COVID-19 pandemic has breathed new life into the debate on neoliberal reforms. It opened space to question how decades of continuous cuts and restrictions on these systems' financial, material, and human resources may have eroded their capacity to address the health crisis. Using a sample of 147 countries, Assa and Calderón (2020) show that higher rates of private health expenditure at the national level are associated with both higher prevalence and mortality rates related to COVID-19. The authors argue that the decades of austerity and reforms preceding the pandemic have contributed to reducing equipment and personnel in public systems, undermining countries' preparedness to fight the virus. Also, previous measures would have increased inequality in health care coverage, leading individuals to respond differently to the disease and making it more difficult to control it.

Popic (2020) reminds us that, as the hospitals that deliver costly specialized care in Europe are still predominantly public, one of the key cost-containment measures since the 1990s has been to reduce the number of hospital beds in the sector. The main targets of these measures were beds dedicated to treating severe and long-term conditions, which are more expensive to maintain than those for short-term stays. But these included the beds suited to treating the worse symptoms associated with COVID. In Italy, the number of acute care beds per 1,000 people dropped from 7 in 1990 to 2.6 in 2017 (Prante et al., 2020). In France, the number of long-term hospital beds fell by more than 50,000 since 2003 (DREES, 2019a), while the public hospital budget lost approximately €12 billion over the last decade (Petit, 2020). It is inconceivable to imagine that such types of cutbacks, similarly observed in several other countries, did not affect the capacity to fight the pandemic.

In light of the fact that neoliberal reforms in PHS seem far from over and do not seem to favor the population at large, since acting against universality and equity, it is important to ask ourselves: what are the pressures leading to transformations in public systems today? Who do they truly benefit? One may argue that the answers to these questions are not the same as those of nearly fifty years ago, when the first neoliberal reforms began reshaping public health policies.

Some ideas and concepts have been ritually cited to describe neoliberal reforms of public health systems over the past four decades. They include, most notably, the idea of austerity (pressures to limit public spending with social provision) and privatization (an "umbrella term" to account for trends pushing for a greater space of private activities in and out of the public sector). But the concepts we employ determine the changes we see. Without denying the relevance of such notions, they no longer seem sufficient to grasp the nature of present-day developments in public systems. Today, such a task requires acknowledging and investigating the role of one of the key processes driving transformations in neoliberal capitalism: financialization, or the unchecked expansion of the financial sector in size, scale, and power. This allows us to better understand the pressures leading to changes in public health systems today, the mechanisms through which they occur, and who benefits the most from them.

2   Incorporating the Concept of Financialization into Public Health Systems Research

One of the main points I seek to advance in this book is that the concepts commonly used to understand PHS reforms are no longer sufficient to capture the full extent of the drivers, characteristics, and impacts of such developments. It is hard to imagine how the colossal expansion of financial actors in the global economy over the past decades would not have a direct impact on the paths taken by PHS reforms.

There is mounting evidence that financial institutions and investors have been influencing public policy-making processes according to their interests. In reviewing the literature on financialization, one can find authors demonstrating the transformative effects of financialization on both ends of social provision. On the one hand, governments seem ever more reliant on financial instruments and institutions to finance and provide goods and services in areas associated with social rights (Chiapello, 2017; Karwowski, 2019); on the other, individuals are increasingly dependent on financial instruments and institutions to access them, largely encouraged by governments themselves (Fine, 2014; Lavinas, 2018b). Financialization trends in social provision are of particular concern in light of their potential to undermine principles of universality, equity, and solidarity. The expansion of financial capital in such areas pressures in favor of decisions that maximize returns and minimize risks for investors, often at the expense of increasing investments and expanding service provision (Bayliss, 2016; Fine, *op. cit.*; Lavinas and Gentil, 2018; Mulligan, 2016; Vural, 2017).

There is no *a priori* reason why this greater influence of finance over public policymaking wouldn't reach public health policy. Although existing research shows that financialization has been driving major transformations in how the public sector works, we know little about the mechanisms through which it has been reshaping public health systems. The investigations that apply the concept of financialization to understand changes in health care have been mainly focused on global health policies and private health activities, where changes driven by the financial sector can be more easily perceived (Hunter and Murray, 2019; Mulligan, 2016; Vural, 2017). As noted by Bayliss et al. (2016a), public services often remain free or highly subsidized at the point of access, making it more difficult for users and even policymakers to understand restructurings taking place due to the pressures of global finance. Studies looking at public health activities tend to focus on how this process would boost austerity measures, limiting the volume of funds available to public health policies (including PHS). There is also attention to specific points of the chain of provision, notably the phenomenal growth of private investments to build public infrastructure, including public hospitals (Bayliss and Waeyenberge, 2017; Fine, 2020; Loxley and Hajer, 2019).

In sum, the effects of financialization in PHS are almost always associated with austerity and cuts in public provision, which would consequently reduce the space these systems occupy in the economy and for society. And, at the same time, the growth of private activities in and out of public chains of provision would favor the financial actors involved in private health care. One can conclude, therefore, that PHS still seem to appear as mostly passive agents in the process of financialization of health, subsidizing and favoring the expansion of private, financialized health provision.

I argue that the impacts of financialization on PHS go beyond the developments described above. There are also internal restructuring processes that need to be taken into account. Public systems today do not only favor the expansion of financial capital by withdrawing coverage, which favors the private, financialized health sector. They also do so by resorting to financial actors and markets themselves.

PHS account for a significant, often the largest share of financial, material, and human resources for health care provision at the national level. This translates into large funding requirements and a vast existing infrastructure with the potential to grow further. They need money and investment, and public funds seem increasingly insufficient to cover these financing requirements. This is where financial players come in. Banks, financial institutions, and investors more broadly are willing to cover financing gaps, build infrastructure, and any other activity in PHS that may provide them with financial profits. They are likely to be interested in investing in and lending to PHS (or the government agencies that finance the latter), benefitting from government incentives and the secure flows of public revenue that cover investment returns. Therefore, there are sound reasons to argue that PHS also play an active role in the process of financialization of health, turning to financial markets, institutions, and investors to continue operating. It is important to understand the mechanisms through which this occurs and explore the inherent contradictions between, on the one hand, the goal of financing public health, and, on the other, the choice of using financial capital to achieve it.

Reassessing the trajectory of PHS from the fresh theoretical background of financialization represents a relatively new approach in relation to the existing literature on health systems change, as explained next.

3   Research Design

This book offers a fresh reading of the path of public health systems in the neoliberal period by specifically incorporating financialization into the analysis of their recent trajectory. It interrogates how financial actors, instruments, and interests have reshaped these systems over the past decades, and what are some of the main consequences of such developments. It answers these questions by combining a theoretical discussion with an original empirical analysis of real-world systems.

The arguments in this book are informed by critical research on financialization, one of the most prominent areas of study within political economy today. I understand financialization as a multifaceted process involving the growing size of finance in the global economy, its expansion in scope, and its progressive concentration of wealth and power relative to other actors (Gabor, 2018; see Mader et al., 2020 for a review). This open approach is important when seeking to grasp the channels and impacts of financialization in public health systems, where these cannot be predicted in advance. Emphasis is placed on contributions from scholars within the Marxist school, bringing in contributions from other heterodox schools such as the Post-Keynesian and the French regulationist ones to enrich the discussion.

The main underlying assumption of this book, that financialization will change the inner workings of PHS, finds extensive support in the strand of the financialization literature concerned with the public sector. I refer, more specifically, to the research on the financialization of the State (Karwowski, 2019; Pagliari and Young, 2020; Schwan et al., 2020; Wang, 2015, 2020) and the financialization of public policies (Chiapello, 2017). This is a flourishing field of study dedicated to examining the ways in which finance has been altering the internal structures of the public sphere. The research on the financialization of the public sector stands out by showing that, beyond facilitating the expansion of financial markets through regulatory shifts, States and public entities have been actively participating in financial markets and resorting to the financial sector to finance and provide the goods and services still under their responsibility.

Once PHS belong to the public sector and are responsible for funding and delivering public services, the literature on public sector financialization provides the basis to argue that such systems will be restructured in light of the financialization process. Drawing from this body of knowledge, I propose an original way to conceptualize and investigate how this unfolds in the case of PHS. This method draws from the organizational framework proposed by Karwowski (2019) to investigate the process of State financialization, which she defines as the increasing influence of financial logics, instruments, markets, and accumulation strategies over public institutions and policies. Her framework identifies different types of policies leading public bodies to adopt financial logics, engage with financial innovations, and deploy strategies for financial accumulation. In doing so, it acknowledges that the policies leading to State financialization, defined in the terms above, may vary significantly from one country to another. In the realm of fiscal policy, financialization trends arise may come as a result of policy shifts in the revenue side (how public entities raise funds), with measures that transform public entities into active market players and make them engage with financial innovations. They can also derive from changes on the expenditure side of fiscal policy (how public entities spend these revenues), through policies that allow public provision to become the basis for the creation of financial assets. In the realm of monetary policy, the transformation of the State in line with the financialization process seems to come most often via inflation-targeting policies and actions focused on short-term liquidity management, which preserve the value of financial assets.

Considering the strong ties between the notions of State and PHS, I draw from this approach to devise a method to investigate the latter. Applying Karwowski's methodology to the present research object, the financialization in PHS is conceptualized here as the changed relationship between these systems and financial markets and practices, with the increasing influence of financial logics, instruments, markets, and accumulation strategies in their activities. I applied this methodology to reassess the past trajectory of two PHS, in France and Brazil, looking for changes in both the realms of fiscal and monetary policy in each country leading these systems to become more dependent on financial capital. More specifically, I reassess the path of transformations in fiscal and monetary policy in each country from 1990 to 2018 to examine policy shifts leading the national PHS to adopt financial logics, engage with financial instruments, and participate in financial accumulation strategies. The choice for this period is justified as the 1990s decade marks the beginning of the era in which both the processes of neoliberal reforms in PHS and the financialization of the world economy accelerated (André and Hermann, 2009; Fine and Saad-Filho, 2017). I then follow a mixed-method approach combining quantitative and qualitative information to examine the most significant shifts that stand out during the investigation.

I focus on investigating policy shifts in the side of revenues, which includes not only the volume of funds entering the system but also who provided them, and at what costs and conditions. This is the most straightforward way to apprehend how financial capital has been increasing its participation and influence within PHS. I organize the discussion by systematizing the advance of financialized policies in three key areas: long-term financing (strategies that affect the system's financing over the years), short-term financing (strategies for managing funds within the fiscal year), and the financing of service providers (strategies to fund hospitals working for the system).

Figure 1 below illustrates how the framework on State financialization mentioned above serves as a guiding point for elaborating the research method applied for PHS.

Another strand of the financialization literature informing the research is that of subordinate and peripheral financialization, which shows that this process tends to take on distinct traits across both the high-income center and lower-income peripheral countries. Indeed, the findings of this book are in line with those from earlier works on peripheral financialization. While the case study of the high-income country shows that the PHS started to engage in financial markets as an active player, the PHS of the middle-income country has been mostly tied to financial capital via a permanent, high interest debt burden.

4   The Case for Country Studies

To develop the idea of financialization in PHS, I combine a theoretical discussion with an empirical investigation of two countries with universal public systems. Considering that PHS follow distinctive arrangements in each place and function within unique social, political, and economic backgrounds, country studies seem the most appropriate way to capture the complexity of the phenomenon we seek to apprehend. The countries selected for an in-depth analysis were France and Brazil, precisely because of the major differences between them.

France is a core country with a health system of the social insurance type. The French system was once considered the best in the world by the World

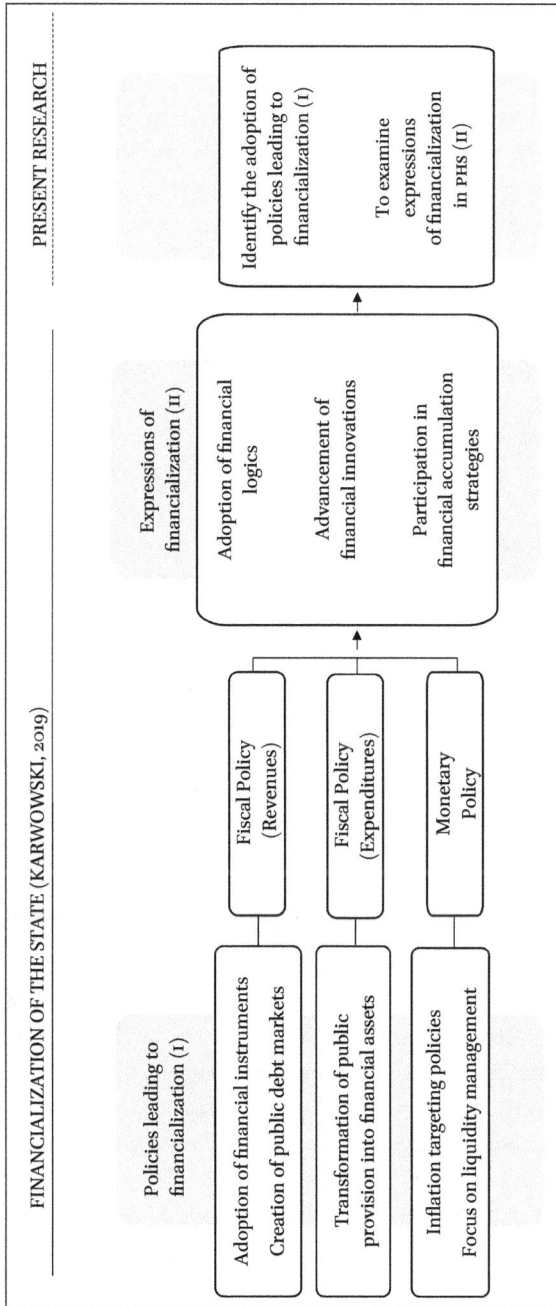

FIGURE 1 Empirical framework: typologies of state financialization and application for Public Health Systems (PHS)

SOURCE: AUTHOR'S ELABORATION BASED ON KARWOWSKI (2019)

Health Organization (WHO, 2000). At the same time, it also seems to be in the lead when it comes to implementing financialized strategies to run the system, which reach a degree of complexity unseen in other countries. Brazil, for its part, is a peripheral country with a health system of the national health service type. The Brazilian PHS is considered the largest system in the world in terms of population coverage, as more than 200 million people are entitled to use the system. Different from core countries, the Brazilian system was subjected to the pressures of financialization since its early years. Its creation at the end of the 20th century represents a milestone in the history of public health, going against worldwide trends toward restricting public intervention taking place at that time. Meanwhile, the attempts to consolidate the system over the next years took place when neoliberalism (and financialization) was already in full swing.

It is of great interest to study how these different dynamics will play out. On the one hand, both countries are committed to providing universal health care for the population. On the other, they are at different stages of economic development and their health systems work differently – one under the logic of social insurance, and the other under the logic of direct service provision. This choice of countries offers thus a particularly valuable combination to gain further understanding of the process of financialization in PHS. More than a comparative study, looking at the French and Brazilian systems allows us to apprehend simultaneous yet different trajectories toward financialization. It can demonstrate the global reach of the process of financialization in PHS, proving that this process is not restricted to the realm of wealthy countries with developed financial systems. In particular, examining these countries offers insights into how a country's position as a core or peripheral economy may influence how the process of financialization impacts its PHS.

Focusing on certain countries and dimensions gives us the ability to capture dynamics that would be nearly impossible to grasp using less specific approaches. Even so, there are major challenges in obtaining high-quality data for financial investments and instruments in the context of PHS. The reasons for this are many, from transparency problems and methodologies ill-suited to capturing this kind of information to outdated and conflicting databases. In cases where the available information was considered deficient, I opted for analyzing the data during relatively short periods of time but for which there was reliable information. Appendix 1 contains details on further data sources and adjustments.

The findings reveal that, together with policy shifts that have been cutting public revenues (through austerity) and bringing in private service providers (through privatization), there is also a lesser-known but equally important trend of bringing revenues from the financial system into PHS financing and diverting the latter's revenues back to the financial system (which are better explained through the concept of financialization). Based on these findings, I take a critical stance on policy options that expand the participation and influence of finance within public health systems. I argue that financialized policies turn public systems into vehicles of income concentration, decrease the stability of funding, and hinder civil society participation. In this way, they undermine some of the principles that constitute the very reasons for public health systems to exist.

The research presented in this book offers the first systematic investigation of the influence of the process of financialization in PHS across different countries. In particular, it provides an in-depth analysis of a central and a peripheral economy, with original data compiled for this investigation. The findings of the empirical chapters provide solid evidence against the widespread but mistaken belief that comprehensive systems of public provision are somehow shielded from the process of financialization.

This discussion is of potential interest to those interested in public health, for which it provides a greater understanding of its evolution and challenges in contemporary capitalism. It provides vital inputs for understanding not only the direction that public health systems have been taking but also their challenges ahead, since these systems are likely to be increasingly encouraged to turn toward the financial sector to address funding problems arising from austerity policies, pandemics, and all manner of other crises. The book can also serve those working with social policies more broadly, since the developments described here illustrate a transformation in the logic of financing social provision that may also be seen in other areas. Finally, for those interested in the topic of financialization, this book offers insights into how financial processes unfold in ways that have remained largely unexplored.

5   Structure of the Book

The book is structured into two parts. The first part grounds the research in the existing literature and suggests how to address research gaps related to financialization and public health systems. It provides answers to some key and still open questions, such as: what does it mean to say that a public health system is undergoing a process of "financialization"? How to examine this in practice? And how to contextualize events related to financialization within the long-standing path of health system change in the neoliberal era?

To answer these questions, Chapter 1 discusses how the existing knowledge on financialization can contribute to refining our approach to health systems change. It starts with a description of the inner workings of finance and financial institutions to explain why financial actors and instruments are likely to be interested in participating in public structures of financing and provision. I then introduce the critical scholarship on financialization, which allows us to assess this process from a critical perspective. After a general presentation, I focus on two strands of the financialization literature that are vital to the present discussion: first, I look at the regional question, differentiating processes of financialization in central and periphery countries; next, I consider the sectoral question, discussing the existing research on how this process reshapes social provision. I build on works presented in this section to suggest a way to define and empirically investigate how financialization reshapes public health systems.

Chapter 2 bridges the discussions between financialization, on the one hand, and health system change, on the other. It clarifies why financialization represents a distinctive type of reform in public health systems and how this is likely to appear in practice. The chapter starts with an overview of the trajectory of reforms in public health systems over the neoliberal period and the conventional approach to examining them. In doing so, I demonstrate that finance remains largely on the sidelines. Next, I review the literature on the financialization of health to gather available evidence of how finance has been changing health activities. I present findings for areas such as global health policy and private health care, and point out the research gaps when it comes to public systems. I close the chapter justifying why financialization represents a specific type of public health system change. This is done by looking at the narratives, actors, and policy decisions involved in typical processes of privatization, the core notion used in the literature on public health systems change so far. I highlight how developments that I associate with financialization involve different types of narratives, actors, and policy decisions, which are related but not the same as those that prevail in privatization processes. Lastly, I acknowledge the common causes and connections between processes of privatization, financialization, and other paths of health care reforms. This serves better contextualize the changes discussed in this book within the longstanding process of PHS reforms in neoliberal capitalism.

The second part of the book moves from theory to practice, demonstrating how the process of financialization steered the trajectory of two real-world PHS. The analysis answers the following questions: what are the mechanisms through which financial actors, instruments, and interests have shaped reforms in public health systems over the past three decades? What have been the consequences of this expanded participation of finance in these systems?

Chapter 3 provides answers to such questions in the case of the French public health system, *Assurance Maladie*. I provide original evidence of innovations in the financing circuits of the French universal system allowing it to welcome money from financial markets and adapt itself to meet their requirements. Looking at long-term financing, I describe how the French Social Security system, which finances public health care, started issuing securities to refinance existing debts in the financial markets. The following section turns to short-term financing, showing how a similar strategy of securities issuance was adopted to raise revenues for covering expenses falling due in the near future. I conclude by addressing changes in hospital financing, I describe the creation of programs through which public hospitals started funding infrastructure by contracting loans with commercial banks and issuing debt bonds in financial markets.

Chapter 4 follows the same approach to study transformations in the Brazilian public health system. Starting with changes at the level of long-term financing, I unpack how a set of government budget rules ensures that revenues expected to fund public health can be systematically diverted to remunerate public debt investors. Next, I delve into issues of short-term financing, describing how public health agencies have been using the system's revenues to invest in short-term assets. I conclude by looking at hospital financing, more specifically at government-sponsored programs pushing hospitals to borrow directly from banks in order to finance services for the public system.

The closing chapter draws from both the theoretical discussion and empirical investigation to argue that public health systems are being reshaped in ways that are functional for the expansion of the financial sector and the accumulation of financial capital. First, I systematize the main findings of the French and the Brazilian cases, demonstrating the variegated yet global character of the financialization process in public health systems. I also assess the role played by the State in this process. I claim that governments have had an active role in orchestrating the financialization of national health systems through regulatory shifts and a vast array of legal and economic incentives for financial activities.

The book ends by considering the impacts of opening the financing of public health systems to greater participation of financial capital. Differently from what is often argued when implementing pro-finance measures, these policies are far from neutral. Financialization reforms undermine the capacity of these systems to act according to some of the principles upon which they were founded, such as redistribution, solidarity, stability, and democratic participation. By the end of the book, readers are expected to have a better understanding of the mechanisms driving the increasing participation of financial capital within PHS, as well as the reasons why these changes should be studied and contested.

PART 1

Financialization as a New Concept to Examine Public Health Systems Change

∴

CHAPTER 1

Financialization and Its Inroads into Public Policy

This chapter introduces the conceptual framework that informs the investigation of financialization within public health systems. It introduces the topic of financialization and shows how it has been used to examine changes in areas strategically important to the present discussion, with focus on how it seems to be reshaping public policymaking. In the first part of the chapter, I review the critical scholarship on financialization, presenting influential definitions of this concept, stylized facts, and how different theoretical strands in Economics have approached the subject. In the second part, I explore how financialization has manifested differently across the globe, describing the paths followed by central and peripheral economies as well as the particularities of the French and Brazilian experiences. The final part of the chapter looks at how this concept has been used to examine transformations in social provision across the world – that is, the provision of public services in areas associated with social rights. I propose an original organization of the existing literature on the topic to show that financialization has been reshaping both sides of social provision: on the one hand, how individuals are accessing essential goods and services, and, on the other, how public entities are financing and providing them.

1 Finance and Its Workings

We live in an era when financial players are influencing events beyond their traditional spheres of operation, to a degree unknown until the late 20th century. The acknowledgment of this trend is at the heart of the current usage of the term "financialization", which encapsulates the increasing role of globalized finance in ever more areas of economic and social life (Fine and Saad-Filho, 2017). The onset of this process is usually associated with the liberalization of capital flows and the integration of financial markets following the end of the Bretton Woods system in the 1970s. The continuous development of new technologies and financial innovations during the following decades, along with profound changes in domestic monetary policy and the international financial system, have enabled an unprecedented increase in the volume, speed, and reach of financial flows. Along with them, there was a dramatic growth in the size and power of the financial institutions, the actors responsible for organizing these flows (Chiapello, 2019; Guttmann, 2016).

Although its origins are obscure, the term "financialization" started to appear with increasing frequency in the 1990s and underwent a boom in the 2000s (Foster, 2007). This was when a thematically coherent body of academic work from various disciplines engaged with the phenomenon sparked off (Erturk, 2020). The number of journal articles with "financialization" among the keywords has more than quadrupled between 2000 and 2018, which illustrates the growing relevance of the term for academic research (Mader et al., 2020). Despite its increasing popularity and widespread use, there is no universally accepted definition for the concept of financialization.

Perhaps most famously, Epstein (2005) defines it as "the increasing role of financial motives, markets, actors, and institutions in the operation of the domestic and international economies" (p. 3). Aalbers' (2019) has expanded the scope of this popular definition to include other dimensions of social and political life, referring to it as "the increasing dominance of financial actors, markets, practices, measurements, and narratives, resulting in a structural transformation of economies, firms, States, and households" (p. 4).

Along with these broad definitions of financialization, the literature also offers narrow interpretations of this process. They include, for example, the understanding of financialization as "a new form of competition which involves a change in [the] orientation [of firms] towards financial results" (Froud et al., 2000, p. 104) or a "pattern of accumulation in which profit-making occurs increasingly through financial channels rather than through trade and commodity production" (Krippner, 2005, p. 181). Mader et al. (2020) demonstrate that narrow and broad notions of financialization tend to be mostly in agreement with each other; in general, the former is concerned with specific phenomena encompassed by the latter.

The absence of a commonly agreed meaning for financialization is not accidental. From a theoretical standpoint, the academic debate on the topic is large and diverse. It comprises works from different scientific backgrounds, and that look at the implications of financialization over a wide range of topics (Mader et al., 2020). From a practical perspective, the process of financialization exhibits considerable variation across countries and sectors (Bayliss et al., 2016a; Fine, 2014; Lavinas, 2017). In light of this diversity, it is neither possible nor useful to insist on finding a universal definition of the term (Golka, 2019; Lapavitsas and Soydan, 2020). Instead, it seems more useful to draw on the richness of this scientific debate to refine the analytical framework used to study present-day developments in different realms, including PHS.

Beyond their differences, all of these definitions of financialization converge to the understanding of financialization as a three-sided process involving the growing size of finance in the global economy, its expansion in scope, and its progressive concentration of wealth and power relative to other actors (Gabor, 2018). But what is actually expanding, and how? In the literature on financialization, it is common to find studies that address the topic without first addressing a number of important questions – such as what allows something to be labeled as "financial", who are these so-called "financial actors", what activities they engage in, and what mechanisms could allow them to gain such amount of power over other actors. Addressing these questions can provide a much clearer idea of how financialization is interpreted in this work and how it can contribute to the research on PHS.

1.1   Conventional Views of Finance

First, what is finance? In dictionary definitions, the term "finance" appears in at least three correlated ways: (i) the system allowing for the provision and management of funds in an economy, based on a wide array of activities such as the circulation of money, the granting of credit, the making of investments, and the provision of banking facilities; (ii) the scientific field dedicated to the study of such activities; and (iii) the volume of funds available for undertaking a certain action (Oxford University Press, 2006; Merriam-Webster Dictionary, 2021). There is also a wide array of technical definitions provided by specialized institutions to explain what finance means. The Swedish International Development Cooperation Agency (SIDA) offers a comprehensive description of the financial system, including its actors, instruments, and markets, as well as of the broader structure upon which they work. According to the agency,

> The financial sector forms the structure of arrangements in an economy which facilitates the conduct and growth of economic transactions through the use of money for payments, savings, and investments. It consists of financial policies and financial infrastructure which support the financial system (institutions, instruments, and markets).
>
> As to *financial institutions* they include: (...) financial intermediaries such as banks, microcredit institutions, rural and informal finance institutions, pension funds, insurance companies, leasing companies, risk capital funds and other specialized institutions; financial facilitators such as brokers, credit information agencies, and rating agencies.
>
> *Financial markets* comprise money markets ([for] short-term debt instruments) and capital markets ([for] equities and long-term debt instruments).

> *Financial instruments* represent claims to real resources, and they may
> consist of demand and time deposits, bank loans, bonds, debentures, cer-
> tificates of deposits, and shares.
>
> SIDA, 2004, p. 4, emphasis added[1]

These sorts of definitions do not engage in a critical debate over the financial system, which is why they are considered here as *mainstream* notions of
finance (as opposed to the critical debate on the financial system promoted
by the scholarship on financialization). The scientific literature backing this
conventional approach to finance is heavily grounded in the "functionalist"
perspective of the financial system (Bodie and Merton, 1995; Crane et al., 1995;
Merton, 1995). According to this perspective, the financial system serves six
main functions in an economy: organizing a payment system for the exchange
of goods and services, providing mechanisms for pooling funds, transferring
economic resources through time and across geographic regions and indus-
tries, setting up devices for risk management, disclosing information that
helps in decision-making processes, and addressing incentive problems arising
from asymmetric information.

Neoclassical economists tend to agree with this functionalist perspective
of finance. Moreover, given the usual assumptions of neoclassical theory, the
financial system is usually portrayed as an intrinsically efficient system, operated according to the perfectly rational decisions of the agents that participate
in it. The financial system would be a self-balancing system with fluctuations in
price corrected by changes in the supply and demand for funds. In this way, they
would serve as an appropriate mechanism to optimize resource allocation in the
economy (Karwowski and Stockhammer, 2017; Lavoie, 2014; Tadjeddine, 2018).

In this neutral place of exchange, financial institutions would play the role
of mere intermediaries, connecting those who have money (savers) and those
who need it in order to invest in production (Chambost et al., 2018; Davis and
Walsh, 2017; Rowden, 2019). As explained by Guttmann (2016), the standard
neoclassical approach divides the economy into "real" and "monetary" spheres,
and reduces finance to a passive channel connecting savings to investments
in the monetary dimension. Financial institutions and markets would simply
operate this intermediation process between savers and investors, with no
capacity to impact the real economy.

---

1   In the original report, the agency also includes financial institutions from the public sector,
    such as central banks. When talking about financial institutions, I focus mainly on private
    entities, the reason being that I seek to examine how private finance is being incorporated
    into public structures.

1.2   *The Heterodox Critique*

The neoclassical approach to finance is heavily criticized by heterodox economists. Heterodox scholars use real-world evidence to argue that the financial system is far from balanced and neutral. They also suggest that the conventional view of finance reflects a limited understanding of the purposes of financial activities and the power of financial institutions today.

The Heterodox tradition encompasses a variety of schools of thought sharing fundamental principles and premises that differentiate them from mainstream neoclassical theory. These include the search for realistic assumptions and explanations of real-world phenomena, the consideration of individuals as social beings (influenced by habits, conventions, and norms), and the rejection of the assumption that markets alone can lead to the best possible economic and social outcomes (Lavoie, 2014). Such principles render the heterodox approach much more apt to explain the current size of the financial system and the roles it plays today.

Each heterodox school examines economic and social developments from a particular angle, leading to a multifaceted critique of the mainstream view of finance. Comparative reviews (Epstein, 2018; Hein et al., 2015; Karwowski and Stockhammer, 2017) suggest that post-Keynesians, for example, tend to focus on issues of fundamental uncertainty and non-rational behavior, demonstrating how they undermine the supposed efficiency of financial markets; Marxists would pay greater attention to asymmetries of power and how finance deepens and multiplies them; French regulationists, in turn, emphasize the influence of institutions (organizations, conventions, and rules more generally) in shaping the interactions at play.[2] However, there is not usually a conflict between these views; on the contrary, they are often combined to form a more general critique of finance.

Given the broad common ground shared by heterodox theories, scholars from different strands tend to draw upon each other's ideas to develop a critical analysis of the financial system. To discuss the essence of the heterodox critique, it is useful to point out one crucial aspect of finance, largely underestimated by the mainstream view: the system's capacity to organize the transfer of revenues and risks across time, space, and agents. According to Durand (2017), the ability to break temporal and spatial constraints is important because it allows wealth to be created on what is yet to be produced, this process of anticipation being a key factor in allowing for the expansion of the financial system.

---

2 Some works present the French Regulation School as part of the Institutionalist School, although this is a matter of debate (see, e.g., Boyer, 2003; Lavoie, 2014).

Krippner (2005) suggests that future expectations are at the very essence of financial activities and profits. By financial activities, the author means "activities related to the provision or transfer of liquid capital in expectation of future interests, dividends, or capital gains" (p. 174). In a similar vein, Sarlat (2009) contends that all goods, currencies, and capital traded on financial markets are judged according to their present value and by the future income they are likely to bring; in this way, "by buying and selling products on the financial markets, we are (...) buying and selling future income" (p. 543). Concrete examples of how financial instruments break time, space, and individual constraints are loans and bonds, for example, as these represent claims on the repayment of the principal and interests by the borrower in the future. Another example are equity securities (e.g., company shares), which guarantee rights to part of the future earnings and assets of another entity. Weber (2020) concludes that any financial instrument, whatever the final form it assumes, is first and foremost a "promise to pay": savings accounts, demand deposits, shares, bonds, derivatives, and others, could be similarly characterized as "contracts wherein an issuer promises to pay money at some future date under specified conditions" (p. 459).[3]

Such characteristics of the financial system could open windows of opportunity for speculation and resource accumulation.[4] According to Guttman (2016), financial instruments would serve as channels for resource accumulation, for example, by allowing creditors to yield income as compensations from previous lending, through interests; another possible channel would be from investments disconnected from the so-called "real economy" of production and exchange, which is mainly the case of capital gains from betting on price movements in financial markets. The author also argues that, in the current period of capitalism, the activity of accumulating financial assets for income generation in the future, disconnected from the financing of productive activities, seems to have become the main purpose of financial activity.

---

3   It is interesting to note that the idea of a "promise to pay" is at the origins of the own term "finance". According to Cresswell (2010), the roots of the English term finance can be found in the Old French *finer*, "the payment of a debt, compensation, or ransom", from the Latin *finis*, "to end". Szendy (2020) draws attention to the fact that the etymology of *finance* is closely related to that of *fine*, which means "to punish (a person) for an illegal or illicit act by requiring him or her to pay a sum of money".

4   Speculation denotes the purchase or sale of something for the sole purpose of making a capital gain, irrespective of the underlying activity generating the investment. The goal is obtaining profit from the variation of prices or other variables, without the intention of keeping the investment for long.

The developments described above – the capacity of some actors to reap gains from lending and speculation through financial instruments, often disconnected from the financing of production – are embodied in the concepts of "interest-bearing capital" and "fictitious capital", which are widely used in the financialization literature.

The concepts of interest-bearing and fictitious capital have been discussed by Marx (1894) and are frequently used by heterodox economists to make sense of contemporary processes of financial expansion and accumulation. For Durand (2017), interest-bearing capital could be explained as capital that is lent and remunerated through the payment of interest. It may or may not generate fictitious capital, which generates revenues from the anticipation of the capital valorization process. Guttmann (2016) offers a synthesis of this second and much trickier concept of fictitious capital:

> fictitious capital involves the trading of claims in financial markets especially created for their circulation. Their value has no material basis in production (hence is "fictitious") and rests instead on the capitalization of future income their holders anticipate.
>
> While the notion of fictitious capital dates back a century and a half, it has not lost its relevance today. In the era of finance-led capitalism we have witnessed an amazing proliferation of tradable financial claims, which investors trade for capital gains (...) these are objects of speculation by investors seeking to profit from their trading without direct connection to the underlying monetary production economy; hence arguably this is fictitious capital.
>
> pp. 69–70, 72

The heterodox critique suggests that finance serves as a channel of accumulation rather than intermediation. The unbridled expansion of the financial sector over the past decades has come hand in hand with the accumulation of wealth via interest-bearing and fictitious capital, even if the boundaries between these forms of capital are the object of ongoing discussion (see, e.g., Durand, 2017; Fine, 2013; Guttmann, 2016; Lapavitsas, 2013). The fact that financial institutions, markets, and instruments serve as the platform for unprecedented levels of capital accumulation via interest-bearing and fictitious capital is at odds with finance's supposed neutrality. On the contrary, finance would serve as a channel for the appropriation of a rising share of global income, largely disconnected from the financing needs of the global economy.

Together with the recognition that the purposes of financial activities go beyond financing production, another fundamental distinction between the conventional and heterodox approaches to finance concerns how they perceive financial actors. Heterodox scholars claim that financial institutions play roles that go far beyond the intermediation between savers and investors, having a systemic power over the global economy (Durand, 2017; Guttmann, 2016; Tadjeddine, 2018). Emphasis is placed on those actors at the top of the "financial pyramid", who run and control the financial system. This notion of financial actors includes banks, insurance companies, and investment funds such as hedge funds and private equity funds, to name a few. Sometimes, it also includes the wealthy individuals who rule the system and whose property materializes in the holding of financial assets (see, e.g., Chesnais, 2016; Duménil and Lévy, 2004; Guillen, 2014).[5]

Financial players profit from key privileges in today's economy, which allow them to concentrate power and resources. On the one hand, they have the capacity to create money and organize investment circuits; on the other, they have an unparalleled ability to undertake and influence investments in these same circuits (Guttmann, 2016). Such prerogatives and powers would grant financial players an unprecedented capacity to "make money from money" (Mulligan, 2016, p. 47) for themselves and others. They can create money *ex nihilo* ("out of nowhere"), for example, through credit concession (which requires little to virtually no backup in "real" money today). They can also multiply the funds they manage through loans, investments, and speculation in financial markets (Appadurai, 2015; Chesnais, 2016).

It is virtually impossible to obtain precise figures on the volume of financial assets and the size of the financial sector at the global level due to several factors including complexity and lack of transparency. A significant share of financial transactions occurs in the so-called "shadow banking" sector – a set of highly heterogeneous entities and activities lying outside the regular banking system (Financial Stability Board, 2018), poorly regulated and monitored. Still, figures for regulated activities only can already give a sense of the disproportionate evolution of the financial sector relative to the "real economy", and serves as empirical evidence against the idea of finance's role as a mere

---

5   The heterodox literature often employs the term "financial sector" with an implicit meaning, referring to these largest players with a systemic power to influence developments in the sector and in the economy more broadly. Following this view, I employ the terms "financial sector", "finance", "financial institutions", and "financial actors" interchangeably in reference to those agents. I also use the concept of "financial capital" broadly as the volume of funds they manage.

channel of intermediation. According to estimates from McKinsey (2005), the value of global financial assets increased more than tenfold between 1980 and 2005, from around US$12 trillion to 118 trillion. Comparing it to the size of the global economy, the global stock of financial assets has more than tripled in this period, from 110% to 325% of the world GDP.[6] More recent estimates from Macquarie Research (2017), which attempts to grasp at least part of the "shadow banking" sector, identify a rise in the value of global financial assets from approximately 2.6 times the world GDP in 1990 to more than five times in 2016. More recent data from the OECD indicates that the total value of global financial assets reached nearly US$380 trillion in 2018, with the value of domestic assets representing on average six times the national GDP in high-income economies and three times in middle-income ones (OECD, 2020).

The soaring value of financial assets has been accompanied by a dramatic growth of the institutions that create, manage, and profit from them. Assessments of the world's largest companies suggest that the financial sector outperforms all other sectors in terms of retained wealth and profits, surpassing even sectors such as energy and technology. The Forbes' ranking of the 2,000 largest listed companies of 2019 shows that financial companies (banks, insurance companies, and other financial companies combined) represented more than a quarter of entries on the list – no other sector came close to that. Together, the financial companies on Forbes' list reaped over US$12 trillion in profits in 2019, more than double the amount earned by the second most profitable sector (oil and gas companies) (Ponciano and Hansen, 2019). Equally impressive is the observation that, today, each one of the world's largest asset management firms has a volume of assets under management worth more than the GDP of several countries (Epstein, 2019; Plihon, 2019).

In light of this evidence, examining the hegemony of finance today requires questioning the legitimacy of the economic rents received by these actors and the true nature of the services they provide (Tadjeddine, 2018). This debate is at the heart of the research field of financialization, which has been allowing scholars to further develop the heterodox critique of finance.

1.3 *The Academic Scholarship on Financialization*

The academic scholarship on financialization is now a solid body of research attentive to the growing dominance of finance and its impacts on the social, economic, and political spheres. This critical literature brings together

---

6 This value of financial assets encompasses "traditional" instruments only – bank deposits, government bonds, private debt securities, and equities. Figures are in nominal values.

contributions from different scientific fields, including economics, anthropology, history, geography, sociology, and political sciences (Mader et al., 2020; Van der Zwan, 2014). Diversity can be regarded as a strength rather than a weakness of the financialization literature: as suggested by Mader et al. (2020), combining various streams of scientific research allows for a deeper comprehension of the object under investigation, as each discipline can highlight aspects that others are less inclined to grasp.

Within the field of Economics, the heterodox approach leads the debate on financialization. Marxist, Post-Keynesian, and French Regulationist authors are particularly active in the field (Hein et al., 2015; Karwowski and Stockhammer, 2017; Lapavitsas, 2011).[7] Authors from these different schools tend to inspire and conceptually borrow from each other when defining and featuring the process of financialization (Hein et al., 2015; Karwowski and Stockhammer, 2017; Mader et al., 2020). As concluded by Hein et al. (*op. cit.*) when comparing different approaches to economics, "when it comes to the main characteristics of the financialization period, we see some convergence among different approaches, and no fundamental differences but some complementarities" (p. 50). This overlap between schools of thought explains why so many works, including the present one, opt to bring together contributions from authors of different theoretical approaches to characterize the process of financialization.

Some fundamental traits unite this seemingly heterogeneous array of works and justify its unification into a single body of research. The most important trait seems to be the view of finance beyond its traditional role as a provider of capital for the productive economy. Instead, financialization studies believe in the increasingly autonomous character of global finance and its capacity to alter the behavior of economics, governments, and people (Van der Zwan, 2014). The scope of the financialization literature has expanded considerably over the last decade to study the impacts of financial expansion over an increasing number of agents (e.g. non-financial corporations, households, public sector entities), markets (e.g., commodity, energy, food, and labor markets), policy fields (e.g., housing, education, health care, and environmental policies), and geographical areas (e.g., central economies, emerging countries, post-soviet countries). The financialization literature has a critical view of the growing size of the financial sector over the last decades, making inroads into these different spheres. The ever-growing volume and complexity of financial

---

7   Reference to the French regulation school sometimes appears implicit in mentions of the institutionalist school (see footnote 2 of this chapter).

instruments would have detrimental impacts on financial stability, growth, and income equality, among others (Karwowski, 2019).

Summing up this debate and contrasting it with the mainstream view on finance, Mader et al. (2020) list three key affinities shared by financialization scholars: (i) they recognize finance as not subservient to the productive economy, but as an autonomous realm that increasingly influences and dominates other dimensions; (ii) they have a critical stance on such expansion and emancipation of finance, linking them with negative socio-economic and political developments; and (iii) they deny the mainstream view of finance that studies financial expansion as a primarily economic issue; instead, they articulate changes in finance with shifts in politics, economics, social relations, and culture.

Several works have sought to make sense of this rich literature on financialization by mapping subfields of research. The most cited systematization so far is arguably the one proposed by Van der Zwan (2014), who distinguishes existing studies into macro-, meso-, and micro-level approaches. According to this view, macro-level studies look at the capitalist system more broadly and examine financialization as a new regime of accumulation. They are concerned with structural shifts in the patterns of capital accumulation, the evolution of macroeconomic aggregates, and the empowerment of the "rentier" class. Meso-level studies focus on transformations at the firm level, considering financialization as a distinctive behavioral pattern of modern corporations prioritizing shareholder value maximization. They investigate the reorientation of investment expenditures by these firms and redistributive processes between managers, shareholders, and employees. Finally, micro-level studies are most interested in individuals and households, with financialization associated with a transformation in "everyday life". This transformation is perceived through a wide range of shifts, from a cultural revolution that leads them to perceive themselves as investors to concrete events through which they are treated as such.

One can list some "stylized facts" of financialization – consistent empirical findings that, although not always present, are regular enough to characterize this process. The literature of financialization has often associated this process with trends such as: (i) the growth of the financial sector in the economy, including the share of financial activity as a proportion of total economic activity and of financial profits as a share of total profits; (ii) the increasing importance of financial activities for non-financial firms, with traditionally non-financial firms engaging with financial investments and earning a larger share of their revenues from the latter; (iii) changes in investment patterns, with the decrease in the overall levels and returns of real investments compared to financial ones; (iv) changes in the governance of firms, with the prioritization of shareholder value maximization (the increase in the volume of revenues addressed to shareholders, often at the expense of reinvesting profits or increasing wages and workforce); (v) a surge in speculative activities by financial and non-financial entities; (vi) the decline in real wages and the wage share; (v) mounting levels of household, corporate, and public debt; (vii) increasing income inequality arising out of greater financial rewards along with lower real wages; (viii) the slowdown of economic growth; (ix) higher levels of financial instability and frequency of economic crisis; (x) shifts in the structure of public revenues and expenditures (Ashman and Fine, 2013; Hein and Treeck, 2010; Stockhammer, 2008). It is important to keep in mind that these are general tendencies, which do not necessarily need to be present to characterize the financialization of an economy.

Having presented the main traits of the financialization literature, it is important to clarify where exactly lies the originality of this scholarship. The novelty brought by the concept of financialization is not necessarily the awareness of the expansion of financial activities. It is well-recognized that individuals have engaged with financial transactions and instruments since the beginning of recorded history, and that creditor-debtor relations organized social life many centuries before the emergence of capitalism (Bodie and Merton, 1995; Graeber, 2011; Lazzarato, 2012). Similarly, there are long-standing debates in the academic literature regarding the idea that financial markets follow a relatively autonomous behavior in relation to other markets (Keynes, 1936; Marx, 1894) and that the financial sector will naturally outgrow other economic sectors at certain points of capitalist cycles (Arrighi, 1994).

The contemporary theory of financialization distinguishes the processes cited above, temporally and spatially bounded, from the changes in capitalist accumulation taking place today (Bonizzi et al., 2020; Powell, 2018). The current meaning of financialization designates not simply the existence of financial relations or a quantitative phenomenon associated with the growth of the financial relative to the productive sphere, but a qualitative transformation in the pattern of capital accumulation (Guillen, 2014). Scholars working with the notion of financialization argue that, in contrast with previous historical periods, the last decades have seen finance not only expand but also determine developments outside of the financial sphere, including patterns of economic production, social reproduction, and resource distribution. These qualitative transformations justify framing the present phase of capitalism as a distinctive stage *underpinned* or *dominated* by finance (Fine and Saad-Filho, 2017). Recent developments in finance would contribute to the formation of a new stage of capitalism where finance plays a catalytic role in the extension, expansion, and intensification of capitalist accumulation, increasing opportunities for exploitation and expropriation (Bonizzi et al., 2020).[8]

While the use of the term "financialization" is an object of controversy (Christophers, 2015; Fine and Saad-Filho, 2017; Amable et al., 2019), the idea of a distinctive era of capitalism subjected to the power of finance finds much less contestation the academic community.[9] This can be illustrated by the myriad of terms coined by scholars from different theoretical schools reflecting the same idea; one can mention, for example, the notions of *finance-dominated capitalism* presented by post-Keynesians (Hein, 2012; Stockhammer, 2008); the discussions on *capitalism underpinned by financialization* and *financialized capitalism* carried by authors within the Marxist framework (Fine and Saad-Filho, 2017; Lapavitsas, 2013); and the idea of a *finance-led growth regime* or *finance-led capitalism* based on the French Regulation school's approach (Boyer, 2000; Guttmann, 2008).

Although heterodox approaches follow different criteria to distinguish the stages of modern capitalism, Fine and Saad-Filho (2017) identify some uniformity in the periodizations proposed by them: a *laissez-faire* period in the 19th century, giving way to a more monopolistic stage in the first half of the 20th century, followed by an era of active and explicit State intervention around the post-war period, and a neoliberal stage emerging from the 1980s on. Associating financialization with the present stage of capitalism requires thus clarifying how this concept is connected to the idea of neoliberalism. While it is impossible to do justice to the entire discussion on the topic, these authors suggest that neoliberalism can be understood as a set of economic and political ideas, and a set of policies, institutions, and practices accompanying these ideas, in favor of private capital in general and financial capital in particular.[10]

---

8   According to Fine and Saad-Filho (2017), what characterizes a stage of capitalism are the distinctive ways in which the accumulation, distribution, and exchange of value are organized and reorganized, as well as its implications for social reproduction. It follows, then, that the rise of financialization over the past decades would have profoundly transformed such foundations, shaping a new stage of accumulation.

9   To avoid overgeneralization, scholars underscore the importance of setting boundaries for the use of the term and distinguishing it from other processes that also influence the course of contemporary economies, such as commodification, commercialization, globalization, privatization, digitalization, and work precarization (Christophers, 2015; Mader et al., 2020; Stockhammer, 2008). In the second chapter of this book, I clarify the specific way in which I understand the process of financialization in PHS and differentiate it from other processes with a recognized influence on these systems, namely privatization.

10   For syntheses of the ways in which the term "neoliberalism" has been employed in social sciences and its relations with the idea of financialization, see Fine and Saad-Filho (2017) and Davis and Walsh (2017).

They would be articulated through the power of the State to impose, drive, underwrite and manage the internationalization of production and finance in each territory, often concealed under the narrative of non-interventionism. In this way, the neoliberal paradigm would set the context for the continuing expansion of finance in scale and power (that is, for financialization), which in turn strengthens the neoliberal paradigm in place.

2   Together but Different: Financialization in Central and Peripheral Countries

Although the process of financialization is global in nature, there are no two countries in which it manifests in the same way (Aalbers et al., 2020). Therefore, it is critically important to consider the specificities of each case to apprehend the variegated nature of financialization across the world (Bayliss et al., 2017; Fine, 2013).

The early research on financialization focused on individual countries, mainly Anglo-Saxon economies (the United States and, to a lesser degree, the United Kingdom). This has encouraged a biased approach to examine how other countries might have been undergoing financialization processes, leading to the idea that there would be a "standard" financialization model that could be applied to all experiences (Aalbers et al., 2020; Karwowski et al., 2020). Over time, a more inclusive approach to studying financialization has emerged, studying various regions and taking into account the social, spatial, economic, political, and historical context of each place. This fresh perspective on the topic demonstrated that financialization is not restricted to a few countries and there is no unique model of financialization that can apply to them all (Aalbers et al., 2020; Bonizzi, 2013; Massó et al., 2020).

Indeed, financial flows are not bounded by national frontiers – at least not in any significant way that could have halted the dramatic financial expansion over the past decades. A common way to make sense of different paths of financialization without losing sight of its global character is thus by contrasting the experiences of central and peripheral countries.[11] The research distinguishing

---

11   The terms "peripheral", "emerging", and "developing" countries are all common nomenclatures to refer to countries with a lower level of capitalist development and a relatively weak position in the global hierarchies of currencies and institutions (Lapavitsas and Soydan, 2020). In practice, they refer mostly to middle-income countries. These are examined in relation to "central", "core", or "advanced" economies, a term used in reference to high-income and industrialized nations. This book uses the term "peripheral" and

financialization in central and peripheral economies has greatly expanded our knowledge of the theme, unraveling how both domestic and foreign pressures shape national experiences (Becker et al., 2010; Bonizzi et al., 2020; Karwowski et al., 2020).

In the case of central economies, several studies acknowledge many commonalities in their processes of financialization. They include, first and foremost, the significant weight of domestic factors in driving this process. Karwowski et al. (2020) find that the three key factors driving financialization in core countries have been asset price inflation, financial deregulation, and debt accumulation, which corroborates the importance of domestic forces in these cases (see also Bortz and Kaltenbrunner, 2018; Karwowski and Stockhammer, 2017; Stockhammer, 2008).

By contrast, research on peripheral countries emphasizes the role of external forces in driving financialization. According to Bonizzi (2013), "peripheral countries are subject to shifts similar to those experienced by core countries, but at the same time these are mediated by their subordinate position, which determines how financialization takes place" (p. 86). The recognition of a distinctive dynamic of financialization in certain countries directly shaped by the relations with the most industrialized nations has informed the literature on "subordinate" (Bonizzi et al., 2020; Powell, 2013) and "peripheral" (Becker et al., 2010) financialization. Both approaches share considerable common ground in which they stress the derivative character of financialization in the periphery of capitalism – that is, shaped by financialized activity in the center (Karwowski, 2019; Lapavitsas and Soydan, 2020).

To make the distinction between domestic and external drivers of financialization clearer, it is necessary to systematize the factors shaping this process in the periphery. These include, in particular, the subordinated position that these countries occupy in the circuits of global trade and the international monetary system. This positioning would determine the behavior of capital flows in peripheral countries, the global hierarchy of currencies, the influence of international and foreign financial institutions on domestic policies, and the quest for accumulating foreign reserves, to name a few (Bonizzi et al., 2020; Kaltenbrunner and Painceira, 2018).

---

distinguishes it from "central". This is because the idea behind *emergence* or *development* is that there is a process of catching up in relation to wealthy countries, which is not the case for Latin America. Bértola and Ocampo (2012) show that the income and technological gaps of countries in relation to the wealthiest nations in the region have been widening rather than narrowing during the neoliberal period.

The pressures arising out of this subordinated condition would play a crucial role in shaping domestic processes of financialization. Most notably, both trade and the most liquid capital markets are denominated in the currency of central economies, leading to a disproportionately high dependence on foreign capital and currencies. As shown by several authors, processes of peripheral financialization seem heavily driven by attempts to attract external funds (Kaltenbrunner and Painceira, 2018; Karwowski and Stockhammer, 2017; Lapavitsas and Soydan, 2020). Domestic policies geared toward attracting foreign capital and discouraging capital flights would often appear in the form of high domestic interest rates. These would generate high interest rates differentials in relation to central economies, becoming relatively more attractive to international investors than they would otherwise (Bonizzi et al., 2020). Especially in Latin America, the chronic need to attract foreign capital is frequently accompanied by the goal of fighting domestic inflation (Becker et al., 2010; Bonizzi, 2013). High interest rates would thus serve a dual objective in these countries: both attracting capital flows and controlling domestic prices. Several peripheral countries have combined high interest rates with inflation-targeting policies since the 1990s to assure that the value of foreign investments would not be eroded by inflation (Epstein and Yeldan, 2008; Frenkel, 2006; Lapavitsas and Soydan, 2020).

Summing up the debate, Becker et al. (2010) identify two chief forms of financialization: the first type would be the most recurrent form in central economies, driven by the rising prices of financial assets; the second type seems to predominate in peripheral regions, particularly in Latin America, and would be fueled by earnings from interest-bearing capital (see also Bonizzi et al., 2020; Lavinas et al., 2019). High interest rates are therefore considered one of the chief drivers of financialization in Latin American countries, as they would promote capital accumulation and concentration via interest-bearing capital.[12] Moreover, high interest rates would set the conditions for the permanent extraction of a significant share of domestically generated surpluses by foreign agents via interest gains, reinforcing dependency bonds (Becker et al., 2010; Bonizzi et al., 2020; Powell, 2013). Financialization and high interest rates have also been associated with the difficulties for peripheral countries to advance in their processes of industrialization and achieve higher positions

---

12   This does not mean that all Latin American countries have undergone similar processes of financialization. This process has spread unevenly in the region, with Brazil and Chile leading the way (Becker et al., 2010; Lavinas et al., 2019). There are also marked differences between the patterns of financialization of "emerging" countries from Latin America and from Asia (see Bonizzi, 2013; Karwowski and Stockhammer, 2017).

in the hierarchy of foreign trade.[13] Karwowski (2020) summarizes the role of high interest rates as a driver of financialization in peripheral countries positing that "they open up avenues for financial accumulation to domestic capital potentially at the expense of supporting productive enterprise, while feeding the international search for yield of (mostly rich-country) financial investors" (p. 164).

A closer look at the process of financialization in France and Brazil reveals that these countries have followed the general trends typically associated with financialization in central and peripheral countries, respectively. However, it also shows that national circumstances have deeply influenced how these general trends appeared in each case, as explored in the next sections.

2.1   *Financialization in France*

According to Plihon (2003), France is one of the advanced countries whose economy has undergone one of the most dramatic shifts toward financial markets since the beginning of the process of financial globalization in the 1970s.

There are two main strands of literature discussing the process of financialization in the country (Foureault, 2018). The first strand examines transformations at the macroeconomic level since the 1970s, such as the increasing weight of the financial sector in the domestic economy and the massive entrance of foreign capital. This approach encompasses, notably, studies framing such changes as part of a new pattern of capital accumulation; being home to the French regulation school, these studies usually refer to the onset of a distinctive "mode of regulation" driven by finance (e.g., Aglietta and Rebérioux, 2004; Clevenot, 2006).[14] Works along these lines highlight the role of the State in fostering this process, associating such developments with the deliberate withdrawal of government participation in the French economy in favor of the private and financial sectors (Coriat, 2008).

---

13 The effects of financialization in holding back long-term productive investments seem an important part of the explanation for the paradoxical fact that Latin American countries underwent a period of deindustrialization in the 2000s even if going through a moment of significant economic growth, led not by manufacture but commodity exports (Bortz and Kaltenbrunner, 2018; Bruno and Paulani, 2019; Lavinas et al., 2019).

14 The French regulation school seeks to explain how inherently contradictory capitalist economic models can be stabilized over relatively extended periods of time. A key element of regulationist theories is that there are distinctive regimes of accumulation throughout the history of capitalism, each one having its particular mode of regulation – a set of institutions, regularities, and policies that make economic and social reproduction feasible in that particular context (Becker et al., 2010; Bonizzi, 2013; Boyer, 2003).

The second strand of literature focuses on transformations at the micro-level, namely the changing behavior of managers and firms in light of increasing pressures coming from financial expansion. A prominent body of research on corporate financialization in France emphasizes that traditional management structures were not *replaced* by financialized ones (as seems to be the case in other countries, such as the US); rather, traditional managers seem to have *converted* themselves into financial ones, adapting to the expansion of finance while preserving much of their power and control (Dudouet and Grémont, 2009; François and Lemercier, 2017).

Apart from these major axes of research, one can also find a fair amount of literature focusing on specific themes related to financialization. I highlight that which looks at public investment bodies and how they incorporated reasonings and practices typical of financial institutions (Ducastel, 2019). The findings of this strand of research are particularly aligned with the ones presented in this book. One of the public bodies that is the object of study by financialization works, the *Caisse des Dépôts et Consignations*, adopted a new approach toward Social Security agencies in the mid-1990s that has had an important role in explaining the latter's greater dependence on financial capital (see Chapter 3).

Not only has France seen dramatic shifts due to financial expansion, but it is also considered one of the countries where the government played one of the most active roles in leading this process. Several scholars concur that France has undergone a strong process of financialization with unique characteristics that can be largely attributed to a reorientation of State policies (Coriat, 2008; Lemoine, 2016).

One can only grasp the impacts of the shifts in the French State's approach since the late 1960s and early 1970s and how they favored the financial sector by understanding how it participated in the economy up to that point. Until the middle of the century, the French State had a chief role in both the financing and production of a wide range of goods and services, significantly larger than in neighboring countries, and exerted a major influence over other sectors. To mention a few examples, the State (including the central government and other parts of the public administration): (i) controlled the largest share of banks and financial institutions in the country; (ii) was responsible for the intermediation of most of the financing of productive enterprise; (iii) administered domestic interest rates, with an important share offered below market conditions; (iv) exerted direct control over credit and money creation, through the central bank; and (v) was an important shareholder in most of the large industrial and financial companies in the country (Coriat, 2008; Firmin, 2008; Plihon, 2003).

The shift in the State's approach toward private capital was marked by wide-scale privatization programs reaching public banks and companies (Coriat, 2008; Dudouet and Grémont, 2009) and major regulatory shifts in the financial system, including both financial deregulation and the State's let go of total control over monetary and credit emission (Lemoine, 2016). Ducastel (2019) describes these changes as part of a context marked by "the advent of the 'neo-liberal State' which abandons central planning tools in favor of market instruments in all areas of activity". The author goes on to say that the liberalization of the financial markets, to which one could add the other reforms previously mentioned, "[provoked] a movement of financialization that translates itself into the increased dependence of companies, households, but also of the State and its administrations on their creditors" (p. 35–6).

Coriat (2006) illustrates the deliberate nature of the State's changing approach toward the financial sector by listing some of the main policies upon which it was based:

> *The French State* (...) *was itself responsible* (...) *for the genesis of its own disintegration as a key industrial player. Whether in terms of privatization, securitization of the public debt,* the general reform of stock and money markets to increase both their depth and liquidity, or again tax measures designed to shift private savings over to financial markets, these measures represent (...) an *impressive collection of "new regulations",* distilled, promoted, and instilled continually over the last decades, and *which are at the origin of the ongoing establishment of the new liberalized finance regime.*
>
>   p. 79, emphasis added

These shifts in State policies promoted the expansion of capital markets and the inflation of financial asset prices, which is in line with the overall observations of how financialization expresses itself in wealthy nations (Becker et al., 2010). It is worth mentioning that these changes came about through consistent measures adopted by successive governments from both sides of the political spectrum; although they were mostly initiated by right-wing governments, the left-wing administrations that followed suit continued and, in many instances, pushed these measures further (Coriat, 2008; Firmin, 2008; Lemoine, 2017).[15]

---

15   During an important part of the initial period of reforms, France was governed by Georges Pompidou (1969–1974) and Valéry Giscard (1974–1981), right-wing presidents. They were

The starting point of this process were changes in State financing – the way the government financed itself and refinanced its debt. The progressive shift in the orientation of government debt management came about as the State started abandoning administered forms of financing and opted instead to raise funds in the financial markets. In this way, it expanded its sources of financing, but at the expense of becoming dependent on private investors to carry on public policies and subjected to their conditions for servicing the public debt.

Lemoine (2016; 2017; 2018) offers the most comprehensive account of how the French State progressively abdicated its control over the national financial system in favor of private finance. As shown by the author, until the 1960s, the government had significant control over its financing sources and actively controlled monetary and credit creation. It did so based on a complex system of non-market financing instruments between the government and financial institutions known as the "Treasury Circuit" (*le Circuit du Trésor*). This public financing arrangement was based on asymmetrical relations between the State and its creditors, with the former holding legal powers to rule on the sources and costs of its own funding. It guaranteed multiple revenue sources for the government that did not require the issuance of marketable bonds, providing funds under conditions and interest rates largely set by the government itself.[16] At the same time, the Central Bank, controlled by the State, had direct control over money creation, fixing the volume of credit each establishment could offer and regulating interest rates (see also Plihon, 2003).

The late 1960s marked the beginning of the "financialization of the public debt" in the country, with the progressive abandonment of administered financing mechanisms in detriment to market-based financing.[17] From this moment on, the State started issuing securities to borrow from financial markets. More specifically, it engaged in a new financing modality by offering bonds in auctions, at market interest rates. The government securities offered in the markets were standardized and exchangeable, generating therefore financial assets traded by financial investors in secondary markets.

---

followed by François Mitterrand (1981–1995), who led a nearly fifteen-year term of the socialist party.

16   Among the various revenue sources that composed the "Treasury Circuit", one can mention the deposits of public banks, public companies, and other financial institutions linked to the State in the French Treasury, the issuance of non-negotiable debt obligations, and the mandatory subscriptions to Treasury obligations imposed on banks. For a detailed description of this "circuit", see Lemoine (2015).

17   The process of "financialization of the public debt" is discussed in greater detail later in this chapter; it refers, *grosso modo*, to the process through which the State issues securities in financial markets to the detriment of previous forms of sovereign debt management.

The reasons leading the State to turn to financial markets seem to have been both ideological and practical. Lemoine (2017) draws attention to the emerging ideological context of the period, which focused on countering inflation and deemed the existing government financing modalities as highly inflationary. The emerging tensions surrounding the issue of inflation would have pressured the government to search for alternatives. At this time, the appeal to international savings and foreign investors was advertised as the only "healthy" and non-inflationary means to finance the public sector (see also Lemoine and Ravelli, 2017). Plihon (2003) adds that the increase in public debt levels around the time made it impossible for the Treasury to continue relying on domestic investors, leading to the use of market instruments to incorporate foreign capital. The government implemented far-reaching policies to modernize and liberalize domestic financial markets in this period, serving both to allow foreign investors to buy French government bonds and meet their demands. Putting these elements together, there is reason to believe that the government's decision to resort to the markets in a systematic fashion resulted from a dual political aim to both curb inflation and develop liquid capital markets (Lemoine, 2017).

The changes in the government's approach to public financing would mark the beginning of the financialization of the State to the extent that, from this moment on, "the State had to live as a borrower, not as an economic sovereign. (...) It became a debt issuer among others and began competing with other States to finance itself in the markets" (Lemoine, 2017, pp. 242, 253). This had implications for policy-making processes and public expenditures. As the State became exposed to the judgment of globalized private capital markets to obtain credit, it was now subject to their conditions to keep running the public machine. This involved, in particular, expectations to pursue a balanced budget and maintain a sustainable level of indebtedness (Lemoine, *op. cit.*).

The State's turn to the markets and the financialization of the public debt played a central role in the financialization of the French economy in many ways. Firmin (2008) notes that the State emerged as a gigantic source of demand for credit that could be covered by private investors. Moreover, the dismantling of existing arrangements for public financing and credit creation, along with the waves of denationalization, meant that companies could no longer count on the government to control credit and cover their capital requirements. Dudouet and Grémont (2009) explain that this change fostered a growing importance of financial markets in France to the extent that domestic companies turned to private financing instruments to raise funds, namely in the form of credit obtained from private banks and securities issued in financial markets.

Aside from the government, French businesses and families also formed new and deeper ties with the private financial sector from the second half of the 20th century onward. According to Firmin (2008), the financialization of financial and non-financial firms can be perceived in the rise of the profit share in the country, the increase in the external financing of companies through securities issuance, the intensification of shareholder value orientation as a consequence of this new financing modality, a larger share of profits distributed as dividends, and a downward trend in the rate of accumulation (see also Karwowski et al., 2020; Plihon, 2003; Stockhammer, 2004).

Compared to the existing literature on the State and firms, there seem to be fewer published works investigating how households in France have been incorporated into the process of financialization (Lazarus and Lacan, 2020). The regulatory changes carried out by the government throughout the second half of the 20th century also reached households, mainly by encouraging them to hold financial wealth. The government created a vast range of regulatory and tax incentives attempting to promote the reorientation of household savings from the acquisition of housing and capital goods to investments in financial assets. These included government securities, life insurance plans, voluntary pension savings, and allocations in investment funds, to name a few (Coriat, 2008; Firmin, 2008). While these incentives increased the volume of households' financial investments, the latter remained concentrated in the hands of a relatively small and wealthy segment of the population. Several studies examine data for household wealth in France and find indisputable evidence that the upper classes hold the vast majority of the financial assets in the household sector until today. Accordingly, they also receive the largest share of financial income addressed to households (Firmin 2008; Lemoine 2019; Plihon 2003).

Apart from financial investments, one must mention the bonds between households and the financial sector formed through debt. Evidence suggests that household indebtedness has increased significantly in France over the past decades. Data from the French Central Bank point to a rise in household debt-to-income ratio from 52% in 2000 to 94% in 2018. Moreover, the share of household debt due to consumer credit is now higher than that from mortgage loans, which had been historically the most important modality in the country (Banque de France, 2019a; Eurostat, 2021; *La finance pour tous*, 2019). Notwithstanding this rise, some authors remark that household debt levels in France remain inferior to those of some neighboring countries (Karwowski et al., 2020; Lazarus, 2017).

It remains an open question whether the process of financialization in France has gone through different phases over time. Firmin (2008) acknowledges the difficulties in establishing a periodization of the process of financialization in France. The most popular systematization of different stages of this process, carried out by François and Lemercier (2017; 2016), is restricted to the micro-level of firms.[18] Despite its relatively narrow scope, this research uncovered an interesting particularity of the French process of financialization: the fact that existing corporate structures and their bonds with State actors were largely preserved during this process. As shown by the authors, traditional managers from listed firms, the so-called *grands patrons* ("big bosses"), did not lose their place to financial managers since the 1970s – a trait that marks other trajectories such as that of the United States. Instead, the corporate elite absorbed financial practices and behaviors, "converting" themselves into financial elites. The long-standing personal and professional connections between the corporate sector and the public administration were largely preserved during this process, resulting in extremely permeable boundaries between the public, corporate, and financial spheres (see also Dudouet and Grémont, 2009).

2.2   *Financialization in Brazil*

Brazil seems to be a case of early financialization, and the first attempts to theorize this process in the country came before the international literature on the subject took off. Already in the mid-1980s, Braga (1985) was explaining how Brazil did not escape the logic of "financial dominance" governing economic decisions at the time and argued that this seemed to be a trademark of contemporary capitalism.

Concerning the changes paving the way for financialization in Brazil, authors give different emphases to foreign or domestic forces in creating the conditions for this process to come about. Looking at the external events, Paulani (2010) emphasizes the country's role as a major source of demand for international credit in the 1970s, contributing to expanding financial accumulation in core countries both in the period of indebtment and during the subsequent foreign debt crisis. Moreover, Brazil's involvement in the expansion of global financial markets would have continued in the 1990s as the country emerged as an international platform for financial valorization. Far-reaching reforms in this period turned the country into an emerging economy opened to foreign capital and offering some of the highest interest rates in the world,

---

18   The authors distinguish two phases of corporate financialization in France: the first phase, around the 1970s, was marked by the growth of financial firms in size and influence; in the second phase, around the turn of the century, what stand out were changes inside financial and nonfinancial firms, including in their shapes and objectives (the greater orientation toward shareholder value being a case in point).

creating spectacular earnings opportunities for strong currency investors (see also Freitas and Prates, 2001; Campello and Fontana, 2020).

With an eye toward internal events, other authors put greater emphasis on how changes in domestic policies since the 1970s led national companies and banks to prioritize the accumulation of financial assets instead of productive investments (Braga, 1985; Bruno et al., 2011; Lavinas et al., 2019). This would have been mainly due to domestic policies to control inflation since the 1980s, including high interest rate policies from the following decade on. Due to its importance in understanding the financialization of public policies in the country, this latter perspective will be the focus of my discussion throughout this section.

The literature on financialization in Brazil also focuses on some core topics. The most prominent strand of research is arguably the one looking at macroeconomic policies and indicators, which addresses how macroeconomic policies contribute to financial accumulation and have an effect on macroeconomic aggregates. A case in point would be the high interest rates paid on public bonds and their connection to the slowdown of the industrial GDP in the country, as these rates would provide investors with profitable and low-risk opportunities to place their money outside of the productive sphere. These structural changes would configure a distinctive "macroeconomic regime" or "accumulation regime" in the country, driven by finance (Araújo et al., 2012; Bresser-Pereira et al., 2020; Bruno et al., 2011; Lavinas et al., 2020, 2019; Paulani, 2010). In addition to macroeconomics, there is also systematic research at the micro-level of firms, especially studies that investigate to what extent financial imperatives alter the behavior of non-financial companies (Attílio and Cavalcante, 2019; Branco, 2010; Feijó et al., 2016; Fellows, 2019). Lastly, the impacts of financialization on areas of social provision, such as health care, education, and pensions, have also been a subject of sustained research activity in the country over the past decade (e.g., Bahia et al., 2016; Bressan, 2020; Lavinas, 2015a, 2017; Lavinas and Gentil, 2018; Martins et al., 2021; Sestelo, 2017a).

Like France, Brazil went through an early process of financialization heavily led by the State (Bruno et al., 2011; Lavinas et al., 2019). While the role of the government in leading this process can also be traced back to a changing approach to public financing in the 1960s, offering bonds in the markets, this appears to have been important not so much for promoting private capital markets (like in the French case), but because it allowed protecting financial investments in times of high inflation. The ways in which policies concerning public debt management favored financial investments varied over time and will be detailed in the next paragraphs.

There is a cohesive body of literature offering a periodization of financialization in Brazil, explaining its origins and different phases up to today (Araújo et al., 2012; Bruno et al., 2011; Lavinas et al., 2020, 2019). These works identify three main phases of financial accumulation in the country since the 1970s, with shifts in State policies being the decisive factor triggering the transition from one phase to another. Despite the differences that separate the several governments in office over this period, both right-and left-wing presidencies have played an active role in creating, maintaining, and expanding the policy framework that allowed financialization to advance (see also Bruno and Paulani, 2019; Gentil and Hermann, 2017).[19] Overall, there seems to be a shared understanding that these policy changes had to do with the fight against inflation, which is therefore considered to be at the heart of the financialization process in Brazil.

The first stage of financialization started in the 1980s, but it was rooted in changes in State financing and debt management practices undertaken as early as the 1960s. This was when the Brazilian government started on its path of financialization of the public debt by issuing standardized and negotiable public debt bonds in auctions. A defining aspect of the Brazilian experience has been the government's concern, since the very beginning, with protecting investors against the depreciation of their investments in public bonds due to inflation. It is telling that the first government negotiable bonds, created in 1964, were called "Readjustable National Treasury Bonds" (*Obrigações Reajustáveis do Tesouro Nacional*) for having their value periodically adjusted according to price indexes. Over the following decades, the public debt market expanded significantly with the creation of several other types of public securities, including fixed-rate and inflation-linked bonds (Araújo, 2002; Pedras, 2009).

This shifting approach to State financing and debt management set the foundations for the takeoff of the first stage of financialization from the 1980s to 1994 based on what was called "inflationary gains", a particularity of the Brazilian case. Bruno et al. (2011) offer a detailed account of this mechanism. As explained by the authors, in the context of a long-lasting inflationary crisis,

---

19   One can highlight a number of important political turnarounds in Brazil during the period under discussion: the rise of the military dictatorship in 1964, the transition to a democratic regime during the late 1980s, the election of a right-wing president in 1995 (Fernando Henrique Cardoso), his replacement for left-wing leaders from 2003 to mid-2016 (Luiz Inácio "Lula" da Silva and Dilma Rousseff), and a process of impeachment in 2016 that paved the way for right-wing, highly conservative governments over the following years (Michel Temer and Jair Bolsonaro).

indexed public debt bonds served to create an "alternative currency" unique to the financial system, which allowed for significant financial gains.[20] This "dual currency" system was based on the coexistence of two currencies: the official one, issued by the State, and the alternative ("financial") currency, issued and managed endogenously by the banking sector. While the former had its value continuously eroded by inflation, the latter was backed by the indexed public debt bonds mentioned above, meaning their value was continuously adjusted according to price indexes (Araújo et al., 2012; Bruno et al., 2011).

This system became both the primary policy strategy to cope with inflation in the country and the main channel for financial accumulation. The "pegged currency" served to create very short-term contracts with positive real interest rates (offered by the indexed bonds) and very low risk, in times of inflation. This allowed financial institutions and privileged investors from the upper middle classes to reap financial gains thanks to monetary correction mechanisms (Lavinas et al., 2019; Oliveira, 2010). The implementation of this system, albeit limited in scope and scale, is considered the trigger of financialization in Brazil: it set the conditions for a period of intense rentier accumulation by financial institutions and high-profile investors, as well as a significant expansion of these institutions based on operations with highly liquid and profitable assets (see also Araújo et al., 2012; Lavinas et al., 2020, 2019).

The previous mechanisms of financial accumulation from indexed public debt instruments were shattered in 1995 due to the sharp fall in inflation rates as a result of far-reaching monetary reforms to keep it under control.[21] However, rather than disappearing, new structures of financial accumulation emerged in line with the newly established policy framework. This came due to strict inflation targets imposed by the government since the mid-1990s and the implementation of an inflation-targeting regime in 1999, which justified permanently high real interest rates to reach them (Bruno et al., 2011). This concerns, in particular, the basic interest rate set by the Central Bank (the "Selic rate"), which influences the remaining interest rates in the economy.[22]

---

20 Inflation rates in Brazil reached 431% p.a. on average between 1980–9 and 1,321% p.a. in 1990–4, measured by the National Consumer Price Index (IBGE).

21 This was mainly due to a new stabilization program, the Real Plan, launched in 1993–4. As will be explained in Chapter 4, this stabilization plan managed to control inflation not only because high interest rates constrained demand, but mainly due to the fact that they countered currency devaluation. The currency devaluation was a product of the inflow of large volumes of foreign capital attracted by high interest rate differentials.

22 The Selic fulfills multiple roles in the Brazilian economy. Among them, it serves as the interbank lending rate, as the reference for the remuneration of a significant part of public debt bonds, and as a parameter for other interest rates.

Several studies demonstrate that both the basic and average interest rates in Brazil have been among the highest in the world since the mid-1990s (Bresser-Pereira et al., 2020; Bruno and Paulani, 2019; Lavinas, 2017).

The second phase of financialization, from the mid-1990s to the mid-2010s, was thus based not on inflationary gains but on interest income *per se*. The chief sources of financial profits in this period came from possessing high-yielding public debt bonds and investments tied to the latter. Furthermore, the rise in general interest rates fueled gains in other important sources of profits such as bank loans, once general interest rates tend to follow the behavior of the prime rate. In contrast to the former, "eliticized" phase of financialization, this stage of financialization reached an entirely new scale from the 2000s onward. With the massive expansion of bank credit to middle and low-income households, it is characterized as the moment of "mass-based financialization" (Lavinas et al., 2019). Salient features of this stage include the expansion of financial services to acquire services traditionally associated with the public sphere, with a dramatic boom in the areas of private pensions, health insurance, and student loans. Another characteristic was the use of social policy benefits by households as collateral to acquire debts (Lavinas, 2018b, 2017). This context allowed for extraordinary financial accumulation from sovereign bonds, loans, and derivative assets, remunerated at interest rates far higher than their foreign counterparts. Banks, investment firms, large national and foreign companies, and rentiers were among those that profited the most in this period (Araújo et al., 2012; Bruno et al., 2011; Lavinas et al., *op. cit.*).

As a result of a sharp economic slowdown starting in 2014 (with negative growth rates of the GDP in 2015–16 and sluggish recovery afterward), the government started reducing the basic interest rate. This seemed to have weakened, once again, the existing structures of financial accumulation. The late 2010s seem to mark a third phase of financialization, based on capital gains. While interest rates followed a downward path in the second half of the decade, the volume and value of stock market operations soared to unprecedented levels.[23] Market capitalization accelerated from 2016 onward, reaching historical highs in 2019. Corporate credit was also on the rise. The opposed trajectories between interest rates and stock market capitalization led Lavinas

---

23   As shown by Freitas and Prates (2001) and Lavinas et al. (2020), Brazilian governments made continuous efforts to promote the expansion of the country's capital markets since the 1990s, which nonetheless was kept in check during most of the financialization period. The level of the Brazilian basic interest rate was the main reason for poorly developed capital markets, making government bonds far more attractive than riskier investments.

et al. (2020) to formulate and test the hypothesis of a transition to a new financialization pattern driven by investments in shares and corporate credit. The authors find robust evidence of a change in the locus of financial accumulation from interest income toward both capital gains from shares and the extension of credit to companies. Another interesting finding is that the increase in market capitalization and corporate debt did not encourage innovation and productive investments; on the contrary, companies turned to debt to buy back their shares for securing future appreciation and speculate on other companies' shares. Despite the convincing results, the recent nature of this process calls for continued research to confirm this as a new phase of financialization.

The body of research presented above demonstrates that the State directly sponsored the process of rentier accumulation in Brazil by setting high interest rates and creating investment opportunities to reap interest income on a permanent basis. These results are in line with the idea that financialization in peripheral countries, especially Latin American ones, is based on the accumulation of interest-bearing capital and unfolds in a context of fighting inflation (Becker et al., 2010; Bonizzi, 2013).

Beyond new relations between the State and finance, the process of financialization also entailed changes in how businesses and households interacted with the financial sector. In the context of underdeveloped financial markets and attractive interest-bearing investments, non-financial Brazilian companies shifted behaviors from their typical activities toward rent accumulation. Several studies find positive correlations between high interest rates, overvalued exchange rates, and low rates of fixed capital formation (Bruno et al., 2011; Feijó et al., 2016; Lavinas et al., 2020, 2019). Micro-level analyses further support this view by showing that the quest for financial income was a determinant driver of investment decisions in Brazilian non-financial companies, leading them to increase the volume of funds invested in interest-bearing assets and remitted to the financial sector (Fellows, 2019; Rabinovich and Artica, 2020). Unsurprisingly, the country followed a path of precocious and progressive deindustrialization since the 1990s, which can be at least partially attributed to the process of financialization (Araújo et al., 2012; Bruno and Paulani, 2019; Lavinas et al., 2019).

To end, the incorporation of Brazilian households into the financial system is one of the most remarkable aspects of its financialization process. Since the 1990s, and particularly after the 2000s, the scope of individuals engaged with loans and insurance contracts has grown dramatically, reaching medium-and low-income households (Lavinas, 2015a, 2017; Lavinas and Gentil, 2018). However, households participate and benefit very differently from the expanded access to the financial system according to their level of income. Given the extreme concentration of the stock of real and financial wealth, the possibility of profiting from financial investments remains limited to the highest income brackets. The richest segments of the population own the largest share of financial assets held by families and receive most of the financial income provided by the latter. It is worth noting that the much-heralded decrease in social inequality in Brazil during the 2000s is skewed toward methodologies based on labor income; when accounting for financial rents as well, the results point to an increase in income concentration at the top of the distribution, much driven by financial gains (Medeiros and Castro, 2018; Morgan, 2017, 2015).

Different from financial investments, debt has advanced significantly toward the middle-and low-income classes. Interestingly, the financialization of households in Brazil followed a dynamic that escaped the usual observations of financialization studies: household indebtedness increased simultaneously with rising wages, lower unemployment rates, and declining labor income inequality (Bruno and Paulani, 2019; Lavinas et al., 2019).[24] Lavinas (2017) explains this paradox by noting that the social reforms in the neoliberal period prioritized monetary benefits over universal service provision, making individuals resort to credit and financial instruments to access essential and non-essential goods and services. The credit boom was heavily encouraged by the government through programs to promote "financial inclusion" and regulatory changes to facilitate individuals to take out loans. Civil servants, pensioners, and the groups at the bottom half of the distribution became a fast-growing market niche for loans and insurance instruments, typically of low value and limited coverage, including for services related to housing, pensions, education, and health care (see also Bruno and Caffe, 2014; Sciré, 2011; Lavinas et al., 2019). Household debt-to-income ratio more than doubled in less than fifteen years, from approximately 20% in 2005 to over 45% in 2018 (Banco Central, 2020). The volume of debts relative to average income is significantly higher for low-income than for middle-and high-income households. The same goes for the share of household income dedicated to covering the costs of debts (Banco Central, 2019; Lavinas, 2017).

---

24   Becker et al. (2010) use the concept of "popular" financialization to denote the incorporation of masses into this process. The authors do not consider this to be the case of Brazil due to a series of social reforms carried out the 2000s, which would have countered financialization trends. However, the studies shows in this section provide evidence that social reforms and financial inclusion went hand in hand in the more recent period of Brazilian financialization.

Taken together, the elements presented so far suggest that the process of financialization of the Brazilian economy shares important commonalities with trends documented in the literature on financialization at large and observed in the French case. Among them, Bruno et al. (2011) and Lavinas et al. (2019) highlight the unprecedented financial expansion and banking concentration since the 1970s, a rise in the personal and functional concentration of income and wealth, the decline in productive investment rates, the mounting levels of household indebtedness, and the affirmation of rentier behaviors in non-financial firms and high-income households. Another trait identified by these authors, and consistent with the previous discussion, is the apparent loss of State autonomy in the formulation of public policies, with an increase in the political power of the rentier classes and capital owners over the State apparatus.

3   Financialization and Social Provision

The inroads of finance into areas of social provision, changing their inner workings, is one of the distinctive traits of the process of financialization of the world economy (Bryan and Rafferty, 2014; Fine, 2014, 2009; Lavinas, 2020, 2018b; Leyshon and Thrift, 2007; Storm, 2018; Thomson and Dutta, 2015). When referring to areas of social provision, or social policy, I refer to those policy fields traditionally associated with social rights and provisions such as health care, pensions, housing, education, and income support (Karwowski, 2019; Lavinas, 2018a). The involvement of financial players in such activities, previously limited and regulated, has expanded dramatically over the past decades. Due to their strategic importance to the present investigation, the last part of this chapter engages in the discussion of how financialization has been reframing State action in areas of social provision. To make sense of this phenomenon, I propose an original systematization of the existing research on the topic, differentiating the ways in which financialization reshapes, on the one hand, how the population accesses essential services, and, on the other, how governments finance and provide these services to the population.

3.1   *The Inroads of Finance in Areas of Social Provision*
Leyshon and Thrift (2007) offer an insightful explanation as to why financial actors would be interested in participating in areas of social provision. According to the authors, financial players would be interested in expanding their participation in those areas due to their desire and need to find new spaces for financial profit extraction, which is necessary for the continuous

accumulation of financial capital. In this process, they need to continue incorporating regular income flows from other sectors and manipulate them so
these income flows can serve as a source of liquidity and solvency for financial
transactions. In the authors' words, "financial capitalism is dependent on the
constant searching out, or the construction of, new asset streams (...) previously considered trivial or off-limits and their incorporation into the financial
system" (pp. 98, 101). These income streams could serve as collateral for lending, investing, and trading, allowing agents to expand financial activities and
therefore the potential for financial returns.

In the process of prospecting for new sources of revenues, anything that
might provide a stable stream of income for capitalization and speculation can
be brought into play (Leyshon and Thrift, *op. cit.*). Areas critical to social reproduction are particularly attractive once they rely on relatively secure revenue
streams. Areas of social reproduction will be continually funded, no matter
their source, not least because human survival depends on them. Examples
of secure revenue streams include the disbursements made by governments,
households, and firms to finance the provision and access to goods and services in health, housing, and education, to name a few. Changes in social policy
can enable and foster the creation of financial assets and collateral based on
these revenue streams. In this way, part of cash flows originally channeled to
areas considered essential to human subsistence and development is diverted
to the financial sector.[25]

But what type of changes will allow finance to enter sectors of social provision? A review of the literature on financialization across different areas provides evidence of the transformative effects of financialization on both ends –
the forms through which the public sector finances and provides goods and
services as well as the ways in which individuals access them. In each case,
there seems to be an increased dependence on financial instruments and institutions. Following a chronological order of when most of these studies were
published, I begin by reviewing those that look at individuals and households,
examining how their conditions of access to goods and services are changing
in the period of financialization. They often characterize such changes as part
of the process of "financialization of social policy". Next, I present the discussion offered by studies demonstrating how governments and public sector
institutions are redesigning the ways to finance and deliver social goods and

---

25   The case studies in chapters 3 and 4 will illustrate how this occurs in the case of PHS, an
      area where this discussion is still in its infancy.

services in the context of financialization, which has been explored in further detail within the research on the "financialization of the State".

3.2   *The Financialization of Social Policy*

Works on the "financialization of social policy" (Fine, 2014, 2009; Lavinas, 2018b, 2017, 2015b) were the first to engage in continued and systematic research on the impacts of financialization in areas of social provision.[26] I argue that their discussion offers an account of the transformations in social policy from the perspective of citizens, addressing how their conditions of access to essential goods and services change in financialized capitalism and critically examining the role of the State in driving this shift.

From a collective reading, the main phenomenon that seems to characterize the financialization of social policy is the increasing weight of financial institutions and products as means to access consumer goods, essential services, and investment in life opportunities, replacing what was previously fulfilled (or expected to be fulfilled) by public provision. In other words, financial instruments are assigned with new purposes, including offsetting the deterioration of public provision. This thrives on the deterioration of comprehensive public provision, leading individuals to turn to the markets to access basic goods and services intermediated by financial instruments. Loans and insurance are two examples of financial instruments that can cover needs in essential areas of human life where the State is stepping back.

Fine (2009) refrains from providing a specific definition of the financialization of social policy, underscoring its variegated nature across countries and sectors. The author argues, however, that any transformation in social policy that creates a stream of revenue consolidated into assets traded in financial markets could be potentially interpreted as such:

> Neoliberalism (...) [is] heavily underpinned by an extraordinary expansion and promotion of financial activity. This goes far beyond the proliferation of the financial markets themselves (...) to an ever-expanding range of activities associated with both economic and social reproduction.
>
> (...) the relationship between financialization and social policy is neither uniform nor always or even primarily direct. *It is more so where the private has displaced the public sector with corresponding incorporation of financial markets into the process of provision*, as most notable with

---

26   For further empirical evidence, see the several studies carried out under the Financialization Economy Society and Sustainable Development (FESSUD) project (www.soas.ac.uk/fessud/).

housing and pensions. But any form of privatization has the potential to induce financialization since it creates a stream of revenue that can be consolidated into assets that can become part of a derivative that is speculatively traded.

> p. 5, emphasis added

Lavinas (2017) conceptualizes the financialization of social policy as the "uncoupling of social policy from its previous modus operandi, now rewarded by institutional arrangements based on the prerogatives of the financialization process" (p. 9). The distinguishing feature of the present historical moment, in her view, lies in the role that the financial sector takes on as a gateway to access social goods and services previously considered under the State's mandate. This would be most glaringly seen in the expansion of financial instruments in areas whose access has been traditionally associated with social rights, where public provision is expected to be universal and irrespective of the citizen's ability to pay. Consumer credit, payday loans, microcredit, student loans, private pension plans, and health insurance are cases in point. The growing availability of such products over the past decades indicates that consumers are appealing to markets to ensure access and protection against risks in sectors like health, old age, and education, as well as to complement income (Lavinas, 2018b, 2018a, 2017). This dramatic expansion of credit and insurance products come with a new scope, reaching middle-and low-income classes.

These studies contribute to dispelling the misconceived idea that the impacts of financialization on social policy are restricted to budget cuts and pressures in favor of the privatization of public services. Instead, they show that these are only the "tip of the iceberg" (Lavinas et al., 2019) of a far deeper transformation in social policies in the period of neoliberalism and financialization. The conclusion is that free, universal provision of in-kind goods and services by the State has to retreat so as to private, financialized alternatives advance. The financialization of social policy can be regarded as a two-sided process in which "more and more households will rely on financial markets for the provision of social goods, while public provision shrinks and deteriorates" (Lavinas, 2017, p. 83).

The financialization of social policy does not mean that social policies necessarily diminish in importance, but that their nature and scope change. The paradigm of social policy forged in the aftermath of the Second World War was based on a specific approach to State provision (Fine 2014, Lavinas, 2018b), promoting universal and publicly provided (or highly subsidized and regulated) services in all levels of complexity. In the case of monetary transfers, it prioritized comprehensive schemes of pension and assistance benefits. Even if heterogeneously and with pitfalls, such an approach oriented much of the formulation of social policies worldwide up until the neoliberal era.

In contrast, in the period of neoliberal, financialized capitalism, the blueprint of social policy is characterized by an increasing focus on basic service provision and conditional transfers. One can observe the widespread presence of this new approach to social policy as governments from both central and peripheral countries have become increasingly inclined to prioritize social spending in the form of low-value monetary benefits (such as minimum pensions and anti-poverty transfers) and service provision focused on basic services and vulnerable individuals (for instance, primary health care and primary education).[27] This logic of social provision based on principles of targeting, residualism, and selectivity opens space for the expansion of finance in areas of social policy.

On the one hand, the current approach to social policy supports the expansion of finance to the extent that areas of social provision constitute market niches in which financial instruments can only gain participation if public, universal options are removed or minimized (Bayliss et al., 2016a; Lavinas, 2020).[28] Cash transfers can be used for citizens to acquire those services in the markets, with the help of financial products, as well as to withdraw risks for the financial institutions providing the latter. Lavinas (2018b) elaborates on this idea of the "collateralization of social policy" with the example of instances where regular State payments (pensions, assistance benefits, and others) serve as collateral to access credit. She shows that this phenomenon was key in boosting the process of financial inclusion in some countries, enabling even welfare recipients to become potential borrowers.

On the other hand, the State focuses on "basic" services, usually riskier and less profitable activities, and often targeted toward the most vulnerable population groups. This also contributes to the expansion of financial activities.

---

27   This "residual" approach to social policy has been expanding with the support of multilateral institutions and international organizations. A telling example is the "Universal Health Coverage" proposal from the World Health Organization. Despite its name, this proposal is based on concepts of universality much more restricted than those of the post-war period (see Chapter 2).

28   Some authors note that private finance and social policy serve similar purposes, such as providing individuals with means to prevent and manage risks, smoothing out consumption throughout the life cycle, and increasing the level of disposable income. This is the case even though they work under different principles and leading, therefore, to different outcomes (Lo Vuolo, 2016; Sarlat, 2012). The acknowledgement of such (to some extent) interchangeable roles further supports the idea that the restriction of public provision opens space for financial activity.

While public provision covers areas in which profit margins are unattractive and for the "hard to serve", finance can act only where and when there is potential for profit extraction (Bayliss et al., 2016b; Fine and Bayliss, 2016; Lavinas and Gentil, 2018). Summing up, instead of promoting comprehensive systems of public provision, this neoliberal approach to social policy serves to increase the demand for financial assets, promote "financial inclusion", and underwrite risks for the financial sector, feeding the latter's continued expansion.

The literature on the financialization of social policy is closely related to the body of studies on household indebtedness (e.g., Fraser, 2016; González, 2020; Mader, 2015; Mertens, 2017; Montgomerie, 2020, 2006; Roberts, 2016; Soederberg, 2014), which associates the process of financialization with the significant rise in household debt over the last decades. Given the deterioration of wages, working conditions, and universal public provision associated with this process, credit would allow households to cover increasing financing gaps to access durable goods, meet daily needs, and cope with contingencies (Lavinas, 2018b). As explained by Roberts (2016), "debt has emerged as a key means through which households have sought to meet the costs of social reproduction being offloaded by the State (through welfare retrenchment) and capital (through low wages and precarious working conditions)" (p. 145). Recent studies have noted that household debt can grow even in the context of rising salaries and average income (ECLAC 2018; González, 2020; Lavinas et al., 2019). This suggests that the financial system is playing a role in domestic life that goes beyond that of compensating for falling wages, a typical trait found in the financialization literature looking at wealthy countries.

The most significant impact associated with such a transformation in social policy is the deepening of social inequalities. Greater inequality comes as a result of the progressive dismantling of policies based on universalism and comprehensive provision, which are essential for promoting basic standards and equal opportunities among individuals. These transformations undermine one of the chief goals of State intervention in areas of social provision, which is promoting social equity: in the context of the financialization of social policies, the quantity and quality of access to services become differentiated according to income levels, which determine how each individual will be able to engage with the financial system. The conditions of access to financial assets, insurance, and debt depend on each one's capacity to pay for them and to provide collateral (Fine, 2014; Lavinas, 2018a, 2018b).

Authors often mention the heterogeneous impacts of household debt across income groups to illustrate the social disparities generated by present forms of financial inclusion. Lapavitsas (2013) proposes the term "financial expropriation" to describe the transfer of income from households directly to the profits of the financial institutions that have played this mediating role for the private provision of goods and services. Once the rich and the poor are unevenly integrated into the financial system, their risks are also unevenly distributed (Mertens 2017). The costs of debt are a particularly important and unequal risk: the literature on household financialization presented in this section underscores that much of the recent credit growth originated from lower-income households, who usually cope with a larger debt burden relative to their income, face worse borrowing conditions, and are the most exposed to economic shocks (ECLAC, 2018; IMF, 2017).

The factors discussed in this section allow us to pinpoint a first effect of austerity on social policy: legitimizing and promoting the downsizing of public, comprehensive provision. In the neoliberal period, there is a rhetoric that public provision systems are overspending (Bayliss and Fine, 2020; Fine and Bayliss, 2016) and that the State must cut public expenditures with the latter to balance the public budget, a requirement of creditors and the international community (Lemoine, 2016; Streeck, 2014). This justifies reducing the scale and scope of universal, publicly provided services, which "run counter to the neoliberal principles of a slim State" (Lavinas, 2018b, p. 509). In their place arise cheaper options of social policy, the targeted and residual services and transfers that create opportunities for private finance. At the same time, austerity and finance also work together in another dimension, reshaping how the public sector will finance the service provision still under its responsibility – the object of the following section.

3.3   *The Financialization of the State*

Notwithstanding their value as reference works, studies on the financialization of social policy focus on examining developments from the perspective of citizens, unveiling how "modern finance has upended the logic of access to rights" (Lavinas, 2020, p. 312). They underscore how the State plays a crucial role in orchestrating these changes by reshaping its approach to social policy in ways that feed the expansion of financial instruments, institutions, and markets. Yet, social provision involves not only the population and the ways in which they access essential goods and services; it also involves public entities and how they finance and provide the latter. While it is true that part of public services is being narrowed or scaled down, there is still a part that remains under the State's responsibility, including in the case of services provided free or highly subsidized at the point of delivery (such as in the case of public hospitals and schools). As a result, there is a need to investigate the mechanisms through which financialization reshapes those parts of service provision that continue to be public and universal. This requires inquiring whether and how governments and public bodies at large may also be turning to financial instruments, institutions, and markets to fund and provide the goods and services that remain within their purview.

A second line of research within the financialization literature can help further understand how public actors are also resorting to financial capital to ensure social reproduction. I include in this strand works concerned with what they refer to as the "financialization of the State" (e.g., Fastenrath et al., 2017; Karwowski, 2019; Lagna, 2016; Pagliari and Young, 2020; Schwan et al., 2020; Wang, 2020, 2015) and the "financialization of public policies" (Chiapello, 2020, 2019, 2017).[29] The notion of "State" appears here in a broad meaning, encompassing the ensemble of entities and policies that make up the public administration. These scholars use the concept of financialization to examine the changing relationships between the financial sector and central governments, local governments, public service departments, state-owned institutions, and Social Security agencies, to name a few.[30] This reflects an interpretation of the State not as a cohesive entity, but as a varied array of apparatuses and branches where different interests are under permanent dispute. Within this literature, there is a widespread understanding that these areas can carry contradictory policies between them, and that the pendulum tends to swing in favor of policies that favor the dominant groups.[31] Although this research does not focus exclusively on issues related to social policy, it provides insights into developments in the latter. It does so by illustrating how financialization reshapes the ways in which public sector entities operate and carry public policies, which

---

29   For the sake of simplicity, I address these body of works collectively as the literature on the "financialization of the State", and use it interchangeably with the expression "financialization of the public sector".

30   In this book, I refer to the "State" in the broad sense applied by this literature, using it interchangeably with the concepts of the "public sector" and the "public administration". This differs from the usage of the term in systems of national accounts, which vary according to the country. In France, for example, the "State" denotes a specific branch of the public administration identified with the central government and separated from other branches, such as local governments and social security entities. In other countries, such as Brazil, the term encompasses all segments of the public administration.

31   See Lemoine (2018) for an insightful review of various interpretations of the "State" in social sciences and their contributions to examine the process of State financialization. In the period of financialization, dominant groups include investors and financial institutions. Several studies (Fastenrath et al., 2017; Lemoine, *op. cit.*; Schwan et al., 2020) demonstrate how public sector agencies, departments, ministers, and personnel working close to the financial sector have been gaining the upper hand over the remainder of the public administration during the past decades.

naturally extends to the entities responsible for social provision and the policies related to it.

Karwowski (2019) conceptualizes the financialization of the State as "the changed relationship between the State (...) and financial markets and practices" or, alternatively, as "the increasing influence of financial logics, instruments, markets, and accumulation strategies in State activities" (pp. 1001–2). Similarly, for Wang (2020), the scholarship on State financialization interrogates "how State ideas, State organizations, and State-making processes dovetail with the expansive mechanisms of finance" (p. 192). Pagliari and Young (2020) argue that such a revolution in the relationship between the State and finance can be observed in practice through various instances where public actors are relying on financial markets, indicators, and instruments. Wang (2020) emphasizes the relevance of such transformations insofar as they represent "a rising paradigm of governance and a new form of statecraft" (p. 188) in which States strategically turn to finance for several purposes such as refinancing the public debt, providing public goods, and stimulating growth. This changing form of governance entails a novel approach to public policies. Taking the latter as a starting point, Chiapello (2017) defines the financialization of public policies as "the penetration of financialized logics and forms of evaluation in the formulation and implementation of policies, even when these do not involve the financial sector" (p. 27). Said otherwise, the distinguishing feature of the financialization period would be that these processes entail changes in how States act, including when it comes to areas unrelated to the financial sector.

As in the case of the literature reviewed in the previous section, which shows that financialization does not simply "shrink" social policies, this body of works also contributes to dispelling some misguided beliefs associated with this process. One of the chief contributions of this strand of research is to challenge the idea that the State contributes to the financialization process mostly by facilitating the advancement of financial activities in the private sector.

There is a fairly generalized perception that the mechanisms through which the State participates in the expansion of finance are related almost exclusively to its role as a regulator, promoting shifts that enable and encourage the expansion of financial markets (Pagliari and Young, 2020). The State is typically constructed as an important actor, facilitator, and promoter in fostering financialization (Sokol, 2017). The problem, according to Sokol (*op. cit.*), is that "the literature on financialization has paid only limited attention to the way in which the State itself is increasingly subjected to the power of financial markets" (p. 680). The research on State financialization shows that the transformations occurring in the public sector in this period include, but are not limited to, promoting private sector financialization. In the words of Schwan et al. (2020), they are concerned with studying not only the process of financialization "*by* the State", but also the financialization "*of* the State". In a similar vein, for Chiapello (2017), there is the need to incorporate an approach to financialization that goes beyond an "externalist view" of the State, which looks at the financialization of the economy through public policies, and includes an "internalist view", concerned with the financialization of public policies themselves.

Wang (2020) offers an insightful account of the widespread misconceptions in the literature and the contributions of this recent body of works:

> Scholarly discussion on the rise of finance (...) tended to implicitly assume that finance expanded at the expense of the State. The contraction of the State was seen as symptomatic of a general net loss of political capacities (...). *We were reminded that everywhere we turned, public sectors were privatized, fiscal spending of the State was constrained, and government regulations were curtailed.* Losing assets and capacity, States were left toothless in the face of the rising global finance.
>
> *The facilitation explanation treated State actions as external to the economy. It did not include state motives and political interests as forces in their own rights driving financialization.* In the past several years, a growing body of scholarship has emerged to call for an extensive and intensive examination of the state-finance nexus (...). [*It*] *shows states to be more than just promoters and facilitators of financial markets. States have used financial instruments and institutions to solve political problems associated with public finance.*
>
> pp. 189, 190, 196, emphasis added

Based on a collective reading, the new relations between State and finance seem to manifest in at least two levels. First, the financialization of the State could be observed through shifts in ideas and structures. The process of financialization is associated with a reformulation of the vocabulary, techniques, indicators, instruments, and institutional arrangements of public entities, which start mimicking those typically employed by financial companies. The creation of financial agencies and units within the public administration, the hiring of new staff from the private financial sector to work in them, and the "training" of existing public servants according to their views are just a few examples of how finance has "colonized" the public sector (Chiapello, 2017; see also Fastenrath et al., 2017; Fine and Hall, 2012; Karwowski, 2019). Such shifts at the intangible level of ideas and organizational models shape public bodies' decision-making criteria in favor of measures that minimize financial costs and risks. Social costs and risks, in turn, are generally left out of the equation. They also make it seem possible, justifiable, and desirable to raise revenues in the private sector, touted as cheaper than traditional forms of funding. This creates an environment conducive to the resort to financial capital (Chiapello, 2017).

Second, these seemingly subtle ideological shifts can lead to transformations at the more concrete level of financing circuits – which includes how public entities raise money, from whom, and at what costs and conditions. Incorporating financial capital in public financing circuits means changing the ways in which public services, policies, and bodies are funded, introducing new instruments and strategies to bring in money that ultimately emanates from financial institutions and investors. This can occur, for example, when public entities issue securities, offer contracts that encourage investors to put money into specific projects, and create financial arrangements to pool money from different sources. Such innovations allow the public sector to mobilize funds voluntarily (as opposed to compulsory taxation on individuals and companies), notably from foreign investors (Chiapello, *op. cit.*; Fastenrath et al., 2017).

The vast majority of what has been written about transformations in public financing in times of financialization focuses on *quantitative* trends, specifically the steady and significant rise in public debt levels. This rise is associated with the economic, social, and political changes that emerged along with financialization, and is considered to fuel the ongoing expansion of financial markets (Lemoine, 2016; Streeck, 2014). The literature on State financialization, however, calls attention to a vast array of *qualitative* changes that are also underway. The diversification of instruments to finance public policies, some of which were mentioned in the previous paragraph, is an important example. Karwowski (2019) underscores the importance of considering the qualitative dimension of State transformations, commenting that "it is difficult to fully comprehend State financialization using quantitative measures alone, as major changes to fiscal and monetary policy have been qualitative in nature"; for instance, "it is not merely the size of public debt that indicates the presence (or absence) of financialization, but rather how debt instruments are designed, issued and managed" (p. 1004; see also Fastenrath et al., 2017).

The literature on State financialization presents two main explanations as to why governments and public entities engage with financial instruments and institutions. Aalbers et al. (2017) frame them as "constraint-driven" and "opportunity-driven" financialization. The idea of constraint-driven financialization embodies the assumption that public entities adopt financially innovative techniques as an attempt to circumvent budget constraints in times of austerity (Karwowski, 2019; Quinn, 2017). Financial practices are interpreted as "defensive measures" (Løding, 2018, p. 4) in an era when public entities face increasing difficulties to obtain revenues from traditional sources. Apart from increasing income, the use of market instruments could also offer, at least in a first moment, other compelling advantages such as low interest rates (Dodd, 2010; Løding, 2018) and the opportunity to bypass regulatory constraints, as they allow to reallocate revenue and spending items across the public budget (Chiapello, 2017; Lagna, 2016; Quinn, 2017; Whitfield, 2015). Following this line of reasoning, it can be argued that austerity would favor not only a more residual approach to public policies but also new strategies to finance them, as this context imposes limits to usual sources of revenues and stricter budget rules on public entities.

Even Schick (2013), who departs from a rather positive view on the use of private finance by public entities, acknowledges the potential for using these strategies to bypass regulatory constraints. He writes that, on some occasions, welcoming private capital

> can be a means of *evading fiscal constraints by shifting expenditures off the budget*. In many cases, contingent liabilities can substitute for direct expenditures, but with the critical difference that the latter are recognized on financial statements and the former usually are not. For example, governments (...) can directly finance road construction through budgeted expenditures or through off-budget guarantees embedded in Public-Private Partnerships. *The choice of policy instrument is not driven solely by efficiency considerations, but is strongly influenced by how various arrangements are treated in the budget.*
>
> p. 48, emphasis added

Opportunity-driven financialization, in turn, reflects the idea that the observed transformations in public finances are considered a result of public entities seizing opportunities to generate income and conduct statecraft in ways that were previously inaccessible to them (Lagna, 2016; Løding, 2018). Aalbers (2019) contends that these two sets of explanations are not necessarily opposed, suggesting that the reality seems to be better understood as a "bricolaged" response to both fiscal constraints and financial market euphoria.

There are at least four prominent research themes within the research on State financialization. These are focused on how financialization has changed the workings of central governments, local governments, public investment institutions, and areas of social provision. Considering that these spheres are all directly or indirectly involved in the organization, financing, and service provision of PHS, understanding how financialization reshapes them can bring valuable insights to the discussion presented in the following chapters.

3.3.1   Financialization and Central Governments: Changes in Public Debt Management

The so-called "financialization of government debt management" is arguably the most researched topic in the literature on State financialization (Fastenrath et al., 2017; Lagna, 2016; Lemoine, 2018, 2016; Pagliari and Young, 2020; Preunkert, 2017; Schwan et al., 2020b; Wang, 2020). At the heart of this transformation is the marketization of the public debt – the process through which governments started borrowing from financial investors in global financial markets instead of relying on administered sources of funding. The central agent driving these transformations is the central government, which issues these securities to finance itself and refinance its debt (also known as "sovereign debt").

As described throughout these different accounts (and exemplified by the French and Brazilian cases presented earlier), until the 1960s, States financed themselves by borrowing from individual agents and issuing their debts in the form of bonds with politically controlled interests and to targeted buyers, with whom they negotiated directly. This form of financing can be referred to as "classical debt". It implied stable, long-standing relationships with creditors, who provided loans or purchased bonds intending to hold them to maturity. Along with the beginning of the financialization of the world economy in the 1970s, there was a structural shift in the way that governments raised revenues and refinanced their debts. This went from borrowing from specific lenders via long-term arrangements to selling public bonds to financial investors in order to raise funds. The novel approach allowed governments to raise funds from financial investors willing to buy these securities, both national and foreign. These securities consist of negotiable assets, meaning that investors are not obliged to hold them until maturity, but can sell them at a profit at any time. Issuing bonds quickly became the primary means of government financing, accumulating what is sometimes referred to as "financial debt".

The financialization of the public debt is marked not only by a shift in the instruments used for public debt management but also by the changing balance of power between the State and its creditors as a consequence of such a shift. The public debt ceased to rely on non-tradeable obligations based on a stable bilateral relationship between the State and individual creditors; instead, it became a tradeable financial product that could be bought and sold on financial markets to make short-term assets (Preunkert, 2017). Marketable public bonds are sold at auctions and have their interest rates influenced by the conditions of supply and demand in the markets; as highlighted by Lemoine (2018, 2016), this means governments are deprived of their power to regulate the volume and cost of their own financing. By issuing securities to obtain funding, States become market creators and players (Karwowski, 2019; Pagliari and Young, 2020). At the same time, global financial actors acquire the power to influence their decision-making processes, determining the availability and costs of government financing (Fastenrath et al., 2017; Preunkert, 2017).

Blakeley (2020) goes over some of the chief mechanisms through which markets manage to gain influence over governments through the channel of the public debt, as well as the role played by austerity ("fiscal rectitude") in this process:

> Part of the reason governments considered such a demonstration [of fiscal rectitude] necessary is that they needed private investors to believe that they will honor their debts. Demand for government debt is inversely correlated with yield: the higher the demand, the lower the interest payments. This gives the markets power to discipline states that fail to demonstrate a commitment to creditworthiness. States that fail to implement neoliberal policies can be punished through bond selloffs and runs on their currencies, giving international investors significant power to influence democratically elected governments. It doesn't matter that forcing States to implement neoliberal economic policy actually reduces their creditworthiness over the long term; the time horizons of financial capitalism are shorter than at any other period in history.
>
> pp. 7–8

Issuing debt instruments in financial markets has been justified because they would offer governments the possibility of expanding the scope of revenue sources, especially by reaching out to foreign investors (e.g., Plihon, 2003). It would also reduce debt costs due to the assumption that competition among lenders tends to lower the interest rates charged to provide funds (Fastenrath et al., 2017; Karwowski, 2019; Preunkert, 2017).

A number of authors put these explanations into perspective, suggesting that this shift in public financing should be understood as part of a far deeper transformation in the relations between States and financial markets in the context of the financialization of the world economy. One of them is Streeck (2014, 2013), who distinguishes three paradigms governing States' approach toward public financing, expenditures, and debt management over the past centuries. According to the author, until the post-war period, governments relied on taxation as their primary source of funding, configuring the so-called "Tax State". Amidst the rise of neoliberalism in the 1970s, the declining taxation on capital and the globalization of production shrank the volume of public revenues relative to the economy, leading States to face growing financing needs. Seeking to conciliate profit incentives with social demands, governments "came to rely on borrowing from elites instead of taxing them" (Hager, 2016, p. 7, commenting on Streeck's work). In this context, States carried institutional reforms to raise funds through the process of marketization of the public debt and started borrowing at a much faster pace. This marks the emergence of the "Debt State", a State that finances itself increasingly through debt borrowed in the financial markets. Such developments were contingent on the financialization of the economy, including the deregulation of financial markets, their geographic integration, and the enormous expansion of their institutions and instruments. At the same time, creditors started a permanent onslaught to maintain a political-economic arrangement favorable to States' continuous indebtedness.

Streeck also argues that the continuous growth of public debt amidst a context of heightened global instability, especially since the late 2000s, has steered governments in a slightly different direction. Creditors started calling for implicit and explicit guarantees of governments' capacity to honor their debts. These include the implementation of "fiscal consolidation" policies by governments – measures to reduce the fiscal deficit and the debt-to-GDP ratio (Ortiz et al., 2015). This context set the stage for the third stage known as the "Consolidation State", marked by government attempts to stabilize and bring down the public debt under the narrative that the latter is unsustainable. Despite the differences between the last two stages of public debt management, one thing remains the same: the prioritization of the use of public resources to service the public debt.

From a different perspective, Lemoine (2018, 2016) also discusses how changes in public debt management are connected to the financialization of the world economy, and the implications for the use of public funds. The author suggests the concept of the "Debt Order" to describe the formation of "a political society that makes sacred the credit of the State vis-à-vis financial investors" (2018, p. 316), prioritizing the use of funds to serve the public debt rather than financing social provision. Lemoine puts greater emphasis on the variegated ways in which a specific approach toward public debt management affects different sectors of society. Beyond their differences, both Streeck and Lemoine agree that this particular mode through which governments operate, subordinated to financial markets, was contingent on financial expansion and contributed to boosting it even further.

More importantly, both Streeck's concepts of "Debt State" and "Consolidation State" and Lemoine's idea of "Debt Order" describe the existence of a hierarchy in public decision-making policies in favor of State creditors, a consequence of this particular *modus operandi* on public debt management. Such a hierarchy in government priorities has direct implications for fiscal policy, including for social spending in health care, pensions, education, and so on. This is because governments must save funds to honor their debts – meaning, in practice, pay for interests and amortizations on sovereign bonds. In a political setting averse to increasing taxation, especially on capital, these revenues come mainly from cutting spending in areas other than the public debt service, notably investments and social expenditures. Cuts in these areas are among the most common measures carried by governments to save funds for public debt repayments and reassure the markets about their creditworthiness (see also Deruytter and Möller, 2020; Sokol, 2017). Another common type of reform to save funds for public expenditures consists of regulatory shifts imposing legal constraints on public spending, such as balanced budget amendments to the national constitution (Deruytter and Möller, 2020; Streeck, 2013).

It is worth noting that these shifts in State financing entail not only a particular paradigm of fiscal policy, but of monetary policy as well. The standard approach to monetary policy in the present stage of public debt management also seems to prioritize the interests of financial investors and impose constraints on public spending to do so. The literature on the *modus operandi* of financialized States mentioned above (Lemoine, 2018, 2016; Streeck, 2014) highlights that fiscal policies typical of the financialization period are accompanied by a specific orientation to monetary policies focused on fighting inflation. The fight against inflation is crucial for preserving the social and political order subordinated to global financial markets: as explained by Epstein (2001), financial profits are positively correlated to asset appreciation and negatively affected by price inflation. This means that price stability preserves the value of financial assets, while inflation erodes it once the currency loses its value (see also Karwowski, 2019; Lemoine, 2018; Palley, 1997). Especially in the case of developing countries, this concern with inflation often reinforces high interest rate policies, which take a heavy toll on the public budget (Becker et al., 2010).

The consolidation of a "pro-finance" monetary policy framework became evident in the 1990s as a growing number of central and peripheral economies started adopting inflation-targeting policies. This means establishing a low inflation goal and directing monetary policy to achieve it, almost always to the exclusion of other goals such as reducing unemployment or stimulating investments (Epstein, 2001). Tellingly, the inflation-targeting framework takes into account the inflation of general prices while leaving aside financial asset inflation (Karwowski, 2019). This indicates that "central banks across the globe have internalized the financial motives of private investors and creditors through inflation targeting, aimed at preserving the value of financial investments" (*op. cit.*, p. 1017). Empirical studies support this argument by confirming that the only effect of inflation targets over the past decades has been to curb inflation, with no significant improvements in other macroeconomic aggregates (Epstein, 2001; Epstein and Yeldan, 2008). In light of these results, these studies conclude that the explanations for the spread of inflation-targeting regimes over the last decades are to be found in "the increased power of rentier interests which have been promoting inflation targeting and central bank independence as ways of keeping inflation low", which consequently "increase the share of income going to rentiers" (Epstein, 2001, p. 5).

From what has been exposed so far, it becomes clear that the marketization of the public debt, tight fiscal policies, and anti-inflation monetary policies go hand in hand, consolidating a form of governance where the interests of creditors are placed above those of other agents. In the case studies presented here, it will become clear how such developments imposed unprecedented challenges for the financing of public health and favored the financialization of PHS. Before delving into this discussion, it is worth devoting a few lines to some emerging topics in the literature on State financialization that are likely to be important for future research on the topic.

3.3.2   Emerging Themes on State Financialization: Local Governments, Public Investments, and Social Provision

Among emerging themes in the literature on State financialization, one of the most rapidly growing areas of research is the one on local governments. The research on the "financialization of local governments" (Ferlazzo, 2018; Løding, 2018) calls attention to the fact that local and regional governments are engaging in new relations with the financial system. It shows, in particular, how the latter are employing strategies to raise and manage funds independently from the central government. Case studies and reviews show that local governments are issuing their own bonds, capitalizing future income streams from public services and utilities, engaging with derivatives and off-balance sheet transactions, using local revenues to invest in financial markets, and contracting structured loans (including "toxic loans"), to mention a few examples (Aalbers, 2019; Beswick and Penny, 2018; Deruytter and Möller, 2020; Dodd, 2010; Løding, 2018; Wang, 2020).[32] The fact that local governments in both France and Brazil are experimenting with financial innovations demonstrates how quickly this phenomenon is spreading across the globe: for example, French "local communities" have been issuing bonds and engaging in structured loans (Ferlazzo,

---

32   Some authors also call attention to the use of such instruments by central governments, although in this case the research is mostly focused on derivatives and swaps (e.g., Fastenrath et al., 2017; Lagna, 2016; Schwan et al., 2020).

2018), while Brazilian municipal governments (*governos municipais*) are increasingly interested in securitizing local tax revenues (Fattorelli, 2017).

Aside from governments, two research areas attracting considerable attention in recent years are those looking at the impacts of financialization on public investments and service provision. In the case of investments, studies note that bodies responsible for managing public assets and investing public funds have been relating differently to financial markets, practices, and institutions over the past years (Dixon, 2020; Schwan et al., 2020b; Wang, 2020, 2015). This novel approach to public investment and asset management could be observed by looking at State-run investment funds, State-owned enterprises, and bodies responsible for managing State assets, among others. There is growing evidence that some of these entities are behaving similarly to private shareholders and institutional investors, making decisions that prioritize shareholder value maximization or increase the share of revenues coming from financial investments. Wang's (2015) concept of the "shareholder State" is particularly illustrative of the nature of such shifts, describing a State that has "refashioned itself as a shareholder and institutional investor in the economy and resorted to financial means to manage its ownership, assets, and public investments" (p. 1).

Finally, we reach the area of social provision. The literature on State financialization also opened an avenue of research into the transformations taking place inside the public entities that organize the financing and delivery of social services. These include governments, ministries, social security institutions, specialized agencies, and other bodies directly or indirectly responsible for policies related to health care, education, pensions, housing, and other realms related to social reproduction. Given that these are an integral part of the public sector, this approach also considers whether and how these entities are leaning toward financial instruments and strategies to carry out such activities. Wang (2020) captures the essence of these developments observing that "welfare state institutions moved closer to financial markets" as "State agencies for pensions, housing, education, and health care have invested in the market, borrowed from the market, and subsidized market-based financing" (p. 190).

Initially, the investigation on how financialization reshapes the ways in which public entities finance and organize social provision paid particular attention to the areas of pensions and housing (Bayliss et al., 2017, 2016b; Fine, 2014, 2009; Karwowski, 2019).[33] The role of household credit as a means

---

33   Although some of these works are not explicitly informed by the theory of State financialization, they have been important to bring awareness to the field. While part of them suggests that the largest amount of research is dedicated to pensions, there is reason to

of accessing housing, in the first case, and the shift from public risk-sharing pension schemes to increasingly individualized fully funded schemes, in the second, have been presented as particularly prominent aspects of financialization in social provision. This is not to say that these have been the only sectors under investigation, but simply that they seem to have been the object of more continuing research over time, especially in earlier stages of research. This focus is understandable; the own nature of these services makes them relatively more dependent on financial intermediation than other sectors (even if sometimes subject to State regulation), which contributes to making new relations with financial markets more evident in these cases. In contrast, there seems to be less published research on how the financing of activities in sectors of service delivery, such as public health and public education, might have been subjected to financial practices, institutions, and markets.[34]

Over the last decade, academic research began to pay greater attention to other financing instruments, broadening the research on the financialization of social provision. These include, for example, public-private partnerships and social impact investment (e.g., Andreu, 2018; Bayliss and Van Waeyenberge, 2017; Bryan et al., 2020; Karwowski, 2019; Whitfield, 2015). Public-Private Partnerships (PPPs), mostly used for infrastructure financing, consist of long-term contracts between the government and private actors in which the latter assumes part or all of the financing, building, and operational tasks of a public project. Financial actors participate and profit from PPPs in different ways; for example, banks, investments funds, and investors can provide credit, acquire assets, or even securitize income flows to create securities traded in secondary markets (Bayliss and Waeyenberge, 2017; Loxley and Hajer, 2019). Social Impact Bonds (SIBs) and other variations of "social impact investing" are used to finance specific interventions, raising funds from investors against future repayments and compensations based on results (Andreu, 2018; Lavinas, 2018b; Ryan and Young, 2018). In both cases, these strategies allow financial investors to provide upfront financing for public actions in several areas related to social provision.

Given the diversity of social policy across place, time, and program (Bayliss and Fine, 2020; Fine, 2014, 2009), understanding how public entities are turning toward finance to maintain social provision requires systematic and in-depth investigations for a wide scope of countries, sectors, and strategies. In

---

argue that the research on the housing sector has also received a great deal of attention (see, e.g., Aalbers et al., 2020, 2017; Bayliss et al., 2016a; Beswick and Penny, 2018; Wijburg and Waldron, 2020).

34   The existing research for health care will be discussed in Chapter 2.

the remaining part of this book, I delve into the case of health and in particular of public systems of health care, which have received scant attention from the literature so far. The goal is to unpack how these systems are responding to the constraints they face in the period of financialized capitalism and how they are drawing on the growing array of solutions offered by the financial sector to do so.

CHAPTER 2

Public Health Systems in Times of Financialization

During the 20th century, several countries recognized health care as a fundamental right and instituted public health systems (PHS) seeking to guarantee this right to the population. Over time, these systems have expanded both in terms of service and population coverage, reflecting their centrality as a mechanism to promote social well-being. This successful trajectory, however, seems to be increasingly questioned and reversed.

At the same time, it is virtually impossible to describe current transformations in the health sector without mentioning financial actors and instruments. Considering that PHS are responsible for a significant, often the largest share of health care financing and provision at the national level, the rampant expansion of finance will most likely influence the direction taken by these systems in the 21st century. In this way, it is crucial to look at the process of financialization and how it might be shaping public policy-making decisions related to PHS.

This chapter seeks answers to two key and still open questions that are crucial to examine how financialization reshapes PHS: One, what does it mean to say that a PHS is undergoing a process of "financialization"? Two, how to contextualize this process in the long-standing path of health system transformations in the neoliberal era? I argue that the fresh perspective offered by the concept of financialization can provide a clearer view of the instruments and strategies through which part of reforms in PHS from the 1990s onward have been implemented. Using this concept can also shed light on who are the agents that have been driving and profiting from such shifts, as well as the potential implications for how these systems operate.

The first section of this chapter introduces the topic of PHS, clarifying to which institutions I am referring to and the main institutional arrangements guiding existing systems worldwide. The second section systematizes the most common terms that have been used to examine neoliberal reforms in PHS. It will also highlight the limitations of the traditional literature on health systems change, in particular the lack of in-depth analyses of financialization. The final section recovers the concept of financialization and elaborates on how one could apply it to examine reforms in PHS. I draw insights from two sources to conceptualize the process of financialization in PHS: one, the existing literature on financialization in global health policies and private health activities; two, empirical evidence on how public health activities, especially in countries with comprehensive public provision, have become more dependent on financial instruments and markets. I contrast these developments with the shifts that are typically associated with the notion of privatization. In doing so, I contend that they reflect a distinctive type of PHS reform aligned with the idea of financialization. The working definition and typical features of financialization in PHS suggested here offer a common analytical grid for the empirical investigation carried out in the upcoming chapters.

1   Public Health Systems (PHS)

1.1   *Reasons for State Intervention in Health Care*
State intervention in health care has been justified on both moral and economic grounds. First, many societies, for generally accepted ethical reasons, have decreed that certain goods and services should be excluded from usual market relations (Barr, 1998). There are compelling arguments to explain why nations would agree with State intervention in health goods and services markets. A good state of physical and mental health is necessary for individuals to survive, function as agents in their societies, and develop their potential as human beings (Sen, 2004, 1992). It is no surprise that people tend to express greater concern with inequalities in health than with inequalities in the distribution of income or regular commodities: the former is considered a constraint on what people can *be* and *do*, representing inequalities in the most basic freedoms and opportunities that people can enjoy (Anand, 2004).

Adding to the intrinsic value of health and health care, there is the realization that individuals may lack the opportunity to access a good state of health not out of personal choices but because of factors beyond their control (Sen, 2004, 1992). Some health problems may arise from the choice for a certain lifestyle; others, however, can be directly related to the existing modes of living and production typical of modern capitalist societies. By shaping the conditions in which people live and work, modern capitalist structures may enable healthy lives, or, conversely, sicken, disable, and kill (Schrecker, 2020). State intervention in health can thus be justified as a means to guarantee that individuals receive the assistance they need regardless of factors that would otherwise prevent them to receive care in market economies, such as personal income or occupational status (Barr, 1998).

Besides the moral case for public health care, related to the idea of social justice and equality, economic reasons have also served to justify the need for State action in the distribution of health goods and services. The efficiency case for State intervention in health care is based on the argument that they are not like other types of goods and services. It is possible to show that the conditions for unregulated private markets to function properly are mostly absent when it comes to health goods, services, and insurance. The assumption of private market efficiency depends on some conditions including perfect information, perfect competition, and the absence of market failures; health care activities fail to meet these conditions in several ways. There are, for example, serious information problems caused by the inherently unequal levels of power and knowledge between health providers and patients. Similarly, several aspects undermine perfect competition: it is no exaggeration to state that obtaining health assistance is often a matter of life and death. It is thus difficult to argue that individuals can make "rational choices" between service providers when decisions are surrounded by a heavy weight of emotions, fear, and urgency. There are hardly any other sectors where the so-called "rational consumer choice", so dear to advocates of private markets, is as compromised as in health care. These are only some of many distortions commonly seen in private health markets that undermine efficiency, understood as the allocation of resources that could bring the greatest improvements to health at the lowest cost at the national level (Barr, 1998).

One can make a similar case with the conditions that are necessary for health insurance markets to work. The reasons why free private health insurance would be prone to gaps and inefficiencies have mainly to do with the fact that private insurance is governed by the logic of actuarial accounting, based on the estimation of individual risks (which is not the case for public insurance). For private schemes to work, such risks must be assessable, independent among members, and cannot be certain. Fulfilling these requirements may be difficult or even impossible in the case of health. For example, it is difficult to estimate individuals' health care needs in the long run, risks may not be independent (talk about contagious diseases and natural disasters), and there are many events in which the need for insurance is certain (as in the case of chronic illnesses). To cope with these distortions, private insurers often resort to practices known as "cherry-picking" or "cream-skimming", where they refuse to cover high-risk individuals, or instead charge them much more. The gaps in medical insurance coverage are thus particularly harmful to the most vulnerable individuals, including the elderly and those suffering from complex and long-term diseases (Arrow 1963; Barr, 1998).

The many distortions across service and insurance markets explain why there is an overwhelming presumption that an unrestricted private health market will be highly inefficient and inconsistent with notions of social justice (Barr, 1998). Due to its exclusive capacities to regulate activities, organize production, and redistribute resources across individuals and sectors, the State has been considered by many as a better candidate to foster equity and efficiency in health care. In fact, many countries have chosen to not rely on private payments and insurance as the primary method of health care financing; in those cases, public entities provide citizens with access to service provision or insurance, protecting them against the risks of diseases and the costs of treatments.

1.2   *Defining Public Systems*

But how can we define a public health system (PHS)? According to the World Health Organization (2010a), a health system can be conceptualized as the ensemble of institutions, resources, and people involved in the financing, organization, and delivery of health services at the national level. Every country has a unique health system, which reflects its history, level of economic development, and dominant political ideology (Roemer, 1993). Although the literature presents numerous proposals for classifying and characterizing national health systems, there is no commonly agreed-upon definition of what a *public* health system is, nor a standard set of criteria to identify it (Jarvis et al., 2020; Papanicolas, 2013; Stuckler et al., 2010). For the sake of illustration, Jarvis et al. (*op. cit.*) assess 67 studies on public health systems and find that only twenty of them have formally defined the term, half of the time proposing an original definition.

The challenges for delimiting the boundaries between public and private in health care can be understood by considering the very notion of "system"; as the term suggests, the organization of health care services at the national level depends on the coordination between several parts of the public and private sector, including the government, public bodies, non-profit entities, private for-profit companies, health professionals, and users. Each country will end up with a unique combination of these elements. Moreover, these agents will work under particular forms of cooperation and competition in each case. In light of these factors, the boundaries between public and private tend to be more blurred in the case of health care than in most other sectors (André et al., 2015; André and Hermann, 2009).

In this work, the notion of public system encompasses all health systems organized by the public sector and informed by the principles of universality, equity, solidarity, and comprehensive care. The public sector referred to here can be either the government or another public body, which takes on a central role in the management and financing of services. The principle of universality establishes that the system covers the entire population of a country, legally entitled to receive health care through insurance coverage or direct service provision. The notion of equity implies that all members have access to the same standards of services, delivered according to medical needs rather than the capacity to pay. Solidarity means that each individual contributes to the system's financing according to his or her means, which is possible through compulsory taxation (e.g., income taxes and contributions on wages). Comprehensive care denotes the State's commitment to cover services at all levels of complexity, comprising the full spectrum of actions individuals may need, from prevention to treatment and rehabilitation. Additionally, these systems are formally inscribed in the national constitution or relevant legislation, which makes their existence relatively shielded from the dispositions of incumbent governments. Several central and peripheral countries present health systems that fit into these criteria, with varied institutional arrangements and at different levels of consolidation in each case.

In the countries in which they exist, PHS represent the main gateway to services for the majority of the population. They also mitigate inequalities and exclusions of access to health care, which tend to be deeper in countries heavily dependent on private financing and provision. Studies show that nations with comprehensive and compulsorily financed systems tend to present lower levels of health care inequalities, greater efficiency in resource allocation, superior indicators of population health, and lower levels of total health spending compared to countries reliant on private and poorly regulated markets (Agartan, 2012; Giovanella et al., 2018; Mackintosh and Koivusalo, 2005; WHO, 2010b; Yi et al., 2017). Public systems also foster a shared sense of community (Dao and Mulligan, 2016) and serve as blueprints for countries still in the process of establishing universal access to health care.

1.3 *Common Institutional Arrangements of PHS*

The different paths taken by each country to organize the provision of health services and insurance led to a vast body of literature seeking to classify health systems (Beckfield et al., 2013; Böhm et al., 2012; Rothgang, 2010a; Toth, 2016; Wendt, 2009; Wendt et al., 2009). This research field adopts an international comparative approach to cluster different experiences and identify "health system types" – theoretical constructs grouping real experiences that resemble each other on some key points (Rothgang, *op. cit.*).

Financing and provision are the two main dimensions used to differentiate health systems (Beckfield et al., 2013; Wendt et al., 2009). The dimension of financing considers the way in which the system is funded – how much it raises in revenues, how these revenues are collected, and where health agents spend them. The dimension of provision takes into account the organization of the scheme – the type and quantity of the services offered, as well as the arrangement between public and private entities to offer them.[1] Rothgang (2010a) includes regulation as a third important dimension to classify health systems. In this way, "health care systems can be visualized as a house, with financing and service provision as its two pillars resting on a foundation of shared values", and "with the roof representing the regulation of the interactions between service providers, financing agencies, and potential beneficiaries" (p. 11).

The degree and forms of State intervention in the financing, delivery, and regulation of health care are the main criteria that distinguish different types of health systems (Roemer, 1993; Rothgang, 2010a). Within this three-dimensional framework, public entities can fulfill several roles: first, they can finance services and insurance; second, they can organize service provision; lastly, even if public actors do not finance or provide services directly, the government can be more or less engaged in regulating private actors.

Once unregulated activities lead to distortions both in health services and insurance markets, the two primary models of PHS that have been created to achieve universal and equal access to care are based on public provision (direct public service delivery) and public insurance (collective and regulated insurance schemes). There is a vast number of works distinguishing health system types and, although each one proposes a unique form of classifying these systems, it is common practice to distinguish three ideal types: the "national health service", the "social insurance", and the "private insurance" model (see, e.g., Böhm et al., 2012; Freeman and Frisina, 2010; Rothgang, 2010a; Wendt et al., 2009).[2] The breakdown of health care systems into these three models is the standard typology that most authors have been sharing and using as a basis to develop their analysis (Toth, 2016). To avoid the danger of oversimplification, several authors have sought to broaden the scope of possible arrangements and empirically test how real-world systems fit into them (e.g., Moran, 2000; Reibling et al., 2019; Toth, 2016; Wendt, 2009; Wendt et al., 2009).

In "national health service" models, the government is directly responsible for health care financing and service provision. The system is financed

---

1   Conventionally, in the health systems literature, "public entities" include government units, public sector institutions, and social security branches, while "private entities" include mutual companies, for-profit insurers, not-for-profit insurers, and sickness funds, among others (OECD, 2004).

2   Some scholars (e.g., Beckfield et al., 2013) also mention a fourth type of health system, the *semashko* model. This was the typical model of soviet countries, based on universal health care fully funded and provided by the State.

through the government budget, mainly from general taxation. Services are publicly provided, free at the point of delivery, and the providers are government employees or contractors. The underlying value is equity: every citizen should enjoy equal access to care. These systems are sometimes referred to as "Beveridgean systems" after William Beveridge, the British civil servant and politician whose ideas influenced the creation of the first system of this type in the United Kingdom. Despite the many reforms in its national health system carried forward over the last decades, the United Kingdom continues to be the main reference for national health service models; several other countries followed the same blueprint, such as Sweden, Norway, Denmark, Finland, Iceland, New Zealand, Italy, Portugal, Spain, Brazil, and Cuba.

In "social insurance" models, societal actors take on the responsibility for health care financing and provision. These are defined as non-governmental actors entrusted with responsibilities to support the public interest (Frisina et al., 2021). They manage the mandatory insurance funds that finance the health system. The bulk of revenues comes from social contributions, typically payroll taxes paid by employers and employees. Social health insurance funds represent a collective form of financing and management, with mechanisms to allow members to take part in decision-making processes. The government may participate in the overall financing of the scheme, regulate conditions of access and the value of premiums, and guarantee the benefits. Service provision is also considered societal, coming from a mix of public and private entities and with the important participation of non-profit providers. The underlying value is solidarity – equal access to services for all members of the fund. These systems are also known as "Bismarckian systems" in a reference to Otto von Bismarck, the German chancellor who first instituted a mandatory national health insurance. Germany remains the archetype of this model; other countries that implemented mandatory insurance include France, Belgium, the Netherlands, Japan, Switzerland, Canada, Taiwan, and South Korea.

In "private health care" models, market actors control health care financing and provision. Private financing comes in two ways: private insurance premiums and out-of-pocket payments. Service provision is in private ownership, from both for-and not-for-profit providers. There is no or limited government regulation on private sector prices and insurance coverage. Different from the social insurance model, insurers have much more freedom to select beneficiaries and adjust premiums according to individual risks. The underlying value is equivalence: services are provided according to the ability to pay for them. Although mandatory or State-sponsored health care schemes may exist in countries that follow this model, they do not cover the entire population, and coverage is heterogeneous across schemes. The United States is the single large, high-income country in which this model better describes the reality, while Chile is a case in point in peripheral countries. In general, one can infer that any country that does not count with significant State intervention in service provision or insurance will fit into this category.[3]

The notion of PHS employed in this book encompasses systems following either one of the two first categories above, national health service and social insurance models. This is because countries following both approaches have been able to foster principles of universality, equity, solidarity, and comprehensiveness in health care through their national health system. In particular, countries following either one of these models have been able to approve universality, the legal right to health care coverage for every citizen. This can be explained in light of the process of (partial) "convergence" between these models since the late 20th century, as countries with national health service models have been incorporating features typical of social insurance models and vice-versa. Countries with social insurance systems have progressively implemented universalization measures so that all citizens, and not only those with a formal labor contract, could be incorporated into collective insurance schemes (Abecassis et al., 2017; Barbier and Théret, 2009; Batifoulier, 2015). This process of convergence gave rise to what are now much more "hybrid" health systems (Rothgang, 2010b). Nevertheless, it remains a "partial" convergence given that the original institutional features of each group were largely preserved throughout this process (Fine, 2014; Palier, 2010b; Palier and Hay, 2017).

The literature on health systems type is connected to that which seeks to classify different types of welfare states, a research line that flourished in the late 20th century following the works of Esping-Andersen (1990).[4] However, several scholars critically remark that areas of service delivery, such as health, have been relatively neglected in the welfare systems research (Bambra, 2005; Freeman and Frisina, 2010), making the literature on health care systems types a crucial strand of research to capture the specificities of State intervention in the case of health.

---

3 The descriptions of the overarching logic of each type of health system are based on Rothgang (2010a; et al., 2005). See also Hermann (2010) for institutional features, Serapioni and Tesser (2020) for empirical examples, and OECD (2004) for technical definitions.

4 The idea of "welfare state" encompasses a wide range of State interventions aimed at improving the population's well-being, including both social policies (e.g., pensions, health, social assistance) and policy interventions in other areas, such as tax, monetary, and occupational policies (Barr, 1998; Esping-Andersen, 1990; Lavinas, 2018a; Titmuss, 1956).

1.4   PHS *in Historical Perspective*

Up to this point, I have covered the technical aspects of State intervention in health and the objective criteria used to classify health systems. But it is important to consider how this applies in practice. This section seeks to briefly describe how public systems emerged and how have evolved from their early years until the present day.

Any attempt to place a start-point on public health history is bound to be arbitrary (Gorsky, 2011). The beginning of public health policies, in the sense of collective actions that prevent or alleviate diseases, could probably be traced back to the start of human civilization. Looking at modern history, the sources of health care assistance until the 19th century varied from one country to another but most often included private services from liberal professionals acquired via direct payments, voluntarist and charitable work, and financial support provided by self-help associations such as mutual aid societies (Immergut, 1992; Porter, 1999). Public health policies, when available, were residual, fragmented, and uncoordinated, failing to reach the majority of the population.

States have become increasingly involved with health policies since the beginning of the industrialization period in the 19th century. Public authorities' increased concern for the health conditions of communities and individuals has been explained as a consequence of both material and ideological transformations coming together with the industrialization process. Overall, there was an increasingly widespread recognition that the advance of industrial capitalism imposed a specific set of risks that threatened individual and social life and needed to be dealt with. Some factors frequently mentioned to explain the growth of public health policies from this moment onward include the detrimental impacts of industrialization and urbanization on the living conditions of the population, scientific discoveries, and the rise of working-class movements and socialist ideals (Valin and Meslé, 2006; Barr, 1998; Gorsky, 2011; Porter, 1999). In this context, authorities started to actively engage in collective and individualized policies to counteract pandemics, diseases, and workplace injuries. Examples include sanitary policies and vaccination programs, the enacting of workplace regulations, financial and regulatory support to mutual insurance funds, and the creation of public hospitals (Bryant and Rhodes, 2020; Goldsteen et al., 2010; Gorsky, 2011; Tulchinsky and Varavikova, 2014).

Over the past one and a half century, several of these nations started to express greater concern with issues of equity and solidarity in health care access. The creation of PHS resulted from the gradual extension of the scope of State intervention through both legislative measures and the creation of public programs to organize health insurance and service delivery (Maarse,

2006). Europe pioneered the creation of public systems, with the institutionalization of national, mandatory arrangements to finance and provide health care. Lobato and Giovanella (2012) identify three moments that marked the constitution of the first expanded systems of health protection in the continent: at the end of the 19th century, a first wave of legal reforms extended government subsidies to voluntary mutual societies in various countries of the region; in the first decades of the 20th century, a second wave led to the creation of social health insurance models, disseminating the German experience with a national compulsory health insurance introduced in 1883; following World War II, a third wave of regulations universalized the right to health care and created universal systems (see also Immergut, 1992 and Lewalle, 2006). In some European countries, principles of universality came with a paradigmatic shift, with governments establishing free public health provision (the path typically followed by national service models); in others, universality was the result of successive measures to expand the eligibility for insurance coverage (the case of social insurance models).

The developments described so far focused on the wealthiest and most industrialized economies, which spearheaded the creation of PHS. But peripheral countries also embarked on this process later on. Several of them extended social protection benefits and health care policies during the 20th and early 21st centuries. Looking at the history of national health systems in Latin America, Giovanella and Faria (2015) and Laurell and Giovanella (2018) show that some countries in the region introduced Bismarckian systems of social protection still in the 1930s and 1940s. In the following decades, public coverage was extended to rural and deprived areas under the influence of "health for all" proposals and the Beveridge model. Chile was the first country to set up a national health care system in the 1950s, inspired by the British model (later dismantled under the Pinochet dictatorship). In 1988, Brazil instituted a national health service system. Following its steps, Venezuela, Ecuador, and Bolivia promulgated constitutions that defined health as a fundamental social right. One can also mention the case of Cuba, which implemented a public and free system in the early 1960s following the institution of the socialist regime. Nevertheless, the landscape of public health in those countries remains characterized by the coexistence of several subsystems covering different population groups. Individuals are subject to distinct rules for financing, affiliation, access, and service network, determined by income levels and occupational status. Even though these inequalities also exist in core countries, they seem to be much more pronounced in the periphery (Lobato and Giovanella, 2012).

The conditions under which peripheral countries operate might contribute to explaining the challenges they face to consolidate national PHS. In central economies, the expansion of public systems in the post-war period and the associated increase in social expenditures coexisted with high levels of employment, economic growth, and financial stability. Amidst processes of "catching up", other countries sought to replicate these institutions under profoundly different circumstances. Taking the example of Latin America, the region was (and continues to be) characterized by high degrees of labor market informality, economic volatility, and political instability. Moreover, many countries in the region attempted to create or expand public systems already in the neoliberal period, under a policy paradigm that runs counter to substantial increases in public health spending. Unsurprisingly, the systems in the region have never been able to achieve the standards of services and levels of redistribution of their European counterparts (Fleury, 2017; Lavinas, 2013; Lavinas and Simões, 2015; Lo Vuolo, 2012).

PHS in both central and peripheral countries entered a new phase in the last decades of the 20th century. Similar to the shifts that led to the creation of the first systems in the post-war period, the structural reforms imposed on them from this moment on can be associated with material and ideological transformations in the global capitalist system. Public budget crises, the arrival of right-wing governments to power, and the emergence of the neoliberal paradigm are some of the factors contributing to the presumed need to carry out major reforms in PHS since the late 1970s and early 1980s (André and Hermann, 2009; Böhm, 2017; Yilmaz, 2017, Fine and Saad-Filho, 2017).

Public budget deficits have been used as the primary justification for changing governments' approach to health care. The dominant discourse explained these deficits as the result of allegedly uncontrolled public spending resulting from the post-war paradigm. It should be noted that the slowdown in public revenues is a much less debated but equally, if not more, relevant factor in explaining the deterioration of public accounts during the neoliberal period. Revenue collection was increasingly constrained since the late 1970s by factors such as the slowdown of economic growth, rising unemployment, tax cuts on private profits, and the erosion of tax bases due to the internationalization of production and capital flows. At the same time, governments were less willing to tax private and notably financial capital, creating room for vast amounts of poorly taxed income and wealth (Hermann, 2010; Huffschmid, 2009; Sell, 2019; Streeck, 2013).

Along with the slowdown of revenue collection, public expenditures in health care were on the rise. This was largely driven by the natural trend of rising costs in the industry, consistent with increasing life expectancies, the incorporation of technology and medical discoveries into health services, and population growth (André et al., 2015; Böhm, 2017; Yilmaz, 2017).[5] The resulting increase in public health spending eventually clashed with the slowdown of government revenues, feeding a discourse of spiraling health care costs that needed to be put under control (André and Hermann, 2009). According to Moran (2000), no policy area of social provision has been more dominated by the search for cost containment since the end of the long boom than the health sector.

Ideological and political factors also played a role in PHS reforms. In several countries, the financial challenges faced by public systems paired with the rise of neo-conservative parties to power (André and Hermann, 2009; Hermann, 2010). These governments upheld a neoliberal agenda that aimed at "rolling back the State", downscaling public provision in favor of private initiative and private capital (Fine, 1999). The neoliberal agenda not only resisted the expansion of public provision but also contributed to the financial difficulties faced by public systems due to its stronger resistance to tax capital. The prevailing discourse of politicians at the time was that public deficits should be reduced, including in health, and that controlling expenditures was the primary means for doing so (Yilmaz, 2017; Agartan, 2012; André and Hermann, 2009; Hermann, 2010).

Neoliberal reforms did not necessarily reduce the importance of PHS for the economy and society, but did lead to substantial changes in how these systems work. In countries with consolidated systems, governments imposed spending limits to reduce budget deficits, constraining the expansion of public provision and coverage. Other typical "adjustment measures" in this period included caps on hospital budgets, the rationalization of costs in public facilities, the introduction of co-payments and performance indicators, wage cuts for medical staff, and the outsourcing of services to private providers, to mention a few (André et al., 2015; Hassenteufel and Palier, 2007; Ortiz et al., 2015).

In the case of peripheral countries, one distinctive trait of their experiences was that the pressures against the expansion of public spending and services fell upon systems that were already much more fragile. Another trait was the role of international institutions in pressuring for reforms and shaping how they would play out. After the external debt crises that ravaged peripheral countries in the 1980s, debt restructuring processes allowed international actors to exert considerable influence on policy decisions in these countries. Central to this influence was the so-called "Washington Consensus" – a set of

---

5 In the context of the pharmaceutical industry, price manipulation from pharmaceutical companies has been another crucial factor to explain rising costs (Abecassis and Coutinet, 2017; Lazonick et al., 2017).

policy recommendations promoted by the United States government, international organizations (namely the International Monetary Fund and the World Bank), and international creditors as the "standard" reform package for crisis-wracked countries. Reflecting the neoliberal ideology, the "structural adjustment policies" informed by the Washington Consensus combined measures for liberalization, privatization, deregulation, and budget austerity, among others (Bayliss et al., 2016a; Fine and Hall, 2012). These measures were touted as necessary to restore the "fiscal soundness" of indebted economies and their capacity to repay their obligations. International institutions attached such recommendations as loan conditionalities in lending agreements to enforce them (Ruckert et al., 2015).

Up to this moment, most health care policies carried out in the so-called "emerging countries" aimed at extending the scope of services and facilitating access to them. Especially from the 1990s onward, this was somehow hindered due to the conditionalities imposed by structural adjustment programs (Ruckert et al., 2015; Yilmaz, 2017). Following the pressures of the international community, governments across Latin America, Africa, and Asia limited public health expenditures and promoted pro-market reforms (Bayliss and Fine, 2008; Dao and Nichter, 2016). The reforms took highly different forms in each case, but studies often mention fiscal austerity, service cutbacks, the introduction of user fees, selective insurance packages, and other measures that increased the burden of health care financing borne by individuals and the private sector (Dao and Nichter, 2016; Ruckert et al., 2015; Yilmaz, 2017). This policy approach also hindered public investments, preventing peripheral countries from breaking with their historical legacy of segmented and exclusionary health systems (Giovanella and Faria, 2015).

Ruckert et al. (2015) offer an insightful example of how the financialization of the global economy connects to the shifts in health policies in peripheral countries informed by the Washington Consensus. The authors argue that the pressures made by international financial institutions (and the private creditors behind them) on these countries' governments aimed at guaranteeing that the latter could serve their foreign debts. A crucial way to save funds for that was by restraining public spending, including in health. As explained by the authors,

> Given globally integrated financial markets (another outcome of neoliberal economics), governments require the confidence of International Financial Institutions to fund their operations through sovereign debt markets. Financial markets generally remain closed to governments lacking IMF [International Monetary Fund] support, fiscally coercing them

to remain on track with IMF lending agreements and to follow IMF policy advice. (...) *The influence of structural adjustment policies on national policies (...) resulted in resources being diverted away from health care due to IFIs pressure to pay off debts first.* (...) At times, even development aid for health has been found to be diverted by developing countries to the repayment of national debts.

     p. 41–2, emphasis added

Since the turn of the century, evidence of the negative impacts of structural adjustment policies on people's lives in peripheral countries has led to growing criticism of the Washington Consensus. This gave rise to the so-called "Post-Washington Consensus", an apparent rethinking of the standard policy framework prescribed to indebted countries. At the surface, the revised policy approach seemed to distance itself from the previous paradigm by adopting a more favorable position regarding State intervention and less radical measures to promote private markets. It acknowledged space for governments to address market imperfections and counter the adverse distributional effects emerging from privatization, always through piecemeal interventions. In practice, thus, the policies carried out under the new "consensus" seemed to depart very little from the previous paradigm. In many cases, it added further conditionalities that favored free trade, privatization, deregulation, and fiscal austerity – only this time with a more explicit call for governments to address their failures (Bayliss and Fine, 2008; Fine and Hall, 2012; Ruckert et al., 2015).

More recently, a new vision of "universality" started taking over the health policy agenda for peripheral countries. Since the early 2000s, policy recommendations for these countries often incorporate ideas of "health for all". The blueprint of public health policies for middle-and low-income countries today is based on the "Universal Health Coverage" (UHC) approach, championed by the World Health Organization (WHO) with the support of other multilateral institutions (WHO, 2005). Since 2010, the WHO and the World Bank have provided technical assistance to more than one hundred countries so they could implement the UHC framework (WHO, 2015). The approach also became one of the core recommendations for countries to meet the health-related targets of the *Sustainable Development Goals*, established by the United Nations and signed by 193 member states in 2015.

However, the notion of universality as applied to peripheral countries today differs significantly from that which guided the creation of universal systems in wealthy countries during the previous century (Dao and Nichter, 2016; Global Health Watch, 2014; Sengupta, 2013; Stuckler et al., 2010). The idea of universality used in this book resonates with the classic idea of *universal care* from the first PHS and should not be confused with today's much-heralded concept of *universal coverage*. This minor difference in name carries a major difference in meaning. Universal care stands for equal access to services at all levels of care – from prevention to healing and rehabilitation. The UHC framework does not propose a new form of achieving universal health care, but rather a reinterpretation of the concept. The focus of government action is on subsidizing demand to avoid individuals facing significant financial hardship when dealing with health risks. In practice, universal coverage implies government coverage for primary care (basic needs) and public subsidies to access more complex services through private services and insurance (Giovanella et al., 2018). This model of health care financing often calls for "affordable" user fees, (possibly subsidized) health insurance, private services, and the expansion of privately owned health care infrastructure (Hunter and Murray, 2019). In this way, access to all levels of health care is only possible with the high participation of the private sector.

Therefore, in peripheral countries, the idea of the right to public health through a series of preventive, primary, and curative services has been gradually replaced by new blueprints where the notion of public health is associated with the coverage of basic services. This means replacing the policy goal of building a national health system (an integrated network of standard, socially acceptable patterns of services at all levels of care) with a policy approach in which the whole spectrum of health needs can only be met through the combined action of public and private actors, according to purchasing powers (Dentico, 2019).

Putting things into perspective countries, the evolution of public health policies and PHS in central and peripheral over the past century seems to point to two seemingly contradictory trends. On the one hand, there were several universalizing measures allowing individuals previously excluded from the public network to be included and cared for (Abecassis et al., 2017; Barbier and Théret, 2009; Batifoulier, 2015). In some countries, such as France, the universal right to health care was achieved through a gradual process concluded only by the late 1990s (see Chapter 3). On the other hand, neoliberal reforms restricted public health funding and supply, as previously explained. These seemingly paradoxical trends of expansion and retrenchment can be explained by the fact that "neoliberalism has never, in practice, been about withdrawal or minimizing the State's economic role. On the contrary, neoliberalism has concerned State intervention to promote private capital" (Fine and Hall, 2012, p. 53). Neoliberal reforms in PHS were one way to do that: without dismantling public health policies and systems, the reforms transformed the latter into venues for the expansion of private capital into public networks of provision and the private appropriation of public funds. Therefore, one can argue that PHS reforms have a specific role in the neoliberal period: that of contributing to the private appropriation of collective resources.

The process of PHS reforms has been underway for at least four decades now and has been led by policymakers of different political stances. Right-wing governments were the main advocates and often introduced the first reforms in PHS, and therefore tend to be seen as mainly responsible for these shifts. However, right-leaning governments did not come into power at the same time across western countries, and there was usually an alternation of parties over time. Despite being usually seen as a right-wing agenda, center-and left-wing administrations often embraced and expanded the reform agenda. Rather than associating reforms with a certain political stance, it seems much more reasonable to interpret them as part of the broader economic and social restructuring that underpins the expansion of globalized financial capitalism (Fine and Saad-Filho, 2017), a process that goes far beyond individual political wills.

Once the process of neoliberal reforms in PHS has been going on for decades, it is reasonable to think that the mechanisms through which they serve private capital have evolved since the beginning of this period. However, the research on PHS change is yet to fully understand these potentially new mechanisms. The idea of finance and financialization, discussed in the previous chapter, are particularly useful yet overlooked concepts to examine this evolution.

2   Conventional Approaches to Assess Health Systems Change

Neoliberal reforms did not necessarily reduce public health spending, but certainly altered the nature of expenditures, the conditions of access to benefits, and the involvement of the private sector. In light of the process of financialization and its inroads into sectors of social provision, these changes are likely to serve the financial sector. To argue that financialization should be integrated into the conceptual framework used to assess PHS reforms, I will first outline the concepts most commonly used to examine reforms so far and the specific policy shifts they refer to.

Rather than a single movement, the process of neoliberal reforms is a mosaic of policy shifts implemented in varying ways and degrees in each country. This diversity of international experiences led to an extensive body of research dedicated to studying the evolution of health systems since the 1990s, which I refer to as the literature on health systems change. This literature employed a varied array of concepts to grasp the specificities of each type of reform in PHS. Some terms have been frequently used to describe these reforms, including *econom-ization, marketization, privatization, commercialization*, and *commodification*.[6] The latter constitute what I will call the "conventional" conceptual framework of PHS research.

The exact definitions of these concepts vary from author to author, and there is debate as to where their respective boundaries lie (Mercille and Murphy, 2017). Although differences of opinion exist, there is some agreement on the general meaning associated with each one. Beginning with the notion of *economization*, this describes changes in public policies at the level of ideas and methods, with the extension of economic logic, practices, and calculation into new areas (Çalışkan and Callon, 2009; Dempsey, 2017). The introduction of languages, principles, and metrics from private (non-financial) compa-nies, aimed at promoting better governance and the more efficient distribu-tion of limited resources, has been described as evidence of economization (Ewert, 2009; Yilmaz, 2017). The famous "New Public Management" approach developed in the 1990s, calling for the incorporation of managerial and organization techniques from the private into the public sector, is the most glaring example of this process (Mercille and Murphy, 2017; Simonet, 2011; Yilmaz, 2017). In health care, economization processes have been observed when the public bodies responsible for health systems start framing the lat-ter issues in terms of monetary costs and benefits, adopt cost-benefit analy-ses, introduce expenditure and efficiency targets, and manage by metrics, to name a few.

The idea of *marketization* has been used to describe changes at the level of internal practices, which came largely as a consequence of this new approach toward public management previously mentioned. It denotes the process through which market structures are extended to new areas, creating possibilities and incentives for buying and selling where these did not exist before (Agartan, 2012; Dempsey, 2017; Whitfield, 2006). In the public sector, marketization reforms reorganize exchanges in the public system to simulate conventional consumer markets; the underlying assumption is that operating in a competitive environment would create incentives for public bodies to decrease costs and increase efficiency (Ewert, 2009; Hermann and Verhoest, 2012; Yilmaz, 2017). In national health service models, the chief example of marketization reforms concerns the creation of "internal markets", with the

---

6   This should not be seen as an exhaustive list; other terms have also been used to assess reforms, although their use appears to be less common or circumscribed to specific coun-tries. This is the case, for example, with *corporatization* (Preker and Harding, 2003) and *liber-alization* (Filippon et al., 2016).

government splitting public bodies into purchases and providers of services and placing them in competition with one another (and sometimes also private actors) for the best deals. In social insurance systems, the introduction of competition between different insurance funds to attract beneficiaries has been described as a form of marketization (André et al., 2015; Bayliss, 2016; Hermann, 2010).

The most important concept underpinning the research on PHS so far is, nevertheless, that of *privatization*. This is the most widespread term in the literature on health systems change and can encompass several types of reforms in PHS. It is frequently employed as an "umbrella term" to encompass the measures such as those previously described, in addition to any public sector restructuring that leads to greater participation of private actors within public structures. The strict definition of privatization refers to the total transfer of ownership from public to private entities (Savas, 2000), but this definition has little applicability in health, where such experiences have been rare (André et al., 2015). When applied to the public sector, the term privatization usually appears with a fluid meaning to denote any transfer of responsibilities and activities from public to private entities (Hansen and Lindholst, 2016). In the context of health systems change, a more appropriate definition for privatization is the delegation or partial transfer of public management, ownership, financing, or provision of public health activities to private actors (Mercille and Murphy, 2017; Starr, 1988).

The privatization of public health can appear in many ways. Shifts in management can be seen, for example, in the adoption of a private management *rationale* by public actors, which coincides to a large extent with the ideas of *economization* and *marketization* previously described. But privatization reforms also include more tangible shifts in the dimensions of ownership, financing, and provision. Such forms of privatization often involve the externalization of services and costs from public to private actors. Some of the most common measures of privatization within PHS of the national health service type include the outsourcing of public provision to private providers and the authorization of private practice in public facilities; in social insurance models, privatization tends to be associated with the introduction of co-payments, the reduction of the scale or scope of public coverage, and incentives to contract voluntary health insurance. In both cases, these reforms often result from the imposition of measures on the public health budget, such as the establishment of rules for public health expenditure growth and the capping of hospital budgets (Abecassis and Coutinet, 2021; André et al., 2015; Mercille and Murphy, 2017; Starr, 1988).

One of the most important contributions brought by the concept of privatization is drawing attention to the fact that PHS may witness significant shifts on the inside while their overarching structure remains public. Starr (1988), for example, differentiates processes of "partial privatization" from "total privatization"; Savas (2000) opposes "passive" against "conventional" privatization, and André et al. (2015) talk about "internal" and "external" privatization. What these pairs have in common is that, in the first case, the expression denotes policy shifts that increase the participation of principles and actors originally foreign from the public sector without changing the system's nature.

As in the case of privatization, the concept of *commercialization* has been used to examine, within a single framework, several simultaneous and interconnected processes. A particularly well-known work in the case of health care associates commercialization with three main developments: the provision of health care services through market relationships to those able to pay; the investment in, and production of, those services for cash income or profit; and health care finance derived from individual payment and private insurance (Mackintosh and Koivusalo, 2005).

To conclude, *commodification* can be interpreted as the underlying change that underpins the developments described in this section. Commodities are defined as goods that can be valued according to their material properties and can be priced, bought, and sold in markets (McDonald and Ruiters, 2006; Oliver and Robison, 2017). Commodification refers to the process of attributing the meaning and features of a commodity to something previously not considered as such. Therefore, the commodification of health is the process that qualitatively reconstitutes so it starts being seen as a commodity (Vaittinen et al., 2018). Commodification strips health-related activities of their image as special activities with intrinsic value that societies should organize for providing collectively; in doing so, health goods and services can be priced, exchanged, and generate privately appropriated gains (Agartan, 2012; Swyngedouw et al., 2002).

2.1   *Deconstructing the Notion of Privatization*

Financialization is related to, but different from, other forms of PHS change. In order to elaborate this argument, one can look at the agents driving and profiting from the reforms typically described in the literature on PHS change, the context underlying these reforms, the narratives used to justify them, their features and impacts. Because privatization is the most widespread concept employed by this literature, it can serve as the reference point for this task. By deconstructing the notion of privatization across these dimensions, it is possible to show that certain developments currently reshaping health systems do not fit neatly into this category. They seem to be of a different nature, involving other types of agents, narratives, and impacts, which can be better examined through the concept of financialization.[7]

2.1.1   Agents

The most straightforward way to contrast longstanding notions of privatization in systems of social provision and new developments shaped by financialization is by considering the agents involved in each set of shifts. When the concept of privatization first became popular in health systems research, the importance of distinguishing the nature of actors most directly involved in these changes was not immediately clear. However, the present moment gives us the privilege of hindsight. It can be argued that developments associated with privatization refer, most often, to measures that increased the participation of private, non-financial actors in health financing and provision. But the so-called "private sector" also includes financial actors, entities of a significantly different nature. Box 2.1 differentiates financial and non-financial companies, a useful distinction for the sake of the present discussion.

BOX 2.1   Deconstructing the "Private" Sector: Financial and
            Non-financial Companies

National accounting systems (IMF, 2017; UN, 2009) distinguish three types of entities performing economic activities in the private sector: financial corporations, non-financial corporations, and non-profit institutions.

Financial corporations are mainly focused in providing financial services – activities related to the supply, intermediation, and management of funds and investments for other entities. They receive income from performing these activities, which comes in the form of interest payments, dividends, capital gains, and fees. Private financial actors include but are not limited to commercial banks, investment banks, investment funds, insurance companies, pension funds, and asset managers.

Non-financial corporations focus in producing, selling, and trading goods and non-financial services. The latter include any services that do not fit into the category of financial services. These corporations receive income from such activities in the form of business profits.

---

7   The systematization of the main agents involved in the reforms and the typical traits of the health sector described in the present and following sections were elaborated by the author based on a compilation of theoretical and empirical studies for advanced and emerging economies. The full list of references can be found in Table 2.1.

These corporations include manufacturers, suppliers, and retailers, utility companies, and service providers, among others.

Non-profit institutions produce and distribute goods and non-financial services outside of the market logic. They provide most of their output either free or below market prices, and cannot provide profits, financial gains, or any other types of income to the units that control or manage them.

The term "corporation" is used in this context to designate "all entities that are capable of generating a profit or other financial gains" (UN, 2009, p. 66). This definition differs from its typical usage in the United States, associated with large-scale business owned by different shareholders. To avoid misunderstanding, throughout this work, I preferer using the term "companies", which includes several types of business (MacMillan Dictionary, 2021) and converges with the interpretation used in national accounting systems.

In general, notions of privatization employ the term "private" in a broad meaning. The three main types of "private" agents mentioned by privatization studies are individuals, health service providers, and insurance funds (in the latter two cases, both for-and not-for-profit).

In several western countries, until the late 20th century, health service providers operated under traditional ownership structures, belonging to families or individuals with a professional record in the sector. The primary sources of income for these companies came from activities related to health care goods and service provision. Their expansion was largely dependent on expanding the capacity to produce drugs, equipment, and services, as well as the incremental demand for them. Health service providers presented relatively low levels of leveraging and weaker (if any) ties with financial institutions and investors.

Therefore, it can be argued that the type of companies more directly involved in earlier rounds of privatization and benefiting from it were *non-financial companies*, whose main activity was the production and commercialization of health goods and services. These include, for example, private hospitals, clinics, care facilities, and providers of medical goods. For the purposes of this work, I will refer to these agents as private health companies, in contrast to financial companies.[8] There are many ways in which these companies benefit from privatization reforms. Budget cuts or restrictions in health care coverage,

---

8 For the sake of simplification, I include non-profit institutions in the category non-financial companies, once the goal here is to distinguish providers of goods and non-financial services (both for-and not-for-profit) from financial service providers.

for example, increase private health spending, boosting demand for privately provided services. Outsourcing and other measures that increase public health spending with private suppliers have a similar effect.

Along with private service providers, another segment mentioned in traditional privatization studies is that of insurance funds. Although insurance services technically fall into the category of financial services, there is reason to argue that the health insurance funds described in the earlier literature on health systems change operated much differently from today's financial companies. In comparison to today, health insurance companies were larger in number, smaller in size, and a higher share of them specialized in health and related services. A significant part of these companies had autonomous ownership structures, independent from larger financial corporations, and their expansion depended on increasing the number of beneficiaries and the value of premiums. Also, there was a greater market share occupied by non-profit institutions. They also benefitted from health reforms when public coverage, whether through services or insurance, shrank. As shown later in this chapter, the companies involved in health care reforms today are much different from the health funds previously mentioned, including global investment funds and highly concentrated insurance companies guided by profit-maximizing strategies.

2.1.2   Narratives

The narrative created around PHS in the neoliberal period described these systems as overspending and inefficient, justifying privatization reforms (André and Hermann, 2009; Bayliss, 2016; Frangakis and Huffschmid, 2009; Maarse, 2006). The main arguments put forward for introducing private practices, actors, and the logic of competition into public health structures since the 1990s were that this would reduce costs and increase efficiency levels (Stuckler et al., 2010). Besides greater "value for money", other arguments in favor of privatization included the possibilities for higher quality service delivery and expanded consumer choice (André and Hermann, 2009; Fine and Bayliss, 2016; Frangakis and Huffschmid, 2009; Maarse, 2006; Whitfield, 2015).

2.1.3   Theoretical Underpinnings

The theoretical underpinnings of privatization derive from different strands of neoclassical economic theory. The belief that private initiative is inherently cheaper and more efficient than the public sector resulted from the combination of ideas borrowed from different neoclassical theories. These included the theory of property rights, the theory of the firm, the theory of industrial organization, the theory of transaction costs, and other theories suggesting that

profit motive, competition, and ownership rights always lead to the most efficient outcomes (Fine, 2008; Loxley and Hajer, 2019; Maarse, 2006; McDonald
and Ruiters, 2006; Starr, 1988). Their assumptions lead to the conclusion that
private firms can optimize resource allocation, provide better-quality services
to more people, and charge more competitive prices than the public sector
(Mckinley, 2008). Another important reference for privatization measures is
the theory of public choice, which contends that public provision is inherently
prone to inefficiency and corruption (Fine, 1999; Starr, 1988).

Thus, the *rationale* in favor of privatization measures lies in "shaky" theoretical foundations (Fine, 2008), constructed by combining ideas from different sources selected arbitrarily and in the most convenient way to justify
the arguments at stake. The neoliberal idea of "State failure and private success" informed by these theories is reinforced by the often overlooked fact that
the public sector tends to concentrate efforts on essential and less profitable
activities, increasing the profit and efficiency margins of private enterprise.
According to Fine (*op. cit.*),

> A longer view of the choice between public and private provision,
> stretching back into the nineteenth century, reveals that the private sec-
> tor presses to provide when and where it is profitable for it to do so (and
> to use the State to make it so) and, equally, does not embark upon, or
> abandons, provision where profitability fails. In contrast, the State is sad-
> dled with the burden of provision irrespective of commercial viability
> and can be pressured to support private at the expense of public provi-
> sion. (...) The public sector tends to become the provider of last resort as
> opposed to the private or privatized sector that can cream off the more
> commercially viable and readily served markets.[9]
>
>   p. 15, 24

2.1.4   Impacts

The impacts of privatization on PHS are highly debated. Scholars have critically observed that public sector reforms continued despite the absence of systematic evaluations demonstrating superior outcomes for the population or
public finances (Bayliss, 2002; Fine, 2008; Whitfield, 2015). Human rights standards are systematically absent from privatization agreements and evaluation

---

9   For works on how the State tends to cover the "hard to serve" across different segments of
    public activities and health care, see Bayliss (2002), Bayliss et al. (2016b), Sestelo (2017a), and
    Tansey et al. (2021).

processes. As acknowledged by the Secretary-General of the United Nations in 2018, "it is clear both from the evidence that exists and from the basic assumptions underpinning privatization that it negatively affects the lives and rights of people"; still, "few detailed studies have been undertaken and that relevant data are often not collected" (UN, 2018, p. 24).

Scholarly research shows that privatization measures have contributed to deteriorating the quantity and quality of public provision and coverage in PHS as well as to worsening the working conditions of professionals working for the system. Another observed effect of these reforms concerns the increasing costs of health care borne by individuals, directly or through private insurance. Consequently, privatization is also associated with higher levels of total health spending and greater inequalities in access to health care (André et al., 2015; Böhm, 2017; Hassenteufel and Palier, 2007; Hermann, 2010; Laurell, 2016; Maarse, 2006; Ortiz et al., 2015).

3   Financialization in the Health Sector

The review of the literature on health systems presented so far suggests that the usual concepts employed to describe neoliberal reforms in PHS were developed at a time when the process of financialization was not as widespread and apparent as it is today. It focused on how private health companies and health insurance funds were increasingly involved in public activities, with less attention to how financial companies and agents might have been participating in these reforms. However, there is reason to think that financial agents such as banks, investment funds, and individual investors have been gaining increasing influence over the direction taken by the health sector at large and PHS in particular. Recent research on health financialization provides several examples of how financial actors have been influencing developments in the sector. Reviewing this body of literature helps trace the usual strategies that allow these actors to engage in health activities. It also contributes to identifying the research gaps that are yet to be addressed to fully understand the role of financialization in shaping public health activities, the object of discussion in the last part of the chapter.

The literature on health financialization is relatively recent and comprises a diverse array of works that do not necessarily resort to financialization theories to develop their analysis. What brings these studies together and justifies treating them as a branch of financialization research is the acknowledgment that current developments in the health sector are qualitatively and quantitatively different from those established by seminal health policy studies (Bayliss et al., 2017; Sestelo, 2017a). Works on health financialization agree that the involvement of financial actors in health activities entered a new stage since the turn of the century, becoming stronger and spreading across the private for-profit, non-profit, and public spheres. In this way, financial institutions and the infrastructures of financial intermediation have come to play a central role in the health care domain (Dentico, 2019).

Evidence from the literature on the financialization of health supports the claim that some of the reforms underway in the public health sector are not fully captured by the concepts traditionally used to discuss them. Lavinas and Gentil (2018) corroborate this argument when they note that "the topic of privatization alone is no longer sufficient to explain this process of transferring responsibilities, previously in the hands of the State, to profit-oriented companies" (p. 12). Also, Hunter and Murray (2019) describe health financialization as "the latest emerging phase of health system change" (p. 2), representing "a new phase of capital formation that builds on, but is distinct from, previous rounds of privatization" (p. 8). Still, to the best of my knowledge, no work so far has attempted to define the lines between privatization and financialization in the case of health care.

This is not to say that the classic literature on health systems change has been oblivious to the growth of financial investments and actors in health care. Back in the early 2000s, some authors were already calling attention to the involvement of multinational financial corporations in the health insurance and service sectors, including in cases where the latter were part of the public health network (Iriart et al., 2001; Maarse, 2006; see also Hermann, 2010). Yet, at this point, the extent of such events was still seen as relatively constrained. Maarse (*op. cit.*), for example, states that "the role of private investors [in health care investments] has always been limited. Some countries are now witnessing the emergence of private investors in health care", but these are described as a "still small-scale phenomenon" (p. 995).

Some earlier works mention the fact public entities have been resorting to financial capital, but consider them as a form of privatization like any other. In this way, this is far from being the focus of analysis. As privatization studies emphasize, most often, measures seeking to diminish expenditures in the public system, there is less space to examine measures seeking to raise revenues in the private (financial) sector. Authors who mention policy shifts seeking to increase revenues for the public system by borrowing from private actors describe them as a specific form of privatization in the dimension of financing or investments (André et al., 2015; Mercille and Murphy, 2017; Pollock et al., 2002; Whitfield, 2006). Mercille and Murphy (*op. cit.*), for example, describe the privatization of investments as the process "when funding sources of public assets and service providers become private, for instance by raising private capital instead of relying on public funding" (p. 6). Despite paving the way for the discussion of the financialization of PHS, the examples mentioned in these works are mostly limited to one specific instrument: public-private partnerships (where public infrastructure is financed via private investments). The scale and scope of financial activities today, however, suggest that there will be many other ways in which financial actors may be transferring funds to public entities and investing in them.

3.1   *The State of the Art of the Health Financialization Literature*

Over the past decade, some scholars have started using the concept of financialization to investigate the ways in which financial actors, instruments, and interests are shaping changes in the health sector. This body of works, introduced in the previous section, addresses three core (and interrelated) processes: one, the transformation of activities related to health financing and provision into financial assets; two, the related increase in the participation of financial actors in the sector; and three, the incorporation of behaviors typical of financial companies by health actors.

Seddon and Currie (2017) describe the financialization of health as "the exchange of [health] goods and services as financial instruments" (p. 1). Similarly, for Hunter and Murray (2019), health financialization means the process of "transforming population ill-health into zones for investment and creating saleable commodities that can be traded by domestic and transnational private capital" (p. 9). Paying attention to the actors behind such transformations, Vural (2017) contends that, in the health sector, the process of financialization "can be observed by the greater reliance of health care providers on financial markets, as well as the increasing penetration of financial actors and institutions into health care provision and funding" (p. 1). As part of the critical literature on financialization, these studies are skeptical about the capacity of these transformations to improve health care equity and access. Bayliss (2016), for example, argues that "the provision of health is being transformed from a local community service to a segment of global investment portfolios of international private finance" (p. 40) as a consequence of them.

But how can health be transformed into a financial asset? And through what channels do financial actors manage to actually enter the health sector? What we currently know about the financialization of health comes mostly from the evidence provided by studies looking at global health policies, private health activities, and specific segments of the public and non-profit sectors. It is possible to identify at least three core processes that have been reshaping the landscape of health care across these domains: the creation of investment platforms, changes in ownership structures, and the deployment of financial innovations. Although these do not constitute an exhaustive list of the phenomena driving health financialization, they can provide valuable, concrete examples of the transformations mentioned so far.

3.1.1   Investment Platforms: a New Approach to Finance Global Health Policies

First, contemporary finance is changing the approach to funding global health programs. These include initiatives to fight epidemics and pandemics, guarantee primary health care in middle and low-income regions, and achieve the health-related targets of the United Nation's 2015 Sustainable Development Goals. The emergence of *investment platforms* (Hunter and Murray, 2019), offering a new way to collect the necessary resources to finance such actions, is the perfect illustration of the changing approach to global health financing currently underway. The notion of investment platforms encompasses a hybrid category of arrangements allowing actions to coordinate and gather funds from different public and private actors toward a common goal, usually through an independent governance structure (Tchiombiano, 2019). These platforms are becoming a central strategy to raise and centralize revenues for collective interventions, gradually replacing traditional forms of financing (Erikson, 2015; Hunter and Murray, *op. cit.*; Stein and Sridhar, 2018).

The creation of investment platforms is heavily grounded on the logic of "blended finance", a term that has been recently applied to describe a new approach to development financing in middle-and low-income countries (UN, 2018). As the name suggests, the idea of blended finance is to "blend" funds – to pool money from different agents in order to finance a specific project. The proposal of combining funds from different sources through independent financial structures underpins, for example, the "Global Fund to Fight AIDS, Tuberculosis, and Malaria" (a joint initiative of governments and private agents to eradicate these diseases in over 100 countries), the "Pandemic Emergency Financing Facility" (a financing mechanism set up by the World Bank to help to contain pandemics), and the "International Finance Facility for Immunization" (a multi-stakeholder partnership set up by the Bill and Melinda Gates Foundation that funds the Global Alliance for Vaccines and Immunization) (Hunter and Murray, 2019; Stein and Sridhar, 2018).

Investment platforms are designed to attract private funds using multilateral and government funding to entice investors who otherwise would not participate. Governments can place public funds into these arrangements directly or by providing subsidies and guarantees. In any case, government funding serves to de-risk investments and ensure returns, which attracts and leverages

private capital (Jomo and Chowdhury, 2019). Among the actors that participate in these platforms, one can mention national governments, multilateral
organizations (such as the World Bank and the World Health Organization),
philanthropic institutions (e.g., the Bill and Melinda Gates Foundation and
the Rockefeller Foundation), banks, investment funds, other institutional
investors, industry representatives, non-profit organizations, and private
companies (Dentico, 2019; Hunter and Murray, 2019; Stein and Sridhar, 2018;
Tchiombiano, 2019).

Such arrangements "transform new sectors and regions into investor-
friendly asset classes and de-risk opportunities for private investment in those
asset classes" (Hunter and Murray, 2019, p. 6).[10] How these asset classes will be
created, as well as the form and degrees in which financial actors are involved
in this process, can vary greatly from case to case. In general, however, these
funding strategies are managed by financial experts and bring in money from
financial institutions and investors (Tchiombiano, 2019), which can occur, for
example, by contracting loans, restructuring ownership, or issuing securities.
The sources of remuneration for financial players depend on the scheme's
configuration but may include income from intermediation and administration fees, interest payments, tax engineering, and monetary compensation for
upfront investments, to name a few.

Critical scholars call attention to the fact that the volume of funds allocated
to these platforms has been on the rise while traditional forms of humanitarian aid follow a steep decline (Dentico, 2019; Hunter and Murray, 2019). In light
of these trends, they suggest that financial investors and global philanthropic
foundations (the latter closely related to financial and non-financial private
companies) are "leading the way in the transition of global public health
funding models to private financial models featuring shareholder return on
investment" (Erikson, 2015, p. 4). According to Dentico (*op. cit.*), these transformations in global health policy make decisions concerning population health
subject to the imperatives of maximizing returns on investments, which completely redefines how the universal right to health is interpreted and pursued.

3.1.2   Ownership Restructuring: Reshaping the Landscape of
            Private Health
Private health care services and insurance are also undergoing major shifts due
to the expansion of the financial sector. On the one hand, health companies

---

10   Asset classes can be defined as forms of investment that share core characteristics, tend
      to behave similarly, and are subject to the same regulations (Lustig, 2014).

are increasingly relying on debt and financial instruments; on the other, financial firms and investors are gaining ever more control over these companies. These developments occur mainly through processes of *ownership restructuring*, which allow financial firms and investors to expand their participation and influence in health care by acquiring rights over health services and insurance companies. This restructuring often occurs as a result of strategies carried out by health companies themselves to attract investments and raise additional funds. Three examples of processes leading to changes in property rights that have been particularly important in the health sector are: one, the entry of health companies in the stock markets, opening capital and issuing securities; two, mergers and acquisitions deals, increasingly driven and funded by financial companies; and three, the welcoming of investments via investment funds, with important participation of private equity funds (Vural, 2017).[11]

As a result of ownership restructuring processes, health companies may end up listed in financial markets, become part of a highly diverse portfolio of investments managed by global financial corporations, acquire ownership stakes in other companies via open market operations, and take over other companies in transactions leveraged and intermediated by financial institutions (Lavinas and Gentil, 2018; Sestelo, 2018; Vural, 2017). There is extensive empirical literature describing how health actors in both central and peripheral economies are taking this road. They include both for-and not-for-profit health insurers (Abecassis et al., 2018; Abecassis and Coutinet, 2021; Bahia et al., 2016; Martins et al., 2021; Mulligan, 2016; Sestelo, 2017a, 2018), hospitals and other service providers (Alles, 2018; Angeli and Maarse, 2012; Appelbaum and Batt, 2020; Horton, 2017; Lavinas and Gentil, 2018; Vural, 2017), and pharmaceutical companies (Abecassis and Coutinet, 2018; Klinge et al., 2020; Lazonick et al., 2017; Montalban, 2011).[12]

---

11   Securities issuance refers to the offering of stocks and bonds by health companies to investors in exchange for funds. Mergers and acquisitions describe operations in which two companies merge to create a larger one, or when one company purchases another. Private equity is a form of investment in which specialized investment funds raise and centralize money to purchase, restructure, and sell a company for an expected profit. Public-private partnerships are long-term contracts in which the private sector assumes total or part of the financing, building, and/or operation of public projects; these projects can be financed by investment firms and banks, and ownership stakes can generate other assets traded in secondary markets.

12   The discussion of this chapter is mostly based on studies looking at health service and insurance companies. Although some of the discussion can be extended to the pharmaceutical sector, the ways in which financialization unfolds in this case seem to be quite specific and demand a separate analysis.

The case of private equity investments, a trillion-dollar industry, is particularly illustrative of the relevance of health care activities for the financial sector. Undertakings geared toward health companies are known for being some of the most profitable in the private equity world. Bain & Company (2019), a major firm in the field, examined investments across different sectors from 2009 to 2015 to find that health care deals have returned US$2.2 for every US$1 of invested capital, more than in technology, financial services, consumer infrastructure, and other common targets of private equity firms.

3.1.3   Financial Innovations: a Novel Strategy for Public and Non-profit Agencies

Financial innovations are another important movement pushing for the financialization of health. They arise from the creation of new asset classes to finance health activities. Among the plethora of financial innovations appearing each day, the spread of "health bonds" – meaning any financial contract or security created to finance a specific health-related intervention – is a case in point. Health bonds can be considered a form of "impact investing", a new approach to finance interventions seeking to combine investments in activities that can promote positive social or environmental outcomes with the possibility of reaping financial returns (Andreu, 2018; Golka, 2019). Impact investing is generally used to raise funds for a specific policy intervention specified in advance; by engaging in contracts or purchasing securities, financial investors provide the upfront finance for the intervention and are reimbursed (usually with additional compensations) depending on the observed outcomes.

Public entities and non-profit institutions have been particularly interested in attracting funds via "social impact bonds" and similar forms of contracts, as in the case of the "Cameroon Cataract Performance Bond" and the "Israel Type II Diabetes Social Impact Bond" (Clarke et al., 2019; Hunter and Murray, 2019; Lavinas, 2018b). Organizations in charge of global health interventions are following a similar path. Two important examples of health bonds are the "vaccine bonds" issued in 2006 by the International Finance Facility for Immunization (which finances the Global Alliance for Vaccine Immunization, mentioned in the previous section), and the "pandemic bonds" issued in 2017 by the World Bank (more specifically the bank's Pandemic Emergency Financing Facility).

Health bonds became particularly known due to the so-called "Ebola bonds" issued by the World Bank and the controversies they have stirred up. The Ebola bonds offered attractive compensations for investors willing to bet against the spread of the disease in African countries. The World Bank issued these bonds to raise funds that could supposedly aid countries in the event of an Ebola crisis. Investors would receive interest payments during the duration of the bonds, as long as there would be no outbreak of the disease in the countries specified in the contracts (Erikson, 2015). Ebola bonds attracted a large number of investors, offering annual returns of up to 11% – far above other assets of a similar kind; a US$95 million tranche of Ebola bonds due by mid-2020 paid investors more than US$1 million each month (Bloomberg, 2019). Such instruments end up surrounded by large controversies, especially because investors were sometimes getting paid while African countries suffering from the spread of Ebola did not receive funds. The justification was that such countries allegedly did not meet certain conditionalities. However, these conditionalities included some morally questionable terms, such as the requirement for a minimum number of deaths in the territory such as insurance payments could be released.

Notwithstanding the importance of financialization, it is important to recognize that this is not the only relatively new concept that can contribute to explaining transformations in the health sector. Beyond health financing and provision, it is important to pay attention, for example, to processes using health data to create new spaces for profit-making activities. This trend underpins concepts such as datafication and digitization, and can help in understanding the recent entry of Big Tech firms into the sector (Prainsack, 2020; Sharon, 2020, 2018). Similar to what has been discussed for the case of financial actors, these authors show that major consumer technology corporations that had little interest in health in the past, Google, Apple, Facebook, Amazon, Microsoft, and IBM, are now making important inroads into the health and biomedical sector. According to Sharon (2020), not only tech corporations are encroaching into ever-new spheres of social life but "the (legitimate) advantage these actors have accrued in the sphere of the production of digital goods provides them with (illegitimate) access to the spheres of health and medicine, and more worrisome, to the sphere of politics" (p. 2).

3.2   *Gaps in the Existing Research for the Public Sector*

The ways in which the public health sector may become more dependent on financial capital are much less investigated than in the case of global and private health activities. This is especially true when it comes to PHS. The usual view on the impacts of financialization on PHS focuses on external changes, particularly how financialization promotes fiscal austerity and thereby restricts the volume of funding available for these systems. As discussed in the previous chapter, one of the most important ways in which financialization would lead to austerity is through the growing power of financial capital to control government financing, and consequently to influence decisions concerning the public budget. These decisions would reflect a hierarchy of priorities for public expenditures, with those of finance at the top. The results are spending cuts, notably in areas of social provision. Spending cuts would serve to limit public deficits and debts, proving the government's creditworthiness, and saving resources to pay its creditors. Beyond the expenditure side, the growing influence of finance would also affect the revenue side of government accounts. It would push for reduced taxation of capital, with the result of limiting the growth of public revenues and further fueling budget deficits followed by service cuts.

Another common association between PHS and financialization concerns how developments in the public sector would contribute to the expansion of the private, today highly financialized health sector. Austerity and policy reforms in PHS would lead to restrictions in the coverage, quantity, and quality of public services, stimulating the demand for private services and insurance. Beyond PHS, the public sector more broadly would also have a role in developing financial activity in the health sector. Governments would contribute to the financialization of health by changing regulations and providing incentives and guarantees for investors and financial companies involved in health care. Favorable regulations and policies could secure profits, mitigate risks, and enhance the profitability of private investments in health care.

However valid, depicting PHS as a supporting apparatus for the expansion of a private-cum-financialized health sector offers an incomplete picture of developments in the field. From this perspective, PHS would have only a passive role in the process of health financialization. Given the increasing adoption of financial instruments and strategies by public sector bodies, discussed in the previous chapter, there is reason to argue that these trends will also reach PHS. This means they would be taking part in the process of financialization of health in much more active ways than what has been usually acknowledged by the literature in the field.

When it comes to internal changes in public health structures that may be related to financial expansion, it has been shown earlier in this chapter that the existing research focuses on developments related to infrastructure financing, more specifically the resort to PPPs.[13] This is true for both the literature on privatization and financialization: there is also a considerable body of works using this latter concept to draw well-deserved attention to the dramatic rise of such "partnerships" and its growing relevance for health infrastructure (e.g., Bayliss, 2016; Bayliss and Waeyenberge, 2017; Fine, 2020; Loxley and Hajer,

---

13   This contrast between *internal* and *external* processes of financialization is an insight
      from Chiapello (2019, 2017), who distinguishes those developments in the context of public policies more generally.

2019). These works examine in greater detail the various ways in which private capital may participate and profit from these projects. These include providing upfront financing for the building of hospitals as well as purchasing and trading infrastructure assets.

Apart from infrastructure, there is little published research on how financialization might be reshaping the forms in which public health bodies are financing and providing services to the population. This means, for example, how these bodies may be participating in financial markets, partnering with financial institutions, and directly contributing to financial accumulation.

There is a surprising scarcity of studies on health financialization where PHS are at the center of the analysis. The only exception so far seems to be Bayliss' (2016) case study for the English National Health Service (NHS), a state-funded health system. In this seminal work, Bayliss provides robust evidence of mechanisms through which "financialization has evolved within, and impacted upon, the NHS" (p. 2). The author identifies different channels connecting the system with global financial institutions and investors, two of which seem to be particularly important. The first channel consists of Private Finance Initiatives (PFIS), the national equivalent of PPPS. PFIS were introduced in England in the 1990s but gained steam from the 2000s onward. They have become the primary form of financing the construction of NHS hospitals. PFI arrangements are highly leveraged by commercial banks and institutional investors, and their asset streams serve for the creation of assets traded in financial markets. These projects have proven to be costly for the NHS but highly lucrative for the institutional investors involved in them.[14]

Another important channel for financialization highlighted by Bayliss was the outsourcing of services to private providers. This is directly associated with "classic" privatization reforms in the NHS taking place since the 1990s, which have increased the participation of private health actors in public service delivery. As several private health companies providing services for the NHS are now owned or backed up by private equity firms, investment funds, banks, and investors, outsourcing puts the system in much closer contact with global finance than is usually acknowledged. Moreover, an important part of NHS revenues ends up being channeled to these actors as a consequence of such shifts[15]

---

14   Estimates suggest that, over these three decades, NHS hospitals received £13 billion in investments, but will have to pay back around £80 billion by the end of the contracts (Thomas, 2019).

15   The interdependence between the public system and the financial sector can be illustrated by the fact that the announcement of cuts in the NHS budget in 2018 led to a

Bayliss et al. (2016a) deploy the UK case study to offer another important insight for research on financialization in public systems: the realization that it is precisely the public nature of these systems that make it difficult to perceive the transformations brought about by financialization. In the NHS, as in other public systems, access to health care continues to be mostly free or highly subsidized at the point of delivery. This means that processes of financialization tend to be obscured from the daily life of the population, making it more difficult to perceive see the transformations that might be taking place due to this process (see also Bayliss and Fine, 2020).

To provide additional elements that can help us conceptualize the process of financialization in PHS, one can turn to other countries committed to public and universal provision. There is fragmented yet compelling evidence that these systems are incorporating financial capital into their funding sources. As a general rule, similar to the English case, the regulatory shifts laying the ground for the developments described below started in the 1990s and gained momentum from the 2000s onward.

In Italy, Messina (2010; Messina and Denaro, 2006) and Cusseddu (2011) explain how the Italian health service system, the *Servizio Sanitario Nationale* (SSN), started resorting to securitization to pay service providers. Securitization is directly linked to financialization, as it is considered the main practice that allowed the financial sector to reach its current scale and scope (Davis and Kim, 2015; Leyshon and Thrift, 2007). Securitization consists of taking illiquid assets, such as long-term debts, and, through financial engineering, transforming them into securities that can be sold to other agents and traded in financial markets. This practice provides the creditor with immediate liquidity, "securing" its gains, while it renounces at least part of the future reimbursement. The holders of the securities, in turn, receive compensation based on the principal and interest payments of the underlying debt.

In the context of systematic delays in the SSN's payments to its suppliers and mounting debts to the latter, the agencies charged with running the public system began to securitize the SSN suppliers' debts. Securitizing debts would allow these public agencies to collect the funds needed to pay the suppliers. In practice, these agencies securitize the suppliers' "receivables" – their rights to future payments for the goods and services they provided for the public system. In one of the most common modalities of securitization, the health agencies assign the receivables to an external body (a "special purpose vehicle"),

---

decline in the price of shares of the main private hospital group that provided services to the system (Financial Times, 2018).

which issues bonds in the markets backed by the debt claims.[16] This operation provides the health agencies with income to pay the suppliers in the short run; in the future, the public sector does not transfer money to the suppliers (which have already been paid), but to the investors who bought the securities, with added interests.

Cusseddu (2011) explains that securitization practices in the SSN serve the immediate interests of public entities, which need to honor payments so that suppliers are willing to serve the system, as well as the investors, who acquire safe and high-yield assets. The author also highlights that this practice consists of the exchange of one form of debt for another, at a higher cost for the public sector in the long run. Moreover, the assets created from the securitization of SSN providers' debts are often listed, rated by credit rating agencies, and publicly offered in the markets, creating additional profit opportunities for financial actors. Messina (2010) identifies similar strategies of financial engineering to monetize health care receivables in Spain, Portugal, and Greece, countries that also have public, national health systems.

In Canada, a country with a publicly funded health insurance system known as *Medicare*, the government has been resorting to financial instruments to finance hospital infrastructure and health interventions. This is evidenced by the studies of Ryan and Young (2018) and Loxley and Hajer (2019), who assess the spread of PPPs and social impact bonds across several areas of the public sector in the country. Although these studies do not focus exclusively on the health sector, their findings show that health is one of the areas where PPPs and social impact bonds have been growing most rapidly. The main channel for financialization in health in this case seems to be the construction of public hospitals financed by PPPs. The data presented in these studies reveal that the majority of existing PPP projects in Canada are in the health sector, and this is now the predominant mode of infrastructure financing for public hospitals. The strategy to use social impact bonds to finance interventions, in turn, is still in its early stages. It is telling, however, that one of the first bonds sponsored by the Canadian government aimed at financing a health-related policy – the "Community Hypertension Prevention Initiative", launched in 2016 to tackle risk factors for high blood pressure.

Moving on to peripheral countries, Kumar (2016) uses the concept of financialization to explain a shift in the State's approach toward public health care in India. The study describes a clear shift in the orientation of public health

---

16   There are still other modalities, such as when the regional governments assume the responsibility for the operation (see Messina, 2010).

policies in the country since the late 2000s and connects it with the process of financialization. This is because the Indian State seems to have moved away from public investments in the existing tax-based, public health system based on service provision, to promote publicly-funded health insurance schemes for low-income individuals and informal workers. In this context, financialization is not associated with the adoption of specific instruments and strategies, but with a transition from the goal of achieving universal service provision to the use of public funds to subsidize access to care via private providers and financial markets, in this latter case notably through health insurance.[17]

Although exploratory, this exposition supports the hypothesis that private finance is making inroads into PHS. It presented examples of how systems in different countries have been directly or indirectly resorting to financial actors and instruments as a way to complement or replace traditional forms of public financing. Even if providing solid evidence of the influence of financialization in the recent path followed by public systems, these are single-case studies that reflect different theoretical and methodological standpoints. The relevance of the topic and the current research gaps warrant further discussion on how one might conceptualize and examine the process of financialization in PHS.

3.3   *Financialization as a Distinctive Type of PHS Change*

As a research object, PHS lie at the intersection of two domains: the public sector and the health sector, whose processes of financialization were discussed in the previous and present chapters, respectively. Taking inspiration from these bodies of research, I suggest that financialization in PHS can be characterized by the increasing participation of financial instruments and actors in these systems' structures of financing and provision. This can be seen, for example, through the incorporation of instruments and strategies that allow financial actors to lend money to public bodies responsible for the public health system. It may also be seen in the growing influence of financial interests in decision-making processes relative to public health care, favoring financial accumulation.[18] The discussion from here on emphasizes policy shifts in financing structures, the most evident and straightforward way through which the financial sector has been gaining ground in PHS. Changes in financing circuits can occur

---

17   Interestingly, the creation of publicly-sponsored insurance programs targeting the poor, seeking to achieve "universality", has been informed by the WHO's Universal Health Coverage approach – illustrating how current blueprints for universal systems are compatible with the neoliberal paradigm and the advance of financialization.

18   See the introduction for further detail on the definition of financialization in PHS proposed in the book and the indicators chosen to investigate it.

through any instrument and strategy that allows financial investors and institutions to finance bodies responsible for the public health system (simply put, to provide and exchange money with them).

An important question is why the developments previously mentioned should be considered a particular kind of PHS change. Shifts in financing circuits that welcome private capital might be seen as more than just another form of privatization. Throughout the previous sections, we have seen that recent developments changing the financing models of global, private, and public health activities rely on a variety of instruments and strategies that have received little attention in privatization studies. The same can be said about the actors behind such instruments and strategies. We have also seen that these instruments, strategies, and actors are directly linked to the financial sphere. This gives reason to argue that financialization constitutes a particular type of PHS reform that is related but not equal to classic forms of privatization.

Despite the recognition that privatization does not fully capture contemporary trends in the health sector, and the evidence that several of them are better described through the idea of financialization, there have been few attempts to draw clear limits between these concepts. As Karwowski (2019) critically observes, researchers tend to "draw only vague distinctions between financialization and the implementation of neoliberal policies, especially privatization" (p. 1007). In the following paragraphs, I take inspiration from the reviews on the processes of privatization and financialization to delineate some of the boundaries between these processes when it comes to PHS. I do so by highlighting some of the most important features, differences, and relations between t9hese sets of reforms. I revisit the categories explored above in the case of privatization – the agents, narratives, theoretical underpinnings, and impacts most typically associated with this process – and consider the extent to which processes related to financialization bring novelties in these realms.

3.3.1   Agents

Part of policy shifts in PHS today aims at reaching not the providers of private health services and insurance, but the providers of money. The most salient feature of financialization is thus that the private actors involved in these shifts are, to a great extent, financial rather than non-financial actors. Different from health companies, financial companies do not focus on health. Their primary business concerns money and investments, including, but far from limited to, health-related activities. Resorting to these entities is in many ways different from outsourcing public services to private providers or externalizing costs onto mutual health funds.

To be clear, what characterizes financialization is not the presence of financial instruments and actors *per se*. Health insurance, for example, is a long-standing practice in the sector, and in many countries, non-profit insurance funds have been serving as the "hidden public sector" due to their instrumental role in ensuring the right to health (Hood, 1986, cited by Maarse, 2006). It is the centrality that finance assumes today that distinguishes the present phase from previous ones; financial companies are not simply intermediating or backing up policy shifts in the health sector (including in public systems) but leading and benefitting the most from a great part of them.

Concerning the timing of this process, the evidence collected so far suggests that changes in the health sector and within PHS paving the way for the use of financial capital date back from the 1990s, but grew at a much faster pace from the 2000s onwards.

Interestingly, even when there is the incorporation of non-financial actors from the private sector into the public system, this has now the potential to expand the participation and influence of financial agents. This is because the landscape of the private health sector is not the same as it was decades ago. Studies on how financialization has reshaped the landscape of private care providers and insurance companies allow us to observe some differences between traditional business models that used to prevail in the past and emerging ownership structures (see segment "ownership restructuring" above). Traditional ownership structures, with specialized health companies often owned by individuals or families with a professional record in the sector, are losing space to companies controlled by global multi-sector financial firms. When health companies are sold to the latter, health provision enters a vast portfolio of other activities that these financial corporations invest in. By means of ownership restructuring, health care companies have been integrated into the portfolio of firms that also invest in energy distribution companies, restaurant chains, music store chains, airports, and credit card services, to name a few (Bayliss, 2016; Iriart et al., 2001). In several instances in which this has occurred, previous company owners gained a seat on the board of directors and (or) an important part of company shares.

In the case of insurance companies, these are now fewer in number and larger in size compared to the 1990s. Also, non-profit insurers specializing in health have been losing space to for-profit insurers. The latter are usually linked to banks or constitute large financial institutions operating in multiple segments of the insurance industry (e.g., Abecassis and Coutinet, 2021; Sestelo, 2017).

Several health actors have been incorporating principles, practices, and goals typical of financial institutions into their growth strategies and daily *modus*

operandi. This often results from the use of financial instruments and the association with financial actors, which requires them to adapt to the latter's standards and satisfy their requirements. This reflects a movement called by Aalbers
(2019) as "corporate financialization", "when traditionally nonfinancial firms
become dominated by financial narratives, practices, and measurements and
increasingly partaking in practices that have been the domain of the financial
sector" (p. 3). The expansion of health companies and health insurers seems
less dependent on the evolution of operational profits *per se* and more on how
they would contribute to increasing shareholder value and investment returns.
The extent of changes brought about by the need to generate financial returns
extends to the materiality of service provision. It steers decisions on what kind
of services will be provided, where, to whom, and at what costs and conditions, favoring those that can maximize financial gains and drive stock market
appreciation. This can be seen, for example, when hospitals decide the profile
of service provision prioritizing niches that maximize investment returns, or
when insurance companies repress the value of benefits while increasing the
volume of funds allocated in financial investments to maximize their financial
results (e.g., Cordilha and Lavinas, 2018; Vural, 2017).

These transformations seem to go beyond the notion of *commodification* –
treating health as a commodity. According to Birch and Muniesa (2020), it is
impossible to fully grasp the drivers of capital accumulation in the present
stage of capitalism "struggling within prevailing conceptions of the commercialization, marketization, and commodification" (p. 9); the concept of "assetization" – "turning things into assets" (p. 11) is a missing piece in the puzzle.
This seems to be the case with the transformations discussed in this section.
An asset is something that can generate returns in the future. Financial assets
are intangible properties that do so by guaranteeing a claim on ownership or
contractual rights to future payments from one entity over another. They can
be owned or controlled, traded, and capitalized as revenue streams (Birch
and Muniesa, *op. cit.*; Chiapello, 2020). Securities, loans, derivatives, and other
instruments and contracts traded in financial markets are examples of financial assets. As commodification can be considered the underlying process
underpinning privatization, a similar case could be made here with the concepts of assetization and financialization. If the process of commodification
was associated with treating health care activities as commodities, attributing
a "price" to it and putting it to be traded in markets for goods and services,
assetization implies turning health care activities into assets, attributing a
"risk" to them, and putting it to be traded in financial markets.

The transformations described above suggest that the transformation of
health into a financial investment has implications for how health is conceived

and provided, and deviates part of the resources allocated to health activities to other ends. They show many instances where health activities have been treated as assets, as activities related to the financing and provision of medical care, ancillary services, insurance, and infrastructure were partially or entirely dissociated from their previous ownership structures and transformed into investment opportunities. Payments from households, governments, and companies directed to pay for such activities ended up partially appropriated by finance, through, for example, rights to ownership or returns on investments.

3.3.2   Narratives

The differences between earlier rounds of privatization and moves toward financialization go beyond the actors involved in each case. The narrative built around PHS and the justifications for turning toward finance seem to have changed. Whereas in the past these systems were portrayed as inefficient and overspending, criticism today has not eliminated those views but focuses on presenting them as financially strapped. The chief argument used by those advocating in favor of "partnering" with financial actors is not so much the opportunity to reduce expenditures or increase efficiency in the public sector, but the chance to boost investments and raise additional revenues. This has been observed in different contexts, including debates on the use of financial instruments by public and non-profit actors (such as SIBs and PPPs) and funding strategies for global health policies. Bayliss and Waeyenberge's (2017) study of PPPs, for example, observes that "unlike the privatization of the 1990s, PPP policy is now driven far more by the availability of global finance than by the previously perceived potential for efficiency gains through privatization" (p. 5).

Besides raising funds, other arguments supporting a turn toward the financial sector include, first, the possibility to forge "virtuous links" between investors, governments, for-profit companies, non-profit institutions, and the civil society, and second, profiting from (supposedly) more attractive financing conditions. Financial markets and institutions are seen as abundant and cheap sources of funds. Therefore, financialized strategies would allow mobilizing idle capital voluntarily, which could not be raised through compulsory taxation (Chiapello, 2017), and the greater competition and availability of funds in private markets would render them supposedly cheaper than other forms of financing.

3.3.3   Theoretical Underpinnings

Another distinctive trait of recent developments in the health sector is that the theoretical bases supporting financialization reforms are fairly opaque. A favorable stance in favor of incorporating financial capital into health care financing seems to reflect the belief that financial institutions and markets can value and allocate resources efficiently. In particular, they would be much more capable of mobilizing funds than the public sector. This in principle would indicate that the theoretical grounds for financialization rest on the assumptions of the financial system's neutrality and efficiency, informed by neoclassical finance theories (Chapter 1).

Interestingly, however, one can hardly find any mentions to finance theories in proposals that advocate in favor of bringing private finance into the health or the public sector. The latest phase of transformations in the health care sphere seems to be characterized by a "common-sense" policy position that enormous volumes of private financial capital are necessary for promoting development (Hunter and Murray, 2019). In this sense, the resort to finance appears much more as a pragmatic solution for times of financial distress than as a theoretically informed policy option.

3.3.4   Different Paths, Same Driving Force: Austerity Policies

Beyond their specificities, privatization and financialization processes are not disconnected – on the contrary, they are complementary and propelled by the same force: the pressure for public budget austerity. Financialized strategies appear as a novel way to deal with the old challenge of maintaining and expanding public provision while public health revenues do not grow accordingly. If earlier rounds of reforms were focused on cutting and externalizing costs, the invitation now is to find ways to raise revenues without increasing taxation. Governments facing pressures for austerity see in financial instruments and arrangements an opportunity to top up their financing needs. They can raise or borrow funds in the financial sector instead of implementing policies running counter to the neoliberal paradigm, such as taxing capital or allocating a higher share of public revenues to the health budget.

The entities responsible for the financing of PHS have particularly strong incentives for turning toward the financial sector, as they need to accommodate growing financing needs within ever more limited budgets. The implicit idea is that traditional sources of public revenues alone cannot provide the necessary funds to maintain and expand access to health care, and private funding would be necessary for closing the gap. As observed by Bayliss (2016), "growing financial deficits puts attention on financial performance and legitimizes increasing penetration of financial capital in the health system" (p. 34). In a similar vein, Hunter and Murray (2019) suggest that the justification for promoting private investment in health care "has been fueled by gaps in adequate resourcing of unified public systems" (p. 4). Reinforcing this impression, research institutions have presented private investments as a "solution to meeting rising demand in the face of severely constrained public resources" (Fraser et al., 2018, p. 4).

together are reshaping the landscape of PHS today. This is in line with Fine and Hall's (2012) assertion that, "as finance has increasingly come to the fore, so it has both promoted and benefited from privatization" (p. 53).

Privatization and financialization are mutually reinforcing processes. First, privatization can act as a driver of financialization. One reason is that privatization requires regulatory shifts that enable and expand the possibilities of profit-making in activities related to health financing and provision, facilitating the creation of financial undertakings in a second moment (Hunter and Murray, 2019; Vural, 2017). Along these lines, Fine (2009) argues that some sort of privatization is necessary for financialization in the public sector. This is because the process of privatization (understood in its broadest sense as reforms that introduce market logic into the public sector) creates payments for goods and services where these did not exist before. In doing so, it introduces monetary flows in public services, which can then be manipulated to create financial assets and returns. In the case of health, establishing internal markets, introducing user charges, and contracting out services are examples of privatization measures that can create revenue flows, potentially leading to financialization. As explained by Bayliss et al. (2017), "financialization can prosper where there is not necessarily commodity production but the presence of the "commodity form" by which is meant monetary payments". Such payments end up "[generating] revenue streams that can be securitized as assets and be speculatively traded as interest-bearing capital" (p. 5; see also Fine and Bayliss, 2016).

Rather than unintentionally promoting financialization, privatization is now partly motivated by the very own prospects of creating assets and returns. Bayliss' (2016) case study of the English health system demonstrates that

> [Public] health services are interpreted in terms of their potential for financial gain in a more creative way than was the case twenty years ago. *Attention is paid to revenue streams and asset values as well as the potential for securitization to enhance shareholder distributions.* This is in contrast to the 1980s *where privatization was seen as a way to improve productive efficiency by bringing in private owners.*
>
> p. 42

3.3.7   Financialization as a Driver of Privatization

Second, there are also several reasons to think that financialization boosts privatization. An important one is that the accumulation and internationalization of financial capital allow for a vast sum of available funds looking for profitable investment opportunities. In this context, privatization would appear as a prominent outlet for excessive capital (Huffschmid, 2009). According to Fine (2008), "the volume and range of financial services that have been made available [in the period of financialization] have given rise to a wealth of 'idle capital' that makes itself busy by the pursuit of privatization" (p. 15). On top of the returns reaped from directly investing in private projects, Sawyer (2009) remembers that the financial sector may also profit from privatization by arranging these operations, earning significant volumes of money in the form of commissions, fees, and the like (see also André and Hermann, 2009). Huffschmid (*op. cit.*) adds that the reason privatization has been so intense can be at least partially explained by the fact that it meets the interests of both finance and the State:

> In the context of growing private financial assets seeking investment opportunities and at the same time growing pressures upon public finances, privatization appears as a solution to the problems of both the wealthy [investors] and the State: it gives the former a new area for financial investment and relaxes the financial constraints for the latter.
>
> p. 54

Other authors, in turn, highlight that the injection of financial capital boosts the growth of the market's largest private health companies and reinforces existing trends for concentration, creating major players with political and economic power to pressure governments in favor of privatization (Bahia et al., 2016; Sestelo, 2018; Vural, 2017).

More recently, it has become clear that financial capital also promotes privatization in a more straightforward way: public projects financed by financial firms and investors tend to have an ideological bias in favor of private actors for building, maintaining, and operating the services as these are considered more efficient and innovative. The preference for private providers has been evidenced in cases where public services were financed by private investors via SIBS and PPPS (e.g., Andreu, 2018; Bayliss, 2016; Loxley and Hajer, 2019).

The joint analysis of the dynamics of privatization and financialization carried out here, including the differences and interdependencies between these processes, is crucial for better understanding part of recent reforms in these systems. Surprisingly, to date, there have been few efforts to systematize these differences and connections, and even less so for the specific case of PHS. Table 2.1 systematizes the fundamental characteristics of each of these processes and how they relate to each other. In the following chapters, I will move from theory to practice, investigating how these developments have unfolded in two universal systems over the past three decades.

TABLE 2.1 Privatization and financialization in the health sector: systematizing prominent features

	Privatization	Financialization
Period of most intense measures[a]	1980s–1990s	2000s onwards
Common aspects covered in definitions	The adoption of a corporate rationale (e.g., languages, metrics, goals of nonfinancial private companies) by public bodies The incorporation of practices and actors from the private health sector into public structures of management, financing, and provision	The adoption of a financial rationale (e.g., languages, metrics, goals of financial companies) by public bodies The incorporation of practices and actors from the private financial sector into public structures of financing, management, and provision
Examples of policy shifts	Introduction of private practice in public establishments Outsourcing of public services to private providers Cost-shifting onto patients and insurers (e.g., introduction or rise of co-payments)	Public-Private Partnerships Social Impact Bonds Issuance of securities Contracting of debt Undertaking of financial investments
Main private actors concerned	Private providers of health goods, services, and insurance ("private non-financial sector")[2] Examples: for- and not-for-profit hospitals, clinics, laboratories, health insurance funds	Private providers of funds and investments ("private financial sector") Examples: for- and not-for-profit banks, investment funds, financial investors, multinational non-specialized insurance companies

(cont.)

	Privatization	Financialization
Main features of private actors concerned: health companies	Family or individual ownership, often owned by health professionals. Weaker connections with financial institutions and investors. Lower levels of leveraging. Specialized in health activities (producing and trading health goods and services) Goal of generating operating profits Expansion led by the incremental consumption of drugs, services, and equipment	Corporate ownership, often owned, controlled, or highly leveraged by financial companies and investors. Previous owners (individuals or family representatives) can be integrated into the newly formed structures Not specialized in health activities (companies with a diverse investment portfolio) Increasing goal of generating financial income (e.g., interest payments, dividends, capital gains, fees)
Main features of private actors concerned: insurance companies[b]	Smaller companies, lower levels of concentration in the sector Often dissociated from other financial institutions Important non-profit segment, benefits based on solidarity principles	Larger companies, higher levels of concentration in the sector Increasingly associated with larger financial institutions Expanding for-profit segment, with benefits defined according to the value of contributions In both cases (health and insurance companies), Expansion led by investment strategies (e.g., mergers and acquisitions, internationalization, private equity investments)

(cont.)

	Privatization	Financialization
Narrative and arguments pro-reforms	Public sector portrayed as overspending and inefficient. Public actors are inherently prone to corruption and inefficiency. Profit motive, competition, and ownership rights can render superior outcomes. Privatization reforms would reduce public costs and promote efficiency gains.	Public sector portrayed as financially strapped. The financial sector can price and allocate resources efficiently. In particular, it can raise a higher amount of funds at lower costs than the public sector. Financialization reforms would bring revenues into the public system and reduce the costs of financing.
Underlying process	"Commodification": assigning properties of a commodity to something previously not treated as such. In health, commodification can be seen when activities for health financing and provision are given a monetary value and start being negotiated according to the market logic, with different agents buying and selling health goods and services.	"Assetization": assigning properties of a financial asset to something previously not treated as such. In health, assetization can be seen when activities for health financing and provision are assessed based on risks and returns and transformed into investment opportunities, representing a claim on ownership or contractual rights to future payments.

(*cont.*)

	Privatization	Financialization
Theoretical underpinnings	Assumptions from different theories grounded on neoclassical Economics (e.g., theory of property rights, theory of the firm, theory of public choice). More explicit attempt to anchor the case for privatization in theoretical arguments.	Assumptions from finance theories grounded on neoclassical Economics (e.g., "efficient market hypothesis") Hardly any explicit reference to finance theories to make the case for financialization; measures presented as pragmatic solutions rather than theoretically-informed policy shifts.
Adverse impacts according to critical studies	Deterioration in the quality and quantity of public provision Deterioration of employment conditions Increase in private health spending Increase in inequalities of access to health services from the downsizing of public provision and the externalization of costs	Intensification of impacts associated with privatization Loss of transparency and accountability Heightened volatility of public financing Increase in income concentration from the use of public funds to pay for financial returns

(cont.)

	Privatization	Financialization
References[c]	Starr (1988), Agartan (2012), André and Hermann (2009), Ewert (2009), André et al. (2015), Böhm (2017), Fine (1999, 2008), Fine and Hall (2012), Yilmaz (2017), Hassenteufel and Palier (2007), Ortiz et al. (2015), Starr (1988), Swyngedouw et al. (2002), Mackintosh and Koivusalo (2005), Mercille and Murphy (2017), Hermann (2010).	Bayliss and Waeyenberge (2017), Birch and Muniesa (2020), Cordilha and Lavinas (2018), Dentico (2019), Chiapello (2017), Bahia et al. (2016), Bayliss (2016), Bayliss et al. (2016), Kumar (2016) Hooda (2016), Hunter and Murray (2019), Alles (2018), Sestelo (2017), Karwowski (2019), Lavinas and Gentil (2018), Vural (2017), Stein and Sridhar (2018), Maarse (2006), Souza et al. (2019), Whitfield (2006, 2015), Martins et al. (2021), Mulligan (2016), Lewalle (2006), Abecassis and Coutinet (2021), Hermann (2010), Angeli and Maarse (2012), Hirakuta et al. (2016), Iriart et al. (2001).

SOURCES: AUTHOR'S ELABORATION BASED ON THE REFERENCES LISTED ABOVE

Notes:

a This differentiation does not mean that privatization and financialization are seen as exclusionary processes: privatization processes occur up to today, and developments associated with financialization started to emerge before the 2000s. The columns attempt to contrast the features of actors and processes leading transformations in the sector in each period.

b Although insurance companies are formally classified as financial actors, the private health insurance companies from the past had significant different features compared to the financial companies taking over the health sector today; therefore, for the sake of simplification, I consider the former together with health companies.

c The references were classified according to the core concept of the study; however, there is an overlap in references, meaning that in some cases they contributed to characterize both phases.

PART 2

*From Theory to Practice: How Financialization
Reshapes Public Health Systems*

∴

The French System

Pioneering Financialized Strategies in PHS

Assurance Maladie, the French PHS, has been subjected to major changes in its financing model leading to an increasing dependence on financial capital. The French State was directly responsible for the implementation of financialized strategies within the system. Even if part of these strategies rewired the financing of the Social Security system more broadly, they have a direct influence on public health funding. This is because the French PHS is one of the branches that constitute the French Social Security system. More than that, it is usually the branch of Social Security that most need additional funding. The financing requirements of the health branch (the PHS) were thus an important part of the argument used by the government to justify turning to financial capital to manage Social Security accounts.

The analysis begins by presenting the institutional features of the French Social Security and health care systems, as well as the latter's evolution over the past half-century. I then examine three sets of transformations through which the financing of public health care became increasingly dependent on financial capital throughout this period. Starting with long-term financing, I describe how the Social Security system started issuing securities for refinancing its debt in the financial markets. The following section turns to short-term financing, showing how a similar strategy was adopted to cover expenses falling due in the near future. The concluding section deals with changes in hospital financing, examining the use of both loans and securities to fund public hospital infrastructure.

1   Social Security and Public Health Care in France

The French PHS is embedded in a more comprehensive institutional framework known as the Social Security system. Its principles of organization, financing, and provision are closely linked to those governing Social Security at large. Moreover, part of the policies described in this chapter targets the broader system of Social Security, reaching all its branches – including, but not limited to, the health system's branch. It seems therefore important to understand how the national Social Security system works before explaining the ways in which the French PHS connects to the financial sector.[1]

1.1   *The French System of Social Security*

La Sécurité Sociale – the French Social Security system – was created in 1945, following a regional trend of expansion of welfare policies in the post-war period. The 1946 Constitution formally introduced Social Security in the country, through which "the French nation" (sic) committed itself to protect citizens against risks and contingencies that could prevent them from attaining socially acceptable living standards (France, 1946).

Some fundamental principles were established during the creation of Social Security to ensure that the system would run in accordance with its original values and objectives. Among the most important principles, one can mention national solidarity (all individuals should participate in the system), redistribution (part of resources should go from the most to the least favored ones), mutualization (the participants would contribute according to their means and receive according to their needs), universality (the system would cover the entire population of the country), and integrality (it should protect against a wide array of social risks).

As of 2018, the system of Social Security was divided into four branches:[2]
- The Illness branch (*branche maladie*) is the French PHS. It covers health-related risks – that is, it provides benefits to protect against risks related to the loss of physical and mental health. These benefits include both reimbursements (cash benefits) and direct public service provision (in-kind benefits).
- The Retirement branch (*branche retraite*) provides cash benefits to cover events related to aging and inactivity, mainly in the form of retirement pensions and allowances;
- The Family branch (*branche famille*) covers events related to family costs and poverty. It provides minimum maintenance benefits ("safety nets"), birth and early childcare benefits, housing subsidies, and other welfare benefits;

---

1   This description of the French Social Security system is based on Abecassis et al. (2018), Abecassis and Coutinet (2021), ACOSS (2018a, 2018b), Batifoulier (2015), Batifoulier et al. (2018), Batifoulier and Touzé (2000), Damon and Ferras (2015), Direction de la Sécurité Sociale (2018), and Palier (2010a).

2   The description presented here refers to the organization of the system for the largest part of the period under investigation (1990–2018).

- The Accidents at Work and Occupational Diseases branch (*branche acci-dents du travail et maladies professionnelles*) covers injuries and illnesses from work activity. It provides benefits ranging from daily indemnities to lifetime disability pensions.

The French Social Security system follows the logic of social insurance, inherited from the earliest forms of Bismarckian State protection in the 19th century (Chapter 2). In reality, it is not a single system, but a combination of different public schemes separated according to one's occupational status and sector of activity. When these schemes were first created, the prevailing idea was that they would be governed together by employers and employees, and financed by both via contributions on wages. These systems underwent several reforms over the years, some of which have distanced them from these principles (Damon and Ferras, 2015; Palier, 2010c; Vahabi et al., 2020). Yet, the logic of "social insurance" remains in place to the extent that there are different social security schemes, separated from the central government and expected to be funded and governed collectively.

As of 2018, the Social Security system was formed by three "basic" schemes (*régimes de base*): the General Regime, the regime for agricultural workers, and the set of "special regimes" dedicated to particular categories of workers (e.g., public servants, the military, and employees of specific public enterprises).[3] These are mandatory schemes covering the full range of risks guaranteed by the Constitution. The General Regime is the focus of the present analysis. It covers covering most wage-earners from the private sector, the self-employed, and those not eligible for any other scheme, reaching almost 90% of the population (DSS, 2018).

The French "State" and the "Social Security" are considered different spheres of the public administration, with separate budgets.[4] The chief sources of

---

3   The term "Social Security system" is usually employed to refer to the ensemble of basic regimes. Nonetheless, it is possible to find other usages. Some use the term to refer to the group of all mandatory basic and complementary schemes, or even the whole scope of institutions classified as "Social Security administrations". For reasons of scope and data availability, the present investigation focuses on the General Regime.

4   There are four spheres of public administration in France: the State, Social Security administrations, other central government agencies, and local public administrations. Social security administrations comprise the compulsory Social Security regimes, the unemployment benefit scheme, auxiliary funds (such as the Fund for Old-Age Solidarity – Fonds de Solidarité Vieillesse/FSV, the Pension Reserve Fund – Fonds de Réserve pour les Retraites/FRR, and the Social Debt Amortization Fund – Caisse d'Amortissement de la Dette Sociale/CADES), and "organizations dependent on social insurance" (public hospitals, private non-profit health establishments, and social works).

revenues for Social Security are earmarked taxes known as "social contributions". These include contributions on the payroll paid by employers and
employees (*cotisations*) and general contributions levied on different sources
of income such as wages, retirement pensions, property income, and investment income (*contributions généralisées*). Social Security also receives funds
from general taxation, which enter the system through State transfers. In 2017,
approximately 55% of Social Security's revenues came from contributions on
the payroll, 20% from the "general social contribution" (*contribution sociale
généralisée*), and 25% from State transfers and proceeds from other taxes, contributions, and fees (DSS, 2018). This list comprises the permanent sources
of revenues of the Social Security system; it does not take into account the
"non-permanent" revenues that Social Security raises in order to manage its
accounts, including in financial markets, which are discussed in the following
sections.

The circuit from tax collection to benefit payments depends on a network
of bodies, each one in charge of a specific stage – collection, centralization,
and redistribution of revenues (Figure 3.1). The collection unions (*Unions
de recouvrement des cotisations de sécurité sociale et d'allocations familiales –
URSSAFs*) are in charge of gathering revenues from contributors (companies,
public administrations, independent workers, and individuals) and addressing
them to the agency that centralizes the resources. This is the Central Agency
of Social Security Organizations (*Agence Centrale des Organismes de Sécurité
Sociale – ACOSS*). After pooling the resources, the Central Agency distributes
them across the Social Security branches. To do so, it transfers the money to
the Social Security Funds (*Caisses de Sécurité Sociale*) – the "accounts" of each
Social Security branch in the Central Agency.

The general regime has three national Social Security Funds: one for the
Illness and Occupational injuries branches (combined), one for the Retirement
branch, and one for the Family branch. The Funds operate at the national level.
Together with its subordinated local funds, they execute Social Security payments to individuals, public and private entities. Apart from this central circuit, Social Security can also reach for external sources of financing including
the State, other public agencies, and financial institutions and markets.

1.2   The French Public Health System: Assurance Maladie

Each Social Security regime in France has its own health insurance scheme,
with different rules for enrollment, contribution, and benefits. The term
Assurance Maladie (literally, "Illness Insurance") is usually employed in a
broad sense to encompass the public health insurance schemes provided by
the various regimes of Social Security. This study focuses on the public health

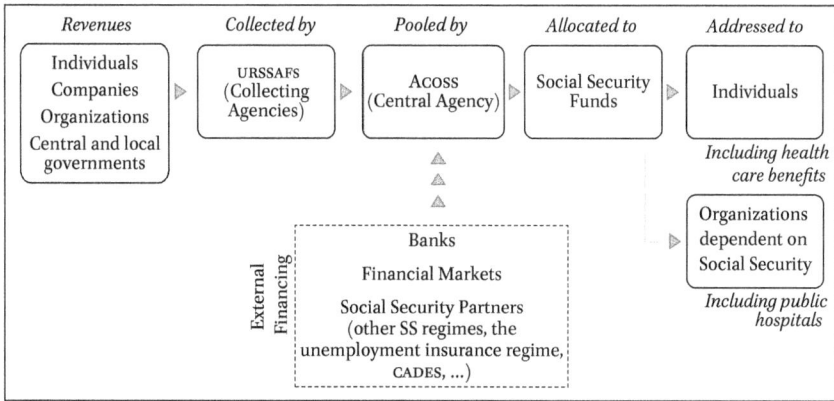

Revenues	Collected by	Pooled by	Allocated to	Addressed to
Individuals Companies Organizations Central and local governments	URSSAFS (Collecting Agencies)	ACOSS (Central Agency)	Social Security Funds	Individuals

Including health care benefits

Banks
Financial Markets
Social Security Partners (other SS regimes, the unemployment insurance regime, CADES, ...)

External Financing

Organizations dependent on Social Security

Including public hospitals

FIGURE 3.1   France, Social Security (General Regime), simplified scheme of financial flows
SOURCE: AUTHOR'S ELABORATION. REFERS TO THE GENERAL REGIME OF
SOCIAL SECURITY

insurance system from the General Regime, which, as observed in the previous section, covers the vast majority of the population in the country.[5]

Besides working in line with the general principles of Social Security, *Assurance Maladie* must also follow an additional set of principles that includes equality of access, solidarity, and quality of provision (France, Social Security Code, Article L111-2-1).

The revenues to finance *Assurance Maladie* come primarily from the Social Security system. Consequently, social contributions are its main source of funds. In 2017, 43% of *Assurance Maladie*'s revenues came from contributions on wages, 31% from the General Social Contribution, and 26% from State taxes and other sources of revenues (DSS, 2018). Additionally, health benefits provided under universalization programs (see below) are co-financed by a fee levied on complementary health insurance premiums. A small share of activities and programs carried by *Assurance Maladie* are financed directly by the State (not by Social Security), such as certain actions related to prevention, medical and pharmaceutical research, professional training, health insurance programs for the poorest or irregular residents, endowments for military hospitals, and emergency medical care.

As a model of social insurance, part of *Assurance Maladie*'s expenditures come in the form of reimbursements or cost-coverage for medical goods and

---

5   Unless stated otherwise, the term "Assurance Maladie" will be employed here in reference to the public insurance scheme of the General Regime and used interchangeably with "French PHS" and the "Illness branch of Social Security" (as seen in official reports).

services, acquired either in the public or the private sector. The extent of public coverage depends on a number of factors, namely the type of good or service and the beneficiary's health and financial conditions. As a general rule, by 2018, *Assurance Maladie* reimbursed approximately 70% of the standard price for medical appointments and laboratory tests, 80%-90% of hospitalization costs, 60% of services and goods related to optics and orthopedics, and from 0% to 100% of drugs.[6] The share of costs paid by *Assurance Maladie* is referred to as the "obligatory part". Under certain conditions, health professionals may bill additional charges not covered by the public system (*dépassement d'honoraires*). This does not apply to all circumstances and may vary depending on the patient's financial situation, the practitioner's decision, and the complexity of the procedure.

After public coverage, the remaining payables are left to the patient and can be paid either directly (*out-of-pocket*) or by a private insurance plan. This is known as the "complementary part" of medical coverage. The public and private insurance segments in France follow thus a complementary logic (OECD, 2004), in the sense that private insurance works *in tandem* with the public system covering the residual costs left unpaid by the latter. Approximately 95% of the French population benefits from "complementary" health insurance plans (DREES, 2019b). This widespread presence of private insurance can be traced back to the historical role of mutual companies in covering health risks. They managed to preserve their power and autonomy amidst the creation of Social Security in the 1940s, continuing to have an important role in the full coverage of health care costs.

Despite the fast growth of for-profit companies in the last decades, complementary insurance remains mostly in the hands of non-profit institutions. In 2017, 78% of establishments proposing complementary health insurance contracts were classified as non-profit, receiving 70% of the total revenues from complementary health insurance premiums (DREES, 2018a). Several studies show, however, that these non-profit insurance funds have been abandoning solidarity values and behaving similarly to for-profit insurance companies (Abecassis et al., 2018, 2017, 2014; Abecassis and Coutinet, 2021).

Besides public insurance, the French PHS also provides health care services directly, through public hospitals. The public sector is responsible for the largest share of hospital care in the country. In 2016, 62% of hospital beds were in public health establishments. *Assurance Maladie* and public hospitals have

---

6 The standard price, or "convention tariff", is a fixed price determined *ex-ante* between *Assurance Maladie* and health professionals. See www.ameli.fr/assure/remboursements.

separate budgets. The latter are still part of the Social Security system, but they are classified as a special category of entities known as "organizations dependent on social insurance", separated from social insurance schemes. Yet, public hospitals are mostly financed by *Assurance Maladie*, which provides around 70% of their revenues. Individuals, private insurance, and the State together account for the remaining 30% of public hospital revenues (DREES, 2018b).

1.3   *The Trajectory toward Universalization*

Although the principle of universal health care dates back to the creation of Social Security, the extension of the right to participate in public schemes to all the population was a gradual process, completed only by the end of the 20th century. The first efforts to extend social protection started in the 1960s in the context of an increasingly diversified working class, with the creation of Social Security schemes for specific professional activities. Despite substantial signs of progress toward universalization since then, there were still significant gaps in terms of the population covered by the public system by the 1990s. The most important reason was that a significant number of individuals could not benefit from Social Security because their employment status did not make them eligible for any existing scheme.

At the end of the century, the State began a more consistent strategy to universalize access to health care with the creation of programs to guarantee public and private insurance coverage regardless of one's occupational status. In 1999, the government universalized access to public insurance by altering the eligibility criteria of the General Regime of Social Security, allowing any individual unaffiliated to a mandatory scheme the right to enroll in the General Regime. This device is known as the Basic Universal Illness Coverage (*Couverture Maladie Universelle de Base*, CMU). Yet, administrative barriers kept preventing individuals from either joining the scheme or staying in it after eventual changes in their personal or professional statuses. In order to address those issues, the CMU was transformed into the Universal Illness Protection (*Protection Universelle Maladie*, PUMA) in 2016. With PUMA, residence criteria became the norm: any individual living in France with a permanent and regular status was automatically entitled to the General Regime. As of 2015, two million people in the General Regime joined the scheme thanks to these universalization programs (Fonds CMU, 2016). In parallel, in 1999, the government also created the State Medical Aid (*Aide Médicale de l'État*, AME) for residents with irregular statuses, providing health assistance to them. In this case, participation in the scheme is temporary and subject to conditionalities.

The generalization of private insurance represented another core pillar of the government's universalization strategy. This is because the CMU/PUMA programs guarantee the coverage of the share of health expenses normally included in the public system, the "obligatory part". Consequently, the members who entered the system through these programs are still left with a "complementary part" to pay. To extend access to private insurance schemes, the government created the Complementary Universal Illness Coverage (*Couverture Maladie Universelle Complémentaire*, CMU-C) together with the CMU in 1999. The CMU-C entitles low-income individuals to complementary health insurance free of charge, chosen from a set of institutions selected by the government. In 2004, those earning slightly above the maximum eligible for the CMU-C received support with a new program called the Aid for the Acquisition of a Complementary Health Plan (*Aide à l'Acquisition d'une Complémentaire Santé*, ACS), giving discounts on premium payments. By the end of 2017, 5.5 million people benefited from the CMU-C and 1.6 million from the ACS, amounting to around 10% of the French population (Fonds CMU, 2016). Both programs, CMU-C and ACS, were financed by taxes levied on complementary insurance premiums.

Individuals are also entitled to the coverage of health care costs in case they suffer from illnesses that require expensive or continuous treatments (*Affections de Longue Durée*, ALD). As of 2017, there were thirty health conditions allowing individuals to obtain free treatment for these diseases, and more than ten million people enrolled in the general scheme were classified as ALD patients (Assurance Maladie, 2018).

1.4 *The Path of Neoliberal Reforms in Assurance Maladie*

From 1975 to 2015, the French Social Security system was subjected to a series of structural changes, including a constitutional reform (1996) and frequent adjustments imposed by two organic laws (1996 and 2005) and eighteen financing laws (from 1997 to 2015) (Franchet, 2015). Along with the reforms in Social Security, which naturally impact the Illness branch of the system (*Assurance Maladie*), there were also numerous reforms directed specifically at the latter.

Until the 1980s, *Assurance Maladie* underwent changes in its institutional framework, eligibility criteria, and value of benefits. However, these reforms were mostly to expand public coverage and provision (with the consequence of also expanding public health spending). After that, the government started a systematic process of reforms in the opposite direction. Its reform agenda, aimed at achieving "financial equilibrium", imposed a combination of measures to increase revenues, curb expenditures, and increase the State's grip on decisions relative to the Social Security system.[7]

A particularly important set of measures to contain public coverage and costs sought to increase the share of health care costs borne by patients, with the rise in co-payments. While these measures were largely justified as a way to "foster responsibility" in patients (creating disincentives for supposedly unnecessary demands), they also allowed for the relative decline in the costs covered by the French PHS in many areas. Along with that, there were measures to limit expenditures by service providers, namely through the imposition of budget ceilings for public hospitals and outpatient care providers.

In the 1990s, the progressive deterioration of Social Security accounts led the government to intensify measures for increasing revenues and curbing costs in the PHS. It sought to raise funds by increasing rates on contributions, withdrawing caps on existing ones, and introducing the General Social Contribution (which became one of the primary sources of revenues for Social Security). Meanwhile, the government continued to implement devices to control spending, diminishing the share of *Assurance Maladies'* reimbursements for certain medical consultations, examinations, and drugs.

In the second half of the 1990s decade, the Social Security system underwent a structural reform allowing for the almost automatic adoption of cost-containment measures. The 1996 Constitutional Reform of the Social Security system did so by creating a new category of laws, the Social Security Financing Laws (*Lois de Financement de la Sécurité Sociale* – LFSSS). With these Financing Laws, Social Security policies started being formally subjected to guidelines and spending targets voted by the Parliament each year. The government also created a specific set of spending targets for the PHS, the *Assurance Maladie's* National Spending Target (*Objectif National des Dépenses d'Assurance Maladie*, ONDAM). Through this device, the government could set an expected growth rate of health care expenditures for the following year ("no more than x%") and adopt the necessary measures to achieve such targets.

The financial pressures on *Assurance Maladie* continued into the 2000s and 2010s. The French government continued to diminish public coverage for part of health goods and services and impose budgetary rules. In 2004, the PHS underwent a far-reaching institutional reform taking co-payments and budget constraints to a new level. The most telling example was the redesign of the

---

7 For extensive reviews of *Assurance Maladie* reforms, see IRDES (2017, 2015), Jansen (2016), Nay et al. (2016), and the Projects for the Financing Laws for Social Security (Assemblée Nationale, various years). The measures listed in this section were extracted from these sources.

traditional form to access public health coverage, implementing a protocol for patients to follow so they could benefit from the full reimbursement expected from the public system (*parcours de soins coordonnés*).

While the introduction of devices increasing the share borne by patients continued in the 2010s, these were combined with more significant shifts in the conditions and values of transfers from *Assurance Maladie* to hospitals and health professionals. The diversification of measures extended to reach cost-saving agreements for hospital procurements and the de-listing or decrease in reimbursements for drugs, to name a few.

The magnitude of the French public health system can be perceived in figures (Table 3.1). The health sector has a significant weight in the economy, accounting for around 11% of the French GDP in 2016. The public sector exerts a chief role in health spending, far greater than the share borne by the private sector (including individuals and insurance). Government spending on health accounted for 8.4% of GDP this year, while the average in OECD countries was 6.1%. The share of national health spending borne by the public sector is above the OECD average, accounting for approximately 73% in France against 70% in the OECD region in 2016. Public health spending *per capita* is also above the OECD average, US$3,100 against US$2,396 this year.

TABLE 3.1   Health spending, total and public, France and selected regions, 2016

	Share of total health spending (%)	Share of the GDP (%)		Per capita spending (USD)	
	Public	Public	Total	Public	Total
France	73	8.4	11.5	3,100	4,268
United Kingdom	80	7.9	9.9	3,268	4,066
United States	50	8.6	17	4,977	9,878
OECD average	70	6.1	8.8	2,396	3,426
World average	52	3.5	6.6	686	1,028

SOURCE: WHO (2020). OWN ELABORATION
Public spending refers to domestic general government health expenditure (GGHE-D). Per capita spending in current values. The share of public spending in total spending may vary depending on the selected indicator, for reasons related to methodology and rounding

1.5   Assurance Maladie's Accounts in Perspective

The turn of the French Social Security system toward financial markets since the late 20th century coincides with two parallel trends that marked this period: on the one hand, the acceleration of the process of financialization of the global economy, and, on the other, the deterioration of the system's financial accounts in historical perspective. Around this time, financial imbalances in Social Security began to serve as a justification for reforms in PHS. Some of these reforms were in the direction of reducing expenditures, as described in the previous section. But these imbalances also led to another and far less discussed set of reforms, those leading the system to resort to financial capital to raise additional revenues. This section briefly reviews the evolution of Social Security and public health accounts over this period once they provided the context that justified the adoption of financialized strategies within the French Social Security system.

Social security results, meaning the balance between the revenues and expenditures of its four branches combined, presented positive values throughout the 1980s (DREES, 2008). During the first half of the 1990s, this balance started eroding at a fast pace, reaching a deficit of *minus* €14 billion in 1995. More than half came from the Illness branch (*Assurance Maladie*), which attained a deficit of €8 billion this year.[8] In the second half of the decade, the gaps between revenues and expenditures started to close again, leading to a positive balance by the early 2000s (Table 3.2). These improvements, however, were short-lived; after 2002, both the Social Security system and the Illness branch started facing deficits due to the combination of an adverse macroeconomic context, decelerating revenues, and expenditure growth (Assemblée Nationale, 2002). Social Security accounts started recovering again in 2004, but this recovery was once again temporary: following the Great Financial Crisis of 2008 and the Eurozone crisis of 2009, the accounts of both Social Security and the health branch reached a new bottom. The 2010s decade presented a slow but steady recovery, with diminishing deficits until 2018.

Table 3.2 also reveals the weight of the PHS (*Assurance Maladie*) in Social Security accounts, represented by the Illness branch. *Assurance Maladie* absorbs most of the Social Security budget and is the primary source of the so-called "Social Security deficits", when revenues fall short of expenditures

---

8   Although historical trends are clear, I do not make a continuous data series since the 1980s due to changes in methodology and data sources that occurred since then (DREES, 2008). Unless stated otherwise, figures in this section are in constant values of 2018, adjusted according to the Consumer Price Index (IPC), and refer to the General Regime.

TABLE 3.2 France, Social Security and Illness branch (General Regime), financial balance, 2000–2017, billions of euros of 2018 and as a % of GDP

	2000	2001	2002	2003	2004	2005	2006	2007	2008	2009	2010	2011	2012	2013	2014	2015	2016	2017	2018
Billions of euros of 2018																			
Illness branch	-2.1	-2.7	-7.6	-13.6	-13.9	-9.4	-6.8	-5.2	-4.9	-11.7	-12.6	-9.2	-6.2	-7.1	-6.7	-6	-4.9	-5	-0.7
Social Security	0.9	1.4	-4.4	-12.5	-14.2	-13.6	-10.1	-10.8	-11.2	-22.4	-26.1	-18.6	-13.9	-13	-10	-7	-4.2	-2.2	1.2
% GDP																			
Illness branch	-0.1	-0.2	-0.5	-0.8	-0.8	-0.5	-0.4	-0.3	-0.2	-0.6	-0.6	-0.4	-0.3	-0.3	-0.3	-0.3	-0.2	-0.2	0.0
Social Security	0.1	0.1	-0.3	-0.8	-0.8	-0.8	-0.5	-0.6	-0.6	-1.2	-1.3	-0.9	-0.7	-0.6	-0.5	-0.3	-0.2	-0.1	0.1

SOURCE: AUTHOR'S ELABORATION BASED ON CCSS (2000–2018). REAL VALUES OF 2018 ADJUSTED FOR INFLATION ACCORDING TO THE CONSUMER PRICE INDEX. FOR 2018, ESTIMATED GDP. SOCIAL SECURITY REFERS TO THE SUM OF THE FOUR BRANCHES (ILLNESS, OLD AGE, FAMILY, AND WORKPLACE CONTINGENCIES)

for a given year. In 2017, *Assurance Maladie* received about half of the revenues transferred from Social Security to its branches. Its deficit (€4.9 billion) was even larger than that of Social Security at large (€2.2 billion), as the latter was partially offset by positive results in other branches.

Regarding *Assurance Maladie*'s deficits (Table 3.3), their causes are a matter of dispute in the literature. The government attributed the deficits mainly to expenditure growth. Nevertheless, there is evidence that the country's economic slowdown in the 2000–2010 decade and the consequent decrease in revenues played a major role in the negative results observed in Social Security accounts in this period (Cornilleau, 2009, cited by Nay et al., 2016). By breaking down *Assurance Maladie*'s accounts over the last decade, one can see that expenditures grew slower than revenues, challenging the widespread idea that these financial imbalances were primarily driven by rising costs.

Data suggests that public health spending became increasingly concentrated on the most expensive, riskier, and complex area of service provision over the years – represented here by the item "hospital care" (Table 3.4).[9] The share of hospitalization costs covered by *Assurance Maladie* increased from less than 60% in the 1960s to more than 90% in the 1990s. The share of public spending in relation to total spending remained significantly lower in other areas, and even decreased in the case of ambulatory care. As of 2015, the Social Security budget covered 91% of the total consumption of hospital care, against 65% for ambulatory care, 69% for drugs, and 55% for other medical goods.

Another evidence that Social Security focuses on assisting the individuals of highest risks and costs is that patients with chronic and long-term illnesses ("ALD" patients) represent a minor share of the population, but they receive the largest share of Social Security revenues allocated to health care. In 2015, 17% of the population was classified as ALD patients, while 62% of the health care reimbursements provided by Social Security sought to pay for the treatments associated with such conditions (Assurance Maladie, 2018).

---

9   The "Consumption of Care and Medical Goods" (*Consommation de Soins et de Biens Médicaux*, *CSBM*) is a popular indicator to assess health care spending in France. It discriminates the consumption of medical services and goods according to categories and sources of financing. The central categories of care and goods are: (i) hospital care; (ii) ambulatory care (doctors, dentists, medical auxiliaries, and analysis laboratories); (iii) medical transportation; (iv) drugs; and (v) other medical goods (optics, prostheses, minor equipment, and dressings). The sources of financing are divided into: (i) the public insurance scheme ("Social Security"); (ii) the State and local collectivities; (iii) complementary private insurance ("complementary organizations"); and (iv) individuals ("households").

TABLE 3.3   France, Illness Branch (General Regime), revenues, expenditure, and balance,
            2000–2017, billions of euros of 2018 and % growth rate

	2010	2011	2012	2013	2014	2015	2016	2017
Billions of euros of 2018								
Revenues (I)	154.6	158.1	162.2	163.7	167.0	172.6	200.2	205.1
Expenditures (II)	167.2	167.2	168.4	170.8	173.7	178.6	205.2	210.1
Balance (I–II)	*-12.6*	*-9.2*	*-6.2*	*-7.1*	*-6.7*	*-6.0*	*-4.9*	*-5.0*
Growth rate (% relative to the previous year)								
Revenues	-	4.4%	4.7%	1.9%	2.5%	3.5%	16.2%	3.4%
Expenditures	-	2.1%	2.7%	2.4%	2.2%	2.9%	15.1%	3.4%

SOURCE: AUTHOR'S ELABORATION BASED ON CCSS (2011–2018). REAL VALUES OF 2018
ADJUSTED FOR INFLATION ACCORDING TO THE CONSUMER PRICE INDEX

The path of neoliberal reforms can be evidenced by the data on the long-term evolution of health care spending by funding source. The participation of Social Security in total health care financing has been stable for several decades, at around 77% (Table 3.5). The State's participation – meaning that of central and local governments – fell significantly over the decades, from 10% in the 1960s to 1% in 2015. The participation of complementary insurance and households in health costs declined until the 1980s and became relatively stable afterward, at around 13% and 9%, respectively.

TABLE 3.4   France, Social Security's share in the consumption of care and medical goods,
            1960–2015, % of total spending in each category

	1960	1970	1980	1990	2000	2010	2015
Hospital care	59%	79%	88%	92%	92%	91%	91%
Ambulatory care	58%	74%	77%	67%	66%	63%	65%
Transportation	100%	100%	96%	96%	95%	94%	93%
Drugs	49%	64%	66%	61%	65%	67%	69%
Other medical goods	30%	39%	45%	45%	50%	54%	55%

SOURCE: AUTHOR'S ELABORATION BASED ON DREES (2020, 2017). INCLUDES ALL STATU-
TORY REGIMES

TABLE 3.5   France, consumption of care and medical goods by source of funding, 1960–2015, % of total spending

	1960	1970	1980	1990	2000	2010	2015
Social security[a]	55%	73%	80%	77%	77%	76%	77%
Central and local administrations[b]	10%	6%	3%	1%	1%	1%	1%
Complementary organizations & households[c]	36%	22%	17%	21%	22%	22%	21%
Complementary organizations	-	-	-	*10%*	*12%*	*13%*	*13%*
Households	-	-	-	*11%*	*10%*	*9%*	*8%*

SOURCE: AUTHOR'S ELABORATION BASED ON DREES (2020, 2017)
Note:
a   includes all statutory regimes, including basic universal illness coverage and complements of alsace-moselle's regime and CAMIEG
b   free medical assistance/departamental medical assistance/state medical aid, complementary universal illness coverage, veterans' benefits, and urgent care
c   prior to 1990, complementary organizations and households were recorded together

There were also structural shifts in the private insurance sector over the past decades (Table 3.6). Two trends in private insurance stand out: the accelerated concentration of the sector and the increasing market share of for-profit insurance companies. The number of establishments providing complementary insurance contracts halved in ten years – from about 1,631 in the mid-2000s to 825 in 2015. The space occupied by for-profit institutions (insurance companies) grew to the detriment of not-for-profit organizations (mutual companies and pension institutions). Both the number of for-profit insurance companies and the volume of contributions (insurance premiums) appropriated by them increased relative to the other types of entities providing health care insurance.

In contrast to public insurance, private insurance targets individuals with lower health and financial risks. In this way, even though private insurance in France is mostly complementary and not-for-profit, it can still promote discrimination among individuals and intensify inequalities. For example, the cost of premiums and the coverage provided by complementary contracts can vary according to age and occupational status. The working population usually benefits from more favorable conditions, with lower premiums and more extensive coverage. A comparative assessment of different complementary

TABLE 3.6   France, complementary insurance sector, 2001 and 2015, market share indicators

	Market share (% of the number of institutions)		Market share (% of contributions)	
	2001	2015	2001	2015
Mutual companies	90%	77%	60%	53%
Pension institutions	3%	4%	21%	18%
Insurance companies	7%	19%	19%	29%

SOURCE: AUTHOR'S ELABORATION BASED ON DREES (2017)

plans using data for the early 2010s found a 15% difference in the price of premiums for contracts with the same level of coverage, depending on whether they were acquired as part of a working contract or not. The study also showed that private contracts tend to become more expensive and less supportive with age: plans for individuals above 75 years old cost, on average, 75% more than those offered to young adults. Moreover, the share of their health expenses not covered by the insurance contract was more than double that of younger adherents (DREES cited by Cour des Comptes, 2017).

2   Mechanisms of Financialization

As shown in Chapter 1, France has gone through a relatively early process of financialization spearheaded by the State. I argue that a similar development occurred within the Social Security system in this period. To substantiate the argument, this section examines the adoption of financialized policies in the French Social Security system – that is, policies through which the government rewired the system's financing circuits in ways that expanded the participation and influence of financial capital inside these circuits. This can be seen in three key dimensions of financing for Social Security at large and the PHS in particular: long-term debt management, short-term financing, and hospital funding.

2.1   Financialized Strategies for Long-Term Debt Management: the Social Debt Amortization Fund

The first major policy shift in Social Security connecting it to financial capital came in the context of a new strategy for managing the system's debt. Since the mid-1990s, the long-term financing of the Social Security debt became subjected to new arrangements that rely on financial markets. These arrangements were built around the Social Debt Amortization Fund (*Caisse d'Amortissement de la Dette Sociale*, CADES). CADES is an external agency created by the French government to absorb the Social Security debt and convert it into securities that can be sold in the financial markets. From 1996 to 2018, the Fund absorbed approximately €260 billion in debts to be financed in such a way (CADES, 2018a), which represents around 10% of the country's GDP for this last year.[10]

2.1.1   Contextualizing CADES' Creation

Before the creation of CADES, the Social Security debt was mostly refinanced by public institutions. The Central Agency of Social Security (ACOSS), a body created in the late 1960s to administer the system's accounts, was in charge of addressing eventual funding shortfalls and outstanding debts (cf. Figure 3.1). It solved these issues by appealing to cash advances from the Treasury and loans from the *Caisse des Dépôts et Consignations* (CDC), a public bank created in the early 19th century and serving multiple roles for the French public sector.

In the context of mounting deficits in Social Security during the early 1990s, ACOSS was given ever-larger financial imbalances to solve. It became dependent on financial support from the Treasury and the *Caisse des Dépôts* to manage Social Security accounts, resorting to them on a permanent basis. The recurrent deficits in the system led to a mounting debt held by ACOSS and refinanced at high costs with the former institutions. This can be at least partly understood by the fact that, by law, the Central Agency, ACOSS, can only perform short-term operations with other institutions. As a general rule, financing conditions are less favorable for the borrower in short-term than in long-term operations. The high costs of the financial support obtained by ACOSS to refinance the Social Security debt further undermined the system's financial situation. In 1993, the amount of interest paid by the agency to the Treasury and the *Caisse des Dépôts* was estimated at €1.2 billion, one-tenth of the total deficit of €12.3 billion expected for the year (CCSS, 1994). Still in 1993, the State made an

---

10   Total debt taken over (amortized and non-amortized), expressed in constant values of 2018 adjusted for inflation according to the Consumer Price Index (IPC).

exceptional move and assumed the debt of Social Security with the *Caisse des Dépôts*. The expectations for the following years were of continued deficits in the Social Security accounts, aggravated by high interest charges (CCSS, 1996, 1995, 1994, 1993).[11]

The idea that the debt management policy added further pressure on Social Security accounts justified the search for alternative strategies to refinance the system's debt over a longer period and under more favorable conditions. This led to the creation of CADES, the Social Debt Amortization Fund. The French government instituted the Amortization Fund in 1996, amidst a major structural reform in Social Security under a right-wing majority known as the "Juppé Plan" (*Plan Juppé*).[12] One of the main goals of this plan was to address the Social Security deficits and debt. To do so, it set up a special agency, CADES, in charge of writing off the Social Security debt accumulated up to that date. CADES is currently classified as a "special fund" that is part of Social Security but financially independent from the system's regimes. It is subordinated to the joint supervision of the Ministries of the Economy, Finance and Industry, and Social Security affairs.

CADES was assigned with three missions at the time of its creation: (i) take on the Social Security debt with the *Caisse des Dépôts,* of €28 billion; (ii) reimburse the State for taking over past debts for Social Security; and (iii) cover the 1995 and 1996's deficits of the independent workers' regime that existed at that time (France, 1996).[13] CADES' creation law authorized the Fund to borrow funds from external agents in order to accomplish these goals. From the very beginning, these funds were expected to come from the financial markets. As stated in law, the agency was allowed "(...) to take out loans. It may, in particular, to this effect, from its outset, make a public offering and issue any negotiable security representing a debt right" (*op. cit.*, art. 5, I). Just as regular financial securities, the securities issued by CADES work as a type of loan; one party (in this case, CADES) sells a note and receives funds in return, under the commitment of reimbursing the other party (in this case, the investors who purchase

---

11   Values for the general regime, converted from francs to euros of 2018 according to the Consumer Price Index (IPC). As pointed out by the Social Security Audit Commission's reports at the time (CCSS, 1996, 1995, 1994, 1993), these deficits cannot be attributed solely to imbalances between Social Security's revenues and expenditures. Other factors also had an adverse impact on the systems' finances, especially the macroeconomic context and the revenue losses from tax exemptions on social contributions.

12   Named after Alain Juppé, French Prime Minister under Jacques Chirac's first term.

13   Values converted from francs to euros of 2018 according to the Consumer Price Index (IPC).

the securities) with added interests. These debt securities, therefore, provide financial gains for investors in the form of interest payments.

Over time, CADES' responsibilities have increased in scale and scope. Besides amortizing the Social Security debt received from other bodies of the system, its missions were broadened to include absorbing deficits of specific branches, making payments to Social Security bodies, and assisting in the financing of the Central Agency of Social Security by subscribing to the latter's financial securities (as discussed in the following section).

The creation of a public amortization fund to refinance and erase the Social Security debt can be considered a major financial innovation. To my best knowledge, no other country to date has an external agency dedicated exclusively to refinancing the Social Security debt in the global financial markets.

2.1.2   Deconstructing CADES' Strategy

The largest part of the so-called "social debt" passed on from the Central Agency of Social Security to CADES consists of the debt of the General Regime of Social Security.[14] This debt arises from the accumulation of deficits over years. When the total amount of revenues received by the Central Agency to finance the system in a given year is insufficient to cover all expenditures of the Social Security branches – i.e., when it faces a deficit, the agency ends with an outstanding debt in its balance sheet (see Figure 3.1). Such debt stays with the Central Agency until it is transferred to CADES. This transfer is made through an accounting move voted by the Parliament in certain years, with no defined frequency. The amounts transferred from the Central Agency of Social Security to CADES can cover past, present, and even future debts, and are decided based on the expectations for the Social Security deficit in the years to come.

When CADES was first created in 1996, it was conceived as a temporary entity responsible for settling the debt that had been entrusted to it at the time of its creation. This was expected to be done until 2008, after when the agency would close its activities. However, CADES' mandate has been continuously extended in light of new debt transfers. Already in 1998, the end date

---

14   Apart from the debt of the General Regime, the term "social debt" can take on other meanings. These include the debt of all mandatory basic schemes or even of the whole scope of Social Security administrations (encompassing, for example, mandatory complementary schemes and public hospitals). By the end of 2017, the debt of Social Security administrations stood at €226.1 billion, accounting for 10% of total public debt, worth €2.2 trillion. The chief drivers of the Social Security debt were, in this order, CADES (€120.8 billion of outstanding debts – i.e., still not amortized), ACOSS (€27.8 billion), Unédic, which finances unemployment insurance (€33.5 billion), and public hospitals (€29.8 billion by the end of 2016) (Cour des Comptes, 2019).

was postponed to 2014. In 2004, its extinction was suspended during a structural reform in *Assurance Maladie*. Six years later, in 2010, the government reintroduced an end date, this time to 2025. The prorogation of CADES' activities accompanied new rounds of debt transfers from other Social Security entities to the Fund, with important movements in 1996, 1998, 2004, 2009, 2011, and 2019.[15]

CADES can amortize the Social Security debt by taking it from other entities and managing it differently. On the one hand, it can refinance the debt in the medium and long run; on the other, it can raise additional sources of funds to pay for the refinancing costs. To roll the debt over a more extended period of time, CADES issues medium-and long-term debt securities in the financial markets, selling them to domestic and foreign investors. In this way, the Social Security debt is transformed into a financial debt. When the interests and the principal of such securities are paid, that debt is considered amortized.

To pay for the interests and principles on the securities, the Fund receives money from public sources, mainly tax revenues collected from the population at large. It is important to note, therefore, that CADES' strategy is viable not only because it can reschedule the debt in the financial markets, but also because the government provides it with additional revenues that were not available for Social Security before. These revenues are critical to pay the interest and amortizations on the securities and, therefore, allow for the continued reproduction of this strategy.

To raise these revenues for CADES, the government introduced a new social contribution in 1996 whose revenues should be addressed directly to the agency. It also made changes in existing contributions and earmarked part of the additional revenues to the Fund. As of 2018, CADES received revenues from the following sources:

- The Contribution for the Reimbursement of the Social Debt (CRDS), entirely allocated to CADES. It is levied on a wide range of incomes from labor activity, replacement, investment, wealth, and gambling, at a rate of 0.5%;
- The General Social Contribution (CSG), partially allocated to CADES since 2009. It is levied on a similar base, at the rate that goes to the Fund has gradually increased from 0.2% in its first year to 0.6% in 2016 (full rate), and government announcements signaled for further increases;

---

15   Although this investigation is limited to 2018, the relevance of the 2019 debt transfer justifies its inclusion in this paragraph.

- The Pension Reserve Fund, a public fund created to support the payment of future pension benefits, obliged to transfer €2.1 billion per year to CADES since 2011;
- Revenues from the sale of public property, derived from the sale of real estate owned by national Social Security agencies. This rule was instituted in 1996 and provided CADES with over half a billion euros by 2003.[16]

In practice, CADES is almost exclusively funded by the two social contributions in the list, the CRDS and the CSG. In 2017, these accounted for 87% of its revenues (41% and 46%, respectively). The remaining 12% came from the Pension Reserve Fund (FRR). Property sales were particularly important at the beginning but now have marginal relevance, providing around 1% of total revenues (CADES, 2017a, 2017b).

Another interesting way to examine CADES' revenues is by looking at the sources of income on which these taxes are levied. Due to the predominance of social contributions, most of these revenues derive from wages and social benefits. At present, around 60% of the Fund's revenues come from taxation on activity income (wages, agricultural profits, and other bonuses), 20% on replacement income (pensions, daily allowances, unemployment benefits, social benefits, housing subsidies), 4% on wealth, 5% on investments, and 1% on gambling and other revenues. To identify the origins of the remaining 12% coming from the Pension Reserve Fund, one has to go back to the time when the fund was set up, in 2001. The revenues used to constitute the fund came from social contributions, revenues from privatizations and public licenses, and transfers provided by the pension system, to name a few (CADES, 2017a; Mendez and Ragot, 2010).

In the 2000s, the government approved a number of rules to reinforce CADES's financial soundness. The PHS was particularly implicated in this process; in 2004, the government decreed that any future surpluses achieved by *Assurance Maladie* would be allocated to the Fund (France, 2004).

2.1.3   CADES in Numbers

The successive debt transfers to CADES led to a progressive rise in the latter's debt, mostly in the form of financial securities, as well as in the volume of revenues collected to pay for them (Table 3.7, Figure 3.2). By the end of 2018, the volume of debts transferred to CADES each year (1) accumulated to €260

---

16   Equal to €571 billion in real values of 2018 converted according to the Consumer Price Index (IPC). In the beginning, CADES also received taxes levied on capital income; however, the government erased this rule in 2016 and compensated the losses with an increase in the share coming from the CSG.

TABLE 3.7 France, Social Debt Amortization Fund (CADES), debt and revenues, 1996–2018, billions of euros of 2018

	Annual debt transfers (I)	Accumulated debt, total (II)	Accumulated debt, amortized (III)	Accumulated debt, non-amortized (IV)	Annual revenues (V)	Accumulated revenues (VI)
1996	28.1	31.3	2.9	–	4.3	4.3
1997	–	33.4	6.8	26.6	5.2	9.4
1998	17.5	53.2	9.9	43.2	5.3	14.7
1999	–	55.4	13.8	41.6	5.9	20.5
2000	–	57.0	17.8	39.3	6.1	26.3
2001	–	58.4	21.3	37.1	5.8	31.6
2002	–	61.1	24.9	36.2	5.8	36.9
2003	–	65.1	28.5	36.6	5.8	41.9
2004	41.9	110.6	31.9	78.7	5.9	46.9
2005	7.8	119.8	34.4	85.4	6.1	52.1
2006	6.6	124.5	37.1	87.4	6.3	57.6
2007	-0.1	122.6	39.5	83.1	6.5	63.2
2008	11.1	130.4	41.6	88.8	6.6	68.2
2009	18.8	148.7	47.3	101.5	8.9	76.9
2010	–	146.7	52.3	94.5	8.9	84.7
2011	72.4	216.1	63.7	152.5	16.5	99.6
2012	7.0	218.9	74.9	143.9	16.8	114.4
2013	8.0	224.8	87.1	137.7	16.4	129.7
2014	10.3	234.1	99.8	134.3	16.5	145.6

	Annual debt transfers (I)	Accumulated debt, total (II)	Accumulated debt, amortized (III)	Accumulated debt, non-amortized (IV)	Annual revenues (V)	Accumulated revenues (VI)
2015	10.3	244.2	113.7	130.6	17.0	162.4
2016	24.3	268.1	126.2	141.8	16.3	178.4
2017	–	265.4	140.3	125.1	17.5	194.2
2018	–	260.5	153.2	107.3	17.7	208.2

SOURCE: AUTHOR'S ELABORATION BASED ON CADES (2018A)

1996 and 1997 figures converted from francs to euros according to the INSEE franc-euro converter. real values of 2018 adjusted for inflation according to the consumer price index. values of accumulated debt are estimated by CADES. the decrease in total debt in 2018 is explained by the use of nominal, preliminary values

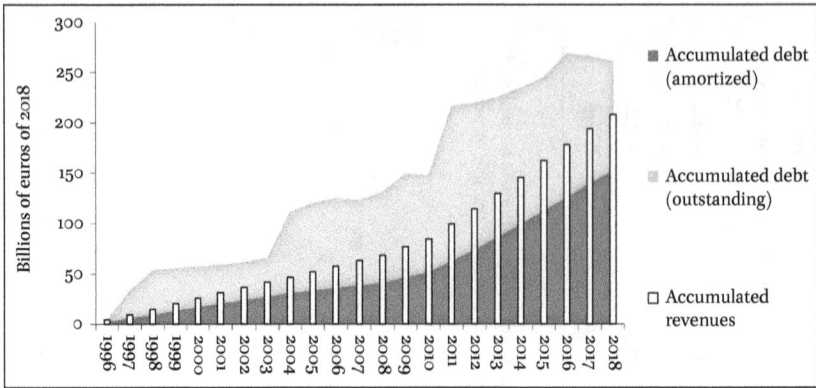

FIGURE 3.2   France, Social Debt Amortization Fund (CADES), accumulated debt and
revenues, 1996–2018, billions of euros of 2018
SOURCE: AUTHOR'S ELABORATION BASED ON (CADES, 2018A). CADES'
ESTIMATIONS. REAL VALUES OF 2018 ADJUSTED FOR INFLATION
ACCORDING TO THE CONSUMER PRICE INDEX. OUTSTANDING DEBT: TOTAL
DEBT TRANSFERRED TO CADES MINUS THE SHARE AMORTIZED. THE
DECREASE IN TOTAL DEBT IN 2018 IS EXPLAINED BY THE USE OF NOMINAL,
PRELIMINARY VALUES

billion in total (II). An additional transfer of €15 billion was already planned
for the following years. From the amount of Social Security debt received by
the Fund, €155 billion had been amortized by 2018 (III). This means that the
principal and interests on the securities were paid, "erasing" this amount of
debt from Social Security accounts. This accounted for 60% of the total debt
transferred until 2018. There were €105 billion still left for amortization (IV),
40% of the total debt. To pay for such a strategy, CADES received €228 billion
in revenues since 1996 (VI).

Figure 3.2 provides a better visualization of the trends described in the
table above.

Data suggests that the Illness branch, which finances the PHS, had the highest weight in the buildup of the debt assigned to CADES. This is because this
branch presents the greatest financial imbalances among the four branches
of Social Security. While the reasons for them are a matter of debate and do
not seem to be driven exclusively by costs (section 1.5), the fact is that those
imbalances contributed significantly to the deficits that accumulated in Social
Security accounts, and therefore to the debt that was eventually transferred to
CADES. Up to 2018, the weight of the Illness branch in the debt transferred to
the Fund was estimated at €147.7 billion (CNAM, 2018).[17]

---

17   Real values of 2018 adjusted for inflation according to the Consumer Price Index (IPC).

2.1.4   Instruments and Costs

CADES issues several types of securities, including commercial papers (US commercial papers, USCP; Euro Commercial Papers, ECP; Negotiable European Commercial Papers, NEU CP; European Medium-Term Notes, EMTN), inflation-linked bonds, Eurobonds, and bonds in other currencies. In general, commercial papers are securities with a maturity of less than one year, medium-term notes mature from one to five years, and long-term securities (bonds), in the case of CADES, last from five to ten years. This array of securities of different durations allows the Fund to engage in short-, medium-, and long-term borrowing operations with financial investors. Besides securities, CADES also uses derivatives to hedge against the risks involved in market borrowing. In particular, it issues interest and currency swaps to hedge against fluctuations in the value of interests and foreign exchange rates.[18] By 2017, the profile of CADES' operations has changed dramatically, and the vast majority of operations were now with short-term securities (commercial papers). They accounted for 81% of the securities issued this year. The remaining 19% came from the issuance of medium-and long-term securities (notes and bonds). Still in 2017, 54% of the outstanding debt (accounting for present and past issuances) was falling due in the medium-run (from one to five years), 31% in the long run (over five years), and 15% in the short-run (one year or less). Most of the outstanding debt this year was in Eurobonds (59%), followed by bonds in other currencies (25%), inflation-linked bonds (8%), and medium-term notes (4%) (CADES, 2017b).

Concerning the costs of this strategy, CADES' securities can be issued at fixed interest rates, variable rates, or rates indexed to inflation. Data for 2017 (CADES, 2017b; France, 2018) show that 34% of the outstanding debt this year was remunerated at fixed rates, 28% at variable rates, and 8% at indexed rates. Since the mid-2010s, the Fund has been able to finance itself at negative interest rates. In other words, it was able to find purchasers for its securities while offering low or negative interest rates. This also means the Fund was able to make financial gains from operations that would typically incur charges for it.[19] Being able to obtain financing at negative rates is a recent phenomenon

---

18   The principle of a rate swap is to compare a floating rate and a fixed rate, with the parties paying each other rate differentials without exchanging capital. Swaps serve as an instrument of protection (for those transferring risks from market fluctuations) and speculation (for those expecting gains from such fluctuations).

19   Negative interest rates have been conventionally explained as an exceptional measure associated with stimulus policies carried out by central banks following the Global Financial Crisis and the Eurozone Crisis of the late 2000s. In this context, governments

most typically associated with wealthy central governments selling their sovereign bonds. These are considered the most liquid and safe assets in the market, which allows governments to find demand for these assets even under negative rates. CADES' securities are perceived as virtually as safe as those offered by the French State, which means it was also able to find demand for its securities under the same conditions. In 2017, CADES' average interest rate was-0.65% for short-term financing and-0.17% for long-term financing. The average rate paid on the outstanding debt at the end of the year was 1.74%.[20]

CADES's securities are implicitly backed up by the State while offering more flexible conditions and higher interest rates for investors than those found in State securities. Although the difference in interest rates between CADES and State's securities seems small (Assemblée Nationale, 2016), the sheer volume of funds mobilized by CADES, to the tune of billions of euros, makes this differential have a significant impact over time. Moreover, unlike the French State, CADES is authorized to operate in other currencies, which can be an advantage for foreign investors.

It is possible to compare CADES' interest rates with those paid by the State on its securities, although bearing in mind that the results must be interpreted with caution due to data constraints and differences in methodology. The interest rates offered by CADES that could be directly compared with those paid by the State would be those offered at a specific point in time, once this is the information available for government securities (Banque de France, 2019b). However, there is limited data on CADES' annual interest rates, which prevents a direct comparison with government data. Considering 2017, CADES' average interest rate for the short-term securities issued this year was-0.063%. These are negative rates, but still less punitive than those offered by Treasury bills, which ranged from-0.64% (12-month Treasury bill) to-0.85% (1-month Treasury bill). This suggests that CADES' securities were more attractive to investors. The picture is reversed when it comes to long-term financing. In the same year, the average interest rate of long-term securities issued by CADES was negative, at-0.172%. The average interest rates of Treasury bonds, on the other hand, were positive, at 0.01% for five-year bonds and 0.8% for ten-year bonds (Banque de France, 2019b; France, 2018).

---

practiced negative basic interest rates to discourage investors from holding their capital in highly secure assets. There is much debate on why they continued to be the case for a long time and the reasons leading agents to lend at negative rates, a discussion that escapes the scope of this analysis (see, e.g., Ainger, 2019; Duarte, 2019).

20   This rate reflects the weighted average of the interest rates offered by CADES' securities, including those issued before the interest rates became negative.

This comparison becomes more difficult when trying to look at the evolution of these interest rates over time. This is because the only data series for CADES' interest rates for a relatively long period of time is the one providing information for the average interest rate paid on its outstanding debt, which takes into account the rates paid on all securities issued in the past (Table 3.8). Bearing in mind that data for the State's interest rates are for a given year and not for its outstanding debt, it is still possible to observe that CADES' average financing costs tended to be higher than the costs of debt financing by the State.[21]

The volume of revenues channeled to the banking and financial sector can be assessed by looking at CADES' financial charges (Table 3.9, Figure 3.3). These charges comprise interest payments from market operations (securities) and bank operations (loans), as well as commissions to financial institutions. From 1996 to 2018, CADES paid almost €68 billion to investors in interest payments

TABLE 3.8   France, Social Debt Amortization Fund (CADES) and State's interest rates, 2009–2017, %

	CADES	French Public Securities						
	Weighted average (outstanding loans)	1-month T. bill	3-month T. bill	6-month T. bill	9-month T. bill	12-month T. bill	5-year T. Bond	10-year bench-mark bond
2009	3.38%	n.a.	n.a.	n.a.	n.a.	n.a.	n.a.	3.60%
2010	3.56%	n.a.	n.a.	n.a.	n.a.	n.a.	n.a.	3.35%
2011	2.84%	n.a.	n.a.	n.a.	n.a.	n.a.	n.a.	3.15%
2012	2.70%	n.a.	n.a.	n.a.	n.a.	n.a.	n.a.	2.25%
2013	2.52%	n.a.	n.a.	n.a.	n.a.	n.a.	n.a.	2.43%
2014	2.42%	n.a.	n.a.	n.a.	n.a.	n.a.	n.a.	0.84%
2015	2.08%	-0.63%	-0.45%	-0.41%	-0.38%	-0.39%	0.08%	1.00%
2016	1.61%	-1.08%	-0.90%	-0.86%	-0.81%	-0.74%	-0.13%	0.68%
2017	1.74%	-0.85%	-0.78%	-0.72%	-0.67%	-0.64%	-0.01%	0.79%

SOURCE: AUTHOR'S ELABORATION BASED ON BANQUE DE FRANCE (2019B) AND FRANCE (2018)
Interest rates in 31/12. n.a: not available. T. bill: Treasury bill. T. bond: Treasury bonds

21   See Crepin (2017) for a different approach reaching a similar conclusion.

TABLE 3.9   France, Social Debt Amortization Fund (CADES), interests and commissions, 1996–2018, millions of euros of 2018

	Interest charges, market operations (I)	Interest charges, bank operations (II)	Total interest charges (III = I + II)	Interest income (IV)	Net interest charges (V = III - IV)	Commissions (VI)	Net financial charges (VII = V + VI)
1996	745	685	1,430	117	1,313	79	1,392
1997	1,567	15	1,582	254	1,328	55	1,383
1998	2,198	268	2,466	270	2,195	57	2,253
1999	2,165	123	2,289	146	2,142	61	2,203
2000	2,195	150	2,345	183	2,162	10	2,171
2001	2,088	184	2,271	297	1,974	9	1,983
2002	1,857	161	2,018	241	1,777	11	1,787
2003	1,816	145	1,961	214	1,747	3	1,750
2004	2,017	188	2,205	376	1,829	30	1,860
2005	3,334	171	3,505	553	2,952	39	2,991
2006	3,507	149	3,655	606	3,049	27	3,077
2007	3,663	133	3,796	272	3,524	9	3,533
2008	3,564	210	3,775	356	3,419	10	3,430
2009	3,320	51	3,371	309	3,062	54	3,115
2010	3,636	12	3,648	382	3,266	19	3,285
2011	4,162	163	4,325	341	3,984	64	4,049
2012	4,775	60	4,835	629	4,206	58	4,263
2013	4,076	43	4,119	621	3,497	25	3,523
2014	3,951	43	3,994	668	3,327	28	3,355
2015	3,658	45	3,703	904	2,799	28	2,827
2016	3,434	42	3,476	1,118	2,359	39	2,398
2017	3,171	43	3,214	1,044	2,170	32	2,202
2018	3,014	44	3,058	874.5	2,184	23	2,207
Total	67,913	3,128	71,041	10,776	60,265	768	61,037

SOURCE: AUTHOR'S ELABORATION BASED ON CADES (2017B, 1996–2018)
FIGURES FOR 1996 AND 1997 CONVERTED FROM FRANCS TO EUROS ACCORDING TO THE INSEE FRANCO-EURO CONVERTER. REAL VALUES OF 2018 ADJUSTED FOR INFLATION ACCORDING TO THE CONSUMER PRICE INDEX

and similar charges on financial securities (I). During the same period, it also paid an additional €3.1 billion in interest payments to credit institutions on both loans and transactions with securities (II). In total, CADES channeled €71 billion to financial actors in the form of interest payments and similar charges (III). The payment of commissions (VI) added €768 million to this figure.[22] These costs are not negligible; in 2017, CADES paid €2.2 billion in interests and commissions, net of interest income. This was the same value as the so-called Social Security "deficit" of that year (CCSS, 2018).[23]

The net costs with interest payments (V) are calculated by deducting the interest income received from securities held by CADES and other types of financial revenues, such as profits from operations in foreign currencies (IV). Since 1996, the Fund made €10.7 billion in financial income. Most of it came in recent years, from the issuance of securities at negative interest rates and securities issued in foreign currencies in the context of favorable exchange rate variations. The value of financial income earned in the year almost tripled during the last decade, from €382 million in 2010 to €1 billion in 2017.

From 1996 to 2017, the amount of resources transferred from CADES to the banking and financial system, already net of financial gains, totaled €61 billion (VII).

Figure 3.3 uses these series to provide a clearer visualization of the costs of CADES' strategy.

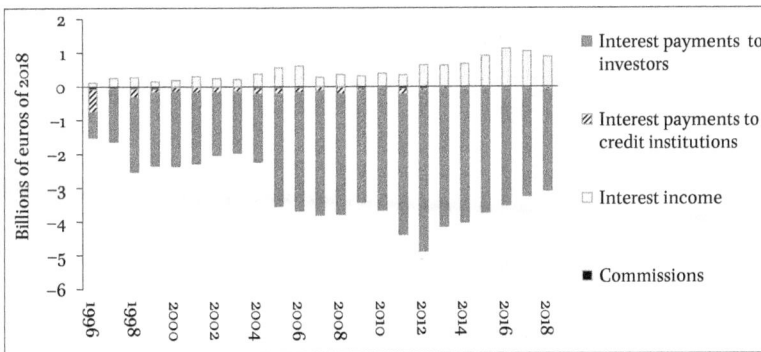

FIGURE 3.3   France, Social Debt Amortization Fund (CADES), financial results per year, 1996–2018
SOURCE: AUTHOR'S ELABORATION BASED ON (CADES, 2017B, 1996). CADES ESTIMATIONS. REAL VALUES OF 2018 ADJUSTED FOR INFLATION ACCORDING TO THE CONSUMER PRICE INDEX

---

22   Real values of 2018 adjusted for inflation according to the Consumer Price Index (IPC).
23   Without the Old Age Solidarity Fund (*Fonds de Solidarité Vieillesse*).

2.1.5   Investors and Intermediaries

Banks are the largest buyers of the CADES' securities in the primary markets, followed by central banks and institutional investors (namely insurance companies and pension funds) (Table 3.10). Besides their role as investors, banks are also the most important actors in the chain of intermediation for CADES' operations. The securities are issued and distributed by domestic and foreign banks, for-and not-for-profit. The banks responsible for placing the securities issued by CADES include private banks from Europe, United States, and Asia, such as Merrill Lynch, BNP Paribas, BRED Banque Populaire, Citigroup, Crédit Agricole, Deutsche Bank, HSBC, Natixis, Nomura, The Royal Bank of Scotland, Société Générale, and UBS (CADES, 2004, 2018b).

Other types of financial institutions also play a crucial role in the success of CADES' issuance programs. These include clearing agencies, which are independent, privately-owned institutions responsible for settling these transactions. The clearing agencies working for CADES are Euroclear and Clearstream, based in Belgium and Luxembourg, respectively. Credit rating agencies are another important type of institution in the context of these operations. They are private companies in charge of assigning grades on financial instruments, signaling to investors the level of risks involved in their purchase. The rating agencies are key for the success of CADES' emission programs, influencing both the volume of demand and the minimum levels of compensation that investors are willing to accept. CADES' securities are rated by Moody's, Standard & Poor's, and Fitch Ratings, the three giants of the global rating industry. The grades they assign to CADES' securities are extremely high, reflecting virtually no risk of default (CADES, 2017b).

TABLE 3.10   France, Social Debt Amortization Fund (CADES), purchase of securities by type of investor, 2009–2017, % of securities issued in the year

	2009	2010	2011	2012	2013	2014	2015	2016	2017
Banks	42%	34%	42%	45%	46%	25%	41%	55%	50%
Central Banks	23%	29%	29%	17%	26%	54%	41%	32%	28%
Institutional investors	35%	36%	28%	38%	29%	21%	17%	13%	21%
Others	0%	1%	1%	0%	0%	0%	0%	0%	1%

SOURCE: AUTHOR'S ELABORATION BASED ON CADES (2017B, 2016)

CADES' strategy is heavily dependent on foreign capital. Most of the investors that buy these securities that refinance the French Social Security debt are based in other European countries, even though there was a marked increase in the participation of American and Asian capital over the past decade. Together, the participation of Asia and America (namely the US) in CADES' financing more than doubled in six years, from 16% of the capital raised in 2011 to nearly 35% in 2017. Asian and American investors bought 19% and 15% of the securities issued in this last year, respectively. French capital has marginal participation, at around 6% of CADES' financing in 2015 and 11% in 2016 (CADES, 2017b, 2016).

CADES issues securities in euros, US dollars, Australian dollars, Hong Kong dollars, Canadian dollars, British pounds, Japanese yens, Swiss francs, and Chinese renminbis (yuans), to cite a few.[24] The authorization granted to CADES to issue securities in foreign currencies and markets is specifically designed to attract foreign investors. The latter see in CADES an opportunity to profit from securities guaranteed by the French state and with additional advantages over traditional government bonds. As explained by CADES' President in 2016, foreign investors often face regulatory barriers and liquidity requirements that prevent them from freely investing in currencies other than their own. Therefore, that CADES can issue securities in other currencies makes them particularly attractive to international capital (Assemblée Nationale, 2016).

2.1.6   State Support

CADES enjoys large State support against liquidity and solvency issues – the capacity of meeting short and long-term financial commitments, respectively. The French State is required to service the debt of national public agencies in the event of their dissolution (France, 1980), which includes that of CADES. Moreover, as determined in CADES' founding law, the French Government is required to ensure that the principal and interests are paid to investors on the expected dates:

> If the annual revenue and expenditure forecasts for the fund for the remainder of the period for which it was created show that it will not be able to meet all of its commitments, the Government shall submit to Parliament the measures necessary to ensure that the principal and interest are paid on the scheduled dates.
>
> FRANCE, 1996, art. 7

---

24   In 2015, CADES issued a bond program in renminbi worth €437 million in 2018 prices. At that time, it was "the first bond in RMB ever launched by France and the largest one in Chinese currency [issued] by an Eurozone issuer" (CADES, 2015, p.1).

Besides solvency and liquidity, the government also guarantees sufficient revenue streams to remunerate investors. CADES' revenues, specified earlier in this section, draw from relatively stable sources of income (namely wages and pension benefits). These sources of revenues are determined by the government, earmarked for the agency, and can increase upon State decision. The State's support is openly acknowledged by credit rating agencies as the primary reason for the high grades assigned to CADES' securities (see, e.g., Euromoney, 2011).

This section described the innovative way in which the French State sought to externalize the Social Security debt by transferring it to an external body so it could be transformed into assets sold in financial markets. CADES' strategy has introduced the large-scale use of financial instruments to manage the Social Security debt and opened space for a greater influence of financial institutions and investors on the system's financing conditions. In the following section, I examine how a similar strategy was introduced ten years later for the management of short-term financing requirements.

2.2   Financialized Strategies for Short-Term Financing by the Central Agency of Social Security

Since the mid-2000s, the use of financial securities has spread to other areas of the French Social Security system. These instruments became the central instrument not only to refinance the debt in the long run, but also to cover funding gaps in the short run. The transition from public to financial capital to address urgent cash requirements was headed by ACOSS, the Central Agency of Social Security Organizations.

2.2.1   Contextualizing the Adoption of Financialized Practices by the Central Agency

ACOSS is a Social Security body created in the 1960s, during the first wave of structural reforms in the system (France, 1967). These reforms separated Social Security into branches for the first time (at the time, Illness, Old-age, and Family). They also introduced ACOSS to serve as a "central body" that could ensure the smooth financing of the system and coordinate the distribution of resources across the newly created branches.

Over time, ACOSS' roles in the Social Security system increased in number and complexity. The agency is often described as the "central bank" of Social Security due to its critical role in guaranteeing a well-functioning system. Among the most important tasks performed by ACOSS, there is, first, managing the financing of the General Regime of Social Security, centralizing revenues from different sources and distributing them across its branches (Figure 3.1). Second, it must ensure that there will be enough funds for paying the Social

Security benefits, borrowing from external sources if necessary. Last, ACOSS is in charge of optimizing financial flows inside the system. This is done by lending to the different bodies that are part of Social Security, borrowing from them, and remunerating the deposits they keep with the agency, to mention a few activities. In 2017, the value of financial transactions that circulated through ACOSS' accounts amounted to €2.3 trillion, equivalent to the country's GDP in that year (ACOSS, 2018b).[25]

Financial capital entered the agency's financing circuits to serve as a source of external funding, helping to fulfill the second of the tasks mentioned above. It served to cover cash requirements, which appear when the amount of funds received by the agency from regular revenue sources is not sufficient to cover the Social Security benefits falling due in the near future (the next days or weeks).[26] This mismatch between the volume of revenues from permanent sources available at a specific date and that which is necessary to cover payments coming due is also known as "cash needs" or "Treasury needs". It is important to note that these cash needs do not necessarily mean an imbalance in Social Security accounts; they can arise from the very nature of the system's revenues and expenditures. For example, most social contributions are collected at the end of the month, while part of social benefits (e.g., some sorts of pensions, reimbursements from *Assurance Maladie*, and welfare benefits) are paid earlier in the month or do not follow a fixed schedule. ACOSS can borrow from other agents to raise additional revenues and cover those funding gaps.

Historically, the agency turned toward public banks to address short-term cash needs. Its main partner was the *Caisse des Dépôts et Consignations* (CDC), the same public bank that refinanced the Social Security debt for the agency before CADES' creation. ACOSS used short-term loans and cash advances from the *Caisse des Dépôts* to obtain the necessary financing to top up financing

---

25   This is possible because a single transaction can be separated into several shorter operations that can be accounted for separately. For the sake of illustration, the circuit to pay for Social Security benefits depends on monetary flows first from taxpayers to collecting agencies, from these to the Central Agency, from the latter to Social Security Funds, and finally from the Funds to individuals (see Figure 3.1).

26   ACOSS' "regular" or "permanent" revenues are those coming from traditional sources such as social contributions, general taxation, and State transfers. They differ from "external" or "non-permanent" revenues, coming from operations with third parties (Figure 3.1). In 2017, nearly 70% of ACOSS' regular revenues came from contributions levied on wages, 17% from reimbursements (mainly State transfers to compensate for benefits paid on its behalf), 10% from other taxes allocated to the Social Security (value-added tax, behavioral taxes), 3% from contributions on replacement income, and 2% from contributions on wealth, investment, and gambling income (ACOSS, 2018a).

gaps. However, the ongoing deterioration of Social Security accounts in the early 2000s turned the bank's support, in principle an exceptional measure, into an integral part of the system's day-to-day operations. They made ACOSS ever more dependent on CDC loans, leading to a growing debt with the latter. The imbalances in ACOSS' accounts at this time can be attributed not only to the mismatch between revenues and expenditures in the General Regime but also to systematic delays in State transfers to compensate for tax exemptions and payments made on its behalf (CCSS, 2003).

As noted in the previous section, the interest rates charged by the *Caisse des Dépôts* were considered significantly high. For the sake of illustration, ACOSS paid €168 million in interest charges to the *Caisse des Dépôts* in 2003. This amounted to more than 10% of the General Regime's deficit in that year (CCSS, 2004).[27]

In 2004, the *Caisse des Dépôts* denied the full coverage of Social Security's cash requirements due to the expectations that the latter's accounts would continue to deteriorate in the following months. The period was marked by intense debates, disputes, and the resort to temporary solutions to finance ACOSS' short-term needs (CCSS 2006, 2005, 2004). Amidst a context of uncertainty concerning the government's disposition to rescue the agency, the *Caisse des Dépôts'* unwillingness to fully cover the demand for funds, and the agency's desire to find cheaper financing solutions than those proposed by the bank, the proposal of "diversifying" ACOSS' revenue sources gained increasing support. This paved the way for the deployment of new strategies geared toward financial markets. Starting in the mid-2000s, the introduction of practices much similar to those adopted by CADES led to a progressive shift in the nature of the creditors covering Social Security's short-term cash needs.

In 2006, the State altered ACOSS' legal framework, authorizing it to issue commercial papers in domestic markets (France, 2008). Later this year, the agency launched its first commercial paper program to complement the financial support from the *Caisse des Dépôts*. In 2010, the government expanded the array of financial instruments available to ACOSS by allowing the agency to issue commercial papers in international markets (2010 Interministerial Directive, cited in France, 2014). The role of the *Caisse des Dépôts* was entirely revised: the public bank went from the lender of last resort to Social Security to a supporting mechanism for market-based financing. A new convention signed between the Central Agency and the bank this year limited its aid to

---

27   Real values of 2018 adjusted for inflation according to the Consumer Price Index (IPC).

one-third of the maximum amount that ACOSS was authorized to borrow each year (ACOSS, 2011).

ACOSS currently has two instruments for meeting cash requirements: loans from the *Caisse des Dépôts* and financial securities. The possibilities to borrow from the *Caisse des Dépôts* are restricted to a few credit lines with pre-defined interest rates. Market financing is much more flexible. ACOSS issues short-term securities, borrowing from investors in money markets – the segment of financial markets dedicated to highly liquid assets. The agency issues commercial papers, more precisely Negotiable European commercial papers (NEU CPs) in France and Euro Commercial papers (ECPs) in foreign markets. ACOSS can also use derivative contracts (namely interest and currency swaps) to hedge against the risks involved in those operations. To a lesser extent, other agents apart from financial investors can also subscribe to ACOSS' securities and thereby provide funds to the agency, including the State (the central government), Social Security administrations, and the Social Debt Amortization Fund (CADES).

Each financing method compensates creditors and intermediaries in a specific way. CDC loans entail the payment of interests and commissions to the bank. Debt securities, in turn, require the payment of interest to investors. The intermediaries (banks) can make profits by placing and trading these instruments. The Central Agency does not specify the sources of funds used to pay for the interests on the securities (e.g., ACOSS, 2019a).

Besides covering short-term financing requirements, financial capital also became central for ACOSS to refinance its debt. When the agency's total expenditures exceed its revenues after the year-end, this leads to a debt that remains in ACOSS' balance sheet until being transferred to CADES. This debt also started being refinanced through securities.[28] Even the traditional relations between the Central Agency and the *Caisse des Dépôts* were reorganized due to the use of securities, as part of the bank's lending to Social Security now occurs through the exchange of such instruments. In the case of short-term loans to pay for pension benefits, for example, the bank now grants these loans via sale and repurchase agreements ("repos"), operations in which the borrower sells a security for the lender in exchange for funds under the commitment to buy it back at a higher price. In a similar vein, the use of financial

---

28   ACOSS' deficits are closely related but not equal to the so-called "Social Security deficit". ACOSS manages the revenues and expenditures of the General Regime, whose difference accounts for most of the Social Security deficit. Nonetheless, the agency also manages other revenues and expenditures – for example, it makes payments on behalf of entities other than the Social Security Funds and engages in operations with bodies outside the scope of Social Security schemes. This explains the difference in the final results of ACOSS and Social Security.

securities shaped the way in which the agency finances other public and Social Security bodies. For example, these bodies can now place their financial surpluses in ACOSS or borrow funds from it using securities and repos.

2.2.2   ACOSS' Financing Strategy in Numbers

Data show a structural shift in the sources of additional capital for ACOSS over the 2010s decade, from public banks to financial markets (Table 3.11, Figure 3.4). Until the mid-2000s, the cash requirements of Social Security were almost entirely covered by loans, mainly from the Caisse des Dépôts. Their participation went from virtually 100% of external borrowing in 2004 to 3% in 2018.[29] By the late 2010s, these requirements were almost entirely covered by financial securities. They went from having no participation in 2006 to 93% of external financing in 2018. It is worth mentioning that the largest share comes of these revenues comes from securities issued in foreign markets, revealing that the new strategy is primarily based on international capital. In 2018, international securities (ECPS) accounted for nearly 80% of the Central Agency's external borrowing. Apart from securities and loans, there are also funds coming from deposits of "social partners" in ACOSS (e.g., CADES and social funds – see footnote 4 of this chapter). These deposits have marginal participation, at around 4% in 2018.

The total value of commercial papers issued by the Central Agency increased each year except for 2011, reaching outstanding values at the end of the series. In total, the agency issued €2 trillion in securities between 2007 and 2018.[30] In this last year, the value of emissions reached nearly €300 billion, consolidating ACOSS' position as one of the world's largest issuers of ECPS. In 2016 and 2017, the agency was the second largest issuer of ECPS in the world, and the largest one among public entities (ACOSS, 2017a).

2.2.3   Instruments and Costs

Similar to what has been observed for long-term financing, the policy changes allowing the Central Agency to issue securities have transformed financial capital into the primary source of funds for short-term financing. As in the case of CADES, ACOSS issues securities in several currencies and works with different

---

29   The data for the relative participation in total borrowing reported by the agency and systematized here is based on the average values of external borrowing at different times of the year.

30   As ACOSS can only borrow in the short run, its securities are continually maturing, and new ones are issued in their place. The high turnover makes the total value of emissions exceeds that of financing requirements, which helps explaining these outstanding values, above the actual value of cash requirements in a given year.

TABLE 3.11 France, Central Agency of Social Security Organizations (ACOSS), external financing by instrument, 2004–2018, billions of euros of 2018 and share in total financing

	2004	2007	2008	2009	2010	2011	2012	2013	2014	2015	2016	2017	2018
Financial securities, amounts issued (billions of euros of 2018)													
Total	0	n.a	171	131	150	142	79	124	175	265	246	230	296
Domestic securities	0	n.a.	171	131	137	129	49	89	132	201	147	141	148
International securities	0	n.a.	0	0	12	13	29	34	43	64	99	89	148
Share in total financing (%)													
CDC loans	100	84	87	69	60	42	8	10	18	14	3	2	3
Partner's deposits	0	0	0	0	0	3	3	14	11	5	4	3	4
Domestic securities	0	16	13	31	34	36	44	39	31	30	31	22	14
International securities	0	0	0	0	6	19	44	38	40	51	62	74	79

SOURCE: AUTHOR'S ELABORATION BASED ON ACOSS (2007–2019A, 2007–2019B) AND FRANCE (2018)

Share in total financing based on average amounts borrowed per instrument over the year. Real values of 2018 adjusted for inflation according to the Consumer Price Index. Divergences in the total may appear as a result of approximations. Domestic securities: CPs/NEU CPs. Foreign-market securities: ECPs. n.a.: not available

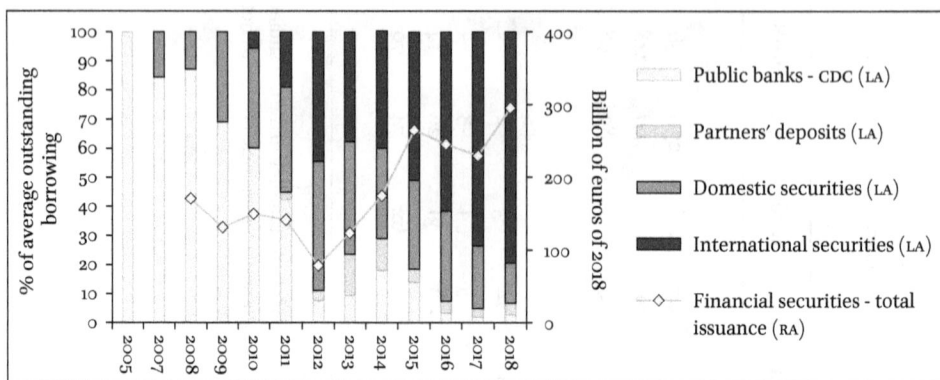

FIGURE 3.4   France, Central Agency of Social Security Organizations (ACOSS), financial securities, 2004–
2018, participation in total short-term borrowing (left axis) and total amounts issued in the
year (right axis)
SOURCE: AUTHOR'S ELABORATION BASED ON ACOSS (2007–2019A, 2007–2019B) AND
FRANCE (2018). LA: LEFT AXIS. RA: RIGHT AXIS. SHARE IN TOTAL FINANCING BASED ON
AVERAGE AMOUNTS BORROWED PER INSTRUMENT OVER THE YEAR. REAL VALUES OF 2018
ADJUSTED FOR INFLATION ACCORDING TO THE CONSUMER PRICE INDEX

types of interest rates. A closer look at its 2017 financing program reveals a
predominance of securities issued in foreign markets, mostly at fixed interest
rates, and with a period until repayment ranging from a few weeks up to three
months (ACOSS, 2018a; France, 2018).

The agency's interest rates followed a downward trend in the long run, from
4% in 2007 to-0.65% in 2017 (Table 3.12).[31] More than falling interest rates,
ACOSS was able to finance itself at negative interest rates after 2015. One can
put the evolution of these rates into perspective by placing them alongside the
reference rate for short-term markets and those offered by State bills (short-
term securities) in the same period. A common way to compare the evolution of ACOSS' interest rates relative to other market rates is by observing their
spread against the Euro Overnight Index Average (Eonia), the overnight interbank lending rate in the European Union and the reference rate for short-term
borrowing. On average, ACOSS' financing costs had a small spread against the
Eonia up to 2015 and fell below this rate afterward.

---

31   Average financing rate – i.e., the average interest rate of each type of instrument, weighted
     by the volume of funds borrowed through each one. The available series do not allow to
     exclude interests on CDC loans, but these have a marginal weight in the average consider-
     ing their low participation in external financing today.

TABLE 3.12   France, ACOSS and State interest rates, annual average, 2007–2017, %

	ACOSS		State securities							
	Average financing rate	Average cost of financing	1-month bill	3-month bill	6-month bill	9-month bill	12-month bill	2-year bond	5-year bond	10-year benchmark bond
2007	4.04	Eonia + 0.141	n.a.	n.a.	n.a.	n.a.	n.a.	n.a.	n.a.	4.30
2008	3.87	Eonia + 0.044	n.a.	n.a.	n.a.	n.a.	n.a.	n.a.	n.a.	4.24
2009	0.78	Eonia + 0.136	n.a.	n.a.	n.a.	n.a.	n.a.	n.a.	n.a.	3.65
2010	0.96	Eonia + 0.506	n.a.	n.a.	n.a.	n.a.	n.a.	n.a.	n.a.	3.11
2011	0.98	Eonia + 0.197	n.a.	n.a.	n.a.	n.a.	n.a.	n.a.	n.a.	3.31
2012	0.18	Eonia + 0.016	n.a.	n.a.	n.a.	n.a.	n.a.	n.a.	n.a.	2.54
2013	0.14	Eonia + 0.043	n.a.	n.a.	n.a.	n.a.	n.a.	n.a.	n.a.	2.21
2014	0.20	Eonia + 0.104	n.a.	n.a.	n.a.	n.a.	n.a.	n.a.	n.a.	1.66
2015	-0.06	Eonia + 0.045	-0.22	-0.20	-0.20	-0.20	-0.20	-0.18	0.14	0.85
2016	-0.45	Eonia − 0.139	-0.58	-0.56	-0.55	-0.55	-0.54	-0.52	-0.23	0.46
2017	-0.65	Eonia − 0.293	-0.67	-0.64	-0.63	-0.61	-0.58	-0.50	-0.05	0.81

SOURCE: AUTHOR'S ELABORATION BASED ON BANQUE DE FRANCE (2019B) AND FRANCE (2018)
For State interest rates, annual average. T. bill: Treasury bill. T. bond: Treasury bond. n.a.: not available. Eonia: Euro Overnight Index Average, the overnight interbank lending rate in the European Union

That the securities issued by the Central Agency are considered virtually as safe as those offered by the State is an important factor explaining why ACOSS, like CADES, can borrow at low or negative interest rates. ACOSS' capacity to finance itself at low interest rates in recent years, even below the interbank rate, is also strongly related to the fact that it can operate in foreign currencies. This allows the agency to strategically place securities where it can explore exchange rate differentials in its favor, paying interest rates that, when converted to euros, end up being lower than the interest rates paid in domestic currency (IGAS, 2018).

Comparisons between ACOSS and the Treasury's interest rates must be made with caution due to methodological differences in how they are calculated. But the figures can still give an idea of how the agency's financing costs stand in relation to those of the debt that is directly financed by the State. In the last years of the series, ACOSS' rates were relatively more advantageous for investors ("less negative") than those offered by the State.

The values of financial charges paid by ACOSS indicate how much the agency channels in revenues to the banking and financial sector each year (Table 3.13, Figure 3.5). Financial charges include interest payments and other costs, namely commissions and guarantees. From 2009 to 2018, ACOSS paid €496 million in charges derived from banking operations (primarily with the *Caisse des Dépôts* and the French Central Bank) and €341 million to financial markets, totaling €837 million in ten years. There was a marked decrease in financial expenditures, particularly until 2012. The primary explanation for this decrease lies in the lower interest rates paid on securities compared with those charged by the *Caisse des Dépôts*.[32] This can be observed by the decline in banking expenditures along with a less than proportionate increase in financial market expenditures. It is important to remind that such a drop in financing costs should be attributed not simply to the use of securities, but also to the fact that this transition accompanied a period of generalized fall in interest rates in the European Union.

Another important trend of the past decade was the increase in financial income. This originates from different sources. One is the interest income from ACOSS' positive accounts at the *Caisse des Dépôts* and the French Central Bank. Another is the profits made by the agency from operations with securities and

---

32   For the sake of comparison, in 2016, ACOSS' average cost of financing stood at -0.45%. Breaking it down by instrument, the average was of -0.22% for NEU CPs issued at variable rates, -0.29% for NEU CPs at fixed rates, -0.47% for ECPs, +0,005% for partner's deposits, and +0.14% for CDC loans (ACOSS, 2017b).

derivatives. There was a sharp increase in the volumes of interest income earned by the Central Agency when it began selling securities at negative interest rates (see the discussion for CADES). The financial income from market operations amounted to €536 million from 2009 to 2018, coming mostly in the last three years of the series. Banking operations, in turn, provided €25 million, all until 2014. In total, the Central Agency of Social Security reaped €561 million in financial income in this period.

Besides interest payments, the greater complexity of the current financing strategy also brought other kinds of revenues and expenditures. For example, ACOSS made €2.2 million in profits from interest rate swap operations in 2016 – a sound illustration of the incorporation of interests and practices typical of financial institutions within Social Security agencies.

TABLE 3.13   France, Central Agency of Social Security Organizations, revenues and expenditures, banking and financial market operations, 2009–2018, millions of euros of 2018

	2009	2010	2011	2012	2013	2014	2015	2016	2017	2018	Total
Financial charges	108	348	158	22	50	115	15	25	17	22	837
Banking operations	78	273	83	6	10	23	14	15	16	22	496
Financial markets	30	76	75	16	41	92	1	10	1	0	341
Financial income	2	3	12	8	27	72	32	118	145	141	561
Banking operations	2	3	11	7	1	1	0	0	0	0	25
Financial markets	0	0	0	1	26	71	32	118	145	141	536

SOURCE: AUTHOR'S ELABORATION BASED ON ACOSS (2009–2018). REAL VALUES OF 2018 ADJUSTED FOR INFLATION ACCORDING TO THE CONSUMER PRICE INDEX. ROUNDED VALUES

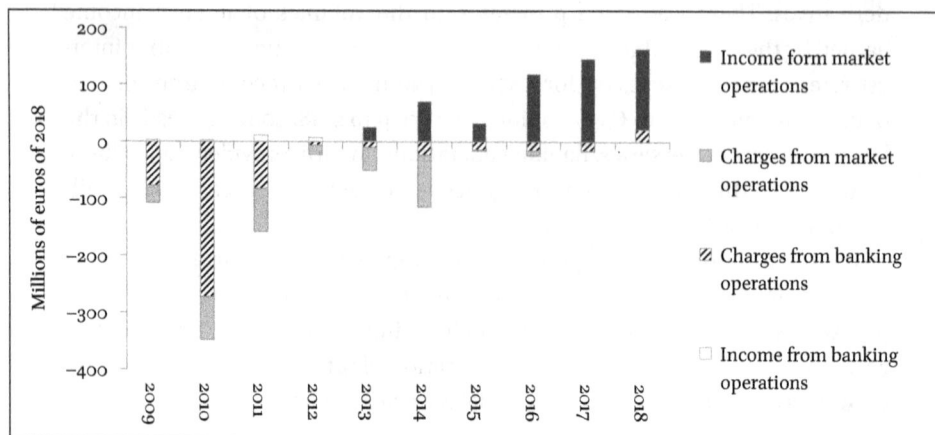

FIGURE 3.5   France, Central Agency of Social Security Organizations, revenues and expenditures, banking and financial market operations, 2009–2018, millions of euros of 2018
SOURCE: AUTHOR'S ELABORATION BASED ON ACOSS COMBINED ACCOUNTS (ACOSS, 2009–2018). REAL VALUES OF 2018 ADJUSTED FOR INFLATION ACCORDING TO THE CONSUMER PRICE INDEX

2.2.4   Investors and Intermediaries

Like in the previous case, ACOSS' market-based strategy depends on a vast array of investors and financial institutions. In the case of investors, the agency does not provide detailed information on the nature of agents who buy its securities. The possibility of knowing the investors' identities is further limited by the speed and non-disclosure of transactions in short-term markets, as well as by exchanges in secondary markets. What we know is that the agency operates in money markets, whose key participants include governments, central banks, private and public banks, mutual funds, insurance companies, non-banking financial institutions, and private companies.

Besides investors, the strategy of refinancing Social Security's short-term cash needs in the financial markets also relies on a large chain of intermediation. The central actors in this chain are banks, both national and foreign. They organize the issuance programs, ensure that legal requirements are met, and find investors, among other roles. The intermediaries include both French and foreign banks, mostly private; the official arranger of ECPs programs in 2018, for example, was UBS (private, headquartered in Switzerland), the domiciliary agent was Citibank (private, headquartered in the United States), and dealers included Bank of America, Merrill Lynch, Barclays, Crédit Agricole, Credit Suisse, Royal Bank of Scotland, UBS, and BRED (private and cooperative banks, headquartered in Europe and the United States). Along the same lines as CADES' instruments, ACOSS' securities flow through clearing houses based in Belgium and Luxembourg, and are evaluated by the three giants of the rating industry. Credit rating agencies classify them as extremely safe investments (ACOSS, 2019b, 2018c).

As previously noted, ACOSS' financing strategy is heavily geared toward attracting foreign capital. Most of its international securities (ECPs) are denominated in US dollars and British pounds, corresponding to 67% and 29% of ECP financing in 2017, respectively. The agency also issues ECPs in other currencies, such as Australian dollars, New Zealand dollars, Canadian dollars, and Polish zlotys (ACOSS, 2018a). Several factors explain the increasing focus on foreign markets. On the one hand, there is a high demand for ACOSS' securities from international investors. This is expected as the latter offers similar returns while also having more flexible conditions than French sovereign bonds, such as the option of having the assets denominated in foreign currency. On the other, for Social Security, foreign markets offer the possibility of increasing the supply of capital and reducing the costs of financing by exploring exchange rate differentials. Such developments have already been noted for CADES and are reinforced by statements and reports that describe ACOSS' strategy (e.g., Assemblée Nationale, 2018; IGAS, 2018).

2.2.5   State Support

ACOSS' securities are implicitly guaranteed by the State and enjoy the same level of creditworthiness assigned to government bonds. Both ACOSS and the rating agencies emphasize the French government's commitment to mitigate and withdraw any risks associated with the securities. The guarantee that the State will protect investors in case of liquidity or solvency problems is clearly stated in ACOSS' issuance programs:

> Should a court order the Issuer to pay any amounts, Law No. 80–539 (...) provides that the Minister in charge of Social Security (...) *may be required to order the Issuer [ACOSS] to pay and, if necessary, the Minister shall find the necessary resources to meet such liability and/or budget for such amounts due* in the accounts of the Issuer. Since ACOSS is a national administrative entity, the State, by way of a decision by the Minister in charge of the Economy, may subscribe for its negotiable debt instruments.
>
> ACOSS, 2018c, p. 9, emphasis added

As stated in Fitch Ratings' credit report, State support is the main reason for the high grades assigned to the securities. The institution emphasizes that "although the French government has no legal obligation to prevent a default

(...) it has a strong incentive to do so and that it has the legal means to enable ACOSS to meet its debt service obligations in a timely manner" (Fitch Ratings, 2017, p. 1).

This section described how internal bodies of the French Social Security system, responsible for administering the financing of the PHS, began embracing financialized strategies to raise funds in domestic and foreign markets. Such a shift followed a path much similar to that which had already been traced by the body responsible for restructuring the Social Security debt. State decisions to facilitate the turn toward markets found a particularly favorable context in the 2000s, when the diversification of financial instruments available for Social Security met a large number of investors eager to lend to the system. While the policy changes discussed so far have dealt with changes at the level of Social Security more broadly, which directly affect the financing of the health system, the last section examines the advance of financialized policies specifically in the latter case by looking at how public hospitals have been financed.

2.3   *Government Policies toward Hospitals: Credit-Based Investment Programs*

The expansion of the financial sector in the past decades also altered the State's approach to financing public hospitals. Since the 2000s, a government-sponsored strategy increased the participation of banks and investors in the financing of public hospital infrastructure. As of 2017, public hospital debt amounted to approximately €30 billion, of which 90% was in bank loans and 10% in debt securities (AP-HP, 2018a). This section briefly characterizes the public hospital sector in France and then examines the programs leading it to turn to banks and financial markets.

2.3.1   The French Hospital Sector at a Glance

The hospital sector in France comprises public, private not-for-profit, and private for-profit health establishments. Most hospital care is provided by the public sector, responsible for 62% of hospital beds in 2016. The remaining share is divided into 24% in private for-profit establishments and 14% in not-for-profit ones. The French hospital sector has suffered important cuts over the past decades: it lost 64,000 full-time beds from 2003 to 2016, partially offset by the creation of 25,000 part-time beds (DREES, 2018b).[33]

Public hospitals are part of the Social Security system but do not belong to any specific regime of Social Security. While public hospital budgets are

---

33   Official figures comprise metropolitan and overseas territories.

formally independent of the Social Security budget, most of their revenues come from the latter in the form of compensation for services rendered to beneficiaries and other kinds of monetary transfers. These revenues derive, more specifically, from the Illness branches of the Social Security Regimes, which together make up what is known as *Assurance Maladie*, the French PHS.[34]

The public hospital sector encompasses different types of units including hospital centers, regional and university hospital centers, specialized hospital centers, and long-term care facilities. Historical records suggest that the early stages of hospital building and expansion were typically financed through a mix of self-funding, State resources, and external borrowing, at different ratios depending on the type of establishment. The State played a central role in the construction of hospitals, especially when it comes to large-scale establishments. This is best exemplified by looking at the case of regional and university hospital centers. These are a central pillar of hospital care in France, providing almost one-third of beds in the public sector and leading hospital teaching, research, and innovation (DREES, 2018b). Regional and university centers were mostly built during the 20th century, largely financed with interest-free State funds (Debeaupuis, 2004; Garnier, 2015). Their expansion and renovation in recent decades, by contrast, have relied on interest-bearing capital provided by commercial banks and financial markets.

2.3.2   Bringing Hospitals and Banks Closer Together: a New Approach to Finance Investments

Bank credit became increasingly important for public hospital financing over the 2000s decade. This was mainly the result of two five-year government programs aimed at restructuring the public hospital sector, the 2007 Hospital Plan, launched in 2002, and the 2012 Hospital Plan, signed in 2007. One of the primary goals of these programs was to expand and renovate the public health infrastructure. Such tasks required massive amounts of investments. However, the possibility of financing such investments through State funding was constrained by several measures to contain public spending in general and health care spending in particular (section 1.4).

In the context of fiscal austerity, the French government sought to boost public hospital investment by providing incentives to hospitals so they could borrow from financial institutions. These incentives consisted mainly of

---

34   As a reminder, the discussions carried in the previous sections focused on the Illness branch of the General Regime of Social Security, but *Assurance Maladie* also encompass the health schemes provided by other minor regimes.

regulatory shifts that made it easier for public hospitals to obtain loans and provided subsidies to help them pay the interests and amortizations.

The Hospital Plan approved in 2002 set a target of increasing public hospitals' investment by 30% in five years (2003–2007) (France, 2003). To put the plan into action, the government announced it would provide €7.5 billion in grants to public hospitals to help them finance investment projects. The financial aid from the government came gradually and in two main forms. The first one was via capital grants from the "Fund for the Modernization of Public and Private Health Facilities" (FMESPP), a fund sourced from revenues of the PHS (*Assurance Maladie*). These grants amounted to €1.9 billion. The second and most relevant one consisted of subventions to hospitals, at approximately €536 million per year. They consisted in increasing the value of regular transfers from *Assurance Maladie* to the hospitals to encourage them to take out loans (since they would have more financial security to reimburse the loans). Throughout the course of the plan, the government had to provide a greater volume of funds than was originally planned, as the debt charges were increasing above initial expectations (Cour des Comptes, 2014).[35]

Besides pecuniary incentives, regulatory shifts also gave a major boost to public hospital borrowing. The simplification of public hospitals' legal framework in 2005 (France, 2005) was particularly important for the credit boom observed in the following years. Among several measures that facilitated public hospitals to obtain bank loans, the new legislation eliminated the need for prior authorization from a supervisory body before taking credit. Facing lower regulatory constraints, hospitals began borrowing at a much faster pace in the following years (Cour des Comptes, 2014).

As the 2002 five-year plan came to an end, the government renewed the strategy in 2007 to continue the previous strategy for another five years (France, 2007). The goal of the new plan was to increase investments in the public hospital sector by another €11.4 billion, half of which (€5.7 billion) financed by the public sector, especially in the form of subventions from *Assurance Maladie* to facilitate loan repayments.

At first, the government-sponsored programs to increase public hospital investment via private credit were successful to the extent that the investments carried by these hospitals almost doubled in six years, from €4.4 billion in 2003 to €7.4 billion in 2009 (Table 3.14). The share of hospital revenues allocated to investments (the "investment effort") rose from 7.9% in 2003 to almost 11% in

---

35   Excepted when stated otherwise, all values in this section are expressed in real values of 2018 adjusted for inflation according to the Consumer Price Index.

TABLE 3.14 France, public hospital sector, investment, and debt indicators, 2003, 2009–2018

	2003	2009	2010	2011	2012	2013	2014	2015	2016	2017	2018
Investment effort[a] (%)	7.9	10.9	10.2	9.4	8.8	7.6	7.1	6.6	5.9	5.7	5.2
Indebtedness ratio[b] (%)	33.1	46.0	47.4	48.7	49.6	49.8	50.0	50.5	51.5	51.6	51.6
Investments[c] (€ billion of 2018)	4.4	7.4	n.a.	n.a.	n.a.	5.2	5.0	4.5	4.2	4.1	3.7
Outstanding debt (€ billion of 2018)	11.9	24.2	26.3	28.1	29.4	30.2	30.2	30.6	30.8	30.4	29.4

SOURCE: AUTHOR'S ELABORATION BASED ON DREES (2010–2014, 2015–2019) AND COUR DES COMPTES (2014)
Data for 2003–2017 in real values of 2018 adjusted for inflation according to the Consumer Price Index. n.a.: non-available
a Investment spending relative to revenues
b Share of outstanding debts relative to stable resources (equity, provisions, and debts)
c DREES does not publish the absolute value of investments for the period before 2013; the figures for 2003 and 2009 are from Cour des Comptes (2014)

2009. In the 2010s decade, however, investments began to decelerate amidst a context of crisis and over-indebtedness. The investment effort decreased continuously to reach 5.2% of revenues in 2018. Public hospital investments amounted to €3.7 billion in that year – adjusted for inflation, this was less than the value observed at the beginning of the strategy.

The investment boom was accompanied by a major increase in credit borrowing and indebtedness. Different from investments, these did not decelerate in the transition for the 2010s decade. The public hospital debt more than doubled during the first decade of the plan, from €11.9 billion in 2003 to €24.2 billion in 2009. In relative terms, the indebtedness ratio (the volume of debts in relation to hospitals' "stable resources", comprising equity and financial liabilities) rose from 33% to 46%. While investments declined during the 2010s, debt levels continued to rise. The total debt of public hospitals peaked in 2016, at €30.8 billion, and ended the series at €29.4 billion in 2018 (Cour des Comptes, 2014; DREES, 2019c).

The relatively high costs of debt, coupled with the financial practices adopted by the banks (discussed below) and the insufficient rise in hospital revenues to cover the costs of the loans, contributed to a generalized over-indebtedness crisis in the public hospital sector at the beginning of the 2010s. In 2015, around one-third of public health establishments were considered to be in a critical situation, considered "excessively indebted".[36] The average length of public hospital debt was of 13 years in the mid-2000s and stabilized at an average range from sixteen to eighteen years from then on, although some contracts extend for over forty years (Finance Active, 2016).[37]

2.3.3 Delving into the Credit-Based Financing Strategy

The business of lending to public hospitals was controlled by a few banks. The main creditors were private banks, both for-profit and cooperative (formally non-profit) institutions. As of 2010, the lion's share of hospital debt was in the hands of five institutions: *Dexia* (32.3%), *Caisse d'Épargne* (15%), *Crédit Agricole* (12.2%), *Société Générale* (9.9%), and *Crédit Foncier de France* (8.7%) (Cour des Comptes, 2014). The financial crisis of 2008, coupled with a looming debt crisis

---

36   In 2011, the government established a set of criteria for deciding if a hospital was "excessively indebted", which could help them obtaining government support. The institution should meet least two of the following situations: (i) a financial independence ratio (the ratio between its long-term debt and permanent capital) of more than 50%; (ii) an "apparent duration of the debt" exceeding 10 years; and (iii) a ratio of outstanding debt to total income over 30%.

37   The scope of Finance Active's survey is based on a set of approximately 400 public health institutions, representing more than three-quarters of the sector's debt.

in the public hospital sector in the same period in light of the increasing burden of debt service costs, led traditional lenders to refrain from continuing to provide credit to these establishments. Public financial institutions had to step in to avoid the drying up of hospital financing, which would worsen the latter's already critical situation (Cour des Comptes, 2018, 2014). Despite the greater participation of public institutions in the 2010s, the largest share of public hospital debt remained in the hands of private banks (Finance Active, 2016). The greatest lender was *Dexia*, which made massive profits lending to the French public sector in the 2000s; in the aftermath of the 2008 crisis, the bank was bailed out by the French State, at a cost of over six billion euros (Financial Times, 2013).

Among the features of the private banking sector that contributed to the financing-cum-indebtedness boom, one can mention the use of financial innovations to provide credit and the adoption of aggressive marketing strategies to push them onto hospitals. This is particularly the case of the so-called "structured loans", an important financial innovation that exploded in the 2000s. Part of them became known as "toxic loans" after the 2008 financial crisis. These loans contrasted with regular ones by applying different financing conditions over the duration of the contract. These conditions were extremely appealing at the beginning of the contract, such as a long grace period and zero or low interest rates on the first installments. However, they could be significantly revised at a later stage, imposing a significant burden on the debtor. The terms of structured loans were determined according to complex regulations and calculation formulas, making them more risky and opaque than ordinary loans. Official reports and statements from professionals working in the financial industry at the time consider structured loans as one of the main causes of the over-indebtedness problems faced by several hospitals, including due to hospital managers' difficulties in properly assessing the long-term costs of such loans (Assemblée Nationale, 2015; Cour des Comptes, 2018).

Banks had a sound marketing strategy for distributing structured loans to hospitals in the context of government-sponsored investment plans. This was described by the director of a fintech company as follows:

> the market was guided by banks – some of which had teams of more than 300 sales representatives – and throughout the day, financial managers from local governments and public health institutions were called upon to engage in this type of product. (...) The market was perfectly organized by the banks at the time: Dexia in the lead, Caisse d'Épargne, Crédit Agricole, Royal Bank of Scotland, etc.
>
> Assemblée Nationale, 2015

The spread of toxic loans within the hospital sector can be assessed through the "Gissler scale", an analysis grid that allows for assessing the risk levels associated with a structured product.[38] Using this scale as a parameter, data suggest that, in 2012, approximately €2.6 billion, or 10% of the public hospital debt, consisted of "extremely risky" loans. From this total, around €1.5 billion, almost 4% of the debt, consisted of "toxic loans", whose risks cannot be assessed. Dexia, the largest lender to public hospitals in the 2000s, was responsible for 70% of the toxic debt held by these institutions by 2012. Public banks, in turn, did not engage in this type of practice (Cour des Comptes 2018).

The debt-based strategy brought significant costs to public hospitals in the form of interest payments. The average interest rate charged by banks remained above 3% per year, peaking at 4.08% just before the financial crisis. The costs of the bank-based strategy seem particularly high when contrasting the interest rates paid by public hospitals on their loans with those paid by the State on Treasury bonds (Table 3.15). During the 2010s, the trajectory of interest rates charged to hospitals declined at a much slower pace than other interest rates in the European Union and the rate paid by government bonds. The spread against the rates of government bonds has widened over the years, which suggests that bank financing became increasingly expensive compared to direct government funding. The same caveats regarding differences in methodology made earlier apply here; still, in 2017, the average interest rate of public hospital debt stood at 2.93% per year, while the interest rate on the French State's benchmark bond (10-year *emprunt phare*) closed the year at 0.79%.

Public hospitals service their debts out of their revenues. As previously noted, the largest share of hospital revenues comes from the PHS (*Assurance Maladie*). Over the last decade, the revenues received from the public system accounted for nearly 80% of their revenues – 78% on average between 2010–2018 (DREES 2010–2014, 2015–2019).[39] Therefore, one might infer that most of the funds used to pay interests to banks were ultimately provided by Social Security.

The decline in investments along with mounting debts suggests that an increasingly larger share of revenues was drifting away from the expansion of public infrastructure to debt repayments. The evolution of the sector's financial

---

38   The Gissler charter evaluates the "quality" of the loan considering the complexity of the underlying index and the formula used to calculate the loan's interest rate. The grades can vary from A to F. Loans graded as D, E, and F are considered extremely risky. Those classified as 6F or "out of the charter" are the so-called "toxic loans", whose risks cannot be assessed (Cour des Comptes, 2018).

39   Figures refer to items of the main budget, which excludes long-term care services.

TABLE 3.15   France, interest rates of public hospital debt and Treasury bonds, 2005–2018, %

	Public hospitals, average interest rates of outstanding debt[a]	French securities, interest rates of 10-year Treasury bond
2005	3.67%	3.29%
2006	4.00%	3.98%
2007	4.08%	4.42%
2008	3.84%	3.41%
2009	3.25%	3.60%
2010	3.31%	3.35%
2011	3.50%	3.15%
2012	3.35%	2.25%
2013	3.43%	2.43%
2014	3.36%	0.84%
2015	3.26%	1.00%
2016	n.a.	0.68%
2017	2.93%	0.79%

SOURCE: AUTHOR'S ELABORATION BASED ON FINANCE ACTIVE (2016) AND BANQUE DE FRANCE (2019B). VALUES OF DECEMBER 31
a   Data for approximately 400 health care establishments covering over three-quarters of public hospital debt. n.a.: not available

results corroborates this view (Figure 3.6). Financial results correspond to the difference between public hospitals' revenues and expenses related to debt and investments. Therefore, a negative result reflects the amount of financial charges paid by hospitals, already discounted from any financial income they might receive. It can therefore be considered an adequate indicator to assess the costs of financial operations. Data show that the volume of financial charges, net of income, doubled from around €500 million per year at the beginning of the 2000s to approximately €1 billion per year by the late 2010s. These values appear in the figure below as negative financial results. Summing up all values for the period 2002–2018, hospitals paid €13.7 billion in financial charges, net of financial income.[40]

---

40   Differently from the previous sections, in this case the item "financial results" include transactions with both banks and financial markets. However, except in some cases (as discussed next), public hospital debt comes primarily from bank loans.

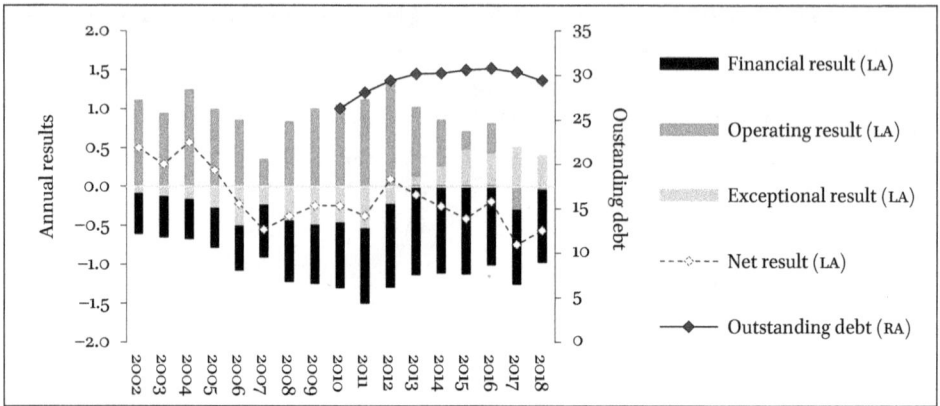

FIGURE 3.6   France, public hospital sector, annual results (left axis) and outstanding debt (right axis),
2002–2018, billions of euros of 2018
SOURCE: AUTHOR'S ELABORATION BASED ON DREES (2010–2014, 2015–2019). LA: LEFT
AXIS. RA: RIGHT AXIS. RESULT: REVENUES MINUS EXPENSES. FINANCIAL RESULT: ITEMS
RELATED TO DEBT AND FINANCIAL INVESTMENTS, INCLUDING INTEREST PAYMENTS
ON BORROWINGS. OPERATING RESULT: ITEMS RELATED TO HEALTH CARE ACTIVITIES.
EXCEPTIONAL RESULT: ITEMS RELATED TO MANAGEMENT AND CAPITAL OPERATIONS,
DEPRECIATION, AND PROVISIONS. NET RESULT: ALL RESULTS CONSIDERED. VALUES
FOR THE GLOBAL HOSPITAL BUDGET. REAL VALUES OF 2018 ADJUSTED ACCORDING
TO THE CONSUMER PRICE INDEX (IPC/INSEE), EXCEPT FOR 2018. 2018: NOMINAL
ESTIMATED VALUES

The increasing burden of interest payments on the hospitals' accounts has
contributed to deteriorating the financial results of these establishments and
weakening their fiscal soundness. The sector's net result, which also takes into
account operating results (revenues and expenditures for regular health care
activities) and exceptional results (for other items) entered a new trajectory
in the mid-2000s. Up to this point, the public hospital sector ended the year
with a surplus. However, starting in 2005, hospitals began to face recurring
deficits in their overall accounts, with net results hitting minus €745 million
in 2017. The financial results, always negative and mostly due to interest payments, played an important part in the poor performance of hospital accounts.
After 2012, this deterioration was aggravated by the steady decline of hospitals'
accounts related to ordinary medical activities (operating results).

2.3.4   The Role of the State
The French State was the chief actor behind the dramatic growth of interest-
bearing capital as a means to finance public health infrastructure. The

government implemented investment programs based on bank credit, simplified regulations to facilitate credit taking by hospitals, and subsidized debt repayments, to name a few. It also provided additional guarantees to investors. For example, amidst the hospital indebtedness crisis during the first half of the 2010s, the government actively countered the credit rationing of private banks by increasing the participation of public institutions. Moreover, it financed hospitals' early exit from toxic debts in 2014, putting in place a special fund to renegotiate the risky structured loans granted to hospitals. This fund was intended to raise money to finance the settlement of these debts before the original end date and to pay for indemnities associated with this early exit. The exit from "extremely high-risk loans" cost €678.8 million in total, from which 51% were financed by the public sector (12% by *Assurance Maladie* and 39% by public hospitals) and 49% by the banks who provided these toxic loans (Cour des Comptes 2018).

The French Supreme Audit Institution has analyzed the bank-based strategy and concluded that the State ended up facilitating access to credit more than effectively financing investments (Cour des Comptes, 2014). The institution highlights that the volume of credit concession and investments grew far more than was initially expected, but State subsidies did not grow accordingly. As a consequence, the guarantees facilitated the take-up of loans at first, but the bulk of the debt burden remained with the hospitals, making them reduce their investment capacity subsequently. The idea that the government facilitated credit-taking but did not provide hospitals with sufficient financial security to repay their debts finds support in the data provided throughout this section. While investments grew in the 2000s but slowed down in the following decade, the rerouting of funds from health care to the financial sector via interest payments remained intense.

2.4   *Addendum: Public Hospitals Venturing into Financial Markets*
Much like Social Security agencies, some hospitals turned to financial markets in the 2000s. A number of public hospitals started issuing financial securities to finance investments and, later on, cover immediate cash needs. In both cases, these movements were pioneered by Assistance Publique – Hôpitaux de Paris (AP-HP), one of the main health care service providers for the French PHS.

AP-HP is a public university hospital consortium that operates in Paris and its surrounding areas. It is the largest medical research center in Europe and the largest employer of the Parisian region. In 2017, over one-tenth of hospital stays in France were in an AP-HP facility. The institution's revenues amounted to €7.9 billion this year, more than 80% from *Assurance Maladie* transfers (AP-HP, 2018a).[41]

The institution entered the financial markets for the first time in 2000, issuing €41.3 million in long-term bonds to finance investments. In 2006, the institution began issuing medium-term notes, raising €173 million in that year. Two years later, AP-HP started issuing bonds in foreign currencies, which led it to also engage in derivatives (swaps) to hedge against currency fluctuations. Starting in 2016, the strategy of borrowing from markets was extended to short-term bonds, with a €308.7 million commercial paper program to cover short-term expenses. Given its size, AP-HP met the minimum legal requirements of scale required for borrowing in the financial markets on its own. Relatively smaller institutions organized collective issuances following AP-HP's steps. In 2009, 24 university hospital centers launched the first joint issuance program in the French public hospital sector, worth €298.3 million, with other programs thereafter (Chambre Régionale des Comptes, 2016; Cour des Comptes, 2014).

2.4.1   Financing Conditions and Intermediaries

One can gain a much better understanding of the conditions under which these programs work and the main financial players involved in them by taking a closer look at AP-HP's strategy. By the end of 2017, AP-HP had an outstanding debt of €1.6 billion in medium-and long-term securities, at a length of approximately 10 years and an average cost (interest rates) of 2.2%. The debt in the form of financial instruments corresponded to 72% of the AP-HP's total debt, of €2.3 billion in total. The remaining 28% was in bank debt, equal to €640.6 million. Bank debt presented a similar length and a slightly higher cost than financial debt, at 2.697% on average. Adding to that, there were still €54 million in debts from PPP contracts. This contrasts with the debt structure of the public hospital sector at large, where the share of debts from securities and bank loans accounted for 11% and 89% of total debt, respectively (AP-HP, 2018a). In 2017, AP-HP paid €52.5 million to investors and banks. From 2010 up to this year, financial charges amounted to €533 million in total (AP-HP, 2018b).[42]

AP-HP separates the buyers of securities into three categories: institutional investors (*institutionnel*), management funds (*fonds de gestion*), and banks. By 2017, these segments held 69%, 19%, and 12% of the institution's outstanding debt, respectively. Most of this debt was held by foreign investors (55%).

---

41   All figures are in real values of 2018 adjusted for inflation according to the Consumer Price Index.

42   Real values of 2018 adjusted for inflation according to the Consumer Price Index.

Seventy-one percent of the financial debt was denominated in euros, 18% in Norwegian krones, 6% in Japanese yens, and 5% in Swiss francs (AP-HP, 2018a). As in the other cases, the figures refer to primary placements, without taking into account eventual exchanges in secondary markets.

Also similar to the model used by CADES and ACOSS, the intermediaries of issuance programs include several private banks, domestic and foreign, such as ABN-AMRO, Natixis, HSBC, BNP Paribas, Merrill Lynch, Barclays, BRED, and Goldman Sachs (AP-HP, 2018b).

3 Taking Stock

This chapter examined mechanisms through which the French PHS has been integrated into the process of financialization. Since the 1990s, the system has been adopting rationalities typical of the financial sector and rewiring its financing circuits to welcome financial capital. This was mainly a result of the adoption of financial instruments to help address imbalances in the social budget. The French Social Security system, responsible for the financing of the PHS, started issuing financial securities to refinance debts and finance short-term expenses. In the case of public hospitals, the backbone of service provision, the hallmark of this period was the massive recourse to bank loans to finance investments. These strategies have come to replace previous arrangements based on public funding (including direct government spending and public banks' support). Such a transition was actively promoted by the French State, which altered regulations, provided implicit and explicit guarantees to the financial sector, and mobilized the necessary funds to pay for its costs.

The use of financial securities and loans opened channels through which domestic and foreign capital entered the French PHS and the Social Security system more broadly, providing funds for various purposes and profiting from these businesses. A particularly relevant outcome of these transformations in the logic of Social Security funding is that they created pathways for part of these systems' revenues to flow to the financial sector. Both Social Security and public hospitals had to address a significant volume of funds to financial institutions in order to remunerate them for the anticipation of resources. In the next chapter, we will see how the process of financialization reshaped the trajectory of the PHS in a peripheral country, in this case the Brazilian system.

The Brazilian System

A Trajectory (Mis)led by Financialization

This chapter shifts the focus of the analysis from the center to the periphery of capitalism. It shows how the Brazilian PHS, *Sistema Único de Saúde,* has been reshaped by financial interests, instruments, and institutions. Unlike the experience of advanced countries, Brazil created its PHS when the financialization of the world economy was already underway. Moreover, the country was integrated into this process from a subordinate condition. This led to distinctive links between financial capital and the PHS: the Brazilian experience is particularly illustrative of how the increasing participation of financial capital in public financing can change not only the ways in which a PHS manage its revenues but the very volume of resources it receives.

The first section provides critical background information on the Social Security and public health systems in Brazil and describes the evolution of their financial accounts over the past decades. Next, I examine how the introduction of financialized policies for public debt management at large and PHS financing in particular has altered how the latter works. Following the same approach as in the French case, I look at transformations in long-term, short-term, and hospital financing. The impacts of financialization on the long-term financing of the Brazilian PHS I will examine here concern the adoption of a monetary policy framework geared toward financial accumulation that constrained the volume of funds available to the system. For short-term financing, I describe how public health agencies themselves have incorporated financial accumulation strategies to manage the system's short-term revenues. I conclude by looking at hospital financing, studying the creation of government-sponsored bank credit lines for hospitals that provide services for the public system.

1   Social Security and Public Health Care in Brazil

The Brazilian PHS, SUS, is part of a broader system of Social Security named *Sistema de Seguridade Social*. Its principles of organization, financing, and provision are heavily influenced by this larger institutional framework.[1]

1.1   *The Brazilian Social Security System*

The Brazilian Social Security system was created in 1988, relatively late compared to the experience of most central countries. Before the creation of Social Security, there was a public system of social protection put in place by the military regime in the 1960s, centered on the Social Insurance system (*Instituto Nacional de Previdência Social*, INPS).[2] The Social Insurance system was a mandatory public pension scheme for private-sector workers, controlled by the State. It provided work-related benefits, such as retirement benefits, pensions for dependents, and unemployment insurance. The system also provided some form of health assistance for pensioners, formal workers, and, in some cases, their dependents. Despite being controlled by the federal government, it had typical "Bismarckian" features: the right to access was restricted to workers with formal labor contracts, benefits were funded by contributions on wages paid by employers and employees, and the value of benefits depended on the worker's contribution record. In addition to employers and employees, the State was also formally required to participate in the system's financing; in practice, however, it often refrained from fulfilling its obligation. In this way, the system had important limitations concerning population coverage and equity of access.

The health assistance coverage provided by the Social Insurance System offered a restricted scope of benefits, centered on access to medical care and hospital treatments within the system's service network. Individuals had access to different ranges of services depending on their occupational category. Once most of the population did not have access to the social insurance system, it was not entitled to its health care network. Unlike what was usually observed

---

1   The characterization presented in this section draws from the compilation of information from Barbosa (1996), Gentil (2019) Lavinas (2021), and Souza et al. (2019).

2   The use of the term "Social Security" in Brazil follows that of Continental Europe, encompassing the entire social protection system including pension, health, and social assistance policies. This differs from how the term is used in Anglo-Saxon countries, where "Social Security" is most often used in reference to the pension system. To avoid conceptual misunderstandings, I refer to the national institute created in Brazil in the 1960s as a "social insurance" scheme (because it was focused on the pension system), in order to contrast it with the more comprehensive system created in 1988 which I refer to as "social security".

in wealthy countries, the share of workers with formal labor contracts in Brazil was small by the second half of the 20th century; as of 1986, less than 40% of Brazilian workers had formal occupations and thus access to social security benefits (ANFIP, 2019). Individuals with the capacity to pay could have access to private health practitioners and facilities via out-of-pocket payments. They could also benefit from private insurance schemes, either privately contracted or sponsored by their employers. The population at large, and especially the most disadvantaged groups, often relied on private charitable and philanthropic health care.

The first attempts to expand access to public pensions and health-related rights came in the 1970s, consisting mainly of federal government initiatives to incorporate more individuals into the social insurance scheme. These initiatives sought to extend the right to contribute to the system to previously excluded categories, such as domestic servants, rural workers, and the self-employed. They also made advances in the direction of universalizing access to emergency care. Despite these efforts, the system of social protection in Brazil remained highly fragmented and exclusionary; even after them, a significant part of the population was still denied the right to participate, lacked the means to make regular contributions, or faced other administrative barriers to joining the Social Insurance System. Estimates suggest that nearly 60% of private sector workers were not effectively covered by the public pension scheme in 1998 (Previdência Social, 2000), which means that even a larger share was excluded from the scheme described here (that prevailed until 1988).

Apart from the health care assistance policies within the Social Insurance system, there were also public health policies carried out directly by the State. These were mostly focused on actions related to collective health, such as vaccination campaigns and actions for preventing and fighting contagious diseases. Another area with some degree of public intervention was hospital care, with government-sponsored referral hospitals specialized in specific conditions and groups of individuals. Overall, this array of systems and policies formed a fragmented public network with significant gaps in the services provided and the population covered.

The key event leading to the creation of the Brazilian Social Security System was the demise of the military government in 1985. This was a time of intense political mobilization to restore democracy and promote reforms to address the flaws of the authoritarian regime. Social demands for a more inclusive social protection system found a particularly favorable context in the setting up of a Constituent Assembly to elaborate a new Constitution. The 1988 Constitution, also known as the "Citizen Constitution" (Brazil, 1988), radically changed the approach to social rights and social protection in Brazil. In one of its opening articles, the State recognized a series of fundamental rights, including health, and acknowledged its responsibility to ensure them to all citizens. It also lays the basis for the creation of the Social Security System, comprising health, pensions, and social assistance policies and institutions.

The 1988 Constitution established a set of fundamental principles for the newly-created Social Security system, which would explicit its core values and serve as a guide for present and future policy decisions. In organizing a Social Security system according to such principles, Brazil sought to emulate the comprehensive and redistributive nature of the European systems created in the post-war period. It instituted features typical of the Beveridgean or universalist model of social protection (Chapter 2), consisting of a State-controlled system that applied common criteria to individuals with different contribution records and counted on a diversified financing pool including revenues from general taxation and social contributions. Among the most important principles, one can mention the universality of coverage, the uniformity and equivalence of benefits among different groups, the equitable participation in funding (matched to income levels), and the democratic administration through the joint management of workers, employers, retirees, and the government (Brazil, 1988).[3]

In terms of organization, the Brazilian Social Security system is divided into three subsystems:

- The public health system, named Unified Health System (*Sistema Único de Saúde* – SUS). It protects the population against health-related risks, providing health care services to all the population free of charge to the patient.
- The public pension system, the General Regime of Social Insurance or (*Regime Geral da Previdência Social* – RGPS). It is a mandatory scheme for formal private sector workers and open to the rest of the population upon contribution. It protects against work-related risks, providing retirement benefits, allowances for dependents, unemployment insurance, sick leave, maternity and parental leave, among others.

---

3   These Beveridgean traits were particularly salient in the case of health and social assistance. In the case of pensions, however, many aspects of the former system of Social Insurance remained in place. For example, instead of conforming to the principle of universality, promoting a single retirement system for all the population, the State preserved privileged schemes within the public administration and subsidized complementary private retirement and health insurance for part of the civil service. In this way, what emerged in practice was a hybrid model conjugating features from the previous logic of Social Insurance and the new logic of Social Security.

– The public system of welfare assistance, named Unified Social Assistance System or (*Sistema Único de Assistência Social* – SUAS). It covers vulnerable groups of the population against risks of subsistence and different forms of exclusion. The essence of its policies consists of cash transfers to low-income individuals who fall into specific categories. Unlike other schemes, social assistance benefits may not constitute vested rights.

The Social Security system has its own budget, the Social Security Budget, separated from the Fiscal Budget of the federal government (named *Orçamento da Seguridade Social* – OSS and *Orçamento Fiscal* – OF, respectively). During its creation, Social Security was endowed with earmarked revenues that in principle could only be allocated to its budget, so as to finance the three areas covered by the system. The Constitution defined that such revenues should come from a wide range of income bases. It presented a list of revenue sources for Social Security that included tax revenues from the fiscal budgets of national and subnational governments, social contributions levied on the revenues of workers and companies, other contributions paid by workers and other individuals insured by Social Security, the revenues of lotteries, and import revenues. In practice, the system's financing depends almost entirely on social contributions, while government provisions from tax revenues account for a marginal share of revenues (Brazil, 1988).[4]

The State, more precisely the federal government, controls the Social Security Budget.[5] About half of the revenues to finance the PHS comes from Social Security, which corresponds to the share of public health financing provided by the federal sphere. However, unlike other sectors of Social Security (namely pensions), the PHS also depends on revenues from subnational governments, receiving money that does not come from the Social Security budget. This is why, especially in the Brazilian case, it is important to look at both the national and the subnational levels of financing when studying transformations linked to financial capital (as demonstrated in the next sections).

In broad terms, the financing circuits of Social Security begin with taxpayers, who address funds to the government. The federal government forwards

---

4   During the period under analysis (1990–2018), the system went through several changes with regard to organization, financing, and provision. This characterization focuses on the prevailing features of the Social Security system throughout this period.

5   Brazil is a Presidential Federated Republic with 26 states, the Federal District, and approximately 5,570 municipalities. There are three levels of government: federal, state, and municipal. The federal government administers the national territory, and it is often referred to as the "Union". States and municipal governments rule within their jurisdictions and will be collectively referred to as "subnational governments".

revenues from federal taxes and social contributions to the Ministries in charge of health, pension, and social assistance policies. Each Ministry allocates the incoming revenues in its respective budgetary entity, known as "Funds" – the National Health Fund, the General Social Insurance Regime Fund, and the National Social Assistance Fund, respectively. The Ministries and subordinate bodies execute the payments. In the case of health care, Social Security revenues are used to make direct payments to service providers and other organizations to cover the costs of health actions and service provision. They are also channeled to state and municipal governments via monetary transfers, contributing to the implementation of public health policies at subnational levels. The financing circuits of the PHS described here are illustrated in Figure 4.1, presented in the next section after introducing the channels of subnational financing as well.

1.2   The Brazilian Public Health System: Sistema Único de Saúde

Brazil is one of the few middle-income countries with a public and universal health system covering all levels of care. The Brazilian PHS, SUS, is the largest universal health system in the world in terms of population coverage, reaching more than two hundred million people. The system represents a milestone in the history of universal health care since it was created under the yoke of neoliberalism and financialization, when several other countries were waging campaigns against State intervention in health. Yet, the constraints imposed by this context posed enormous difficulties in making universal access to health care a reality in the country. The particular trajectory of the Brazilian PHS in the neoliberal period led to a case full of contradictions: Brazil is also the only country with a universal health system where private health spending exceeds public health spending. The next paragraphs continue to deconstruct the ways in which the system organizes, finances, and provides services to the population. This will serve to apprehend some of the mechanisms by which neoliberalism and financialization have influenced SUS' trajectory and contributed to this situation.[6]

As explained in the previous section, before the creation of Social Security in 1988, the range and quality of public health care services available for each individual were determined according to his or her income and occupational

---

6 The overview presented in this section is based on the works mentioned in the previous section, in addition to Bahia and Scheffer (2018), Piola and Barros (2016), Funcia (2019), Giovanella et al. (2012), Mendes (2012), Nugem et al. (2019), and Senado Federal (2018). When using a data or idea extracted from one specific work, I indicate the source of information from which it was retrieved.

status. The public health network provided under the Social Insurance scheme was discriminatory and based on a privatized model of provision. A significant part of the services was delivered by private providers, sponsored by the federal government with public resources (especially from pension contributions). This arrangement was heavily criticized by social groups with more progressive agendas, in particular the members of the "sanitary reform" movement, which had a key role in advancing the idea of a public, universal health system during the Constitutional Assembly.[7]

The promulgation of the 1988 Constitution and the creation of the Social Security system brought about a radical change in the State's approach to health care. The new text provided for the universality of health care, stating that "health is a right of all and a duty of the State" (Brazil, 1988). SUS was formally created two years later through the enactment of the so-called "Organic Health Laws" (Brazil, 1990a, 1990b).

Beyond the principles of Social Security, SUS also has its own set of directives to guide future policies according to its founding values. SUS' principles of operation include (i) universality (every citizen is entitled to use the system irrespective of personal income, occupational status, or participation in private schemes), (ii) completeness (it provides services in all levels of care, from simple to complex procedures), (iii) equality (no form of discrimination or privilege in access to services is allowed), and (iv) community participation (decision-making processes involve different social groups, including the civil society). The legislation also provides that SUS services should be entirely free at the point of delivery (Brazil, 1990a). Such principles bring the model followed by Brazil closer to those of some wealthy nations and set it apart from the systems of most other Latin American countries.

SUS has a decentralized management structure. The three levels of government (federal, state, and local governments) are jointly responsible for financing and running the system. The federal government, via the Ministry of Health, is in charge of planning, coordinating, regulating, and overseeing the SUS programs, actions, and services. State governments, more precisely the

---

7 This was an intellectual and political movement created in the 1970s bringing together university professors, medical students, health professionals, trade unionists, left-wing party activists, and other activist groups. The "sanitarists" were highly critical of the system in place and campaigned for a transformation in the country's health system, with the creation of a truly unified and universal scheme. The sanitary reform movement represented a first important step for the creation of SUS: they found space to advance their ideas during the constitutional debates of the late 1980s, countering movements in defense of a privatized system.

State Health Secretariats under their control, are tasked with organizing and articulating sus actions and services across the municipalities within their territory. Municipal governments, through their Municipal Health Secretariats, are responsible for executing policies and delivering services. Higher levels of government may participate in service provision, especially when these involve more complex levels of care.

The system's financing also depends on the three levels of government. The federal government, each state, and each municipality allocate a predefined amount of revenues to health spending each year. Each level of government allocates the revenues earmarked for health spending into its respective Fund – the National Health Fund in the case of the federal government, and the State or Municipal Health Secretariat's Fund in the case of each state and municipality. This amount is defined throughout the annual budgetary process. The Executive branch of each government decides this amount in advance, during the elaboration of the annual budgetary law for the following year. This value is set taking into account government plans and the volume of public revenues expected for the following year. The predefined value for public health spending is approved by the Legislative and can be adjusted over the course of the given year. Once these are expected disbursements, it is often the case that the volume of resources effectively allocated to the health system is smaller than the amount of public health spending originally announced by the government.

Having a clear view of how revenues circulate within the system is crucial for understanding the mechanisms through which these circuits can be rewired and connected to the financial sector. Drawing from the review provided so far, it is possible to trace the key stages of sus financing circuits (Figure 4.1). They start with the population, companies, and other organizations, who pay taxes and contributions to the federal, state, and municipal governments. The federal government allocates its share of funds to the Ministry of Health, which allocates them to the National Health Fund. This represents most of what is considered to come from the Social Security budget (controlled by the federal government). In the case of the federal and state governments, a significant part of health spending does not come in the form of direct payments to health actions and services, but as mandatory and voluntary transfers to the lower levels of administration. The volume of transfers received by each government depends on several factors such as the size of the population and the enrollment in national or state health programs.

States and municipalities, for their part, allocate revenues to their respective Health Secretariats, which places them in the Health Funds. In the case of states, part of their spending consists of transfers to the municipalities within their jurisdiction. The Health Ministry and Secretariats forward funds to public and private entities that work for SUS. These include hospitals, public health units, research institutes, and other parts of the public administration, to cite a few. SUS' funds cover current and capital expenditures, including wages, inputs (materials, equipment, drugs), and infrastructure investment. SUS also provides financial support to other entities responsible for actions such as research and teaching activities, sanitary surveillance, and community health programs.

Over the 2010s, the federal and subnational governments were responsible for around half of SUS' annual revenues each. The sources of these revenues vary. The share from the federal government comes mostly from the Social Security Budget which is almost entirely made of social contributions. State and municipal governments, in turn, provide funds from their Fiscal Budgets, based on tax revenues and transfers from the upper levels of government. There is also a marginal share of funds from complementary sources, such as part of the proceeds from a mandatory fee charged by the federal government on all vehicle owners.

SUS follows what is typically identified as the "national health service" model (Chapter 2). This means that the government is directly responsible for service provision, in this case through public or contracted private providers. The system offers the largest share of health facilities and beds in the country, coming from public and private nonprofit institutions working for the system. According to the Brazilian Federation of Hospitals (FBH, 2019), the public and the non-profit sector together accounted for 68% of hospitals in the country in 2017 (35% in the public and 28% in the non-profit sector).

The interaction between SUS and the private health sector follows a "duplicate" logic (OECD, 2004), meaning that they offer the same services in a parallel fashion. Private health actors are free to operate in the country, and private insurance can be purchased directly or accessed as part of a working contract. Individuals with private health insurance continue enjoying full access to the public system. During the last decade, the share of the population with access to private health insurance has varied between a quarter and a fifth of the total population. They accounted for 47 million in 2018, out of a population of 208 million people (IBGE, 2020a; ANS, 2019a). The number of private insurance beneficiaries turned Brazil into the second largest market of private voluntary health insurance in the world by the mid-2010s, only behind the United States (Deloitte, 2014). Beneficiaries are almost equally distributed across for- and not-for-profit insurance companies (ANS, 2019a).

These figures suggest that the share of the population without private insurance, which corresponds to more than 150 million people, depends entirely

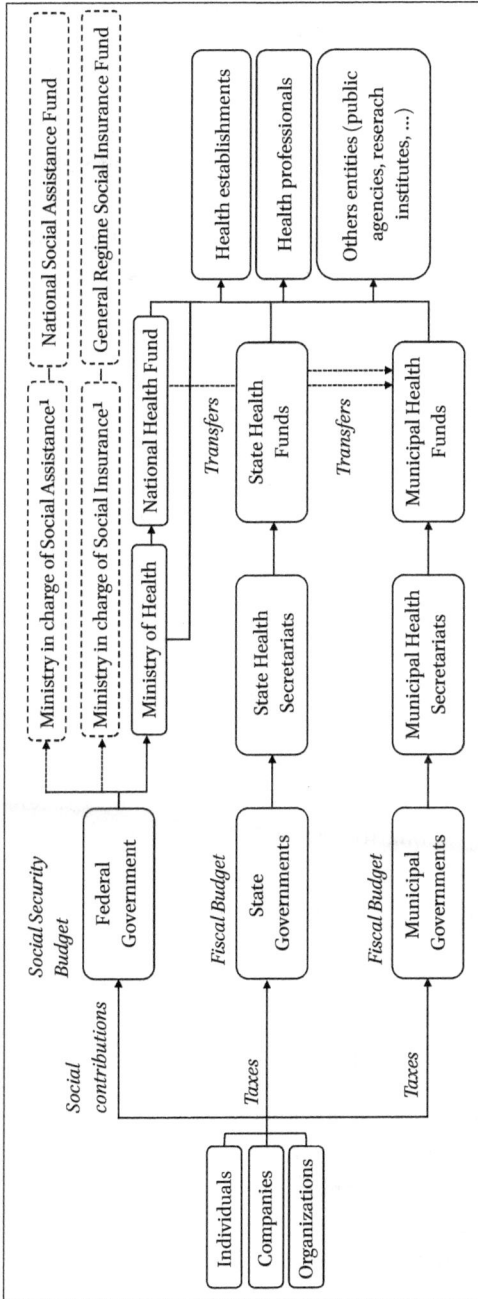

FIGURE 4.1 Brazil, public health system (SUS), simplified scheme of financial flows
SOURCE: AUTHOR'S ELABORATION. [1] THERE HAVE BEEN SEVERAL CHANGES IN THE NAME OF THESE MINISTRIES OVER TIME

on the public system or out-of-pocket payments. Considering the high levels of poverty and inequality in the country, it is thus safe to say that SUS represents the primary or only gateway to health services for the majority of the population.

In practice, the public and the private spheres are interdependent, with one often filling the other's gaps. On the one hand, SUS covers private sector deficiencies in areas in which the latter does not have the capacity or interest to operate. Data on the use of SUS services by privately insured individuals suggest that they resort to the system when needing to access activities of high costs and risks (ANS, 2019b, 2018). This suggests that individuals who are insured or pay for private services still use the public network when their insurance coverage or capacity of payment is insufficient to access services through the market. Moreover, the entire population relies on SUS in some areas that are almost exclusively covered by the latter, such as vaccination, mobile emergency care, and actions of health surveillance and disease control (Bahia and Scheffer, 2018; Paim et al., 2011; Sestelo, 2017a). On the other hand, the private sector has large participation both inside and outside SUS structures. Inside SUS, private entities offer infrastructure and services on behalf of the public system. The private institutions that work for SUS remain private, autonomous, and are paid directly by the latter.

1.3   *The Quest to Consolidate Universal Health Care: Successes and Drawbacks*

In Brazil, the universal right to health care was not achieved gradually, but through a paradigm shift in 1988. Therefore, the creation of SUS was only the beginning of the path toward universalization: making access to health care universal in practice required expanding the system's network to reach the entire population and provide services at all levels of care. Such goals could not be met without structural policy shifts in provision and financing.

The most significant shifts in SUS' structures came in the 2000s. From the side of provision, the government implemented several measures to consolidate and expand SUS programs, actions, services, and infrastructure. The expansion of primary care was the main vector of change. Aside from basic services, SUS also invested in complex levels of care. By the mid-2010s, the system enjoyed international recognition in several areas such as vaccination programs, generic drugs, HIV treatments, and organ transplants. The creation and expansion of the PHS in Brazil brought significant improvements to population health (Bhalotra et al., 2019; Souza et al., 2019; UNICEF, 2019). Life expectancy increased by almost ten years between the early 1990s and the late 2010s (IBGE, 2020a).

Notwithstanding these advances, there were clear privatization tendencies inside SUS. This can be seen in the progressive delegation of public infrastructure construction and management to private organizations, the outsourcing of medical and ancillary services to private providers, and the authorization of private practice in public establishments, to cite a few. The increased participation of the private sector in public structures has been criticized in light of evidence that this contributes to deteriorating working conditions, increases selectivity in the services offered to the public, and creates high compensations for managers based on public revenues, among others (Andreazzi and Bravo, 2014; Bahia and Scheffer, 2018; Lima, 2018; Mendes and Funcia, 2016; Morais et al., 2018).

In the years immediately after the creation of SUS, it was clear that the unstable and insufficient level of revenues allocated to the system represented one of the main obstacles to the consolidation of universal health care in Brazil. Therefore, there were also constitutional reforms targeting financing, seeking to overcome the lack of resources to finance service provision. Although the 1988 Constitution determined that 30% of the Social Security budget should be allocated to the health branch, the federal government never complied with this rule. Instead, it opted for the creation of different financing rules to strengthen the system's financial soundness.

The first type of measures to address SUS funding gaps came still in the mid-1990s, with the introduction of additional sources of revenues for the system. The most significant one was a contribution on financial transactions, the Provisional Contribution on Financial Transactions (CPMF). This contribution was instituted in 1996 and extinguished in 2007, followed by failed attempts to recreate it. A second important revenue source created in 2013 came through the binding of 25% of oil royalty proceeds to health spending.[8] Nevertheless, these incremental measures were insufficient to bring a significant increase in the volume of resources allocated to SUS (Piola et al., 2000; Souza et al., 2019).

The second type of reform in SUS' financing, starting in the 2000s, came from the expenditure side. It was centered on the approval of "spending floors" – a minimum amount that governments were obliged to spend on health each year. These rules were introduced in 2000 and reinforced in 2012 (Brazil, 2012, 2000). In the case of the federal government, the mandatory spending floor was tied to economic growth: the government should spend at least as much on health as it did the year before, plus a percentage equal to

8 Oil royalties are payments made by companies to the State for the right to oil exploration, drilling, and production.

the GDP variation. For subnational governments, expenditures were pegged to fiscal revenues: states and municipalities should spend at least 15% and 12% of their fiscal revenues, respectively. In 2015, the parameter for the federal government was modified and tied to the volume of current revenues (Brazil, 2015a). These rules had a positive and significant effect on public health spending. However, they were partially repealed in 2016. This year, the government completely reversed the logic of spending floors and turned them into ceilings, defining a *maximum* instead of a *minimum* level of federal health expenditures (Brazil, 2016a).[9]

A final set of policies carried out during the thirty years of SUS's existence with a direct impact on its financing are tax exemptions. Although tax exemptions are a common practice in most countries, the particularities of tax incentives in Brazil make these measures particularly harmful to public health financing. The range of activities to which the government grants tax waivers, and the proportion of the public budget they absorb, are far greater in Brazil than in other countries with universal health systems. For example, today, national legislation allows individuals and companies to deduct virtually any spending on private health services and insurance plans from their taxable income. Individuals can deduct expenditures with insurance premiums, consultations, exams, and hospital treatments (even aesthetic surgeries), while companies enjoy large tax breaks on the payment of private insurance premiums to employees. Pharmaceutical companies and philanthropic hospitals also receive massive tax exemptions (Nugem et al., 2019; Ocké-Reis, 2018).

Most importantly, the largest share of tax exemptions is granted through the waiver of social contributions, the chief source of revenues for the Social Security budget. According to estimates from the Federal Revenue Service, between 2010 and 2018, the value of tax exemptions granted by the federal government averaged 4.2% of the GDP per year; more than half of this amount – 52%, on average – came from waivers of Social Security contributions (Receita Federal, 2009–2017). Put otherwise, these benefits are provided by forgoing revenues that would otherwise go to SUS and other areas of social security. Only a marginal share is compensated by the State to avoid direct losses in these areas (ANFIP, 2019, 2014; Gentil, 2019; Ocké-Reis, 2018; Salvador, 2015).[10]

---

9   This latter policy shift will be discussed later in this chapter due to its links with government strategies that promote financial accumulation.

10   Own calculations based on real values of 2018 adjusted for inflation according to the Consumer Price Index (IPCA). Considers tax exemptions to all activities (in health and other sectors). The average exchange rate of December 2018 was of 4.3 Brazilian reais per euro. Studies estimating the share withdrawn from the Social Security budget use

1.4   The Public Health System Today

The Brazilian PHS has never counted on a volume of funding comparable to that of wealthy countries (Table 4.1). The share of public spending in total health spending is close to that of the United States, known for its highly privatized system. It is almost half of the amount spent in France and England, core countries with universal health systems. Public health spending in Brazil is also far below those of wealthy countries in terms of GDP. Moreover, the gap in *per capita* health spending is significantly wide, with public spending accounting for approximately half of the world average and one-tenth of the other selected countries. The private health sector has experienced significant growth over the last two decades, much supported by the lack of sufficient spending in SUS and incentives from the federal government. This can be seen by the fact that total health spending, accounting for public and private sources, is relatively high in terms of the GDP, above the world average and similar to that of European countries.

TABLE 4.1   Brazil and selected countries, total and public health spending, 2016

	Public spending (% of total spending)	Health spending (% GDP)		Per capita health-spending (USD)	
		Public	Total	Public	Total
Brazil	43	4	9.2	344	801
France	73	8.4	11.5	3,100	4,268
United Kingdom	80	7.9	9.9	3,268	4,066
United States	50	8.6	17	4,977	9,878
World average	52	3.5	6.6	686	1,028

SOURCE: WHO (2020). OWN ELABORATION
Per capita spending in current values. The share of public spending in total spending may vary depending on the selected indicator for reasons of methodology and rounding. Public spending: Domestic General Government Health Expenditure

different methodologies but reach similar conclusions (ANFIP, 2019; Cordilha, 2015; Ocké-Reis, 2018).

The restrictions on public spending translate into difficulties for consolidating the universal system. As with the volume of resources, the public system has never been able to reach results like those countries with consolidated public systems. The WHO's 2000 ranking mentioned in the previous chapter placed Brazil in 125th place out of 191 countries in terms of the overall quality of the national health system (WHO, 2000). In 2016, a new classification ranked the country in 96th place among 195 nations (Fullman et al., 2018). Life expectancy indicators, which are heavily influenced by the quality of access to health care, also remain below other countries with universal systems (WHO, 2020). Criticism is often directed at the quantity and quality of the services provided.

From another angle, SUS' supporters argue that the system should be considered highly efficient given the disparity between the vast scope of services it offers and the small amount of money it receives. In 2016, public per capita spending in Brazil was approximately US\$344 per year (Table 4.1), or 0.9 cents per day; as reminded by Funcia (2019), this value is far inferior to both the revenues received by other universal systems and the value that private companies would consider economically feasible if they were to provide the same scale and scope of services offered by SUS.

1.5   *SUS Accounts in Perspective*

In light of the complexity of SUS' financing structure, it is worth unpacking how different actors contribute *de facto* to the system (i.e., who provides funds, how, and how much), the volume of money that entered the system over time, and where it was spent. This information will help to better describe the mechanisms by which financial capital gained participation and influence within the system in the following section.

When looking at the weight of SUS in the Social Security budget, three trends stand out (Table 4.2). First, one can see that a minor share of the Social Security budget goes to the public health system. This can be observed in the share of the Social Security budget granted to the Ministry of Health, responsible for SUS at the federal level. The expenditures from the Ministry of Health represented a relatively low and stable share of total Social Security expenditures during the period under analysis, at around 15%. Since the federal government controls this budget, the share of SUS financing coming from Social Security may serve as a proxy for the amount of financing provided by this government.[11] Second, the expenditures in health increased in absolute terms

---

11   The share coming from the federal budget can vary according to the methodology to account for public health spending, although observed trends usually point to similar directions. The next tables offer an alternative view of federal health spending.

TABLE 4.2 Brazil, Social Security budget, 2005–2018, billions of reais of 2018 and % of the GDP

	2005	2006	2007	2008	2009	2010	2011	2012	2013	2014	2015	2016	2017	2018
Billions of reais of 2018														
Revenues (R)	584	610	667	663	664	735	793	857	891	888	787	770	813	822
Social contributions	559	585	640	636	638	709	765	826	870	861	760	739	785	793
Entities' own revenues	23	22	23	24	24	23	25	28	19	24	24	30	26	27
Transfers from Fiscal Budget[a]	2	2	3	3	2	2	3	3	2	2	3	2	2	2
Expenditures (E)	438	492	535	546	607	643	676	729	772	798	780	829	872	875
Pension benefits	295	325	349	353	382	409	424	452	482	499	500	544	581	587
Ministry of Health[b]	70	78	85	87	97	98	107	113	114	118	116	115	121	120
Others[c]	225	246	264	265	284	311	317	339	368	381	384	429	459	467
Balance (R – E)	146	118	132	116	57	92	117	127	119	90	6	-58	-59	-54
% GDP														
Revenues (R)	13.3	12.9	13.0	12.1	11.7	11.8	12.0	12.5	12.4	12.1	11.5	11.5	11.9	12.0
Social contributions	12.8	12.4	12.5	11.6	11.3	11.4	11.6	12.0	12.1	11.8	11.1	11.0	11.5	11.6
Entities' own revenues	0.5	0.5	0.5	0.4	0.4	0.4	0.4	0.4	0.3	0.3	0.4	0.4	0.4	0.4
Transfers from Fiscal Budget	0.1	0.1	0.1	0.1	0.0	0.0	0.0	0.0	0.0	0.0	0.0	0.0	0.0	0.0
Expenditures (E)	10.0	10.4	10.5	9.9	10.7	10.3	10.3	10.6	10.7	10.9	11.4	12.3	12.8	12.8
Pension benefits	6.7	6.9	6.8	6.4	6.8	6.6	6.4	6.6	6.7	6.8	7.3	8.1	8.5	8.6
Ministry of Health	1.6	1.7	1.7	1.6	1.7	1.6	1.6	1.6	1.6	1.6	1.7	1.7	1.8	1.8
Others	1.7	1.9	2.0	1.9	2.3	2.2	2.2	2.4	2.5	2.5	2.4	2.5	2.5	2.5
Balance (R – E)	3.3	2.5	2.6	2.1	1.0	1.5	1.8	1.9	1.7	1.2	0.1	-0.9	-0.9	-0.8
Min. of Health (% total expenditures)	16	16	16	16	16	15	16	15	15	15	15	14	14	14

SOURCE: AUTHOR'S ELABORATION BASED ON ANFIP (2019)

Real values of 2018 adjusted for inflation according to the Consumer Price Index (IPCA). Average exchange rate of Dec. 2018: 4.3 Reais/Euro. See Lavinas (2017) for an earlier version of this table

a   Counterparts from the fiscal budget for pension-related payments

b   Includes costs with active personnel and other operational and investment expenses

c   Assistance benefits, direct expenditures from Ministries, and others

but remained relatively stable in terms of GDP. Third, as commented earlier, Social Security revenues are almost entirely drawn from social contributions, accounting for more than 95% of total revenues.

There are financial imbalances in the Social Security system (negative financial results, known as "deficits"). The causes of these deficits are a highly debated topic, including for methodological reasons (see Box 4.1). Whether real or artificially created, it is commonly agreed that the deficits in Social Security are mainly caused by the insurance branch (the pension system), which has by far the greatest weight in the Social Security budget. As the health branch has relatively low participation in the budget, it has little influence on the system's apparent deficits. In this way, when referring to the financial challenges faced by the Brazilian health system, the notion of "underfunding" (the insufficient allocation of resources to fund all the actions necessary for adequate coverage) is far more widespread than that of "deficit" (a situation of not receiving sufficient resources to cover already incurred expenditures).[12]

BOX 4.1 **Methodologies to Compute the Social Security Budget in Brazil**

There are two competing methods to compute the Social Security budget in Brazil. The main difference between these methods lies in the items of revenues and expenditures that are considered part of the Social Security budget. This is important because it leads to significantly different results at the end of the fiscal year, including if Social Security presents a "deficit" or not.

The first methodology is the one used by the National Association of Fiscal Auditors of Brazil's Federal Internal Revenue Service (ANFIP). It computes the sources of revenues and expenditures that the 1988 Constitution defined as pertaining to the Social Security budget.

The second methodology is the one adopted by the National Treasury Secretariat (STN) and followed by the government. It computes a number of items that are not part of the Social Security Budget as provided for in the Constitution. Most importantly, the STN considers the revenues and expenditures of the pension system for federal servants and the military, which is not part of Social Security and is historically in deficit. It also discounts revenues from social contributions that are supposed to go to the Social Security system but are redirected to the federal government's fiscal budget through an accounting maneuver (called the "Unbinding of Union Revenues").

---

12   In this sense, it is different from the French case, where reforms are aimed at ending the supposed "deficit" of Assurance Maladie.

Following ANFIP's methodology, the Social Security budget presents surpluses until 2014. The deficits from 2016 onwards are mostly explained by the decrease in revenues. Using the STN's methodology, in turn, the deficits appear at least since 1995, and are mostly attributed to growing expenditures.

For further details on these different methodologies, see ANFIP (2019). For a critical discussion, see Gentil (2019).

The difference between decision-making processes for health and pension expenditures can contribute to explaining why the latter has a larger weight in this budget. In Brazil, health spending is discretionary, depending on the government's decision on how much to spend with in-kind provision. As previously explained, the only requirement for federal health spending was a minimum threshold (replaced by a maximum threshold after 2016). Pension spending, in contrast, is relatively automatic, as it consists of mandatory payments to individuals defined by existing contractual arrangements. In a context where the different areas of Social Security are competing for resources, pensions and related benefits tend to receive priority in resource allocation.

The next set of data moves the analysis from the federal to the national level, presenting the total volume of public health spending and how each sphere (federal government, states, and municipalities) has contributed to it (Table 4.3).[13] The series shows that public health spending grew continuously until 2014 and started declining from then on, triggered by the beginning of a sharp economic downturn. Most of the expansion came from subnational governments, especially municipalities, whose contribution more than doubled in this period. In terms of GDP, however, public health spending remained almost stable, increasing by about one percentage point in two decades, once again almost exclusively due to the greater contribution from subnational spheres. The federal government continued to be responsible for the largest share of public health spending, but this participation diminished significantly to the detriment of subnational governments.

---

13   The official indicator to assess public health spending at the national level is the value of expenditures on "Public Health Actions and Services" (*Ações e Serviços Públicos de Saúde* – ASPS). It includes expenditures with universal health care, epidemiological and sanitary surveillance, salaries, training, scientific and technological development, production, acquisition and distribution of inputs, basic sanitation, disease control, infrastructure spending, and administrative costs. This is not the official indicator used in Social Security accounts, which explains the differences between the values of federal expenditures in Table 4.2 and Table 4.3.

TABLE 4.3 Brazil, expenditures on public health actions and services (ASPS), 1980, 1990, 2005–2017, billions of reais of 2018, % of GDP, and % in total spending

	1980	1990	1995	2005	2006	2007	2008	2009	2010	2011	2012	2013	2014	2015	2016	2017
Billions of reais of 2018																
Total	n.a.	n.a.	n.d.	156	171	182	198	212	223	241	252	263	274	267	266	277
Federal Govt.	n.a.	n.a.	n.d.	75	80	83	86	99	100	109	114	112	116	115	114	120
States Govts.	n.a.	n.a.	n.d.	40	45	49	55	55	60	63	64	70	73	69	68	71
Mun. Govts.	n.a.	n.a.	n.d	41	46	50	57	59	63	69	74	81	85	83	84	86
% GDP																
Total	n.a.	n.a.	3.0	3.6	3.6	3.6	3.6	3.8	3.6	3.7	3.7	3.7	3.8	3.9	4.0	4.1
Federal Govt.	n.a.	n.a.	1.88	1.7	1.7	1.6	1.6	1.8	1.6	1.7	1.7	1.6	1.6	1.7	1.7	1.8
States Govts.	n.a.	n.a.	0.54	0.9	1.0	1.0	1.0	1.0	1.0	1.0	0.9	1.0	1.0	1.0	1.0	1.0
Mun. Govts.	n.a.	n.a.	0.57	0.9	1.0	1.0	1.1	1.0	1.0	1.1	1.1	1.1	1.2	1.2	1.3	1.3
% Total spending																
Federal Govt.	75	74	63	48	47	46	43	47	45	45	45	43	42	43	43	43
States Govts.	18	14	18	26	26	27	28	26	27	26	25	27	27	26	26	26
Mun. Govts.	7	12	19	26	27	27	29	28	28	29	29	31	31	31	32	31

SOURCE: AUTHOR'S ELABORATION
Data for health spending extracted from Mendes (2019) for 1980–1995 and Piola et al. (2018) for 2005–2017. GDP data: IBGE. Real values of 2018 adjusted for inflation according to the Consumer Price Index (IPCA). Average exchange rate of Dec. 2018: 4.3 Reais/Euro. Mun: municipal. Govts: governments. N.a.: not available. Eventual differences between total and partial values are due to rounding

As a general rule, most SUS expenditures are concentrated in activities of higher risks, costs, and technological complexity, represented by hospital and outpatient care. They absorb almost half of federal and municipal disbursements (Table 4.4). Still, there is a marked difference between federal and local spending patterns. While the federal government's participation is diversified, subnational governments, most notably municipalities, allocate most of their funds to primary care and preventive actions.

TABLE 4.4   Health expenditures by subfunction, federal and local governments, 2000, 2005, 2010–2017, % total spending

	2000	2005	2010	2011	2012	2013	2014	2015	2016	2017
Federal Government (Ministry of Health)										
Primary Care	32	21	17	18	18	18	20	19	19	18
Hospital and Outpatient Care	58	69	51	50	49	47	47	47	45	45
Prophylactic/ Therapeutic Support			10	10	11	12	11	13	13	12
Sanitary Surveillance	10	10	0	0	0	0	0	0	0	0
Epidemiological Surveillance		5	5	5	5	5	5	5	6	6
Other Subfunctions			18	17	17	18	17	15	16	18
Total	*100*	*100*	*100*	*100*	*100*	*100*	*100*	*100*	*100*	*100*
Local Governments (Municipalities)										
Primary Care	44.4	48.9	50.1	48.9	48.7	48.9	45.8	45.3	45.4	45.4
Hospital and Outpatient Care	49.2	47.3	44.8	46.0	46.5	46.6	48.9	49.3	48.9	49.3
Prophylactic/ Therapeutic Support	1.4	1.2	2.2	2.2	2.0	1.9	2.2	2.2	2.1	2.2
Sanitary Surveillance	1.1	0.8	0.9	0.9	0.9	0.9	1.1	1.1	1.2	1.1
Epidemiological Surveillance	1.7	1.7	1.9	1.9	1.9	1.7	2.0	2.0	2.1	2.0
Other Subfunctions	2.3	0.1	0.1	0.1	0.1	0.0	0.1	0.1	0.3	0.1
Total	*100*	*100*	*100*	*100*	*100*	*100*	*100*	*100*	*100*	*100*

SOURCE: AUTHOR'S ELABORATION
For the federal government, data from Junior and Mendes (2015) for 2000–2005 and Ministério da Saúde (2019) for 2010–2018. For municipal governments, SIOPS (2019). Settled expenditures. There were significant changes in the way spending was accounted for between the two periods (2000–2005 and 2010–2017), therefore direct comparisons should be taken with caution

TABLE 4.5   Brazil, health spending, public and private, 2000–2017, % in total health spending

	2000	2005	2010	2011	2012	2013	2014	2015	2016	2017
Public	42%	42%	45%	44%	43%	45%	44%	43%	43%	42%
Private	58%	58%	55%	55%	57%	55%	56%	57%	57%	58%
Health Insurance	20%	21%	24%	25%	26%	26%	26%	27%	28%	29%
Out-of-pocket	37%	36%	29%	29%	30%	28%	28%	28%	27%	27%
Total	100%	100%	100%	100%	100%	100%	100%	100%	100%	100%

SOURCE: AUTHOR'S ELABORATION BASED ON WHO (2020)

Last, the challenges and contradictions of public health financing in Brazil become clear when comparing the share of national health care spending coming from the public and private sectors (Table 4.5). Brazil stands out as the only country in the world with a universal health system where private spending outstrips public spending. The weight of each segment remained stable over the past years, averaging 43% of total health spending financed by the public and 57% by the private sector. The private share includes the participation of both insurance companies and individuals paying directly for services ("out-of-pocket" payments). Brazil bears yet another particularity compared with the pattern usually observed in countries with universal systems: the largest share of private spending derives from direct payments (out-of-pocket) rather than cost-sharing mechanisms (insurance), averaging 30% and 25% of total spending, respectively. The combination of private above public spending and direct over socialized cost-coverage suggests a highly inequitable structure of access to health care in the country.

2   Mechanisms of Financialization

The process of financialization has influenced SUS' trajectory from the 1990s onward. As discussed in Chapter 1, this decade marked a new stage in the financialization of the Brazilian economy. It was a time when the country adopted extremely high interest rates to counter inflation, leading to the accelerated accumulation of interest-bearing capital through public debt assets and credit expansion. It is possible to bridge these developments in the domestic economy with changes taking place inside the Brazilian PHS. This section shows how SUS was subjected to policies that tailored the system's financing to ensure the continuation of this macroeconomic regime. It also discusses how such policies ended up transforming SUS into a vehicle for financial accumulation.

I examine how financialization influenced the trajectory of the system's financing in the long run by describing the creation of permanent financial expropriation schemes via interest payments to investors fed by public revenues, including from SUS. The second part deals with short-term financing, more specifically how public bodies started to place the system's revenues in short-term financial investments. Moving to hospital financing, I address the expansion of bank credit for hospitals backed up by public health transfers.

2.1 Public Health Revenues Feeding Financial Accumulation: Policies at the Federal Level

The first and most significant way in which financialization has steered SUS' trajectory was through the channel of monetary policy, more precisely through the adoption of an inflation-targeting regime in Brazil in 1999. As explained in the introduction and Chapter 1, inflation targeting has been considered a "financialized policy", meaning a policy that contributes to financialization, as it prioritizes the protection of financial investments and wealth over other goals that would be more beneficial to the population at large. This is evident in the Brazilian case. The 1999 monetary policy framework led to two key developments in the country: one, permanently high real interest rates to help reach the inflation targets; two, specific fiscal and exchange rate policies to sustain this regime. The fiscal policy agenda focused on creating government budget surpluses to service the public debt. As will be discussed, the government considered that these surpluses were critical for price stability. SUS was incorporated into this process as the government appropriated its revenues to form budget surpluses. In other words, the government saved and reallocated funds from SUS so it could form a surplus addressed to public debt investors. Connecting these dots, one can say that the inflation-targeting regime led to a macroeconomic regime that constrained SUS funding, while the revenues that could potentially go to the system were used to pay financial rents.

The tendency of channeling public funds to the financial sector to the detriment of investing in social provision is not exclusive to Brazil, having been considered a stylized fact of financialized capitalism. Yet, Brazil stands out in this regard due to the rigidity of the macroeconomic policy rules and the implications they have on the national PHS, which do not seem to find parallels with other countries providing universal health care.

There is extensive literature on the relations between the dominance of financial capital in contemporary capitalism and the challenges faced by SUS (e.g., Lavinas, 2017; Mendes and Funcia, 2016; Mendes and Marques, 2009;

Mendes, 2012; Paiva and Lima, 2014; Salvador, 2017; Sestelo et al., 2017). However, as a general rule, the focus of the analysis tends to lie on rules that withdraw resources from the Social Security budget to pay for financial expenditures. While acknowledging the contributions provided by this body of work, the relatively new approach to State financialization, which informs the present research, can shed greater light on the links between financialization and SUS. This approach allows us to widen the scope of analysis in several ways: first, it invites us to examine how this process affects not only the Social Security budget but also the fiscal budget of both the federal and subnational governments. The research on the links between financialization and SUS financing at the subnational level, in particular, has been quite scarce. Second, the State financialization framework allows us to go beyond the perspective of fiscal policy and understand how monetary policies have played a role in the volume of revenues allocated to public health care in the context of financialization. Monetary policy plays a particularly important role in explaining the financialization of the PHS in the Brazilian case.

2.1.1   The 1999 Monetary Policy Regime and Its Associated Fiscal Policy Framework

While it is not possible to pinpoint a single cause for the high inflation rate recorded in Brazil in the 1990s, some events that can help to explain this phenomenon include the international shocks of the 1970s (the 1973 oil crisis and the 1979 United States interest rate hike) and the domestic debt crisis in the 1980s, which came much as a consequence of such shocks. After a series of unsuccessful attempts to control two-digit monthly inflation rates during most of the 1980s and early 1990s, the federal government managed to stabilize the economy in 1994 through a program named the "Real Plan" (Bastos, 2001; Bresser-Pereira, 2010; Brito, 2021).

The Real plan combined far-reaching reforms in three dimensions: monetary, fiscal, and exchange rate policy. It implemented a new currency (the Brazilian Real) and a fiscal adjustment program seeking to eliminate the government's budget deficit, deemed one of the root causes of inflation. The program promoted a major overhaul of the public administration, inducing tax reforms, spending cuts, and the privatization of public companies. In the realm of exchange rate policy, the stabilization plan imposed an overvalued currency, putting downward pressure on domestic prices. This was, in practice, the main policy that allowed for inflation control, although at a major cost for the domestic industry (Iahn and Missio, 2009; Oreiro, 2015; Serrano and Summa, 2011) The immediate years following the onset of the stabilization plan saw significant increases in interest rates to attract foreign capital and maintain the artificially overvalued currency. The period also saw the rise of public debt, trade deficits, and external volatility. In the second half of the decade, the slowdown of domestic growth and financial crises in other countries reached this already fragile economy, leading to balance of payments crises and speculative attacks against the Brazilian currency. The external crisis led Brazil to turn to the IMF in 1998 (Evangelista, 2017; Iahn and Missio, 2009; Ruckert and Borsatto, 1999).

In the context of structural reforms following the IMF agreement, the federal government instituted a macroeconomic policy framework in 1999 known as the "Macroeconomic Tripod".[14] The main goals of this framework were to control the rise of inflation and public debt. It was again based on the government's concerted action in monetary, fiscal, and exchange rate policy, expanding and consolidating some of the practices initiated by the Real plan. Most importantly, the government instituted an inflation-targeting regime this year, accompanied by budget rules that would serve to sustain it. The decisions on public spending, including on health care, became subjected to the need to abide by such rules.

The Tripod's theoretical foundations rested on the idea that price stability was the ultimate objective of monetary policy. It was based on the simultaneous pursuit of inflation targets in the monetary policy domain, budget surplus targets in the fiscal policy domain, and a floating exchange rate regime in the foreign exchange domain. The chief instrument to control inflation was the setting of the basic interest rate by the Central Bank, the "Selic", kept at permanently high levels. The rise in the basic interest rate served to control aggregate demand, but, most importantly, attract foreign capital. This maintained an overvalued exchange rate, curbing the rise of inflation. Although the Tripod's rules have been partially loosened in the following decades, the combination of inflation targets, budget targets, and a floating (now administered) exchange rate remained in place (Bresser-Pereira et al., 2020; Oreiro, 2015; Serrano and Summa, 2011).

Several studies show that the Brazilian interest rates are one of the highest in the world (Attilio, 2020; Bresser-Pereira et al., 2020; Lavinas, 2016; Reis, 2018; Weisbrot et al., 2017). Bresser et al. (*op. cit.*) study ten emerging countries with similar country risk levels between 2010 and 2014 and find that Brazil was home to the highest real short-term interest rate of the sample. Weisbrot et al.

---

14   Oreiro (2015) defines a macroeconomic policy framework as the set of goals, targets, and instruments of monetary, fiscal, and exchange rate policies, as well as the institutional framework within which they are executed.

(*op. cit.*) point out that Brazil had the fourth-highest interest burden in the world out of 183 countries during a similar period. Also important, the level of basic interest rates dictates the direction of the remaining interest rates in the country. According to Lavinas (*op. cit.*), in early 2016, the nominal interest rate for personal loans and consumer credit in Brazil reached 92% and 142% per year, respectively. The author contrasts these rates with those of advanced countries when they experienced consumer credit *booms* during the 20th century, which stood below 20%.

Table 4.6 offers a panorama of the evolution of the basic interest rate in Brazil since the Real Plan. It also includes data for inflation to indicate the interest rate's evolution in real terms. The table reveals that the interest rate fluctuated but remained remarkably high in both nominal and real terms. In the second half of the 1990s (1996–1999), they stood at 27% per year on average, against a 6.3% rate of inflation. From 2000 to 2018, interest and inflation rates were 13.5% and 6.4%, respectively.

TABLE 4.6   Brazil, interest and inflation rates, 1996–2018, % per year

	Basic interest rate (Selic)	Inflation (IPCA)		Basic interest rate (Selic)	Inflation (IPCA)
1996	27.5	9.6	2009	10.0	4.3
1997	25.2	5.2	2010	9.8	5.9
1998	29.3	1.7	2011	11.7	6.5
1999	26.1	8.9	2012	8.5	5.8
2000	17.6	6.0	2013	8.2	5.9
2001	17.5	7.7	2014	10.9	6.4
2002	19.1	12.5	2015	13.4	10.7
2003	23.3	9.3	2016	14.1	6.3
2004	16.2	7.6	2017	10.1	3.0
2005	19.1	5.7	2018	6.5	3.8
2006	15.3	3.1			
2007	12.0	4.5			
2008	12.4	5.9			

SOURCE: AUTHOR'S ELABORATION BASED ON BANCO CENTRAL (2020B) AND IBGE. SELIC: AVERAGE ANNUALIZED RATE 252-DAYS BASE. IPCA: BROAD CONSUMER PRICE INDEX

Against the same background, the federal government praised budget surpluses as the solution to prevent the rise of the public debt and its monetiza-
tion in the long run, seen as a threat to price stabilization. The government
expressed its commitment to controlling and servicing the public debt by
defining budget surplus targets. These budget surpluses refer, more specifically,
to "primary" surpluses. This seemingly unimportant specification has major
implications for the PHS and its incorporation into processes of financial accumulation: in Brazilian public accounting, primary surpluses mean the difference between all public revenues and expenditures, except for financial ones
(those related to the public debt). Reaching primary surpluses implies that the
government spends less than it earns with ordinary public activities within
a year, which allows it to save revenues for financial expenditures – namely
amortization and interest payments on the public debt.[15] The adoption of primary budget targets was already part of the adjustment plans of the mid-1990s,
but it was formally instituted as a permanent practice in 1999 in the context of
the inflation-targeting regime.

The centrality of the budget targets in the "macroeconomic tripod", as well
as the role of spending cuts in sectors of social provision to achieve the latter,
were openly acknowledged in the government's "letter of intent" addressed to
the IMF in 1998 (Brazil, 1998). This evidences how public debt, and the demands
of creditors and international financial institutions, played an important role
in putting this arrangement in place in Brazil.

The Brazilian government defines primary surpluses targets for the following years and promotes the necessary policy adjustments to reach them. The
primary surplus targets have been high. Between 1998 to 2010, they were set
at 3% of the GDP, on average (Evangelista, 2017). From 2011 onwards, the targets were set in nominal values only (not as a percentage of the GDP), but the
observed surpluses remained close to such ratios until the economic crisis of
the mid-2010s. Under the "macroeconomic tripod", the Brazilian economy ran

---

15   The concept of primary revenues and expenditures refers to all public revenues and
     expenditures except for financial ones. Financial revenues and expenditures are those
     related with the public debt. Primary expenditures comprise all government expenses
     except financial ones, namely current and capital expenditures with ordinary functions
     of the public sector (including with public health). The difference between primary rev-
     enues and expenditures is called the primary result. A positive primary result, or primary
     surplus, means the funds "in excess" that can be used to cover financial expenditures. The
     most important items of financial expenditures are the payment of amortizations and
     interests on the public debt. For reasons of simplification, I use the expressions "primary
     result", "budget result", and "fiscal result" as synonyms.

on high interest rates, solid fiscal surpluses, and an overvalued currency for most of the period from 1999 to the late 2010s.

Public sector accounts started to worsen by the end of the 2000s, suffering the effects of international crises. In the mid-2010s, Brazil plunged into a profound economic recession that prevented it from maintaining positive fiscal balances.[16] In 2014, for the first time since the institution of the macroeconomic tripod, the government's primary accounts ended in a deficit rather than a surplus. The country recorded a double-digit inflation rate in the following year, at the same time that public debt was rising at a fast pace. Despite the economic downturn of the mid-2010s and the emergence of deficits in government accounts, the government continued imposing budget targets. The policy was maintained over the second half of the decade, only to move from surplus to deficit targets, which should not exceed a certain threshold (Evangelista, 2017; Gentil and Hermann, 2017).

By not abandoning the fiscal targets, the government could maintain its ability to pay for financial expenditures even under adverse fiscal conditions. Such a hierarchy of priorities in public spending was not only preserved but reinforced as the economic crisis worsened. The prime example of new measures to preserve the existing strategies of financial accumulation was the adoption of spending rules by the federal government. These rules were designed to put the country "back on track", achieving positive primary surpluses. Put otherwise, they would help the government reduce primary spending, saving funds for financial expenditures on the public debt. This would ensure the sustainability of the macroeconomic tripod regime. The spending rules enacted in the second half of the 2000s were particularly problematic for areas of "discretionary" spending, such as health care. They had direct consequences for SUS financing.

2.1.2   Reinforcing the Macroeconomic Regime: Health Spending Rules
Given the unlikelihood of meeting the established fiscal targets in the context of crisis, the federal government created the so-called "New Fiscal Regime" in 2016. This set of policies sought to reinforce the government's capacity to sustain the macroeconomic policy framework described so far. It reinforced the existing macroeconomic policy framework focused on the dual objective of meeting inflation and budget targets. This was done through new rules that automatically limited public spending. Spending limits would help the

---

16   The Brazilian GDP growth rates were of-0.5% in 2014,-3.5% in 2015, and-3.3% in 2016 (IBGE).

government get closer to the annual budget targets and eventually restore the positive fiscal results achieved during the 2000s and early 2010s.

The new fiscal regime and its related spending rules became part of the Constitution. They were introduced through a constitutional amendment, the Constitutional Amendment 95, known as the "spending ceiling rule" (Brazil, 2016a). The law's explanatory memorandum clearly states that its goal was to complement the existing fiscal stability tool (primary fiscal results targets for the following year) with an instrument for the medium and long run (limits to primary spending valid for several years). This would lead to the highest possible primary result and contain the expansion of the public debt (Brazil, 2016b).

In practice, the 2016 spending rule established a twenty-year freeze on federal annual spending – more specifically, on primary spending (which encompasses health-related items). Total primary expenditure would have zero real growth: the federal government was allowed to spend, each year, the values spent in 2016, adjusted only for inflation. Public spending would not be able to increase in line with GDP, revenue, or population growth. In the case of health, the base year was moved to 2017 – meaning expenditures in health care would be frozen in real terms at the values spent in this year.[17] The new fiscal regime focused on the expenditure side, with no comparable measures to increase revenues on a permanent basis.

The rule applies exclusively to primary spending, which means that financial expenditures – public debt interests and amortization payments – are exempted from the ceiling. It becomes clear, thus, that the spending limits were a way to save money on public services and infrastructure to continue remunerating public bondholders. Other authors (Funcia, 2019; Salvador, 2020) concur that, while the explicit objective of the budget ceiling was to stabilize the growth of primary spending to contain the rise in public debt, the implicit goal was to continue saving funds to service the debt even in times of economic turbulence.

The implementation of spending ceilings by way of a constitutional amendment overrode the previous constitutional rule that tied federal spending on SUS to GDP growth.[18] Under the new rule, if the government wants to increase

---

17   The rule considers the values of public spending in monetary values, not in terms of the GDP. The government eventually approved an exceptional rule for education; in this case, federal spending should be equal to 18% of the net federal tax revenues of 2017, adjusted for inflation. The rule applies to the federal government only (although it directly impacts the value of transfers to the subnational spheres).

18   In 2015, the year before the spending ceiling was approved, federal health spending had been altered to keep pace with overall revenue growth.

the amount spent on health relative to the previous year, it must compensate for it by reducing expenditures in other sectors so that the total amount of expenditures remains flat. In a context where different areas of the public administration compete for increasingly scarce funds, there is hardly any room left to expand investments in health, an area of discretionary spending. That there is no space even for an automatic increase in health spending to keep pace with population growth and rising health care costs means a level of restrictions on health care financing unseen in any other country with a universal health system. Dissociating expenditures from such variables leads to a decrease in *per capita* health spending, a trend that started during the crisis (2014) and became almost unavoidable after this rule (Bahia et al., 2021; Funcia, 2019).

Wrapping up the various elements presented in this section, the inflation-targeting policy regime and its associated fiscal rules represent a financialized policy framework that had a direct impact on SUS financing. This framework reallocated federal spending from social services, including health care, to financial expenditures, notably interests on the public debt. In practice, thus, it appropriated from SUS funds to feed financial accumulation. Before comparing data on interest and health spending, it is important to recall some rules on the Social Security budget that also led funds from public provision to be allocated to interest payments.

2.1.3   Backing the Macroeconomic Regime: Rules for Social Security Revenues

The policy changes described so far focused on the fiscal budget of the federal government and the rules allowing it to save revenues to service the public debt. But the Social Security budget was also turned into a key source of revenues to sustain this strategy. The government started enacting rules to channel part of Social Security revenues to the fiscal budget still in 1994, in the context of the Real stabilization plan. They were introduced as urgent and temporary measures. In 2000, following the institution of the inflation-targeting regime, the government approved the current version of this device, known as the "Unbinding of Union Revenues" (Desvinculação de Receitas da União – DRU).

The unbinding of union revenues is a legal device that alters the constitutional rule binding social contributions to the financing of Social Security policies (public pensions, public health, and social assistance). During most of its existence, the DRU allowed the federal government to take up to 20% of social contribution revenues from the Social Security budget and allocate them into the fiscal budget. In 2016, the share rose to 30%.[19] The DRU is approved through constitutional amendments lasting from five to seven years each. Despite its provisional character, this device has been continually renewed over the years. The Executive proposes a new amendment renewing the DRU whenever the one in force is about to expire and sends it for approval by the Legislative Chamber.

The unbinding of revenues does not provide additional revenues for the government, but changes how existing revenues are allocated within the public budget. In doing so, it becomes a central instrument allowing the current macroeconomic regime to remain in place. This is because the revenues moved through the DRU can be freely allocated into any area of public spending, not only those related to Social Security. As previously noted, the payment of public debt interests and amortizations are items of the fiscal budget. The government would not be able to use revenues from social contributions to service the debt without the DRU, as these would be tied to the Social Security budget (Dias, 2008; Salvador, 2017).

The rule is continuously renewed under the justification that it allows for greater flexibility in spending decisions, which would translate into more efficient public resource allocation. Advocates of the DRU also claim that the measure does not harm the financing of Social Security as the revenues would return to the system via government transfers (Brazil, 1993). This latter argument has been contested by several studies, which demonstrate that the largest part of the revenues is withheld in the fiscal budget rather than going to Social Security. As they rightly emphasize, if the goal was not to withdraw revenues from Social Security, there would be no reason to create the rule in the first place (Dias, 2008; Gentil, 2019; Pinto, 2008).

Since the creation of the DRU, the revenues incorporated into the fiscal budget have been sufficiently large to eliminate or significantly diminish primary budget deficits and allow the government to reach the targets defined for the year. As a result, the volume of public funds available to pay for financial expenditures also increased (Dias, 2008; Gentil, 2019; Mendes, 2012; Salvador, 2017). It is telling that the role of the DRU as a tool to achieve fiscal targets and pay for financial expenditures was not openly acknowledged at first but became explicit over time. Unlike the original legislation of the DRU, by the late 2010s, the Senate's webpage on the rule listed among its goals "the management of resources for interest payments on the public debt" (Senado Notícias, 2020).

---

19   Governments from different political stances engaged with the DRU. This increase was approved after the impeachment of the Workers' Party president in office (Dilma Rousseff) that year.

It is possible to know the overall amount of Social Security revenues with-drawn by the DRU, but there is little information on the specific purposes for which they were used afterward. As the government does not disclose the destination of these revenues, it is virtually impossible to be precise about the share of social contributions destined to public debt interests and amortiza-tions and the share used in other items of the fiscal budget. Not even public oversight authorities have full knowledge of where the resources appropri-ated through the DRU go. The Brazilian Federal Court of Accounts, for exam-ple, has recognized that "due to the method for accounting for DRU resources (…) it is not possible to determine the exact amount of the resources unbound from Social Security that would be funding the fiscal budget or returning to the [Social Security] sphere" (TCU, 2007, p. 127, retrieved by Barbosa, 2020). Research seeking to retrace the path followed by DRU funds also underscores the lack of transparency and timely accounting information on how these resources are managed; even so, they find compelling evidence on their use to pay for financial expenditures (Mendes, 2012; Pitombo, 2019; Dias, 2008; Barbosa, *op. cit.*).

Several studies sought to estimate the effects of the DRU on SUS financing. Gentil (2019) finds that the sum withdrawn from the Social Security budget was greater than that allocated to health in all years from 1995 and 2015. Also according to the author's calculations, had these funds been allocated to SUS, they could have roughly doubled the investments in the system during this period, bringing about a radical transformation in the provision of public health services. Looking at the 2000s, Mendes (2012) shows that the propor-tion of resources absorbed by the DRU that returned to the Social Security budget was almost negligible, and even more so the share of such revenues that was allocated to health. Last, Salvador (2010) demonstrates that the DRU was the chief source of funds for the primary surpluses achieved by the federal government during the 2000s. The author's estimations show that the reve-nues appropriated via DRU represented on average 62.5% of the federal gov-ernment's primary surplus from 2000 to 2007. I will revisit this issue in the following section when presenting data to reinforce the argument that SUS funds have been appropriated by financial capital through fiscal rules saving resources for interest payments.

2.1.4   Data Analysis and Interpretation: Health and Financial
         Expenditures in Perspective
The evolution of monetary and fiscal indicators over the past two decades in Brazil demonstrates how this regime imposed a hierarchy in the use of public

funds, prioritizing financial over health expenditures. This quantitative perspective can shed further insight into the links between financialization, the macroeconomic policy regime, and public health financing. First, the primary surplus target policy was successful in saving public funds to pay for public debt interests (Table 4.7). The monetary policy framework enforced permanently high interest rates; as the Brazilian interest rates are one of the highest in the world, so is the interest burden on the public debt. The federal government, responsible for the interest payments on the sovereign debt, committed an average of 4.6% of the GDP per year to interest payments between 2000 and 2018. In contrast to the deterioration of other fiscal indicators, interest payments increased during the recession (2015–2018), peaking at more than 7% of the GDP in 2015. This evolution cannot be attributed solely to the fall of the GDP, once the amount of interest payments rose in absolute values in 2015 compared to the pre-crisis period. In total, the federal government paid R$5 trillion in interest on the public debt over these eighteen years. The value of interest payments is even higher when accounting for the public sector altogether (including subnational governments), at an average of 6.2% of GDP and R$339.4 billion per year.

The federal government achieved high budget surpluses each year from 2000 to 2013 to pay for public debt interests, averaging 2% of GDP. The federal budget began to show primary deficits from 2014 onwards due to the strong economic recession of the period. From 2014 to 2018, the deficits averaged 1.9% of GDP. This did not prevent the continuation of public debt repayments. The enforcement of new budget rules contributed to maintaining a high and sustained volume of interest payments, including during the 2014–2016 economic crisis.

The growth of budget deficits in the last years of the series, coupled with higher interest burdens, was reflected in the evolution of public debt. This followed a downward trend until 2014 and increased from that point on.

One can contrast how much the federal government spent on public debt interest and health care during most of the period following the implementation of the inflation-targeting regime (Table 4.8). The progressive increase in debt spending contrasts with the virtually unchanged levels of health spending. Central bank figures show a sizeable gap between interest and health spending: from 2000 to 2009, the federal government spent an average of 4.5% of GDP per year on public debt interests, against 1.6% on health. This gap widened in the following decade, reaching 4.9% and 1.5% in 2010–2018, respectively. When considering the absolute amounts allocated to each item, the federal government spent approximately three times more on interest payments than on health. Adding up the expenditures for the entire period, the

TABLE 4.7   Brazil, fiscal policy indicators, federal government and total public sector, 2000–2018, % of GDP and billions of reais of 2018

	% GDP					Billions of reais of 2018				
	Primary balance (Federal)	Primary balance (Total)	Interest payments (Federal)	Interest payments (Total)	Public debt (Total)	Primary balance (Federal)	Primary balance (Total)	Interest payments (Federal)	Interest payments (Total)	Public debt (Total)[1]
2000	1.7	3.2	3.6	7.3	n.a.	63.7	116.3	131.3	266.5	n.a.
2001	1.7	3.2	3.8	6.6	51.5	64.2	118.5	140.2	245.9	1,919
2002	2.2	3.2	3.3	7.6	59.9	83.5	121.3	126.6	289.2	2,278
2003	2.3	3.2	6.6	8.4	54.3	89.5	127.8	259.9	332.5	2,144
2004	2.7	3.7	4.4	6.6	50.2	113.1	154.9	183.8	275.6	2,107
2005	2.6	3.7	6	7.3	47.9	113.2	164.1	262.8	319.2	2,100
2006	2.1	3.2	4.9	6.7	46.5	101	148.8	229.9	317.3	2,195
2007	2.2	3.2	4	6.0	44.6	113	165.7	203.3	305.7	2,279
2008	2.3	3.3	3.5	5.3	37.6	126.9	183.1	191.9	292.6	2,066
2009	1.3	1.9	4.6	5.1	40.9	73.1	109.9	258.7	290.1	2,312
2010	2	2.6	3.7	5.0	38	127.3	163.3	228.4	313.8	2,370
2011	2.1	2.9	4.6	5.4	34.5	140.9	193.8	302.8	356.4	2,272
2012	1.8	2.2	3.7	4.4	32.2	123.9	149.8	250.8	305.2	2,212
2013	1.4	1.7	4.1	4.7	30.5	103.4	123.2	293.9	335.7	2,194
2014	-0.4	-0.6	4.7	5.4	32.6	-25.8	-41.2	346.7	394.3	2,384
2015	-1.9	-1.9	7.1	8.4	35.6	-132.9	-127.5	490.8	575.1	2,449

	% GDP					Billions of reais of 2018				
	Primary balance (Federal)	Primary balance (Total)	Interest payments (Federal)	Interest payments (Total)	Public debt (Total)	Primary balance (Federal)	Primary balance (Total)	Interest payments (Federal)	Interest payments (Total)	Public debt (Total)[1]
2016	-2.5	-2.5	5.2	6.5	46.1	-169.8	-166.9	346.2	436.0	3,099
2017	-1.8	-1.7	5.9	6.1	51.4	-122.6	-115.2	402.4	417.7	3,525
2018	-1.7	-1.6	5.5	5.4	52.8	-115.6	-108.4	386.0	379.8	3,701
Avg.	1.1	1.7	4.7	6.2	43.7	45.8	78.0	265.1	339.4	2,422.6

SOURCE: AUTHOR'S ELABORATION BASED ON DATA FROM THE BRAZILIAN CENTRAL BANK (BANCO CENTRAL, 2020B) Primary balance: non-financial revenues minus non-financial expenditures. Total public sector: federal and subnational governments, the Central Bank, and other parts of the public administration. Data for 2000 includes Petrobras and Eletrobras. Real values of 2018 adjusted for inflation according to the Consumer Price Index (IPCA). Average exchange rate as of Dec. 2018: 4.3 Reais/Euro. Net Debt. Nominal interest rates. N.a.: non-available. Avg.: average

TABLE 4.8   Brazil, federal government expenditures on public debt interests and health, 2000–2018, % of GDP and billions of reais of 2018

	% GDP		Billions of reais of 2018	
	Interests	Health	Interests	Health
2000	3.6%	1.7%	131.3	61.8
2001	3.8%	1.8%	140.2	66.9
2002	3.3%	1.7%	126.6	64.9
2003	6.6%	1.6%	259.9	62.5
2004	4.4%	1.7%	183.8	70.7
2005	6.0%	1.7%	262.8	73.7
2006	4.9%	1.6%	229.9	77.9
2007	4.0%	1.4%	203.3	74.2
2008	3.5%	1.4%	191.9	77.1
2009	4.6%	1.5%	258.7	82.6
2010	3.7%	1.4%	228.4	87.6
2011	4.6%	1.4%	302.8	94.3
2012	3.6%	1.5%	250.8	100.3
2013	4.1%	1.4%	293.9	102.3
2014	4.7%	1.5%	346.7	107.8
2015	7.1%	1.5%	490.8	106.5
2016	5.2%	1.6%	346.2	105.8
2017	5.9%	1.5%	402.4	105.7
2018	5.6%	1.6%	386.0	107.9
Average 2000–09	4.5%	1.6%	198.8	71.2
Average 2010–18	4.9%	1.5%	338.7	102.0
Total 2000–18	4.7%	1.6%	5,036.5	1,630.5

SOURCES: AUTHOR'S ELABORATION WITH DATA FROM BANCO CENTRAL (2020B) FOR NOMINAL INTEREST PAYMENTS AND THE FEDERAL GOVERNMENT'S ANNUAL "SUMMARY REPORT ON BUDGET EXECUTION" (RREO) FOR HEALTH EXPENDITURES. REAL VALUES OF 2018 ADJUSTED FOR INFLATION ACCORDING TO THE CONSUMER PRICE INDEX (IPCA). AVERAGE EXCHANGE RATE AS OF DEC. 2018: 4.3 REAIS/EURO

federal government spent R$5 trillion on interests against R$1.6 trillion on health.[20]

Figure 4.2 uses data from this table to better illustrate the difference between the levels of federal spending on public debt interests and health.

Alternatively, one can consider the share of the federal budget dedicated to financial and health expenditures (Figure 4.3). The correct method to estimate this share is an object of controversy in Brazil. However, the overall conclusion on the primacy of interest payments over health care remains unchanged irrespective of the methodology used.[21] Following the first approach, which

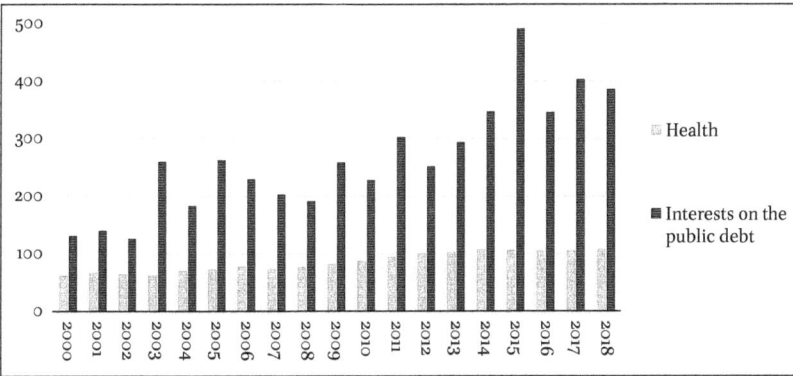

FIGURE 4.2   Brazil, federal government expenditure on health and public debt interests, 2000–2018, billions of Reais of 2018

SOURCE: AUTHOR'S ELABORATION BASED ON BANCO CENTRAL (2020B). REAL VALUES OF 2018 ADJUSTED FOR INFLATION ACCORDING TO THE CONSUMER PRICE INDEX (IPCA). AVERAGE EXCHANGE RATE OF DEC. 2018: 4.3 REAIS/EURO

---

20   I use data from the Central Bank, whose methodology considers net interest on the public debt (interest expenditures minus interest income). It is also possible to assess public debt interest charges with data from the National Treasury Secretariat, which considers gross net interest expenditures on the public debt by the federal government. The institutions also adopt different methodologies to account for health expenditures. Following the National Treasury's methodology, one finds different values for interests and health, but a similar gap between them. Neither of the institutions separates the fiscal from the Social Security budget when providing data on health spending.

21   The first approach, used by many heterodox economists, considers that financial expenditures should include both "debt service" costs (the payment of interest and amortizations using current government revenues) and "debt refinancing" costs (the payment of

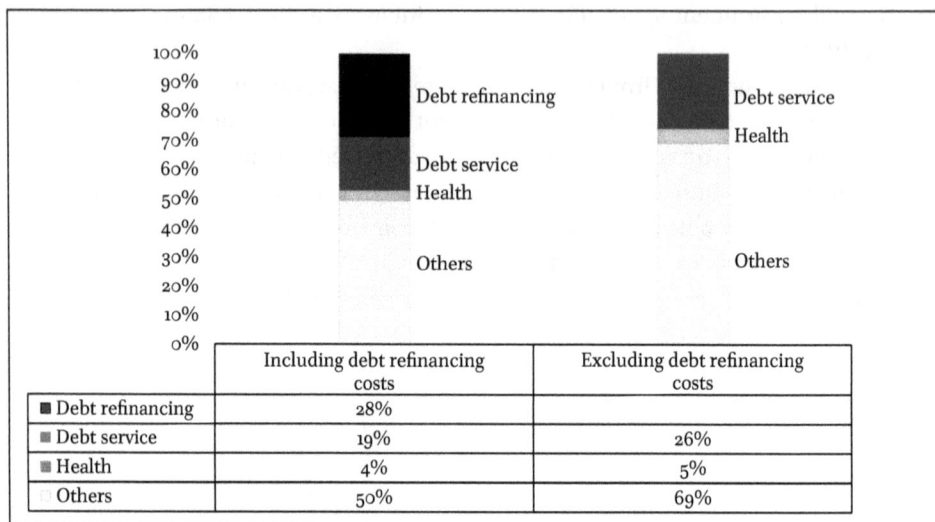

	Including debt refinancing costs	Excluding debt refinancing costs
■ Debt refinancing	28%	
■ Debt service	19%	26%
■ Health	4%	5%
Others	50%	69%

FIGURE 4.3   Brazil, federal government expenditures according to different methodologies, 2018
SOURCE: AUTHOR'S ELABORATION WITH DATA FROM THE BRAZILIAN
GOVERNMENT, TRANSPARENCY PORTAL. UPDATED EXPENSES AS OF FEB 2, 2021.
REFINANCING: PAYMENT OF PRINCIPAL AND MONETARY CORRECTION WITH REVENUES
FROM THE ISSUANCE OF NEW SECURITIES. DEBT SERVICE: PAYMENT OF INTERESTS AND
AMORTIZATIONS

accounts for public debt refinancing costs, data show that almost half of the government budget, 47%, was committed by public debt in 2018, while health absorbed a marginal share, 4%. According to the second approach, excluding refinancing costs, financial expenditures still represented 26% of government expenditures, against 5% for health. In either case, the volume of public funds channeled to the financial sector was nearly five times higher than that destined for health care.

Data for public sector spending based on international accounting standards corroborates the argument that the Brazilian case stands out in international comparison (Figure 4.4). The OECD/UN Classification of Functions of Government (COFOG) uses the indicator "public debt transactions" to

amortizations using revenues coming from the issuance of government bonds). The second approach, adopted by the government, excludes refinancing items, as they supposedly do not compromise existing government funds. The central argument for including refinancing expenditures is that the government seems to use accounting gimmicks to mask interest charges as refinancing costs (Fattorelli and Ávila, 2017).

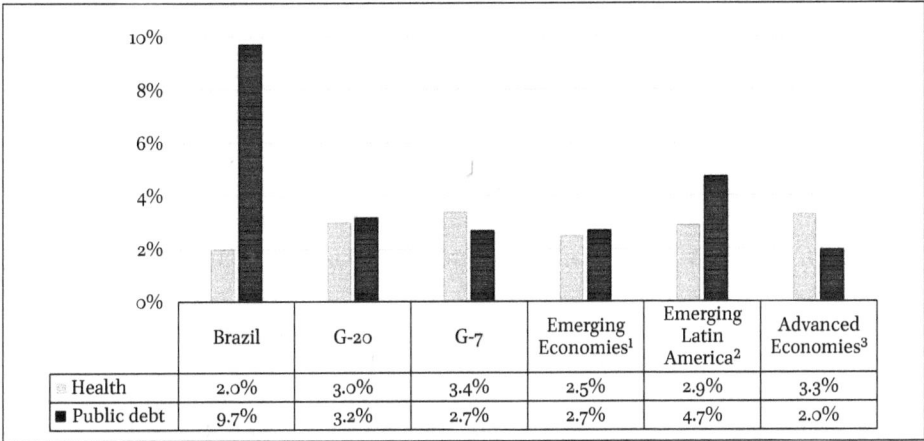

	Brazil	G-20	G-7	Emerging Economies[1]	Emerging Latin America[2]	Advanced Economies[3]
Health	2.0%	3.0%	3.4%	2.5%	2.9%	3.3%
■ Public debt	9.7%	3.2%	2.7%	2.7%	4.7%	2.0%

FIGURE 4.4 Brazil and selected aggregates, central government expenditures with public debt
transactions and health, 2016 (% of GDP)

SOURCE: AUTHOR'S ELABORATION BASED ON DATA FROM THE BRAZILIAN NATIONAL
TREASURY (TESOURO NACIONAL, 2018). PUBLIC DEBT TRANSACTIONS: INTEREST
PAYMENTS AND OUTLAYS FOR UNDERWRITING AND FLOATING GOVERNMENT LOANS.
DATA FOR CENTRAL GOVERNMENTS. [1]SOUTH AFRICA, ARGENTINA, BRAZIL, BULGARIA,
KAZAKHSTAN, CHILE, CHINA, HUNGARY, LITHUANIA, POLAND, RUSSIA, THAILAND,
TURKEY, UKRAINE. [2]ARGENTINA, BRAZIL, CHILE. [3]GERMANY, AUSTRALIA, AUSTRIA,
BELGIUM, SINGAPORE, DENMARK, SLOVAKIA, SLOVENIA, SPAIN, UNITED STATES,
ESTONIA, FINLAND, FRANCE, GREECE, NETHERLANDS, IRELAND, ICELAND, ISRAEL,
ITALY, JAPAN, NORWAY, NEW ZEALAND, PORTUGAL, UNITED KINGDOM, CZECH
REPUBLIC, SWEDEN, SWITZERLAND

compute financial expenditures by central governments, mostly gross interest expenses on the public debt. The results for different countries reveal that
the public debt burden in Brazil is several times larger than that observed in
other emerging and advanced economies – almost twice the Latin American
average in 2016 and three to four times higher than the average in other world
regions. Health spending, in turn, is relatively lower than other regional aver-
ages. Although international comparisons should always be taken with caution, Brazil stands well above all other aggregates when it comes to financial
expenditures and below them regarding health expenditures, suggesting that
the results cannot be fully explained by differences in methodologies.[22]

---

22 In this case, the limits for comparison using the COFOG methodology relate to the fact
    that they consider only central government expenditures. Depending on the country,
    local administrations might have an important weight in the financing of health care and
    (more rarely) of public debt.

To conclude the data analysis, it should be possible to apprehend the role of the Unbinding of Union Revenues (DRU), the rule that withdraws funds from the Social Security system, in supporting interest payments, as well as its impacts on health financing (Table 4.9). Following the same methodology to calculate the Social Security budget items used earlier in this chapter (Table 4.2), one can see that the volume of revenues channeled from Social Security to the fiscal budget via DRU rose almost every year over the past decade, from R$65.6 billion in 2005 to R$120.2 billion in 2018.[23] The DRU unbound

TABLE 4.9   Brazil, Unbinding of Union Revenues (DRU) and selected indicators of federal government accounts, 2010–2018, billions of reais of 2018

	Social contributions unbound via DRU	Health expenditures	Primary fiscal result	Interest expenditures
2005	65.6	73.7	113.2	262.8
2006	65.9	77.9	101.0	229.9
2007	72.3	74.2	113.0	203.3
2008	69.4	77.1	126.9	191.9
2009	65.8	82.6	73.1	258.7
2010	73.7	87.6	127.3	228.4
2011	79.0	94.3	140.9	302.8
2012	82.9	100.3	123.9	250.8
2013	85.6	102.3	103.4	293.9
2014	80.0	107.8	-25.8	346.7
2015	70.7	106.5	-132.9	490.8
2016	106.3	105.8	-169.8	346.2
2017	118.1	105.7	-122.6	402.4
2018	120.2	107.9	-115.6	386.0
Total (2005–2018)	1,155.6	1,303.7	-	4,194.7

SOURCES: AUTHOR'S ELABORATION
Data for DRU, ANFIP (2019); for health expenditures, Tesouro Nacional (2020); for interest expenditures, Banco Central (2020). Values for the federal government only. Real values of 2018 adjusted for inflation according to the Consumer Price Index (IPCA). Average exchange rate of Dec. 2018: 4.3 Reais/Euro

23   Considering that there are different methodologies for computing items of the Social Security Budget (Figure 4.3), there are also different values for the volume of resources

a total of R$1.1 trillion from the Social Security budget in this period. The final balance of the Social Security budget (revenues net of expenditures, presented in Table 4.2) was significantly lower than the revenues withdrawn via DRU each year. This suggests that the system would not have "deficits" during most of its recent history if it were not for this device. The value disconnected by the DRU in 2005–2018 was almost equal to federal spending on health, which totaled R$1.3 trillion.

Data also indicates that the funds appropriated via DRU played a fundamental role in achieving budget targets, and therefore servicing the public debt. The table shows that Brazil had fiscal surpluses until 2013, and that the amount diverted by this device was equivalent to 66% of the annual fiscal surplus, on average. This proportion is sufficiently large to confirm the importance of the DRU in achieving these results. When the federal government's accounts began to present negative results in 2014, the DRU continued to channel significant amounts of funds to the government budget, preventing even larger deficits. It is worth noting, however, that the lack of transparency associated with the measure prevents a more accurate calculation of the volume of funds going to interest payments.

2.1.5   The Role of Financial Institutions

Another way to articulate the process of financialization with the monetary and fiscal reforms presented above is by examining how financial players have worked to sustain this policy framework and profit from it. There are compelling reasons to argue that the regime in place allowed financial actors to gain influence over the State's decision-making processes and boosted financial accumulation, two defining features of financialization.

As in other countries, it is difficult to be precise about the identity of the actors holding public debt securities and profiting from interest payments. Their names are protected by confidentiality agreements and the complexity of financial markets. Policymakers have attempted, so far unsuccessfully, to make this information publicly available (Senado Federal, 2015). Despite transparency issues, aggregate data for the Brazilian public debt market show that financial institutions are the agents that participate more actively and profit the most from these operations. There are twelve "primary dealers" of the public debt in Brazil – institutions with preferential access to Treasury

---

withdrawn via DRU. Yet, the impacts of the DRU over Social Security accounts are significant even when adopting the more conservative methodology used by the National Treasury Secretariat. Following the latter approach, one can still see that the sum of revenues unbound by the DRU corresponded to around two-thirds of the Social Security deficit in 2007–2016 (STN, 2017).

auctions and privileged positions to purchase and trade government bonds. They consist of large banks and brokers, mostly private, some associated with foreign capital. Examples include Bank of America/Merrill Lynch, Goldman Sachs, Credit Suisse, Santander, Bradesco, and Itaú (Tesouro Nacional, 2019a). Financial institutions also hold the largest part of the outstanding public debt. In 2018, approximately 75% of public debt bonds were in the hands of banks, investment funds, and pension funds (Tesouro Nacional, 2019b).[24]

One might argue that these financial institutions operate with public securities on behalf of citizens, not for themselves. Even when this is the case, only a small and wealthy share of the population benefits from financial market operations. According to estimates published by the Brazilian Financial and Capital Markets Association, 3% of Brazilian investors held public bonds and 9% participated in investment and private pension funds in 2018 (ANBIMA, 2019a).[25] Data from the same institution also suggest that the wealthier the individual, the higher the proportion of his or her investments allocated to financial assets (such as bonds and shares) relative to savings deposits (ANBIMA, 2019b). This confirms that the vast majority of the gains made in financial and capital markets are appropriated by a minor (and wealthy) share of the population. Also, the National Treasury Secretariat mentions 786,000 investors buying public bonds directly via the *Tesouro Direto* platform in 2018 (Tesouro Nacional, 2019b), which accounts for less than 3% of the total population.

Apart from their roles as intermediaries and final purchasers of public debt bonds, financial institutions also wield power over the Brazilian macroeconomic regime by influencing the level of domestic interest rates. In doing so, they can influence the remuneration of a large part of their own portfolio as well as of their clients. Therefore, they have incentives to push for higher rates as well as to keep the macroeconomic policy regime in place, as it prioritizes the saving of funds for interest payments.

Bresser et al. (2020) identify two key channels through which financial institutions and investors can influence interest rates in Brazil. The first one is during the process through which the Central Bank decides on the level of the basic interest rates to reach the inflation target. The opinion of financial institution analysts is one of the elements taken into account by the monetary authority, a practice that is openly acknowledged by the latter. The second channel is during public debt auctions. Especially in times of economic

---

24   Data for the Internal Federal Public Securities Debt.
25   According to the same source, 5% invested in private securities. Most invested their money into savings accounts.

distress, financial actors would take advantage of their bargaining power and demand higher interest rates to finance the government. This and several other studies (Bruno et al., 2011; Modenesi, 2011; Oreiro and Passos, 2005; Weisbrot et al., 2017) argue that such a configuration encourages financial institutions to adjust their behavior, pushing for higher interest rates. This is facilitated by the fact that the domestic banking sector is highly concentrated.

This description concludes my analysis of how monetary and fiscal policy shifts that favor the process of financialization have impacted SUS financing. Financialization affected the long-term financing of the PHS through the adoption of inflation targets and permanently high interest rates to reach them. This policy framework served as a fundamental engine for financial accumulation in Brazil while imposing sharp restrictions on public spending. I showed that the federal government advanced measures in both the fiscal and the Social Security budget to save public revenues for interest and amortization payments, thereby sacrificing resources that could go to SUS. The prioritization of financial over health expenditures is clear: health spending evolved at a much slower pace than financial expenditures since the 1990s, in a country with the largest universal health system in terms of population coverage.

This macroeconomic regime has been diverting SUS' existing and potential revenues toward public debt investors almost since the system's creation, and over two decades. In the next sections, I will explore how financialization has also reshaped what happens in the short-term financing of the PHS.

2.2   *Investing SUS Revenues in Short-Term Financial Assets: Policies at the Subnational Level*

This section examines a second dimension of financialization, considering how this process rewires SUS' short-term financing circuits – i.e., the financing of current expenditures within the fiscal year. The central mechanism of financialization identified in this case is the use of SUS revenues to undertake short-term financial investments. These investments are carried by State and Municipal Health Funds, the entities in charge of managing SUS revenues at the subnational level. They can be interpreted as a form of financialized policy to the extent that public health bodies engage with financial instruments to manage their revenues. Moreover, financial investments with SUS' revenues may seem to be related to the mechanism previously examined in that they represent an opportunity to circumvent the shortage of health care resources coming from the public fund.

To understand how SUS revenues can be invested in financial instruments, I describe the role of Health Funds and the evolution of the legal framework allowing them to engage with financialized practices. Concerning data analysis, there is neither a national database providing detailed information on the investments carried by the Health Funds, nor a standard format for the latter to present such information. These limitations make it almost impossible to gather information about financial investments at the national level (including 26 states, the Federal District, and more than 5,500 municipalities). Therefore, I will conduct an empirical analysis on the subject using data for Rio de Janeiro and the Federal District, the country's former and current capital, respectively.[26]

2.2.1   The Role of Health Funds

The 1988 Constitution determined that the resources destined for public health actions and services should be applied through Health Funds (Brazil, 1988, art. 77 ADCT). A Health Fund is strictly defined as a set of accounts through which each government in Brazil receives revenues and executes expenditures related to health actions and services. Each government has its own Health Fund – including the federal government, each state and local government, and the Federal District government. In practice, the term "Health Fund" is commonly employed to refer to the public body in charge of administering these accounts. At the federal level, the Ministry of Health controls the National Health Fund. At the subnational level, State Health Secretariats, bodies from the state governments, control the State Health Funds. The same goes for municipal governments and their Municipal Health Secretariats, which control Municipal Health Funds.

SUS' financing circuits are organized around the Health Funds (Figure 4.1); in principle, all revenues allocated to health actions and services in each unit of the federation should be placed in its respective fund, and all expenditures incurred to pay for these actions and services should originate from the latter.[27]

Health Funds were created as tools to improve SUS' financing and oversight. They allow governments to gather revenues from various sources and centralize them in a single pool. This was considered important to optimize decision-making processes and resource allocation. In addition, having an entity dedicated exclusively to health-related revenues and expenditures was seen as fundamental to improving transparency and accountability. They would make it easier for public authorities and civil society to track the sources, volume, and the destination of funds allocated to SUS.

---

26   See Appendix 1 for further information on the data sources and treatment.
27   Governments are yet to fully obey this rule, but the violations have been falling significantly.

State and Municipal Health Funds can place their revenues in financial assets for a short period of time before allocating them to public health actions and services. These investments must be highly liquid, which includes savings deposits, bank certificates of deposits (CDBs), and short-term investment funds.[28] The main justification presented by the public administration for carrying short-term investments is that the Funds do not disburse the revenues they receive all at once, but pass them on to different public and private entities in charge of health actions and services throughout the upcoming weeks and months. In this context, investing in short-term financial assets would allow them to preserve and increase the value of their revenues by yielding returns and monetary restatement (compensation of losses due to inflation) while these are not applied to health actions and services (Junior et al., 2013; SNA, 2012; TCU, 2010).

SUS' founding regulatory framework (the Federal Constitution of 1988 and the 1990 Organic Health Laws) does not mention the possibility of using the system's revenues to carry financial investments. During most of the time since the 1990s, Health Funds did so based on lax legislation predating the system's creation. This legislation regulates the activities of the so-called "special funds", a broader category of the Brazilian public administration to which they belong.

The concept of "special funds" was introduced by the military government in the 1960s (Brazil, 1969, 1964). They consist of budget units dedicated to managing public resources for a specific public policy program or goal. There is a wide range of special funds in Brazil dedicated to financing specific activities in several areas. One of the features distinguishing special funds from other types of entities within the public administration is that they have the autonomy to decide how to manage the revenues allocated to them. The prerogative to freely manage their resources grants Health Funds the possibility to make financial investments. According to Sanches (2002), special funds can raise revenues from any source that does not violate the prohibitions established by the 1988 Constitution. The author identifies a number of the most common sources of income used by them, which include earmarked taxes, fees,

---

28 Bank certificates of deposit (Certificados de Depósito Bancários, CDB) constitute a popular type of short-term investment in Brazil. They are often presented as a form of investment in which individuals "lend money to banks". Banks issue CDBs and repay the purchaser with the amount invested plus interest payments based on an interest rate agreed in advance. They are, therefore, a fixed income security. Their maturity terms usually range from one month to five years and they can be redeemed before the end date. CDBs represent an important source of funds for the Brazilian banking system.

contributions, government transfers, and other funding sources. The latter item encompasses returns from investing their revenues in financial markets.

The federal government created the National Health Fund (FNS) in 1969 as a special fund to finance programs carried out by the Ministry of Health. With the creation of SUS in 1988, the National Fund became the central entity in charge of managing the revenues that the federal government allocated into the system. State and Municipal Health Funds (FES and FMS, respectively), in turn, are special funds born together with SUS. The 1988 Constitution and the 1990 Organic Health Laws determined that the system's resources should be deposited "in a special account in each sphere of operation" (Brazil, 1990a, art. 33). This obliged subnational governments to create special funds if they wanted to receive transfers from upper spheres of governments. Most subnational Health Funds were created during the 1990s (Pereira, 2013), much because of this rule.

Instead of being subjected to nationwide legislation, each subnational government was left to make its own laws to set up its Health Fund. Due to its status as a special fund, each government could freely determine its sources of income. This served as the gateway for investments in financial markets. The thousands of state and municipal laws instituting Health Funds often included the item "income and interests from financial investments" in their list of potential revenues. During most of the time since the creation of subnational Health Funds, this was not foreseen in SUS legislation. Public bodies most often referred to legislation on special funds dating from the 1960s to justify the practice (SNA, 2012).

Another set of laws that provided (questionable) legal grounds for investing in financial assets relates to the regulation of intergovernmental agreements. These are agreements in which different governments work together to finance public projects and programs. They can be used in several areas (including, but not limited to, health). The monetary transfers from the federal sphere to state and local governments in the context of intergovernmental agreements are subject to specific regulations. In the early 1990s, the federal government determined that revenues from agreement transfers should be mandatorily applied "in savings accounts of official financial institutions if their use is foreseen to be equal or superior to one month", or "in short-term financial application funds or open market operations backed by public debt bonds, when their use will take place in less than one month" (Brazil, 1993). There is no specific reference to SUS or health-related agreements in these laws. Moreover, a minor share of federal revenues received by Health Funds derives from these types of contracts. Even so, public entities have also mentioned the referred law when justifying the application of SUS revenues in financial investments (Bolzan, 2010).

SUS regulatory framework remained oblivious to the practice of financial investments until the mid-2000s. The absence of any specific regulation up to this point is surprising considering that the Brazilian legislation is loaded with special rules for health-related revenues and expenditures. This loose legislation, coupled with the unequal capacity of the more than five thousand State and Municipal Health Funds in Brazil to invest in the markets, led to the uneven and untransparent expansion of this practice across the territory.

In the mid-2010s, the federal government introduced the practice in the legal framework governing SUS the regulation regarding financial investments for the first time. Research in the legislative chamber's databases indicates that the first reference to financial investments within SUS legislation dates from 2014.[29] In an ordinance signed this year, the Ministry of Health determined that the resources from the federal government addressed to State and Municipal Health Funds should be invested in savings or short-term investment funds until they could be allocated to health actions and services. The rule concerns resources from fund-to-fund transfers, which account for most of the revenues they receive from the federal government.[30] Also, these investments became mandatory. As provided for in the new rule,

> The *costing resources transferred by the National Health Fund* to the Health Funds of the other federative entities in the "fund-to-fund" modality, while not used for the purpose for which they were transferred, *will be mandatorily invested* in a federal public financial institution, through the account opened by the National Health Fund, as follows:
>
> I   *in a savings account*, if the expected use of the financial resource is equal or superior to one month; and
>
> II *in short-term financial investment funds or open market operations* backed by public debt securities, when its use is expected for a shorter period than that stipulated in item I.
>
> BRAZIL, 2014, art. 6-C, emphasis added

---

29   As concluded from my searches in the archives of the Chamber of Deputies, the Federal Senate, and the Health Ministry, as well as from the examination of the preceding legislation listed by the laws mentioned in this section.

30   Federal transfers to state and municipal Health Funds are divided into "fund-to-fund transfers" and "agreement transfers". Fund-to-fund transfers are mandatory (the Constitution obliges the federal government to provide them), paid on a continuous and regular basis, and cover operating and capital expenditures. Agreement transfers are voluntary (they depend on agreements signed between the federal and a given subnational government), do not have defined periodicity, and the values vary according to the project or activity they are supposed to finance.

The federal government reinforced this rule in 2017 by approving a new law that turned investments not only mandatory but also automatic. The government determined that the resources coming from fund-to-fund transfers should be directly placed in financial assets. The Fund managers were responsible for the subsequent administration of these resources, deciding on whether they should remain in short-term investments or be transferred to a savings account. This was imposed in the following terms:

> § 1 The resources that make up each financing block will be transferred, fund to fund, on a regular and automatic basis, in a specific and unique current account for each block, held at official federal financial institutions (...)
>
> § 4 While they are not invested for their intended purpose, *the resources referred to in this article shall be automatically placed in short-term financial application funds*, backed by federal public debt securities, with automatic redemptions.
>
> BRAZIL, 2017a, art. 3, emphasis added[31]

The claim that this practice grew in a regulatory gray area finds further support when looking at the way in which the federal government included these rules into SUS legal framework. Both the 2014 and 2017 legislations mentioned above were amendments to laws that did not mention financial investments in the original text. The 2014 ordinance is an amendment to an administrative act approved three years earlier to regulate transactions between the federal government and state and municipalities, with no reference to financial investments. Surprisingly, not even the 2014 rule itself was about financial investments. Its main purpose was to regulate monetary transfers from SUS to individuals under extraordinary circumstances. The article mandating the application of federal revenues in financial instruments by subnational Health Funds was appended as the last item of the text.

Likewise, the 2017 rule is not an original act regulating financial investments, but a rule enacted to alter a previous norm on a different topic. The initial

---

31   The legislation in question and the own Health Secretariats employ the expressions *aplicações financeiras* and *fundos de aplicação financeira*, which I translate into "financial applications" and "financial application funds", respectively. I could not find a technical definition for such expressions in public accounting manuals, domestic or foreign. Based on empirical research, this category seems to include short-term financial instruments such as CDBs (see footnote of this chapter) and quotas of short-term investment funds. In the context of Health Funds, I consider financial applications as any form of pooling and investing resources apart from holding them in savings accounts. I avoided translating

norm established that federal transfers would be organized into six spending categories ("financing blocks"). The new ordinance reorganized this model by dividing federal transfers into two categories only, for current expenditures and investments. Among many items regulating the revised model for federal transfers, there was the item mentioned above, establishing the automatic and mandatory investment of these revenues in financial assets. The lack of legislation specific to the topic suggests that these policy changes were implemented without giving the civil society and other stakeholders in SUS the opportunity to debate whether these practices are acceptable or not. This seems to corroborate what Bahia et al. (2016) have observed when describing the evolution of the regulatory framework for private health activities in Brazil; the national legislation often comes to regulate practices already in place, but which lack legal support. The influence of vested interest groups is presented as an important factor driving these regulatory shifts.

The legislation is highly heterogeneous concerning the nature of the banks where Health Funds should hold accounts to receive federal revenues. The uncertainty is even greater when it comes to the institutions where they can invest the latter. For example, the 2017 law reorganizing Health Funds' accounts into two spending blocks specifies that each block must have a dedicated bank account, opened at a public bank (*Caixa Econômica Federal,* the Federal Savings Bank) or a mixed economy bank (*Banco do Brasil,* the Bank of Brazil). Other laws regulating SUS operations present different specifications as to the nature of the financial institutions involved in the concerned action.[32] Still, the legislation generally refers to the financial institutions where the Health Funds should be received, not where they should be invested. In practice, State and Municipal Funds end up engaging in financial operations in both public and private for-profit institutions, as shown later in this section.

The undertaking of financial investments by State and Municipal Health Funds has attracted little scholarly attention so far. To the best of my knowledge, the only published work examining the practice is Bolzan (2010), who found evidence of this practice in the context of a broader study on the

---

the term *fundos de aplicação financeira* to "financial investment funds", a more common term in English, because instruments such as CDBs do not fit perfectly into this category. When possible, I adopt the terms "financial instruments", "financial assets", and "financial investments", due to their most common usage in English. These expressions are used in reference to both savings deposits and the so-called "financial applications" (CDBs and quotas of investment funds).

32   See, e.g., federal ordinances 3,925/1998, 1,749/2002, 412/2013, decree 7,507/2011, and complementary law 141/2012.

financing of public health activities in the state of Rio Grande do Sul during the 2000s. Inspecting the accounts of the state's Health Fund, the author
observed an increasing volume of revenues invested in financial instruments,
namely in CDBs. According to his calculations, the volume of revenues from
the State Health Fund of Rio Grande do Sul invested in financial markets grew
from R$77 million in 2006 to R$306.5 million in 2009.[33] The author underscores the relevance of these results, as the accumulation of revenues in financial markets means that at least part of them was not being disinvested in due
time to finance public health actions and services.

The following section examines the undertaking of financial investments
by two Health Funds in a more recent period and discusses how they connect
with the process of financialization.

2.2.2   The Rio de Janeiro State Health Fund

The Rio de Janeiro state (Estado do Rio de Janeiro – ERJ) has the second largest GDP among all Brazilian states, accounting for more than one-tenth of the
national output in 2018. It is also one of the most populous states, with over
17 million people (IBGE, 2020a, 2020b). The recession of the Brazilian economy in the mid-2010s was a shock to the state's already fragile accounts. It suffered one of the largest drops in revenues and economic growth rates during
the second half of the decade, along with one of the sharpest rises in public
debt levels (FIRJAN, 2017; Silva, 2017).[34] In 2016, the governor in office declared
a state of public calamity in Rio's financial administration, imposing harsh
measures such as the rationalization of essential public services and postpon-
ing payments to civil servants and suppliers (Rio de Janeiro, 2016).

The ERJ has approximately thirty special funds, among which is the Rio
de Janeiro State Health Fund. The law creating this Fund dates from 1989 and
includes income from investments among its potential sources of revenues.
It states that "the following shall constitute revenues for the Fund: (...) VI –
revenues, increases, interests, and monetary restatements resulting from the
investment of its resources" (Rio de Janeiro, 1989).

The Health Fund has a significant weight in Rio de Janeiro's state finances.
In 2018, it received almost 30% of the revenues allocated to the 24 special
state funds with data available for that year (Rio de Janeiro, 2020). The ERJ

---

33   Real values of 2018 adjusted for inflation according to the Consumer Price Index (IPCA),
      R$38 million and R$152 million in nominal values. Average exchange rate of 2018: 4.3
      Reais/Euro.
34   Rio de Janeiro's GDP grew by an average of 2.5% p.a. in 2010–14, followed by a-2.9% p.a.
      contraction in 2015–17 and a modest recovery of 1.3% p.a. in 2018–19 (IBGE/FIRJAN).

Health Fund is often cited in the government's financial statements as one of the funds with the largest amounts of revenues under management and invested in "financial applications".[35] The government's 2014 year-end report, for example, indicates that the Health Fund was responsible for more than 15% of the money invested in applications in that year, all state funds combined. Moreover, it had 90% of the total amount allocated to savings accounts (SEF-RJ, 2015). Likewise, the 2016 report listed the Health Fund as the state entity with the third largest volume of money allocated to financial investments (SEF-RJ, 2017). Last, the 2018 report shows that the Health Fund was the special fund with the third largest amount of cash and the highest volume of revenues held in savings accounts (SEF-RJ, 2018).

Table 4.10 systematizes the value of financial investments carried out by Rio de Janeiro's State Health Fund from 2012 to 2018 using figures obtained directly from the State Health Secretariat. The data suggests that the Fund had a relevant amount of resources allocated to financial assets until the economic crisis, with more than R$740 million invested in 2012. After dropping together with the deterioration of state finances, investments started to recover in the last years of the series to reach nearly R$150 million in 2018.

The returns on investments fell from 2012–2016, along with the reduction in the value of money placed in those instruments. Despite the recovery of investments at the end of the series, the reported returns continued to fall. These went from around R$40 million per year at the beginning of the series to a value ten times lower in 2018, of R$4 million. The drop in the volume of invested cash in the middle of the series is most certainly linked to the state's financial turmoil and economic recession, which probably led to a greater withdrawal of resources to cover expenditures.

The financial statements provided by the Health Fund Secretariat allow us to break down the share of investments allocated to savings deposits and investment funds. These represented on average 70% and 30% of total investments, respectively. The participation of investment funds followed a pro-cyclical behavior, diminishing in the period of the most acute recession (2014–2016). Their relative participation grew substantially in the last years of the series, exceeding 40% of the total amount of revenues placed in financial assets in 2017–2018.

Figure 4.5 uses data from the previous table to better illustrate the evolution of financial applications and the volume of financial returns obtained by the State Health Fund over the past decade.

---

35   See footnote of this chapter.

TABLE 4.10 Brazil, Rio de Janeiro State Health Fund, financial investments, 2012–2018, millions of reais of 2018 and % in total investments

	2012	2013	2014	2015	2016	2017	2018
Millions of Reais of 2018							
Total	742.7	578.8	331.8	230.8	47.8	79	149.9
Savings deposits	*465*	*402*	*268*	*163*	*40.1*	*41.5*	*88.2*
Short-term investment funds	*278*	*177*	*63.6*	*67.5*	*7.8*	*37.5*	*61.6*
Investment returns[a]	43.2	46.9	33	27.6	11.7	5.8	3.9
% Total investments							
Savings deposits	63%	69%	81%	71%	84%	53%	59%
Short-term investment funds	37%	31%	19%	29%	16%	47%	41%

SOURCE: AUTHOR'S ELABORATION BASED ON DATA FROM THE RIO DE JANEIRO STATE HEALTH SECRETARIAT VIA THE LAW OF ACCESS TO INFORMATION (SEE APPENDIX 1)

a Item "asset variations – remuneration of bank deposits and financial applications". Real values of 2018 adjusted for inflation according to the Consumer Price Index (IPCA). Rounded values. Closing balance as of late December. Average exchange rate of 2018: 4.3 Reais/Euro

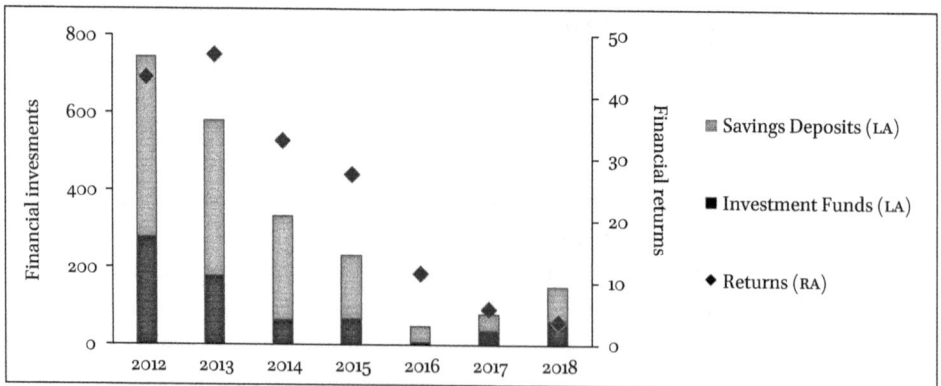

FIGURE 4.5 Brazil, Rio de Janeiro State Health Fund, financial assets (left axis) and returns (right axis), 2012–2018, millions of reais of 2018

SOURCE: AUTHOR'S ELABORATION BASED ON DATA FROM THE RIO DE JANEIRO STATE HEALTH SECRETARIAT VIA THE LAW OF ACCESS TO INFORMATION (SEE APPENDIX 1). LA: LEFT AXIS. RA: RIGHT AXIS. REAL VALUES OF 2018 ADJUSTED FOR INFLATION ACCORDING TO THE CONSUMER PRICE INDEX (IPCA). ROUNDED VALUES. AVERAGE EXCHANGE RATE OF 2018: 4.3 REAIS/EURO

TABLE 4.11   Brazil, Rio de Janeiro State Health Fund, financial assets by nature of institution, 2012–2018, % of investments

	2012	2013	2014	2015	2016	2017	2018
Savings deposits							
Public banks	99.9%	99.9%	99.8%	99.6%	98.5%	98.4%	99.3%
Private banks	0.1%	0.1%	0.2%	0.4%	1.5%	1.6%	0.7%
Short-term investment funds							
Public banks	96.1%	92.1%	90.5%	94.8%	34.3%	84.7%	97.9%
Private banks	3.9%	7.9%	9.5%	5.2%	65.7%	15.3%	2.1%

SOURCE: AUTHOR'S ELABORATION BASED ON DATA FROM THE RIO DE JANEIRO STATE HEALTH SECRETARIAT VIA THE LAW OF ACCESS TO INFORMATION (SEE APPENDIX 1) Results from the aggregation of different accounts in each bank. Average exchange rate of 2018: 4.3 Reais/Euro

The Health Fund had investments in both public and private institutions. The banks where the Fund placed SUS revenues included the two largest private for-profit banks in the country, *Bradesco* and *Itaú*, along with *Caixa Econômica Federal* (entirely public) and *Banco do Brasil* (partially State-controlled). The participation of public/semi-public and private banks varied according to the type of investments. The former held almost the entirety of the Health Fund's savings deposits, while private banks had a relatively larger participation in the case of its short-term investment funds. The weight of public and private banks in total investments varied throughout the period, along with the proportion of revenues allocated to each type of instrument. Table 4.11 breaks down the volume of revenues placed in financial instruments according to the nature of the banks managing the money.

2.2.3   The Federal District Health Fund

The Federal District (Distrito Federal – DF) is home to the current capital of Brazil, Brasília. Apart from being the country's political center, it is also a relevant economic hub. It has the eighth largest GDP among the 27 federative units in the country, amounting to 3.6% of the national GDP in 2018, and the largest GDP *per capita* (IBGE, 2020b, 2020c).[36] The Federal District has a population of

---

36   The Federal District is not officially classified as a state, but as an autonomous territory separated into thirty-three administrative regions. For reasons of simplicity, it is a customary practice to analyze it together with the 26 Brazilian states.

3 million people, and its capital, Brasília, is the third most populous city in the country (IBGE, 2020a). Despite growth rates above the national average during the 2010s, the fiscal crisis in the second half of the decade also hit the region, pushing public deficits and debt levels up. Still, the Federal District remained one of the lowest debt-to-income ratios of the federative units (FIRJAN, 2017).[37]

The Federal District has approximately 32 Special Funds, including the Federal District Health Fund. The Fund was created in 1996, and its founding act foresees income from investments as part of its revenue sources: "the following constitute revenues for the Federal District Health Fund: (...) III-the returns resulting from the investment of its resources in the financial market" (Distrito Federal, 1996). Different from the case of Rio de Janeiro, the Federal District's government does not publish information comparing the levels of revenues and investments of its different Funds. However, it is safe to say that the Health Fund has a significant weight in government finances. According to the Federal District Court of Accounts, it received almost 60% of the revenues allocated to special funds in 2018 by the DF government (TCDF, 2019).

The analysis of the Health Fund's financial portfolio from 2012 to 2018, using information provided directly by the Federal District Health Secretariat, reveals a considerable volume of money invested in banks at the beginning of the decade (Table 4.12). The series starts with more than R$770 million in financial assets. The volume of investments gradually declined in the period of economic crisis but recovered in the last year of the series, ending at R$517 million in 2018. Investment returns went from R$52 million in 2012 to R$20 million in 2018, following an erratic path over the years. They followed the trends of investments until 2017, after which it is possible to observe a detachment; investments resumed growth, while financial income continued to drop.

The largest share of investments carried by the DF Health Fund concerned money in short-term investment funds, followed by bank certificates of deposit (CDBS) and savings deposits. These averaged approximately 50%, 40%, and 10% of total investments in this period, respectively. The relative participation of investment funds grew significantly in the last years of the series, reaching almost 90% of the amount invested in 2018.

Figure 4.6 shows the evolution of investments by type of instrument, both in absolute values and relative to total investments. As for the nature of financial institutions involved, the Federal District Health Secretariat informed that the Fund carried the investments in public institutions.

---

37   GDP growth rates went from an average of 2.9% p.a. in 2010–14 to negative rates of -0.5% in 2015–16, with a slight recovery to 1% in 2017–18 (CODEPLAN, 2019).

TABLE 4.12   Brazil, Federal District Health Fund, financial assets, 2012–2018, millions of reais
of 2018 and % in total investments

	2012	2013	2014	2015	2016	2017	2018
Millions of Reais of 2018							
Total	771	449	237	506	645	510	516
Savings deposits	*31*	*40*	*40*	*41*	*39*	*41*	*41*
Investment funds	*741*	*18*	*19*	*169*	*404*	*387*	*459*
Bank certificates of deposit	*0*	*391*	*178*	*297*	*202*	*82*	*15*
Investment Returns	52	36	30	45	58	37	20
% Total investments							
Savings	*4%*	*9%*	*17%*	*8%*	*6%*	*8%*	*8%*
Investment funds	*96%*	*4%*	*8%*	*33%*	*62%*	*76%*	*89%*
Bank certificates of deposit	*0%*	*87%*	*75%*	*58%*	*31%*	*16%*	*3%*

SOURCE: AUTHOR'S ELABORATION BASED ON DATA FROM THE FEDERAL DISTRICT HEALTH
SECRETARIAT VIA THE LAW OF ACCESS TO INFORMATION (SEE APPENDIX 1)
Real values of 2018 adjusted for inflation according to the Consumer Price Index (IPCA).
Rounded values. Average exchange rate of 2018: 4.3 Reais/Euro

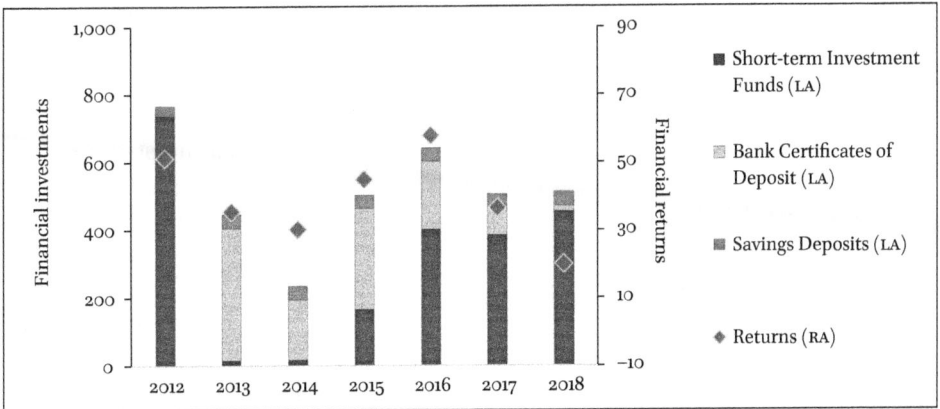

FIGURE 4.6   Brazil, Federal District Health Fund, Financial assets (left axis) and returns (right axis), 2012–
2018, millions of reais of 2018
SOURCE: AUTHOR'S ELABORATION BASED ON DATA FROM THE FEDERAL DISTRICT
HEALTH SECRETARIAT VIA THE LAW OF ACCESS TO INFORMATION (SEE APPENDIX
1). RA: RIGHT AXIS. LA: LEFT AXIS. REAL VALUES OF 2018 ADJUSTED FOR INFLATION
ACCORDING TO THE CONSUMER PRICE INDEX (IPCA). ROUNDED VALUES. AVERAGE
EXCHANGE RATE OF 2018: 4.3 REAIS/EURO

Having covered the technical aspects of this financing strategy underpinned by financial instruments, I can now discuss the extent to which it forges new relations between Health Funds, on the one hand, and financial markets and institutions, on the other. It is also possible to consider the potential impacts of Health Funds' financial investments on public provision by examining evidence of "revenue retention" – when these revenues remain invested in financial instruments instead of being channeled to SUS' actions and services.

2.2.4 When the Financial System Overrides the Health System: Revenue Retention Practices

When Health Funds place their revenues in short-term financial investments, the sums invested are not registered as expenditures. They remain on the side of revenues, as invested revenues. In this way, withholding resources in financial assets opens a window of opportunity for public entities to improve their financial statements, preserving revenues and bringing in extra income from returns on investments. Overseeing entities have found evidence that Health Funds may maintain resources in financial instruments during an extended period of time to improve their accounts, a practice called "resource retention" (*contingenciamento de recursos*). The key problem of resource retention is that it reduces the amount of revenues actually invested in health actions and services, with detrimental effects on the quantity and quality of SUS provision.

The Brazilian Federal Court of Accounts itself has acknowledged that Health Funds may engage in this practice:

> Legally, the fund manager is encouraged to invest the money received through the funds in the financial markets, as long as it is invested ahead of the deadlines for using the money. However, unfortunately, there are cases in which the managers keep the money in financial applications to obtain financial income.
>
> TCU, 2010, p. 70

The challenges in obtaining information on Health Funds' financial statements make it virtually impossible to investigate the possibility of revenue retention using publicly accessible data. Moreover, neither the federal nor subnational governments organize systematic auditing processes by external bodies to monitor the timely disinvestment of these revenues so they can be addressed to health actions and services. It is nevertheless possible to examine this practice by gathering qualitative information from policymakers' statements and audit works for different states and municipalities across the country.

A first piece of evidence regarding resource retention comes from the city of Rio de Janeiro, the capital of the homonymous state examined in the previous section. According to a statement by a then-senator, later mayor of the city during a meeting in the Legislative chamber, leaving the resources earmarked for health expenditures in financial markets for long periods of time was a customary practice in the country by the mid-2000s. The speech took place during a debate about the degradation of health services in Rio de Janeiro observed at this time. Its content suggests that the practice of resource retention has contributed to the critical situation of the city's public health network. Reproducing it *verbatim*,

> There is a very harmful practice that, nowadays, in the 5,561 municipalities of our Brazil, is becoming commonplace. In the first, second, and third year, the mayor reduces expenditures and applies the resources from health and education (...) *making a quarantine for this money to pass through financial markets before, so that in the last year he has enough money* (...)
>
> Your Honor can see Rio de Janeiro's budget, where, in the first three years, spending levels were reduced, and the largest [source of] income was not the tax on services, the urban property tax, or the Municipal Participation Fund, but returns on financial investments.
>
> SENATOR M. CRIVELLA's speech on March 24, 2004, retrieved
> from SENADO FEDERAL, 2020, emphasis added

Press reports published around the same time also drew attention to the issue of resource retention. Nery (2005), for example, describes the results of the auditing work conducted by the Ministry of Health in the Rio de Janeiro Municipal Health Fund in 2004–2005. According to the information released by the Ministry, the auditors found R$30 million worth of financial investments in the Health Fund.[38] Both auditors and journalists called attention to the contrast between, on the one hand, the high volume of funds earmarked for public health kept in banks, and, on the other, the local government's steady buildup of health-related debts (see also Fortes, 2010; Karpov, 2015).[39]

---

38   Nominal values equivalent to approximately R$60.5 million in values of 2018 adjusted for inflation according to the Consumer Price Index (IPCA), or €14.1 million according to the average exchange rate of 2018 (4.3 Reais/Euro).

39   Both the statement and the report mentioned here refer to the city of Rio de Janeiro. There is no *a priori* reason why this could not apply to the state and other regions as well.

Looking at the state of Rio de Janeiro, data presented in the previous section show that the state Health Fund kept a significant volume of resources in financial investments over the 2010s decade. It also suggests that this volume grew since 2016. These tendencies appear to be in stark contrast with the fact that the state's public health network has progressively deteriorated during the decade, collapsing at the very end. Oversight authorities affirm that the state government failed to meet the minimum health spending targets defined by the Constitution during the second half of the 2010s, and that the value allocated was lower each year. In 2016, Rio de Janeiro had the lowest share of government revenues applied to health among all Brazilian states, and health became the area of state administration with the highest indebtedness levels (MPRJ, 2018). In 2017, the Regional Council of Medicine declared a state of technical calamity in the local public health system due to the shortage of resources to keep it in operation (CREMERJ, 2017). The paucity of data makes it impossible to verify if Rio de Janeiro's State Health Fund has engaged in practices of revenue retention during the period under analysis. Still, the existence of revenues held in financial assets, on the one hand, and the growing financing needs of the health system, on the other, suggests that financialized strategies deserve far more attention than they currently receive.

Besides the potentially detrimental effects on service delivery, the case of Rio de Janeiro also shows how engaging with financial instruments can undermine transparency and social control in the use of SUS revenues.[40] Even official oversight authorities face challenges to obtain detailed, updated information on the Funds' operations. To cite one telling example, the Rio de Janeiro State Prosecutor's Office reported difficulties in examining the management of resources by the state Health Fund because much of the data obtained by the institution was outdated, could not be fully accessed, or presented conflicting values. The lack of transparency naturally extends to financial investments. That they are spread over several institutions and different types of assets makes it even more difficult to collect information. When asked to provide information to the Prosecutor's Office, members from the private bank that manages the Health Fund's central account denied the request alleging the right to "bank secrecy" – even though, as noted by the auditors, the transactions involve public money (MPRJ, 2018).

Differently from Rio de Janeiro, the Federal District's Health Fund has been the object of official investigations into possible retention practices. Research

---

40   The idea of "social control" is used here to suggest the capacity of the civil society to steer State actions.

conducted by SUS' audit department found a progressive accumulation of resources in financial assets during the second half of the 2000s. According to the final audit report published in 2012,

> It was found that the SUS manager in the Federal District chose to invest the resources of the Unified Health System (SUS) in bank certificates of deposit, in the financial markets, to the detriment of the offer of health actions and services to the population. At the end of 2006, the amount of resources invested in the financial markets was of R$63.9 million; at the end of 2007, they were of R$124.3 million; on March 31, 2009, the Health State Secretariat had R$238.4 million yielding interest and monetary restatement.
>
> SNA, 2012, p. 45[41]

The audit work also finds that, in several accounts dedicated to specific programs within the Federal District's Fund, the volume of revenues received in a given year was less than the amount allocated in financial investments. This finding is relevant as it illustrates how financial investments may undermine SUS service provision. In 2006, for example, the value of financial investments in the Fund's account dedicated to HIV treatments was more than twice the amount it received from the federal government to finance such activities. The study also found similar evidence of "frozen money" in the accounts dedicated to finance actions related to pharmaceutical assistance, mobile emergency care services, and family health programs. Considering this evidence, the auditors argued that financial investments ended up having a direct and negative effect on public provision. According to them, SUS revenues were kept invested in financial assets to increase returns, "financially benefiting the fund manager (...) [while] causing irreparable social harm to the users of the Unified Health System" (SNA, 2012, p. 45).

The recovery of financial investments in the Federal District's Health Fund by the end of the period examined in the previous section is at odds with the detrimental state of public health provision in the region. Public health services in the Federal District have been continuously underfinanced over the 2010s, to the point the government declared a state of emergency in the local public health network by the middle of the decade (Distrito Federal, 2015). Then again, however, there is limited data to be precise over to what extent

---

41   Nominal values equivalent to R$125 million, R$234 million, and R$416 million in 2018, respectively, adjusted for inflation according to the IPCA. Average exchange rate of 2018: 4.3 Reais/Euro.

rising financial investments may have contributed to diminishing investments in public health services. Public databases fail to provide uniform, up-to-date, easily workable information on the institutions and instruments in which the resources are invested, the volume of returns, and the length of investments, to cite a few.

It is worth noting that the potential retention of SUS revenues in the financial sector is not limited to the cases above. In the late 2000s, SUS' Audit Department inspected the financial operations of several State Health Funds and found evidence of retention in many of them (Fortes, 2010).

What these case studies can safely demonstrate is that the financial investments could not guarantee an increase in revenues significant enough to justify the practice. They were not able to improve the quantity and quality of health service delivery, which deteriorated in both cases studied here. In contrast to the controversial implications for the materiality of health care delivery, these investments were unquestionably beneficial for financial institutions. When the regular and secure income streams from government transfers to the public health system are automatically directed to the purchase of financial assets, they become an important source of liquidity for the financial sector. The following passage from Bolzan's (2010) case study explains this process in detail, describing how the financial investments carried by the State Health Fund under investigation have benefited banks the most:

> The federal resources transferred by the Ministry of Health and that were invested in bank certificates of deposit (...) *were used to generate more fluidity and liquidity to the banking institution* (...) *allowing the excess money to be lent to a financial institution* (...). The manager chose to invest the fund-to-fund resources in the financial market to the detriment of the actions to be carried out with the values transferred by the Ministry of Health.
>
> It is interesting to observe that the federal resources from SUS [were seen] as excess or surplus resources, which allowed such resources to be lent to banking institutions that have a shortage of resources for their operations and financial commitments in order to have more liquidity, to the detriment of users of the public health system. The "liquidity", or "fluidity" of SUS, with its services, flows, referrals, and counter-referrals, is clearly less important for those who choose to invest SUS federal resources in the financial markets instead of in SUS itself. SUS' financial ballast ceases to exist to ensure that of the financial sector.
>
> BOLZAN, 2010, p. 81, emphasis added

This section examined changes in the short-term management of SUS revenues. It focused on the fact that the public entities which administer the system's revenues at the subnational level have been investing their incoming
funds in financial assets before allocating them to health actions and services.
It is possible to contextualize these changes within the process of financialization to the extent that the expansion of financial instruments and actors
created opportunities and incentives to change the forms of managing SUS
resources. Health Funds have been using financial instruments since the 1990s
to prevent their revenues from losing value in the context of inflation and
obtain investment returns. Even more, this practice received a major boost in
the 2010s decade, when new rules rendered investments mandatory and automatic. The same opportunities that enable increased revenues from investment returns also paved the way for resource retention practices, when the
revenues remained invested in the financial sector instead of being used to
finance health actions and services.

This chapter concludes by examining how public health providers, in this
case non-profit hospitals working for SUS, have also been integrated into new
financing strategies dependent on financial instruments and institutions.

2.3   Subsidized Credit Lines for SUS Providers

The changing ways through which the government financed SUS services providers since the late 1990s also reflect a tendency of greater dependence on
financial instruments and banks for public health financing. The third mechanism examined here consists of the deployment of government strategies to
finance non-profit hospitals working for SUS based on bank credit. These strategies target, more specifically, philanthropic hospitals, which play a crucial role
in public health service delivery. I will show that the creation of hospital credit
lines was subsidized by public revenues, including those earmarked to finance
SUS services. In this way, public services provided the basis for the creation
of financial assets and their collateral. To do so, the section describes the role
of philanthropic establishments within SUS and their indebtedness process
over the past decades, followed by the description of financialized approaches
deployed by the federal government to ease their financial distress.

There is no national database providing information on lending operations
to philanthropic health institutions. Therefore, it is virtually impossible to
obtain figures for the total value of loans and other information covering all the
hospitals and financial institutions engaged in this practice. To overcome this
challenge, I combine available information from two sources: the national representative body of philanthropic hospitals (Confederação das Santas Casas de
Misericórdia, Hospitais e Entidades Filantrópicas, CMB), which provides data

on hospital debt, and the National Health Fund database, from which it is possible to draw approximations of the volume of SUS revenues used to repay bank loans.[42]

2.3.1   SUS and the Philanthropic Health Sector

The establishments that financed the provision of SUS services via bank credit were philanthropic hospitals. The Brazilian philanthropic health sector comprises several types of private non-profit health establishments, including clinics, hospitals, and basic health care units.[43] Health care philanthropy has a long trajectory in Brazil: the first "Holy Houses" (*Santas Casas*), medical assistance centers associated with religious organizations, date from the 16th century, and some of them are in operation up to this day (CMB, 2016). Estimates account for approximately 1,800 non-profit hospitals in the country in 2018, most of which working partially or exclusively for the public system (Senado Federal, 2018).

Before the creation of SUS, philanthropic establishments represented the main gateway to medical assistance for those excluded from the public health network run by the Social Insurance system of the time. By serving low-income individuals and informal workers, the sector has played an important (albeit limited) role in mitigating social inequalities in health. Philanthropic providers also had a relevant role within public provision, as an important part of the services offered by the Social Insurance system was delivered by non-profit institutions contracted and paid directly by the government. Given these varied roles, philanthropic actors have long benefited from large volumes of public transfers, tax exemptions, and other State incentives (Nemi, 2020; Ocké-Reis and Santos, 2011; Receita Federal, 2009–2017; Senado Federal, 2018).

The philanthropic sector continued to play a crucial role in access to health care after the creation of the universal health system. Given that philanthropic establishments had a relatively structured network and widespread presence in the country by the time SUS was created, they were considered instruments that would allow the system to reach the entire territory and population. At the same time, philanthropic institutions exerted strong political pressure to maintain their independence and autonomy in relation to the newly created

---

42   See the Appendix 1 for further information on the data sources and treatment.

43   The Brazilian legislation uses different expressions to refer to the philanthropic health sector (Senado Federal, 2018). The discussion in this book encompasses all establishments that fit into the category of "philanthropic institutions", governed by laws no. 12,101/2009 and 13,650/2018. It does not include the private entities identified as the "third sector", such as the "social organizations", governed by laws no. 9,637/1998 and 9,790/1999.

system (Bahia, 2008; Neto, 1997; Senado Federal, 2018). In this way, the government incorporated philanthropic establishments into SUS' chain of provision, while preserving their private nature. In this way, the participation of philanthropic hospitals within SUS was included in the 1988 Constitution and the 1990 Organic Health Laws, which defined that the system may resort to private providers and that non-profit entities would have preference over for-profit ones if the system decides to contract private services (Brazil, 1990a, arts. 24–25).

Philanthropic establishments gained enormous importance within SUS chain of provision over these three decades, being in charge of a significant share of service delivery today. One can find different values for the share of public provision covered by these hospitals, but they converge to about one-third of establishments providing services for SUS and a similar share in terms of hospital beds.[44] What is even more relevant, philanthropic establishments play a central role in providing complex services and treatments for SUS. Data suggest that, by the late 2010s, they were responsible for almost 60% of SUS high-complexity procedures, 40% of medium-complexity ones, and 7% of outpatient care. Also, around the same time, about a thousand municipalities in Brazil did not have public health infrastructure and depended on philanthropic entities to access public services (Instituto Filantropia, 2019; Ministério da Saúde, 2018; Senado Federal, 2018).

The philanthropic institutions that work for SUS remain private and autonomous. The federal government reimburses them for the medical goods and services provided on behalf of the system according to the so-called "SUS table", a list of reference prices defined by the Ministry of Health. Besides working for the public system, these institutions can receive private patients, paying and non-paying. Philanthropic hospitals can also provide services to beneficiaries of private health insurance and sometimes they even run their own health insurance schemes (Pires et al., 2017; Ugá et al., 2008). The relative importance of SUS payments in their total revenue varies. Estimates suggest that around 65% of philanthropic hospitals' revenues come from SUS (Brígida, 2012; CMB, 2013), but this share can reach up to 100% for the many establishments that work exclusively for the public system.

Although it is common practice to refer to the "philanthropic sector" altogether, generalizations must be taken with caution. Under the label of philanthropic entities, there are institutions of various sizes and degrees to which

---

44   The remaining share is predominantly public. For-profit establishments have marginal participation in SUS' chain of provision.

they depend on the public system. Philanthropic establishments range from small "Holy Houses" in remote parts of the country to large hospital centers in affluent urban areas. While the former are most often SUS-dependent, the latter also serve private patients and run health insurance plans. Some of the largest philanthropic hospitals in the country have an annual income of several millions of reais and have even turned to financial markets to raise additional funds (Bahia, 2018; Leis et al., 2003; Nemi, 2020; Sestelo, 2017b; Valor Econômico, 2019).

Whatever their size, philanthropic organizations benefit from massive tax relief and fiscal incentives. According to data compiled by the Brazilian Senate, the federal government spent R$22 billion on philanthropic hospitals in 2017 (Senado Federal, 2018). About 56% of this amount consisted of payments for services rendered to SUS patients, 31% of tax exemptions, 11% of financial incentives, and 2% of monetary transfers in the context of government agreements. Estimates from the Brazilian Revenue Service show that philanthropic organizations working in health-related activities (hospitals and other establishments) profited from a R$6.8 billion federal tax waiver this year (Receita Federal, 2016).[45]

Philanthropic hospitals became increasingly indebted over the past two decades. The reasons for the rising indebtedness levels in the sector are a matter of great controversy. The entities claim that the mismatch between, on the one hand, the remuneration received from SUS for services rendered on its behalf and, on the other, the actual costs of these services, is the main cause for the rising debt levels (ALESP, 2015; Câmara dos Deputados, 2016). Government payments for the services provided to SUS would cover about 65% of the actual costs of these services, leading these hospitals to live in permanent deficits (Alves, 2019; Pires et al., 2017). Philanthropic establishments claim that underpayment brings adverse impacts by forcing them to implement cost-cutting measures such as staff layoffs, salary cuts, and restrictions on the quality and quantity of services (CMB, 2016).

Policymakers, in turn, acknowledge issues of underpayment but relativize them in light of evidence of management problems and corruption scandals in philanthropic hospitals, which would contribute to deteriorating their financial accounts (ALESP, 2009; O Globo, 2015). Several scholars also refute the argument that SUS underfunding is the root cause of philanthropic institutions' financial hardship. They contend that working for SUS grants these

---

45   Nominal values equivalent to R$23 billion and R$7 billion of 2018, respectively, adjusted for inflation according to the IPCA, or €5.3 billion and €1.6 billion according to the average exchange rate of 2018 (4.3 Reais/Euro).

establishments a continuous flow of patients, revenues, and economic benefits, ensuring their financial sustainability and generating positive externalities
for the services they provide outside SUS. They also point out that the sector
comprises entities of significantly different sizes, and large hospitals would be
able to adjust their strategies to generate income and reap financial benefits
from the provision of public services. There is evidence that large-scale philanthropic establishments would use the tax incentives gained from the "philanthropic institution" label to outperform private for-profit competitors (Ocké-
Reis, 2018; Fascina, 2009; Lima et al., 2007; Zatta et al., 2003).

While the reasons for the financial difficulties faced by philanthropic hospitals are a matter of debate, these constraints led them to delay the payments
of suppliers, taxes, labor charges, and financial obligations, resulting in a progressive accumulation of debts. This can be seen through the evolution of the
total volume of philanthropic hospital debt over the last decade, as well as
its structure in the most recent period (Figure 4.7). According to the sector's
representative, the total outstanding debt in the philanthropic hospital sector
grew from R$3.6 billion in 2005 to R$25 billion in 2015. Breaking down the debt
of this latest year, it is possible to observe that more than half of this amount
(56%) was owed to the financial system (banks), followed by debts with suppliers (17%), unpaid taxes (12%), delayed salaries (8%), and labor charges (7%).
The predominance of the financial sector in the debt structure suggests that
these entities were borrowing from banks but were unable to fully honor these
obligations – a point that will be developed in the following sections.

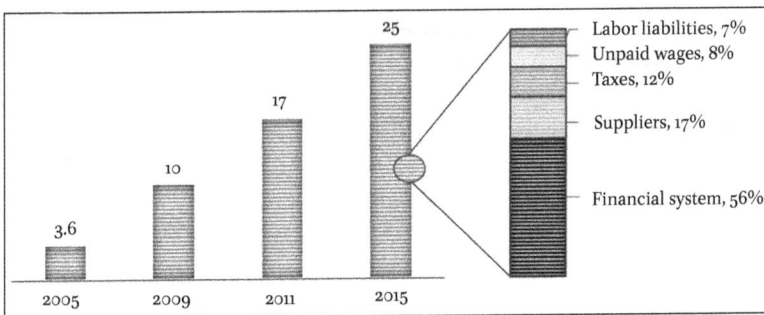

FIGURE 4.7   Brazil, philanthropic health establishments, total sector debt and debt
             structure, 2005–2015, billions of reais of 2018 and % of total debt
             SOURCE: AUTHOR'S ELABORATION BASED ON CMB (2015). ROUNDED
             FIGURES. CONSTANT VALUES OF 2018 ADJUSTED FOR INFLATION
             ACCORDING TO THE IPCA. AVERAGE EXCHANGE RATE OF 2018: 4.3
             REAIS/EURO

2.3.2   Government Programs Connecting Philanthropic Hospitals
               and Banks

The Brazilian government has implemented a series of policies since the end of the 20th century to provide financial support to philanthropic hospitals and help them settle their debts. These policies did not necessarily tackle the causes of the indebtedness problems. Instead, the government opted for alternative strategies to help these entities continue to finance services in the context of resource scarcity and to refinance existing debts. These strategies were heavily dependent on financial instruments and institutions.

Government aid to philanthropic hospitals during the 1990s and 2000s came in two main forms. First, the government designed programs for hospitals to refinance the debts they had with suppliers and public entities. These programs were based on regulatory shifts allowing hospitals to delay debt repayments and get debt discounts. They also provided higher tax breaks to ease the hospitals' financial distress. A review of government measures over the last decade suggests that this first modality had a more prominent place in the State agenda until 2015. It can be considered a "non-financialized" policy orientation in the sense that the measures did not depend directly on the financial sector. For the sake of illustration, one of the largest programs within this category granted philanthropic hospitals the remission of overdue tax debts. It is worth noting, however, that the debts owed to the government, coming from unpaid taxes, constituted a minor share of the philanthropic sector's debt. According to the National Association of Private Hospitals, by the time this program was approved, tax debts represented only one-third of their total outstanding debt (ANAHP, 2013).[46] Unsurprisingly, then, the incentives granted until the first half of the 2010s were unable to solve the problem, and philanthropic hospitals' debts continued to grow.

In the second half of the decade, the federal government began to prioritize a second modality of financial aid to philanthropic hospitals, creating special credit lines in public and private banks to make it easier for them to borrow (Bahia, 2008). In this sense, one can say that the government started leaning toward a "financialized" approach to address philanthropic hospitals' financial difficulties. The credit policies consisted, more specifically, of measures to regulate and promote preferential credit lines for philanthropic hospitals. Through preferential credit lines, these entities would have privileged access

---

46   The 2013 Program for Strengthening Private Philanthropic Entities and Non-Profit Entities Operating in Health Care (PROSUS). For a list of programs and incentives to philanthropic institutions over the last decades, see Senado Federal (2018).

to certain types of loans with more favorable conditions than those offered to typical borrowers. While credit programs were not a novelty in the government agenda, they became the primary focus of State actions to support these institutions since the mid-2010s. Between 2015 and 2018 only, the government approved three key measures reinforcing and expanding this policy approach: the regulation of consigned loans guaranteed by SUS revenues (2015), the revitalization of subsidized credit programs to hospitals (2017), and the mobilization of workers' savings to finance these loans (2018).

2.3.3   Consigned Credit for Philanthropic Health Establishments

Consigned credit is a popular credit modality in Brazil where loan installments (the monthly repayments on the loan) are automatically discounted from a secure stream of income received by the borrower. The money is addressed directly to the bank, making the loan virtually risk-free for the lending institution. In the case of philanthropic hospitals, they can obtain consigned bank credit using SUS revenues to secure the payments.[47] The revenues coming from SUS that can be used to repay the loans are, more precisely, transfers from the federal government to pay for the medium-and high-complexity services provided on behalf of SUS. These are known as "MAC" transfers, an acronym for "Medium and High Complexity" (*Média e Alta Complexidade*).[48]

The federal government transfers resources from the National Health Fund to Municipal and State Health Funds in order to finance medium-and high-complexity services offered by SUS (whether these have been provided by public or private entities). In 2018, MAC transfers accounted for 65% of fund-to-fund transfers from the National to subnational Health Funds (FNS, 2020).[49] After receiving the revenues, the State and Municipal Health Funds remit part

---

47   Consigned credit can be offered to both individuals and legal entities. Lavinas (2017) provides a detailed analysis of consigned credit to individuals and how this was the main driver of the expansion of credit to households in Brazil during 2000–2010. In this case, banks offered consigned loans mainly to public servants and retirees. The repayments were automatically discounted from regular income streams guaranteed by the State – in this case, wages and pension benefits.

48   SUS classifies its services according to ascending levels of complexity and costs (Solla and Chioro, 2012). Medium complexity services are those requiring qualified professionals and specialized infrastructure, such as consultations with specialists, out-patient interventions, and diagnostic imaging tests. High complexity services include procedures such as hemodialysis, chemotherapy, and hospital surgeries.

49   As explained in the previous section, until 2017, nearly the end of the period covered by my research, the federal government organized SUS transfers in six blocks, including for "medium-and high-complexity services". The changes in the model of transfers in 2018 did not alter the use of payments for such services to repay loans.

of these resources to the philanthropic entities that provided such types of services for SUS patients (CGU, 2019; SFC, 2017) (Figure 4.1). Once philanthropic establishments are one of the main providers of medium-and high-complexity care for SUS, the largest source of income they receive from the federal government consists of compensations for having provided these services.

Philanthropic hospitals are authorized to take out interest-bearing loans with financial institutions offering part of their future income from government payments for complex services as collateral for the loans. To put it simply, part of SUS payments to hospitals can be used to service bank loans. These operations are classified as a form of consigned credit to the extent that loan repayments can be discounted from secure income streams received by the hospitals. Once government transfers are, as required by law, regular and automatic, so are the sums deducted from the latter to repay the banks. It is the federal government, through the National Health Fund, which subtracts the corresponding sums from MAC transfers and assigns them to the banks. Some monitoring reports have suggested that the local Health Secretariats, and not the federal government, are the ones executing the payments to financial institutions (e.g., SFC, 2014); in any case, it is a public body that executes the repayment.

The philanthropic hospitals contracted to SUS can engage in multiple contracts with different lenders simultaneously, and may compromise up to 35% of the average revenue received from services rendered to SUS in the last 12 months in automatic repayments. These transfers cover interests and amortizations. The discounts occur each month for the entire duration of the loan until it is paid off. Financial institutions are assured to receive the funds automatically as long as the borrower proves it is providing services to SUS (CGU, 2019; Funcia, 2021; SFC, 2017; Silvestre, 2020). Figure 4.8 below presents a simplified scheme of how the granting of consigned credit to SUS providers works in practice.

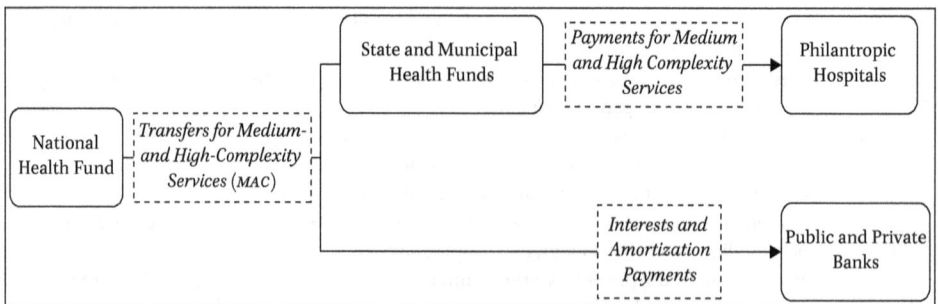

FIGURE 4.8   Consigned credit to philanthropic hospitals (simplified scheme)
SOURCE: AUTHOR'S ELABORATION BASED ON SFC (2017) AND CGU (2019)

It is difficult to determine when exactly philanthropic hospitals started engaging with consigned credit. Banks have been offering special credit facilities to philanthropic hospitals subsidized by government revenues at least since the 1990s (Bahia, 2008). The first line of consigned credit to philanthropic hospitals seems to be *Caixa Hospitais*, created in 1998 by the Federal Savings Bank (*Caixa Econômica Federal*). As of 2008, more than twenty financial institutions, public and private, were offering consigned credit to philanthropic institutions (ANEPS, 2008). Yet, the first regulation from the Ministry of Health mentioning these loans dates from the mid-2010s. One can conclude, therefore, that the practice grew upon a weakly grounded regulatory framework based on norms foreign to SUS legislation. During most of the period under analysis, the consignment contracts gained legal value through agreements signed by the Ministry of Health directly with the financial institution providing the loan. Meanwhile, public entities mentioned broad legal frameworks to justify the use of this credit modality such as the Civil Code (law No. 10,406/2002), which regulates credit operations more broadly and does not make any mention of operations in which the borrowers are health care providers (SFC, 2014).

Within SUS' regulatory framework, the first reference to the use of federal transfers to repay private loans dates from 2015.[50] In an ordinance issued this year, the Ministry of Health mentioned "the need to regulate the procedures relating to the operation of consigned loans through the cession of credit rights to entities providing services to SUS" (Brazil, 2015b, preamble). The expression "the need to regulate" clearly shows that the practice preceded the regulation. More than simply legislating the concession of consigned loans, the 2015 rule expanded it by raising the share of revenues that each hospital could commit to debt repayments. While early records mention that the Ministry of Health allowed hospitals to use up to 30% of federal transfers with loan repayments (SFC, 2014), the norm increased the so-called "consignable margin" to 35% (art. 3).

The federal government justifies the authorization of consigned credit by philanthropic hospitals on the grounds that the existence of repayments guaranteed by the State would allow banks to charge lower interest rates to hospitals, reducing the costs of financing compared to traditional loans (SFC, 2014). The 2015 law, however, does not regulate the interest rates and fees charged by

---

50   As concluded from searches in the Chamber of Deputies, the Federal Senate, and the Health Ministry's archives (available at www.camara.leg.br, www.senado.leg.br, and www .saude.gov.br/saudelegis). Funcia (2015) reaches a similar conclusion. Within SUS' body of norms, the only recent mention in a related topic was ordinance MS No. 220/2007, which authorized State and Municipal Health Secretaries to use revenues from MAC transfers to pay their membership fees to participate in National Health Councils.

the banks. According to information from the press and philanthropic hospitals' representatives, the interest rates charged on consigned loans could reach up to 20–25% per year (ANAHP, 2019; ANEPS, 2008; Instituto Filantropia, 2019; Valor Econômico, 2018), way above inflation rates.[51]

The expansion of bank-based, publicly sponsored strategies to support philanthropic health establishments continued in 2017 when the government launched another large-scale program for loan subsidization. The *Pro-Santas Casas* program introduced two credit lines for philanthropic hospitals, one for the financing of current expenditures and another for asset restructuring (which includes refinancing and paying off outstanding debts) (Brazil, 2017b). In either case, the federal government subsidizes the interest rates so they remain below market rates. Any bank can apply to offer these products. The interest rate for working capital loans corresponds to the reference interest rate for long-term loans practiced by the Brazilian Development Bank, set at 7% p.a. in the year the law came into effect. The interest rate for asset restructuring was capped at 0.5% per year. Interest payments and administration fees remain with the lending institution.

The subsidies for the *Pro-Santas Casas* program come from the Ministry of Health's budget, which transfers the money directly to the banks (Brazil, 2017b, art. 3). The expected cost of the program was R$10 billion by the time of its approval – approximately half of what the public sector spent per year with primary care at the time.[52] Using public funds to sponsor loans was justified, once again, on the basis that this would allow hospitals to obtain more favorable refinancing conditions compared to what they would be able to get through conventional forms of borrowing (Serra, 2018).

In 2018, the federal government reinforced once again the bank-based approach to hospital financing by mobilizing part of workers' compulsory savings to finance the loans. These savings come more precisely from the Length-of-Service Guarantee Fund (*Fundo de Garantia do Tempo de* Serviço – FGTS). The FGTS was created in 1966 as a measure to protect workers from financial hardship upon the termination of their labor contract. It creates a compulsory savings account for each worker during the period of activity, financed by a monthly contribution from the employer proportional to the value of the wage. The account yields a 3% annual return plus monetary restatement, and the worker can withdraw the funds upon dismissal or to finance specific

---

51 See Table 4.6 for the level of basic interest rates and inflation in Brazil during this period.
52 Public expenditures with basic attention amounted to R$19 billion in 2017 in nominal values (Portal da transparência, 2021), equivalent to around €2.3 billion according to the average exchange rate of 2018 (4.3 Reais/Euro).

goods and services (namely home purchasing). While workers do not cash in FGTS benefits, the funds finance government programs related to social and economic development. Since its creation, FGTS contributions have been one of the primary sources of financing for public housing programs, sanitation policies, and infrastructure works (Caixa, 2005).

An official act approved in 2018 determined that part of FGTS funds should be addressed to financial institutions to finance credit operations with philanthropic hospitals. The regulatory shift establishes that 5% of FGTS funds should be transferred to financial institutions to finance philanthropic hospital credit each year. This was equivalent to R$4 billion when the law was approved (Negrão and Sousa, 2018).[53] The rule maintained the share of FGTS funds allocated to housing investments, thereby sacrificing the amount of funds available for sanitation and infrastructure. Following a period of intense disputes, the interest rates of FGTS-financed loans were capped at around 12% per year (CMB, 2019).

2.3.4   The Bank-Based Strategy in Numbers

The quantitative analysis led here will focus on consigned loans since this is an established practice in the country (even before the 2015 law) and for which there is thus more information available. The National Health Fund discloses information on the volume of federal transfers earmarked to pay for medium- and high-complexity services but reassigned to other purposes. These purposes include covering consigned loan repayments. They also include a number of other expenditures such as refinancing philanthropic hospitals' tax debts, granting funds to university hospitals, and paying for the Health Secretariats' participation fees in National Health councils. The available data do not allow us to separate the amount of discounts from MAC transfers between the share used to repay consigned loans and that allocated to other purposes. However, both the events described so far and the conclusions of official auditing reports (CGU, 2019; SFC, 2017, 2014) give reason to believe that consigned loans absorb most of the funds subtracted from federal transfers for complex services. The Office of the Comptroller General, for example, estimates that deductions from MAC transfers to repay consigned loans alone amounted to R$1.6 billion in 2016 (SFC, 2017).[54] This represented more than half of the deductions registered in the National Health Fund's database for this year, all purposes combined (FNS, 2020). Moreover, since credit policies for philanthropic hospitals

---

53   Over €930 million according to the average exchange rate of 2018 (4.3 Reais/Euro).

54   Values adjusted for inflation according to the IPCA equivalent to R$1.5 billion in nominal values and €1.1 billion using the average exchange rate of 2018 (4.3 Reais/Euro).

occupied a large space on the government agenda during the last decade, it is reasonable to think that most of the recent increase in the volume of deductions from complex service transfers is due to consigned credit. Based on the above, I assess the evolution of deductions for consigned loans using as a proxy the values for total deductions from MAC transfers (the part that should be going for complex service provision but is redirected to other purposes).

Table 4.13 displays the values of federal government transfers to states and municipalities destined to finance public health actions and services within SUS, along with the values deducted from the transfers for complex services and used for other purposes. Between 2010 and 2018, R$4.7 billion per year, on average, was subtracted from MAC transfers and used elsewhere. This represented around one-tenth of total MAC transfers. The volume of revenues subtracted from complex services exceeded those spent by the federal government on some core areas of health care provision such as pharmaceutical assistance, health surveillance, and investments (namely infrastructure financing). The volume of funds allocated to each one of those categories was

TABLE 4.13 Brazil, federal transfers for SUS services and deductions from medium-and high-complexity services (MAC), 2010–2018, billions of reais of 2018

	2010	2011	2012	2013	2014	2015	2016	2017	2018[1]	Average
Medium and High Complexity Transfers (MAC)										
Transfers	46.7	48.9	51	49.2	52	50.5	46	48.7	50.9	49.3
Deductions	6.1	5.7	5	4.7	5	4.3	3	4.2	4.1	4.7
Deductions (% Transfers)	*13%*	*12%*	*10%*	*10%*	*10%*	*9%*	*6%*	*9%*	*8%*	*10%*
Other categories										
Primary care	15.5	16.4	19	17.3	18	17.5	17.9	17.9	21.3	17.9
Pharmaceutical assist.	4.2	3.8	2.8	2.5	2.3	2	2.1	1.8	1.9	2.6
Health surveillance	2.5	2.5	2.7	3	2.5	2.2	2.9	2.4	2.7	2.6
Investments	0.7	1	1.7	2.4	3	2.5	2.8	1.2	4.4	2.2
SUS management	0.5	0.3	0.4	0.3	0.1	0.1	0.1	0.1	0.1	0.2

SOURCE: AUTHOR'S ELABORATION BASED ON FNS (2020)
Real values of 2018 adjusted for inflation according to the Consumer Price Index (IPCA). Average exchange rate of 2018: 4.3 Reais/Euro. [1]The method for recording transfers changed in 2018, which explains the surge in investment transfers this year. Due to methodological changes, the series for certain years were adjusted to correspond to the conventional funding blocks (as in 2010, 2011, and 2018)

nearly half of what was deducted from medium-and high-complexity services. The only exception was in the year 2018 due to a sudden rise in investment transfers, which is likely to be explained by methodological changes in the way to account for government transfers this year.

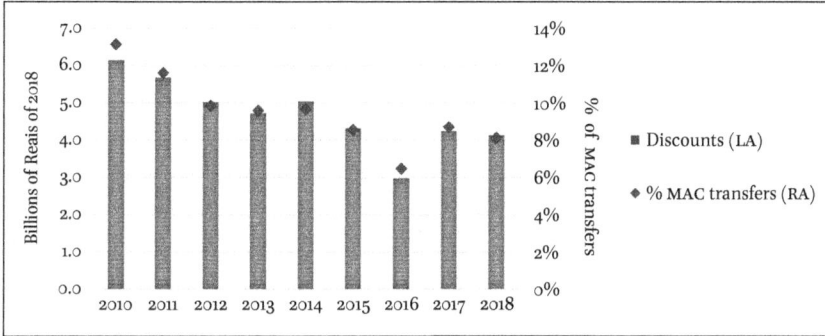

FIGURE 4.9   Brazil, values deducted from federal transfers for medium-and high-complexity services (MAC) for consigned loans and other items[1], 2010–2018, billions of reais of 2018 and as a % of transfers

SOURCE: AUTHOR'S ELABORATION BASED ON FNS (2020). [1]TAX DEBT RELIEF PROGRAMS FOR PHILANTHROPIC HOSPITALS, TRANSFERS TO UNIVERSITY HOSPITALS, FEE PAYMENTS FOR HEALTH SECRETARIATS, AND OTHER FORMS OF COMPENSATIONS AND ADJUSTMENTS. AVERAGE EXCHANGE RATE OF 2018: 4.3 REAIS/EURO. RA: RIGHT AXIS. LA: LEFT AXIS

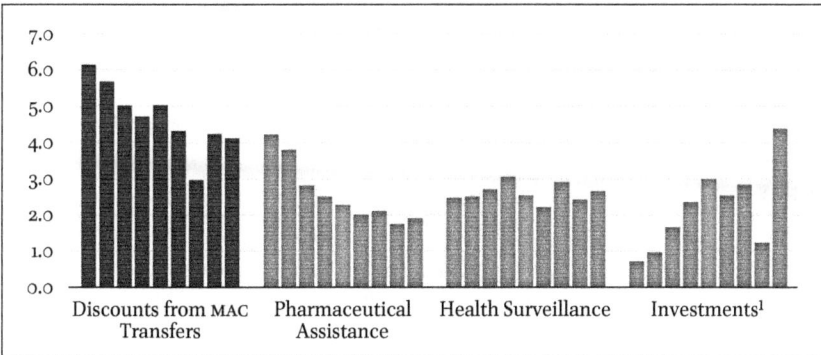

FIGURE 4.10   Brazil, federal transfers for SUS (selected categories) and values deducted from federal transfers for medium-and high-complexity services (MAC), 2010–2018, billions of reais of 2018

SOURCE: AUTHOR'S ELABORATION BASED ON FNS (2020). REAL VALUES OF 2018 ADJUSTED FOR INFLATION ACCORDING TO THE CONSUMER PRICE INDEX (IPCA). AVERAGE EXCHANGE RATE OF 2018: 4.3 REAIS/EURO. SEE SFC (2017) FOR AN EARLIER VERSION OF THIS GRAPH. METHODOLOGICAL CHANGES IN 2018 CAN EXPLAIN THE SUDDEN RISE IN INVESTMENTS THIS YEAR

One can also make a graph out of the figures above to better visualize the evolution of the values deducted from federal transfers to pay for medium-and high-complexity services over time (Figure 4.9). The graph shows this evolution both in constant values of 2018 and as a percentage of the federal transfers for these services.

Figure 4.10 compares the value of these discounts with other groups of transfers.

2.3.5   How Credit-Based Hospital Financing Serves the Financial Sector

Both public and private banks have benefited from federal transfers for consigned loans. The data on the institutions offering consigned credit to hospitals, provided by the National Health Fund upon request, is limited to contracts active in 2019. The records for this year show nearly a thousand contracts on consigned loans, divided into approximately 65% in public banks and 35% in private ones (FNS, 2019).

The strategies discussed in this section are aligned with the process of financialization to the extent that financial institutions acquire a central role within the PHS and manage to profit from it. First, the system becomes dependent on banks to maintain service delivery. The following statement from the National Health Fund to justify the subsidies on loans illustrates how banks started being seen as critical actors to keep SUS in operation:

> The procedure of consignment through a loan agreement (...) serves the public interest, as it provides these entities with the possibility of anticipating revenues through financial institutions (...) which substantially contribute to keeping their "open doors" and thus assisting the population that seeks quality care in SUS network.
>
> FNS, 2014, cited by SFC, 2014

While sectors of the government and philanthropic entities justify hospital credit as a way to preserve the public provision network, a different reading suggests that these strategies serve the interests of the financial sector. Such strategies are based on the use of public revenues to subsidize and secure loans. As a result, financial institutions not only acquire a central role in the system, but they also end up getting a cut of the funds originally addressed to public health services. This means that subsidized credit programs have undoubtedly contributed to financial accumulation, turning financial institutions into one of the main winners of such strategies.

This is even more so considering that this collateral provided by the government turns the financing of SUS providers into a profitable and virtually risk-free activity for the lenders. Consigned loans are a case in point, once SUS transfers guarantee the regular payment of the installments. Not by chance, financial institutions have referred to philanthropic hospital loans as an important avenue of credit expansion. This modality is promoted on the banks' websites and praised by their representatives (ANEPS, 2008; Funcia, 2021, 2015). As recognized by a manager of one of the first banks to engage with this modality, "the advantage of this credit [line] is that it has practically zero risk (...) these are perfectly profitable operations for the bank" (ANEPS, *op. cit.*).

This time again, the capacity of financialized strategies to improve public service delivery can be put into question. Credit programs have the potential to undermine SUS provision, especially when the system's funds are used to pay off debts arising from privately provided services. Investigations from official auditing bodies over the past decade suggest that this might have been the case on several occasions involving consigned loans. Official audit works have found irregularities in these contracts, identifying cases in which SUS transfers were used to repay loans contracted by private hospitals without proof that the money was used to provide services for the public system (CGU, 2019; SFC, 2017, 2014). As concluded by federal auditors,

> It is clear that, from the main actors involved in this process – the citizen, the Federal Government, financial institutions, and private SUS service providers taking out loans, only the citizen and the federal government are bearing the risks of the anticipated discounting operation and its consequences. *These are values financed by the citizen and the Treasury that are not converted into public services.* For their part, the financial institutions and the borrowers continue to have their objectives with the discount operations met. *The latter have already obtained the anticipation of revenues and the former continue, even without ballast for the Treasury, receiving the due monthly installments with their respective accrued interest.*
>
> SFC, 2017, p. 14, emphasis added

This view is supported by Funcia (2015), who examines the potential impacts of consigned credit to hospitals for SUS patients:

The assignment of credit to pay off the service provider's bank debt (…) is harmful to the interests of the population to the extent that it takes away resources intended for health actions and services, more precisely in the medium-and high-complexity (…) for interest payments to the financial sector.

This constitutes the reallocation of public resources originally destined for the financing of universal health actions and services within SUS to remunerate financial institutions and, thereby, offer new profit opportunities for financial capital, characterizing a redistribution of income in favor of the latter.

pp. 3–4

Another characteristic of financialized strategies that becomes clear in this case is the diminishing space for transparency and social control in the use of SUS funds. As noted at the beginning of this section, there is no national database on the loans granted to philanthropic health institutions. The official bodies responsible for auditing public accounts report difficulties in monitoring the use of public resources in these operations due to problems in obtaining data (CGU, 2019; SFC, 2017). That SUS funds flow across banks and private health care facilities makes it even more difficult to monitor the practice, as the latter do not disclose information on the loans to the public. This lack of transparency is at least surprising given the large volume of public resources they involve.

3   Taking Stock

Differently from most wealthy countries, the attempt to consolidate the health system in Brazil took place when financialization was already underway. In this chapter, I have shown how this coincidence of events influenced the structure and trajectory of SUS' financing since its early years. In the 1990s, soon after its creation, the system already began to suffer from the expansion of financial accumulation strategies and started making use of financial instruments itself.

At least three sets of policies were particularly important for this process of internal financialization within SUS. The first and most impactful shift came as a result of the creation of an inflation-targeting regime in the country. To sustain this regime, the federal government implemented fiscal policy measures that directly determined the amount of funds available to SUS each year. This monetary and fiscal policy regime built an arrangement where part of the revenues from the PHS was systematically channeled to pay for interests and amortizations on the public debt, benefitting investors and financial institutions. This included both potential revenues (those that could finance the system had they not been used to cover excessively high charges on the public debt) and effective revenues (those already earmarked to Social Security and reallocated for the same purposes).

The two remaining shifts allowed entities in charge of SUS' short-term financing and service provision to resort to financial institutions to preserve and increase their incoming revenues. Health Funds, the financial managers of the PHS, did so by investing revenues in short-term financial assets seeking monetary returns. More recently, by government decision, these revenues started being automatically placed in financial assets before going to service provision. Private non-profit providers, in turn, raised funds through debt rather than financial assets. The need to maintain SUS service provision served as a justification for the government to create special credit modalities for philanthropic hospitals and use public revenues as collateral for interests and amortizations. The government mobilized several sources of funds to this end, including transfers earmarked for the payment of complex health care treatments and funds from workers' savings.

It is interesting to call attention to the connections between the three mechanisms cited above, not least as macroeconomic policies that have restricted SUS funding to cover financial expenditures have undoubtedly contributed to the severe shortage of funds within the system; this shortage, in turn, may help explain why actors within the system have sought alternative ways to raise money, found in the financial sector. Even though the concept of financialization is not made explicit in this passage from Funcia and Santos (2016), the authors seem to agree with the idea that the broader monetary and fiscal policy paradigm in place is connected to the use of financial instruments by actors involved in public health provision:

> The difficulties in financing public policies, especially in the scope of SUS, is structurally related to the growing commitment of the public debt burden over primary revenues, by obtaining primary surpluses (...) from 2014 onwards, this situation worsened with the fact that primary revenues were no longer sufficient to fund primary expenses, which has amplified the underfunding process of the SUS (...). It is in this scenario that the pragmatic and palliative solution of SUS' consigned loans becomes even more attractive.
>
> p. 4, emphasis added

Summing up, these policies have incorporated sus into financial accumulation strategies by channeling public health revenues to financial expenditures and allowing the own revenues of the public system to be invested in financial instruments. The State played a central role in bringing about these transformations, as the federal government deliberately created and enforced new approaches to sus financing, with other actors involved in the public system following along.

CHAPTER 5

Uncovering the Hidden Costs of Financialized Public Health

Insights from Case Studies

Contrary to common sense, public systems have not been shielded from the advance of financialization. Quite the opposite: it is precisely the magnitude of these systems, universal and comprehensive in nature, that seems to justify the adoption of financialized strategies of similarly large proportions. Deliberate State decisions have been indispensable in facilitating this "marriage" between PHS and financial capital. This is despite the fact that such shifts are far from neutral, having the potential to undermine some of the primary roles for which these systems were created. The concluding chapter of this book elaborates on these affirmations by drawing on empirical evidence presented throughout the previous chapters.

The financialization of PHS was conceptualized here as the increasing participation and influence of financial capital, instruments, interests, and actors in these systems. I conducted in-depth analyses of the French and the Brazilian PHS from the 1990s to 2018 seeking to apprehend if, and how, this process occurs in practice. The methodological framework used to guide the investigation was informed by the typology of different forms of State financialization first proposed by Karwowski (2019), which I adapted to this research object. I searched for policies leading the public system to adopt financial logics, engage with financial instruments, and participate in financial accumulation strategies (which I refer to as "financialized policies"). Although these developments usually go together, differentiating them is useful when differentiating processes in central and peripheral countries, as explained later in this chapter.

More than a comparative study, the goal of using France and Brazil was to demonstrate the global reach of the process of financialization and how it transforms public systems. These cases represent an opportunity to debunk the myth that unchecked financial expansion is a problem in wealthy countries only. In both cases, the national health system turned to finance by their own means and became a venue for the expansion and accumulation of financial capital.

The findings of the empirical investigation have significant implications for the understanding of contemporary reforms in PHS. It is clear that usual concepts, such as privatization, are increasingly insufficient to grasp the nature of these transformations in the period of neoliberal, financialized capitalism. Different conceptual lenses allow us to see different shifts, or at least to better understand the actors and mechanisms behind such shifts.

In the next paragraphs, I systematize and differentiate the mechanisms through which financialization reshapes universal health care systems in the center and the periphery of capitalism. I also make sense of the role of the State in these processes and the harmful implications of financialized policies on principles of equity and solidarity.

1   Systematizing Results: Common Trends

There is no question that financialization had a major influence on the trajectory of the French and Brazilian universal health systems since the 1990s. This influence expressed itself in the increasing incorporation of financial instruments and actors into the financing structures of the PHS. It led to a mounting dependence on financial capital for their continued operation and a greater subjection to financial interests in their decision-making processes. But if the financing of public health services has been captured by the logic of financialization in both central and peripheral economies, the mechanisms through which this occurred were quite specific to each case. These differences can be explained by the institutional arrangements of each system and the country's position in the global balance of powers.

The French system, *Assurance Maladie*, has a unique value for discussing the advance of financialization in public systems. It has been historically recognized as one of the most advanced public systems in the Western world. And yet, it is part of the French Social Security System, a pioneer in the development of strategies to address challenges in public health and social protection financing aimed at international financial markets. France created innovative arrangements that allowed Social Security, responsible for public health financing, to become an active player in financial markets. This was the case for long- and short-term financing, with Social Security agencies adopting innovative ways to raise money by issuing financial securities. The money coming from the issuance of securities serves for debt rescheduling and amortization (in the long run) and to address immediate funding gaps (in the short run). To the best of my knowledge, France is the only country in the world that developed such a complex process of financial engineering to convert social debt into financial debt held by domestic and foreign investors.

There were also transformations reaching service providers more directly, with the expansion of financial logics to fund physical infrastructure.

Government-sponsored programs encouraged public hospitals to finance investments via interest-bearing loans from commercial banks, replacing direct government investment. The extent to which they have spread throughout the sector represented a novelty in relation to previous forms of financing infrastructure based on interest-free government funding.

Table 5.1 explains how the findings for the French case are consistent with the broader framework of public sector financialization that informed this investigation. It identifies the policy instruments characterizing public sector financialization that can be observed in this case.

Brazil is one of the few peripheral countries that succeeded in creating a comprehensive system of Social Security and a universal health system, thus providing insight into how the peripheral condition can influence the ways in which the financialization of PHS unfolds. Moreover, unlike other countries, it created a universal PHS while the financialization of the world economy was already underway. This coincidence of events is a differentiating feature of this

TABLE 5.1   Systematizing findings 1: France (Assurance Maladie)

	Main form of financialization	Policy dimension	Description	Actors Involved
Long-term financing (public debt)	Advancing financial innovations	Fiscal policy (revenue side)	Issuance of financial securities to refinance the Social Security debt	Social Debt Amortization Fund (CADES)
Short-term financing (current expenditures)	Advancing financial innovations	Fiscal policy (revenue side)	Issuance of financial securities to finance immediate cash needs	Central Agency of Social Security Organizations (ACOSS)
Hospital financing	Adopting financial logics	Fiscal policy (expenditure side)	Private bank credit to finance infrastructure	Public hospitals

SOURCE: OWN ELABORATION. SEE FIGURE I FOR REFERENCE

case study that allows us to observe how this process can shape a system's trajectory from its very beginning.

The most relevant way in which financialization influenced the trajectory of the Brazilian PHS, *Sistema Único de Saúde*, was by shaping its structures of long-term financing. The system was incorporated into financial accumulation strategies since its early years, as a result of the implementation of an inflation-targeting regime in the country. This monetary policy regime entailed specific measures on the side of fiscal policy that channeled potential and actual revenues of the PHS to pay interests on the public debt. Brazil is one of the countries that allocates the largest share of public revenues to paying off public debt interests (financial rents), and possibly the one with the strictest rules on health financing to allow this to happen.

In the case of short-term financing, the incorporation of financial logics by the PHS itself is evident as state and municipal Health Funds started investing their revenues in short-term financial instruments, in an attempt to strengthen their financial soundness. Looking at the financing of providers, a similar incorporation of financial logics may be seen in the fact that philanthropic hospitals, a key link on the system's chain of provision, started resorting to interest-bearing loans to finance services. The revenues received from the public system due to services provided on its behalf served as collateral, guaranteeing the automatic repayment of the loans. Similar to the previous case, Table 5.2 systematizes the findings for the case of Brazil in accordance with the broader methodological framework of the research.

The most important trait shared by these experiences is that they have been similarly determined by the global expansion of financial capital in size and power. Although these systems are different in many ways, in both cases one can observe instances where material and financial resources from the Social Security and public health systems were transformed into inputs to create or invest in financial instruments. In doing so, financial operations and actors became critical for these systems to continue running and started absorbing part of the funds originally addressed to public health.

2   Shared Trends, Unique Expressions: Contrasting Central and
       Peripheral Experiences

Looking at the differences between the cases under investigation, at least two factors seemed relevant to determine how financialization unfolded in each PHS: the system's institutional framework and its condition as a central or peripheral economy. France is a wealthy country with solid institutions for the financing of the PHS, presenting relatively high levels of revenue collection and spending. It is also a system based on the social insurance model, where a large part of expenditures consists of reimbursements for services already provided to patients. Both factors seem to make spending have some precedence in relation to financing within the fiscal year. The proof is that the main challenges for the system's financing concerned its "deficits" – the lack of revenues to cover expenditures already incurred by the system. The deficits were, thus, the narrative that triggered financialization within the PHS in the French case. These deficits served as the gateway for financialization mechanisms, which came mainly as strategies to raise additional revenues and refinance debts in the financial markets.

Brazil, in contrast, is a middle-income country whose PHS never reached levels of revenue and spending similar to those of its wealthy counterparts. It is telling that, while core countries with universal systems (such as France)

TABLE 5.2   Systematizing findings 2: Brazil (Sistema Único de Saúde)

	Main form of financialization	Policy dimension	Description	Actors involved
Long-term financing (public debt)	Participating in financial accumulation strategies	Monetary policy (inflation targeting)	Budgetary policies appropriating SUS funds to pay for financial expenditures	Federal government
Short-term financing (current expenditures)	Adopting financial logics	Fiscal policy (revenue side)	Use of SUS revenues to carry financial investments	State and Municipal Health Funds
Hospital financing	Adopting financial logics	Fiscal policy (expenditure side)	Private bank credit to hospitals guaranteedby SUS revenues	Philanthropic hospitals

SOURCE: OWN ELABORATION. SEE FIGURE I FOR REFERENCE

attempt to limit the growth of annual public health spending, part of the financing rules implemented in Brazil during this period sought to force governments to allocate a minimum amount of resources into the system. Also, the Brazilian system is based on the national service model, which means that public health spending is largely discretionary, dependent on government decisions on how much to allocate to service provision in the next fiscal year. Against this background, it becomes easier to understand why the main challenges to financing the system did not appear in the form of "deficits" but rather of underfinancing – the insufficient allocation of resources to carry out all the actions necessary for adequate service provision.

The way that financialization reshaped the system was directly related to the issue of underfinancing. The most longstanding and important mechanism of financialization, the rules on the federal government and Social Security budget that directly impacted sus, did not come to provide financing for expenditures already incurred. Instead, what the rules did were preventing public revenues from entering the PHS in the first place, channeling them to the financial sector instead. This closer relationship between public health and the financial system did not result from any form of upfront financing to the PHS. The peripheral condition seems particularly important to explain these developments. The country's inferior position in the international balance of powers is an important factor in explaining the high levels of interest rates in the country and the influence of external agents in ensuring a monetary and fiscal policy regime that prioritizes servicing the public debt – which led to the measures undermining sus financing described above.

The ways in which financialization expressed itself in each case seem to support the ideas laid down by the theory of peripheral financialization (Becker et al., 2010) concerning how this process usually unfolds in central and peripheral economies. According to this theory, the former are more likely to go through a process of financialization pulled by the valorization of assets in financial markets, while the latter will have this process driven by interest-bearing capital (especially in the case of Latin American countries). And indeed, French Social Security bodies began to create their own financial assets and act as financial market participants themselves. In Brazil, by contrast, the dynamics through which the PHS was impacted by the process of financialization had much to do with strategies favoring the accumulation of interest-bearing capital from public and private debt.

3   A Broader View of Financialized Policies in PHS and the Role of
       the State

The idea that PHS will tend to disappear due to the advance of financialized
capitalism is a misguided interpretation of their transformations in this particular stage. The trajectory of PHS since the 1980s shows that reformulation,
rather than extinction, is what best explains their reality in the neoliberal
period. This reconfiguration of PHS that makes them more dependent on
finance is particularly suited for financialized capitalism, adapting to its conditions and favoring its expansion.

   This specific paradigm of public health in the making is marked by the
extension of indebtedness mechanisms. Both in the Social Security system
more broadly and in the PHS in particular, one can see a tendency to make
the systems indebted to the financial sector on a permanent basis. Debt, either
with banks or financial market investors, appears as a solution to debt itself.
Although many of these mechanisms have been introduced in times of supposed crisis and financing scarcity, they were never removed once in place.
This is the case, for example, of CADES in France and the DRU in Brazil. Even
in cases where financial engineering allowed the system's debt to decrease in
volume, the mechanisms that generate this debt were extended in time and
become an integral part of the system. This permanent indebtedness cycle
means a greater dependence of the PHS on the financial sector, gradually leading to a situation where the former appears unable to work without the latter.
What seems to be facilitating financing mechanisms become instruments of
co-optation of the public by the financial sphere. In this way, while service
provision may remain public, the logic of reproduction of PHS is gradually privatized and financialized.

   There were several occasions where traditional practices and objectives
within Social Security have been overshadowed by the advance of new, typically financialized behaviors. The involvement of Social Security institutions
with derivative markets and strategic decision-making on where to issue bonds
to maximize financial returns are just some examples of the emerging rationalities observed during the investigation. The statement of the then-director of
the French Central Agency of Social Security (ACOSS) at the National Assembly
in 2018 is illustrative of how this market-oriented strategy has reconfigured the
traditional *modus operandi* of Social Security:

> Let us be clear: today, ACOSS has no difficulty in placing the debt it manages on the markets, in a context of the search for good public signatures and extremely low or even negative rates. It is counterintuitive, I agree, but the debt now brings money to the general regime [of Social Security].
>
> Assemblée Nationale, 2018

This reconfiguration would be impossible without the State, meaning here specifically the central government, leading the way. The turn of public systems toward financial markets and their incorporation into financial accumulation strategies were not spontaneous movements, but products of deliberate government policies in these directions. Two key roles taken on by the government in the process of financialization of PHS were, one, turning the health system into a platform for the expansion of financial activities and, two, underwriting risks for these activities to succeed. This was seen in both the French and the Brazilian cases.

Starting with the first of these roles (turning the health system into a platform for the expansion of financial activities), the State has in many cases passed on to the financial sector the responsibility of managing the problems of the public system. This was done by making regulatory changes so that the financial sector could become the ultimate provider of resources to address the financial shortcomings of PHS. In doing so, it opened up possibilities for financial investments based on public health revenues and activities. In the second role (underwriting risks for these activities to succeed), the State also acted as an underwriter of these undertakings, providing direct and indirect guarantees to financial investors and institutions. This has usually come with regulations guaranteeing that public revenues, usually from the PHS or taxpayer money in general, would be allocated to cover amortizations, interests, and intermediations fees.

In France, for example, the State underwrote risks for financial agents by creating new contributions and raising existing ones, with the explicit goal of repaying the holders of Social Security assets. In addition, there were legal guarantees that the State would assume the responsibility to repay them in case of solvency problems in Social Security agencies. In the case of hospitals, the French government granted subsidies for them to repay their loans. In Brazil, the State enforced a regulatory framework designed to channel fiscal and Social Security resources to interest payments addressed to public debt holders, prioritizing the use of public resources for financial over health spending. It also ensured secure revenue streams that bodies linked to the PHS could use to invest in the financial system, in the case of Health Funds, and to borrow from them, in the case of hospitals.

The government, Social Security agencies, and public health bodies have been justifying the deployment of financialized strategies as a way to alleviate public accounts by expanding the sources of income and attracting investments. However, beyond these immediate justifications, there are far deeper, structural factors leading to these developments. As explained through the notion of the Debt Order proposed by Lemoine (2016), the hierarchization of priorities in the formulation of public policies, with finance at the top, is an important factor in explaining why States live under permanent austerity for the social budget in financialized capitalism. Social spending is seen as a "cost" and the social debt, as a "burden". Policy-making decisions work in line with this view, with many consequences from which the financial shortcomings of PHS are but one.

Following this line of reasoning, the state of permanent austerity in public health spending under the neoliberal policy paradigm puts PHS into a constant search for financing alternatives. At the same time, this paradigm pushes these systems to address financing constraints via financial instruments and strategies. When governments and public agencies attempt to overcome budget shortcomings or imbalances by borrowing from banks, investment funds, and investors, they are trying to cope with these challenges without having to address the structural causes of the financing problems of PHS. Addressing these causes would require measures that are considered off-limits in the current fiscal context, such as changes in the level and structure of taxation. Governments' ultimate goals do not seem to be solving the financial problems of bodies related to public health and Social Security but boosting their capacity to contract and cope with debts, either with banks or financial markets. In this way, it is clear that financialized strategies support the advance of a neoliberal State that requires less taxation and runs on lower levels of public health spending.

These results are important in that they show that it is no longer sufficient to fight for public systems: in times of financialized capitalism, it is also necessary to strive for systems that do not depend directly on financial capital to function. To contemplate alternatives, one must question the reasons leading public systems to face such a need for additional funding in the first place. These challenges are strongly related to the fact that Social Security and PHS revenues have not increased sufficiently to keep pace with their expenditures over the past decades. Such a mismatch is inextricably linked to the resistance of neoliberal governments to tax private capital in general and finance in particular, the latter a major *locus* of income and wealth concentration in times of financialized capitalism. In this context, it is no surprise that the continued accumulation of capital in the hands of financial players compromises the volume of resources available to finance public services.

The adoption of financial instruments and strategies did not come alone. In line with what was first observed by Chiapello (2017) looking at public policies more broadly, these shifts followed the incorporation of languages, techniques, metrics, organizational structures, and decision-making criteria typical of financial institutions by the public bodies involved in the PHS. This internal reorganization of the public sector has the effects of depoliticizing and artificially naturalizing choices in favor of financial capital, turning them into a seemingly technical decision. This was evident in our case studies. Several developments discussed here were led by the creation of agencies and departments specialized in financial operations for the Social Security System, or by the adaptation of existing bodies in a similar direction. French Social Security agencies and Brazilian Health Funds were largely autonomous in their decision-making processes concerning financial operations, which was justified on the basis of the complexity and high levels of expertise they involved.

Government choices favoring the openness to financial capital have been artificially turned into pragmatic decisions through longstanding efforts to reorganize spending priorities at the national level. These decisions are taken in a context in which alternatives other than those reliant on financial capital seem hardly feasible. Such a hybridism in the adoption of finance-friendly policies – which are political choices, but constrained by a context that obstructs alternatives – is evident in a statement from CADES' President at the French Senate: "there is the amortization period, the earmarked revenues, and the amount of debt transferred: these are the criteria to be determined, it's mathematical. Then, the choices are political" (Sénat, 2020, p. 120).

4   Impacts of Financialized Policies on the Foundational Principles of PHS

The increasing participation of financial capital within PHS, along with the growth of private activities in their structures facilitated by this movement, produce a silent yet major revolution in how these systems work. In doing so, they alter the capacity of different sectors of society to use these systems' resources, with far-reaching consequences for equity and guaranteed access to health care.

At first, financialized policies may seem advantageous for public systems by offering them the possibilities of raising additional funds, increasing investments, and reducing financing costs. However, closer scrutiny of these policies reveals that these benefits are generally short-lived, or come with major draw-backs. Notably, they entail different forms of monetary and social costs that are excluded from conventional calculations. They also introduce new types of risks from which public systems were previously insulated. One can illustrate the potential problems arising from the adoption of financialized strategies by considering their effects on three key pillars of PHS and Social Security systems: promoting solidarity and redistribution among individuals, guaranteeing stable funding for social provision, and ensuring democratic participation in public policy-making processes.

First, bringing these systems closer to financial actors and markets undermine principles of solidarity by allowing the financial sector to appropriate from public funds. Through the policy shifts described here, part of the money transferred (or that should, in principle, be transferred) to the PHS, directly or through the Social Security system, ended up in the hands of financial agents. This came in the form of payments of amortizations, interests, and fees, or conversely to acquire financial assets. The funds for doing so ultimately derived from taxes levied on the population at large. They were addressed to financial institutions and investors, known to be some of the wealthiest entities and individuals in the economy. In this way, such developments weaken the capacity of public systems to promote solidarity and redistribution among individuals.

The costs of these strategies are far from negligible. To mention a few examples, in France, CADES alone channeled over sixty billion euros to investors and financial institutions in interest payments and commissions from 1996 until 2018, in real values of this last year. In 2017, the volume of interests paid by the agency was almost equivalent to what would be necessary for the General Regime of Social Security to reach financial equilibrium this year. In Brazil, the federal government paid five trillion reais in interest payments to public debt investors from 2000 to 2018 (over one trillion euros, according to the 2018 average exchange rate) while allocating less than one-third of this amount to health care.

Another crucial drawback of financialized strategies concerns their detrimental effects on the stability of funding. Financialization trends within social protection and health care systems render the availability of resources partially determined by the financing conditions practiced by banks and financial markets. This means subordinating the costs of financing to various factors that are constantly changing and escape the State's control. They include domestic and international interest rates, exchange rates, inflation rates, and geopolitical events, to mention a few. Moreover, for the financial sector, financing social protection and health activities is an investment like any other, which is only attractive as long as it outperforms alternative investments. These factors can bring sudden changes in the availability and costs of financing for Social Security and PHS. It follows that making public systems dependent on the financial sector renders them vulnerable to the latter's inherent and ever more frequent cycles, exposing these systems to unprecedented levels of volatility and risks from which they have been previously distant.

When financing becomes contingent on the "moods" of the markets, the availability and costs of funding are more likely to behave in a pro-cyclical fashion. This undermines one of the main roles of social protection policies, which is to make individuals less exposed to the inherent instability of economic cycles. Adding to higher volatility, public bodies are pressed to pursue financial equilibrium at all times to signal to investors the capacity to honor debt obligations, regardless of the economic context. This is also inconsistent with the role of the Social Security system to act as a buffer during economic crises, a role that requires increasing investments and social benefits precisely in moments of downturn and slowdown in economic activity.

Several practices examined in our investigation revealed that the volume of funds mobilized in the markets varied considerably over the years, as did their costs (in the case of debt) or returns (in the case of investments). These variations often accompanied events external to the PHS and Social Security systems. Even if public agencies have been able to reap profits from financial markets operations in some cases, the increased dependence on the latter made the financing of public health care exposed to the reversal of financing conditions. For example, although French Social Security agencies have earned financial income by borrowing at negative interest rates since the mid-2010s, the institutions themselves recognize the role of the meager international interest rates of this period in contributing to these results, and their vulnerability to eventual reversals of this scenario (Assemblée Nationale, 2016; IGAS, 2018). In the case of Brazil, the level of interest rates, conditioned to the market's outlook on the Brazilian economy, determined the volume of revenues spent on the public debt, which in turn dictated what would be available to other areas including the PHS.

A final issue associated with the greater dependence on financial capital concerns the erosion of these systems' capacity to enhance social justice and democratic participation. To the extent that public systems become dependent on investors, banks, and rating agencies to operate, their decision-making processes are increasingly subjected to the interests and requirements of those who provide the funding. Public systems are required to show positive financial results, while social results are left out of the equation. To achieve these results, public agencies are often constrained to reduce the amount of revenue spent on social provision. This research showed several instances where the use of financial instruments led public entities to incorporate an "investor mentality" previously foreign to them and to pursue the maximization of monetary returns against other goals. It is telling, for example, that French Social Security agencies have gambled with interest rate differentials to reap income in international financial markets, and that Brazilian Health Funds have withheld money from the PHS in the financial system to improve their accounts. This suggests a fundamental opposition between the interests of financial actors (focused on maximizing monetary gains and maintaining positive financial results) and the collectivity (based on redistributing resources and investing in public provision).

Despite compelling evidence that financing social provision through financial capital alters the balance of powers in favor of financial actors, it is virtually impossible to determine to what extent this can affect the quantity and quality of services rendered to the population. The proper assessment of the financial and social costs of these strategies is seriously compromised by the transparency problems so typical of how financial markets work. Public databases fail to provide uniform, up-to-date, easily workable data on the institutions and instruments in which the resources were invested, the volume of returns, and the length of investments, to cite a few. In this way, the available information is often insufficient to conduct adequate evaluations. The complexity and opacity of the financial system play a major role in explaining these challenges. When using financial instruments, the origins of the funds to finance Social Security and the PHS cannot be fully known due to confidentiality agreements and the multi-layered, dispersed organization of financial markets. As a consequence, the destination of the reimbursements later on is also partially unknown. This lack of transparency undermines civil society's ability to weigh in and decide on the policies undertaken by Social Security and PHS.

Taken together, the drawbacks described so far disprove common arguments used in favor of pro-market reforms, including the assumptions that all losses can be measured, compensated for, and benefit society in the long run (Arestis et al., 2015). They reveal that the shifts brought about by financialized policies are to a large extent inconsistent with fundamental principles of public systems that represent their very *raison d'être*. The mounting challenges and deteriorating state of several aspects of PHS provision in the last decades reinforce the argument that financial investors and institutions have benefitted from current reforms more than the average citizen. In 2016, the president of CADES himself acknowledged the conflicts of interests inherent to these shifts, stating before the National Assembly that "when CADES was created, I was working as an insurer. At the time, I prohibited the purchase of CADES' securities, considering that Social Security should not be financed in such a way" (Assemblée Nationale, 2016, p. 15).

In light of the fact that austerity policies, market-friendly government agendas, and the growing power of financial actors are common trends in several countries, the financialization of PHS represents a crucial avenue of investigation. The limitations of this work in terms of time and space represent perspectives for further research. The analytical framework suggested here can be applied to other case studies, contributing to understanding how financialization takes place across different national settings. Future research could also seek to apprehend the effects of the coronavirus pandemic starting in 2020 on the creation and deepening of links between PHS and financial capital. This watershed event represented one of the largest shocks that PHS have ever faced, demanding unprecedented levels of material and financial resources to deal with the sanitary crisis. The data available during the period this research was conducted ended in 2018, partially hampered by the delay in the release of data by the government. In this way, it was unable to capture the impacts of the COVID pandemic on the financing strategies of PHS. It would be important to investigate not only the impact of the pandemic on the accounts of health and Social Security systems, but also how financialization may have shaped the ways in which they responded to these pressures. Evidence suggests that the pandemic has only reinforced what has been discussed so far, with the massive transfers of COVID-related debts to CADES being a case in point.

Also, this study focused on the dimension of financing, looking at changes in the management of current expenditures, deficits, and debts. Further research might explore how financialization reshapes the realm of public provision more directly. Evidence from other countries (Bayliss, 2016) shows that there might be a powerful, indirect entrance of financial capital into PHS structures through private providers working for the public system. There is reason to think that the latter are becoming increasingly integrated into financial structures and acting as financial agents themselves. A particularly promising area for further work concerns the case of PPPs, a special type of venture that conjugates aspects of financing and provision. Although there are PPP projects to build and operate public hospitals in both France and Brazil, the resort to these strategies is still limited compared to some other countries with PHS, such as England or Canada. Still, there is reason to think that these proposals are gaining traction over time, making them an important element in this research agenda.

As neoliberal efforts to dismantle public health care systems continue to evolve, it is essential that we remain attentive and critical of the tactics currently used to bend institutions created to achieve collective goals. Examining these tactics is essential for understanding how past measures and future policy recommendations for public health may conflict with the goal of creating a more equitable society. This book is a modest yet sincere contribution to this endeavor.

Appendix
Additional Information on Data Sources and Treatment

The case studies were examined using quantitative data to assess the volume of revenues exchanged between the PHS and the financial sector in each country and area under investigation (long-term, short-term, and hospital financing). The goal was to apprehend the amount of revenues borrowed from, invested in, or channeled to financial actors. The indicators chosen for each country and dimension vary, which is expected given the specificities of the processes of financialization in each case. There were many challenges in the process of data collection, as in many cases the desired information was partially or entirely unavailable. This seems to be related to both the innovative nature of mechanisms of financialization in PHS and the limitations of public information systems. When facing these types of challenges, I added qualitative information to support and refine the results obtained from quantitative analyses.

The primary sources of information were official public sources, including publicly available databases, minutes of legislative debates, as well as annual reports and financial statements from Social Security and public health agencies, statistical agencies, and supervisory auditing bodies. In the French case, they included, namely: (i) annual reports and financial statements from Social Security agencies (ACOSS and CADES), (ii) statistics from the Health and Solidarity Ministerial Statistical Department's database (DREES), (iii) selected reports from the French Supreme Audit Institution (Cour des Comptes), and (iv) documents registered at the national regulatory agency of financial markets (AMF). These data are relatively well systematized, and all the adjustments made to them have been already described in the Introduction (section "data sources and adjustments").

In the case of Brazil, I combined information from: (i) publicly available databases from official public bodies, including the Health Ministry, the Brazilian National Treasury, the Central Bank, and the Federal Revenue Service, (ii) financial statements provided by state Health secretariats in response to information requests send by me through the Law of Access to Information, and (iii) reports from public audit institutions, such as SUS Audit Department and the Public Prosecutor's Office. The information obtained through the Law of Access to Information remains available for consultation with the entities that have responded to the requests. They can be accessed using the following protocol numbers: SICSP 424771913690 and 49696192553 for São Paulo, e-SIC 3772 for Rio de Janeiro, and e-SIC 00060000407201941 for the Federal District. In the cases where the quality or quantity of available data was unsatisfactory,

I complemented the analysis with information retrieved from academic papers and articles from the press.

There were greater challenges in terms of data collection and treatment in the case of Brazil, warranting further explanation of the figures used for this country. In the case of State Health Funds, I have found diverging information on the financial investments carried by the Rio de Janeiro Fund State Health Fund across a number of public databases, such as the state's "Fiscal Transparency Portal" (*Portal Transparência Fiscal do Estado do Rio de Janeiro*), "General Accounting Portal" (*Portal de Contabilidade Geral do Estado do Rio de Janeiro*), and the Treasury Secretariat's website (*Secretaria de Estado de Fazenda*). These sources followed different reporting methods and presented conflicting values for investments in financial instruments by the state Health Fund. In the case of the Federal District, I could not find information for financial investments in public data repositories with information for the Health Fund, including the websites of the Federal District Health Secretariat (*Secretaria de Saúde do Distrito Federal*) and the Federal District Court of Accounts (*Tribunal de Contas do Distrito Federal*). Such inconsistencies prevented the construction of a homogeneous, long-term data series based on these sources. I overcame these challenges by submitting information requests to the State Health Secretariats of both Rio de Janeiro and the Federal District under the Federal Law of Access to Information. I used the data on financial investments provided in response to these requests to build the series examined in this study. I consider this to be the most reliable source of available information to the extent that the Secretariats are the agencies that control the Health Funds and, therefore, can provide the most detailed and up-to-date information on these investments. The initial research scope also included the São Paulo State Health Fund, as São Paulo is the richest and most populous state in the country. However, it was excluded from the final discussion as the data provided by the public administration, in this case, was insufficiently detailed for an adequate analysis.

In the case of philanthropic hospitals, I examined the case of consigned hospital loans using based on the volume of revenues from the National Health Fund used to repay consigned loans. The values used as a proxy were the volume of revenues from the National Health Fund channeled to all purposes other than paying for high and medium-complexity services, which include consigned loans. The use of values for total deductions, including loans but also other items, can be justified given the absence of a series for loan repayments alone. I requested this information from the National Health Fund through the Law of Access to Information, but the entity alleged a lack of operational tools to comply with the request. The protocol numbers for the information requests are e-sic n. 25820006773201995 and n. 25820003194202024. The information available in the National Health Fund's system only allows one to see the revenues destined to loan installments for one health establishment at a time, rendering it infeasible to build a long-term dataset on the total volume of sus transfers for such purposes at the national level. Considering solid evidence that the largest share of the revenues subtracted from the National Health Fund's transfers to subnational Funds is due to loan repayments, I considered that the total volume of discounted revenues was an adequate proxy to examine the evolution of discounts for consigned credit.

The data for each country is presented in domestic currency, Euro (EUR, €) in France and Reais (BRL, R$) in Brazil. To allow a clearer comparison, I indicate the equivalence between these currencies in the tables for the second case study. Unless explicitly stated otherwise, all figures are in constant values of 2018, adjusted for inflation according to the national consumer price index (Indice des Prix à la Consommation – IPC in France and Índice Nacional de Preços ao Consumidor Amplo – IPCA in Brazil). Adjusting the series for inflation provides a more accurate view of the evolution of the selected indicators over the long run.

References

Aalbers, M., 2019. "Financialization", in: *The International Encyclopedia of Geography: People, the Earth, Environment, and Technology*. Oxford: Wiley. pp. 1–12.

Aalbers, M., Loon, J. V. and Fernandez, R., 2017. "The Financialization of a Social Housing Provider", *International Journal of Urban and Regional Research*, 41(4). pp. 572–587.

Aalbers, M., Rolnik, R. and Krijnen, M., 2020. "The Financialization of Housing in Capitalism's Peripheries", *Housing Policy Debate*, 30(4). pp. 481–485.

Abecassis, P. and Coutinet, N., 2017. "Politique d'Austérité et Politique du Médicament en France et au Royaume-Uni", *La Revue de l'Ires*, 1. pp. 111–140.

Abecassis, P. and Coutinet, N., 2018. *Économie du Médicament*. Paris: La Découverte.

Abecassis, P. and Coutinet, N., 2021. "An Increasing Homogenisation of Private Health Insurers Under Solvency II?", in: Benoît, C., Sol, M.D., and Martin, P. (eds) *Private Health Insurance and the European Union*. Cham: Palgrave Macmillan. pp. 129–159.

Abecassis, P., Batifoulier, P., Coutinet, N. and Domin, J.-P., 2017. "Éditorial: la Généralisation de l'Assurance Maladie Complémentaire: Comment Faire Rimer Inefficacité Avec Inégalité", *Revue Française de Socio-Economie*, 18(1). pp. 13–22.

Abecassis, P., Coutinet, N. and Domin, J.-P., 2014. "Les Principes Mutualistes Confrontés Aux Modalités de Regroupement des Organismes Complémentaires d'Assurance Maladie", *Revue Internationale de d'Economie Sociale*, 331. pp. 60–75.

Abecassis, P., Coutinet, N. and Domin, J.-P., 2018. "Les Transformations de d'Assurance Maladie Complémentaire à la Lumière de la Démutualisation/Hybridation des Banques Coopératives", *Revue d'Économie Industrielle*, 161(1). pp. 9–38.

Agartan, T., 2012. "Marketization and Universalism: Crafting the Right Balance in the Turkish Healthcare System", *Current Sociology*, 60(4). pp. 456–471.

Agence Centrale des Organismes de Sécurité Sociale (ACOSS), 2007–2019a. *Comptes Annuels*. Available at: www.urssaf.org/home/lacoss-et-les-urssaf/documents-de -reference/archives.html (Accessed: 28 December 2020).

Agence Centrale des Organismes de Sécurité Sociale (ACOSS), 2007–2019b. *Rapport Thématique Conjoncture et Financement*. Available at: www.urssaf.org /home/lacoss-et-les-urssaf/documents-de-reference/archives.html (Accessed: 28 December 2020).

Agence Centrale des Organismes de Sécurité Sociale (ACOSS), 2009–2018. *Comptes Combinés*. Available at: www.urssaf.org/home/lacoss-et-les-urssaf/documents-de -reference/archives.html (Accessed: 28 December 2020).

Agence Centrale des Organismes de Sécurité Sociale (ACOSS), 2011. *Comptes annuels au 31 decembre 2011, Comptes combinés*. Available at: www.urssaf.org/home/lacoss-et -les-urssaf/documents-de-reference/archives.html (Accessed: 28 December 2020).

Agence Centrale des Organismes de Sécurité Sociale (ACOSS), 2017a. *Acoss Reçoit le Prix CMD du Meilleur Emetteur 2017 Sur le Marché des ECP dans la Catégorie SSA.* Available at: www.urssaf.org/home/journalistes/communiques-de-presse/ListeCommuniquesPresse/lacoss-recoit-le-prix-cmd-du-m-1.html?origine=recherche (Accessed: 2 June 2019).

Agence Centrale des Organismes de Sécurité Sociale (ACOSS), 2017b. *Rapport Thématique Conjoncture et Financement 2016.* Available at: www.urssaf.org /home/lacoss-et-les-urssaf/documents-de-reference/archives.html (Accessed: 28 December 2020).

Agence Centrale des Organismes de Sécurité Sociale (ACOSS), 2018a. *Rapport Thématique Conjoncture et Financement 2017.* Available at: www.urssaf.org /home/lacoss-et-les-urssaf/documents-de-reference/archives.html (Accessed: 28 December 2020).

Agence Centrale des Organismes de Sécurité Sociale (ACOSS), 2018b. *Rapport Annuel 2017.* Available at: www.urssaf.org/home/lacoss-et-les-urssaf/documents-de-reference/archives.html (Accessed: 28 December 2020).

Agence Centrale des Organismes de Sécurité Sociale (ACOSS), 2018c. *Information Memorandum, € 40,000,000,000 Euro-Commercial Paper Programme.* Available at: www.acoss.fr/files/contributed/investisseurs/anglais/fichiers/ACOSS_ECP_InfoMemo_2018.pdf (Accessed: 1 June 2019).

Agence Centrale des Organismes de Sécurité Sociale (ACOSS), 2019a. *Comptes Annuels.* Available at: www.urssaf.org/home/lacoss-et-les-urssaf/documents-de-reference /archives.html (Accessed: 28 December 2020).

Agence Centrale des Organismes de Sécurité Sociale (ACOSS), 2019b. *Investisseurs.* Available at: www.acoss.fr/home/investisseurs.html (Accessed: 2 June 2019).

Agência Nacional de Saúde (ANS), 2018. *Boletim Informativo – Utilização do Sistema Único de Saúde por Beneficiários de Planos de Saúde e Ressarcimento ao SUS.* Available at: www.ans.gov.br/perfil-do-setor/dados-e-indicadores-do-setor (Accessed: 31 January 2018).

Agência Nacional de Saúde (ANS), 2019a. *Dados e Indicadores do Setor.* Available at: www.ans.gov.br/perfil-do-setor/dados-e-indicadores-do-setor (Accessed: 31 January 2018).

Agência Nacional de Saúde (ANS), 2019b. *Boletim Informativo – Utilização do Sistema Único de Saúde por Beneficiários de Planos de Saúde e Ressarcimento ao SUS.* Available at: www.ans.gov.br/perfil-do-setor/dados-e-indicadores-do-setor (Accessed: 31 January 2018).

Aglietta, M. and Rebérioux, A. (2004) *Dérives du Capitalisme Financier.* Paris: Albin Michel.

Ainger, J., 2019. "The Logic Behind the Bonds That Eat Your Money", *Bloomberg.com*, 25 July. Available at: www.bloomberg.com/graphics/2019-negative-yield-debt/ (Accessed: 5 September 2021).

Alles, L., 2018. *Composition et Dynamiques du Paysage Hospitalier Français: Groupes Privés, Investissements Financiers et Marchandisation du Soin.* Master Dissertation. École des Hautes Études en Sciences Sociales, Université Paris Nanterre.

Alves, J. G., 2019. *Impactos Financeiros Provocados Pelo Sistema de Remuneração do SUS e Seus Determinantes.* Master Dissertation. Fucape Fundação de Pesquisa e Ensino. Programa de Pós-Graduação em Ciências Contábeis.

Amable, B., Regan, A., Avdagic, S., Baccaro, L., Pontusson, J., Zwan, N. van der, 2019. "New Approaches to Political Economy". *Socio-Economic Review*, 17(2), pp. 433–459.

Anand, S., 2004. "The Concern for Equity in Health", in: Anand, S., Peter, F., and Sen, A. (eds) *Public health, Ethics, and Equity.* New York: Oxford University Press. pp. 15–20.

André, C. and Hermann, C., 2009. "Privatisation and Marketisation of Health Care Systems in Europe", in: Frangakis, M., Hermann, C., Huffschmid, J., Lorant, K. (Eds.), *Privatisation against the European Social Model.* Basingstoke and New York: Palgrave Macmillan. pp. 129–144.

André, C., Batifoulier, P. and Jansen-Ferreira, M., 2015. "Privatisation de la Santé en Europe: Un Outil de Classification des Réformes", *Document de Travail du CEPN*, 2015–02.

Andreazzi, M. de F. S. de and Bravo, M. I. S., 2014. "Privatização da Gestão e Organizações Sociais na Atenção à Saúde", *Trabalho, Educação e Saúde*, 12. pp. 499–518.

Andreu, M., 2018. "A Responsibility to Profit? Social Impact Bonds as a Form of 'Humanitarian Finance'", *New Political Science*, 40(4). pp. 708–726.

Angeli, F. and Maarse, H., 2012. "Mergers and Acquisitions in Western European Health Care: Exploring the Role of Financial Services Organizations", *Health Policy*, 105(2–3). pp. 265–272.

Appadurai, A., 2015. *Banking on Words.* Chicago: The University of Chicago Press.

Appelbaum, E. and Batt, R., 2020. "Private Equity Buyouts in Healthcare: Who Wins, Who Loses?", *Institute for New Economic Thinking Working Papers*, 118.

Araújo, C. H. V., 2002. "Mercado de Títulos Públicos e Operações de Mercado Aberto no Brasil-Aspectos Históricos e Operacionais", *Notas Técnicas do Banco Central do Brasil*, 12.

Araújo, E., Bruno, M. and Pimentel, D., 2012. "Financialization Against Industrialization: a Regulationist Approach of the Brazilian Paradox", *Revue de la Régulation* [online], 11.

Arestis, P., Charles, A. and Fontana, G., 2015. "Introduction to the Special Issue on Ethics, Global Finance and the Great Recession", *Review of Social Economy*, 73(4). pp. 311–314.

Arrighi, G., 1994. *The Long Twentieth Century: Money, Power, and the Origins of Our Times.* London: Verso.

Arrow, K., 1963. "Uncertainty and the Welfare Economics of Medical Care", *The American Economic Review*, 53(5). pp. 941–973.

Ashman, S. and Fine, B., 2013. "Neo-liberalism, Varieties of Capitalism, and the Shifting Contours of South Africa's Financial System", *Transformation: Critical Perspectives on Southern Africa*, 81(1). pp. 144–178.

Assa, J. and Calderón, M., 2020. "Privatization and Pandemic: A Cross-Country Analysis of COVID-19 Rates and Health-Care Financing Structures", *The New School for Social Research Working Papers*, 08/20.

Assemblée Nationale, 2002. *Rapport sur le Projet de Loi de Financement de la Sécurité Sociale pour 2003*, 330, Tome I. Available at: https://www.assemblee-nationale.fr/12 /rapports/r0330-t1.asp (Accessed: 16 August 2021).

Assemblée Nationale, 2015. *Commission des Affaires Sociales. Compte Rendu de Réunion de la Mission d'Évaluation et de Contrôle des Lois de Financement de la Sécurité Sociale n° 10*. Available at: www.assemblee-nationale.fr/14/cr-mecss/14-15/c1415010.asp#P12 _630 (Accessed: 7 September 2021).

Assemblée Nationale, 2016. *Commission des Finances, d'Économie Générale et du Contrôle Budgétaire. Mission d'évaluation et de Contrôle. La Transparence et la Gestion de la Dette Publique. Compte Rendu n° 15*. Available at: https://www.assemb lee-nationale.fr/14/cr-mec/15-16/c1516015.asp#P7_306 (Accessed: 7 September 2021).

Assemblée Nationale, 2018. *Commission des Affaires Sociales. Compte Rendu de la Semaine du 22 octobre 2018*. Available at: www.senat.fr/compte-rendu-commissi ons/20181022/soc.html (Accessed: 2 June 2019).

Assemblée Nationale, various years. *Projet de Loi de Financement de la Sécurité Sociale*. Available at: www.securite-sociale.fr/la-secu-en-detail/loi-de-financement/ann ees-passees (Accessed: 4 July 2020).

Assembléia Legislativa do Estado de São Paulo (ALESP), 2009. *CPI Santas Casas. Relatório Final*. Available at: www.al.sp.gov.br/comissao/cpi/?idLegislatura=16&idC omissao=99968 (Accessed: 19 September 2020).

Assembléia Legislativa do Estado de São Paulo (ALESP), 2015. *CPI Santas Casas. Entrevista com Sr. Edson Rogatti*. Available at: www.al.sp.gov.br/alesp/cpi/?idLegi slatura=18&idComissao=13144 (Accessed: 19 September 2020).

Assistance Publique-Hôpitaux de Paris (AP-HP), 2018a. *Présentation de l'Institution aux Investisseurs*. Presented on November 15, Paris. Available at: www.calameo.com /books/00402182785dcc74d33fe (Accessed: 6 March 2020).

Assistance Publique-Hôpitaux de Paris (AP-HP), 2018b. *Programme d'Émission €2,500,000,000 Euro Medium Term Note Programme*. Available at: www.aphp.fr/pro- gramme-demissions-de-titres (Accessed: 3 June 2021).

Associação Brasileira das Entidades dos Mercados Financeiro e de Capitais (ANBIMA), 2019a. *Raio X do Investidor, 2a Edição*. Available at: www.anbima.com.br/pt_br /especial/raio-x-do-investidor-2019.htm (Accessed: 20 September 2020).

Associação Brasileira das Entidades dos Mercados Financeiro e de Capitais (ANBIMA), 2019b. *Consolidado Mensal Varejo, Informações consolidadas sobre as pessoas físicas do segmento de varejo bancário*. Available at: www.anbima.com.br/pt_br/infor mar/estatisticas/varejo-private-e-gestores-de-patrimonio/varejo-consolidado-men sal.htm (Accessed: 31 December 2019).

Associação Nacional de Hospitais Privados (ANAHP), 2013. "Santas Casas Terão Parcelamento de Dívidas Tributárias", *ANAHP Notícias*, November 4. Available at: www .anahp.com.br/noticias/noticias-do-mercado/santas-casas-terao-parcelamento -de-dividas-tributarias/ (Accessed: 20 September 2021).

Associação Nacional de Hospitais Privados (ANAHP), 2019. "A Agonia da Saúde Pública", *ANAHP Notícias*, July 8. Available at: www.anahp.com.br/noticias/noticias-do-merc ado/a-agonia-da-saude-publica/ (Accessed: 20 September 2020).

Associação Nacional dos Auditores Fiscais da Receita Federal do Brasil (ANFIP), 2019. *Análise da Seguridade Social 2018*. Brasília: ANFIP.

Associação Nacional dos Auditores Fiscais da Receita Federal do Brasil (ANFIP), 2014. *Análise da Seguridade Social 2013*. Brasília: ANFIP.

Associação Nacional dos Profissionais e Empresas Promotoras de Crédito e Correspondentes no País – ANEPS, 2008. "Bancos Apostam no 'Consignado Hospitalar'", *Imprensa*. Available at: aneps.org.br/leitura/8910/bancos-apostam-no- (Accessed: 3 February 2019).

Assurance Maladie, 2018. *Prévalence des ALD en 2017*. Available at: www.ameli.fr/l -assurance-maladie/statistiques-et-publications/donnees-statistiques/affect ion-de-longue-duree-ald/prevalence/prevalence-des-ald-en-2017.php (Accessed: 1 June 2019).

Attílio, L. and Cavalcante, A., 2019. "Empresas Não Financeiras e o Impacto da Estratégia Maximizing Shareholder Value Sobre o Emprego no Brasil", *Análise Econômica*, 37(73).

Attilio, L., 2020. "A Influência da Financeirização Sobre a Taxa de Juros Real Brasileira", *Revista de Economia Contemporânea*, 24.

Bahia, L., 2008. "A Démarche do Privado e Público no Sistema de Atenção à Saúde no Brasil em Tempos de Democracia e Ajuste Fiscal, 1988–2008", *Estado, Sociedade e Formação Profissional em Saúde: Contradições e Desafios em 20 anos de SUS*, 20, pp. 123–185.

Bahia, L., 2018. "Thirty Years of History in the Brazilian Unified National Health System (SUS): a Necessary but Insufficient Transition", *Cadernos de Saúde Pública*, 34(7).

Bahia, L., Chade, J., Dedecca, C., Domingues, J. M., Gonçalves, G. L., Herz, M., Lavinas, L., Ocké-Reis, C., Ortiz, M. E. R. and Santos, F., 2021. "A Tragédia Brasileira do Coronavírus/Covid-19". Document delivered to the Congressional Committee of Inquiry for Covid-19 of The Federal Senate on April 28, 2021.

Bahia, L., Scheffer, M., 2018. "O sus e o Setor Privado Assistencial: Interpretações e Fatos", *Saúde em Debate*, 42, pp. 158–171.

Bahia, L., Scheffer, M., Tavares, L. R. and Braga, I. F., 2016. "From Health Plan Companies to International Insurance Companies: Changes in the Accumulation Regime and Repercussions on the Healthcare System in Brazil", *Cadernos de Saúde Pública*, 32, pp. S1–S13.

Bain & Company, 2019. *Global Private Equity Report 2019*. Available at: https://www .bain.com/contentassets/875a49e26e9c4775942ec5b86084dfoa/bain_report_pri vate_equity_report_2019.pdf (Accessed: 29 June 2020).

Bambra, C., 2005. "Cash Versus Services: 'Worlds of Welfare' and the Decommodification of Cash Benefits and Health Care Services", *Journal of Social Policy*, 34(2), pp. 195–213.

Banco Central, 2019. *Relatório de Cidadania Financeira 2018*. Available at: www.bcb.gov .br/Nor/relcidfin/index.html (Accessed: 1 June 2020).

Banco Central, 2020. *Time Series Management System Database* (sgs). Available at: www3.bcb.gov.br/sgspub/ (Accessed: 29 June 2021).

Banque de France, 2019a. *Le Surendettement des Ménages – Enquête Typologique 2018*. Available at: particuliers.banque-france.fr/surendettement/etudes-sur-le -surendettement (Accessed: 19 June 2021).

Banque de France, 2019b. *Taux Indicatifs des Bons du Trésor et OAT*. Available at: www .banque-france.fr/statistiques/taux-et-cours/taux-indicatifs-des-bons-du-tresor-et -oat (Accessed: 2 June 2020).

Barbier, J.-C., Théret, B., 2009. *Le Système Français de Protection Sociale*. Paris: La Découverte.

Barbosa, E. de S., 2020. *Desvinculação de Receitas da União e Déficit de Accountability: um Estudo na Política Pública de Saúde no Brasil*. Doctoral Thesis. Universidade de Brasília, Faculdade de Economia, Administração, Contabilidade e Gestão de Políticas Públicas.

Barbosa, F. de H., 1996. "The Brazilian Pension System: Issues and Proposals for Reform". *Site da Fundação Getúlio Vargas*. Available at: www.fgv.br/professor/epge /fholanda/Arquivo/Pension.pdf (Accessed: 2 Mai 2019).

Barr, N., 1998. *The Economics of the Welfare State*. Oxford: Oxford University Press.

Bastos, C. P., 2001. "Inflação e Estabilização", *Polarização Mundial e Crescimento*. *Petrópolis: Vozes*, pp. 201–241.

Batifoulier, P., 2015. *Capital Santé: Quand le Patient Devient Client*. Paris: La Découverte.

Batifoulier, P., da Silva, N., Domin, J.-P., 2018. *Économie de la Santé*. Malakoff (Hauts-de-Seine): Armand Colin.

Batifoulier, P., Touzé, V., 2000. *La Protection Sociale*. Paris: Dunod.

Bayliss, K., 2002. "Privatization and Poverty: The Distributional Impact of Utility Privatization", *Annals of Public and Cooperative Economics*, 73(4), pp. 603–625.

Bayliss, K., 2016. "The Financialisation of Health in England: Lessons from the Water Sector". *FESSUD Working Paper Series*, 131.

Bayliss, K., Churchill, J., Fine, B., Robertson, M., 2016a. "Summary Report on the Impacts of Financialisation and of the Financial Crisis on Household Well-Being". *FESSUD Working Paper Series,* 199.

Bayliss, K., Fine, B., 2008. "Privatization in Practice", in: Bayliss, K. and Fine, B. (eds) *Privatization and Alternative Public Sector Reform in Sub-Saharan Africa: Delivering on Electricity and Water*. Basingstoke and New York: Palgrave Macmillan, pp. 31–54.

Bayliss, K., Fine, B., 2020. *A Guide to the Systems of Provision Approach: Who Gets What, How and Why*. Palgrave Macmillan.

Bayliss, K., Fine, B., Robertson, M., 2016b. "The Role of the State in Financialised Systems of Provision: Social Compacting, Social Policy, and Privatisation". *FESSUD Working Paper Series,* 154.

Bayliss, K., Fine, B., Robertson, M., 2017. "Introduction to Special Issue on the Material Cultures of Financialisation", *New Political Economy*, 22(4), pp. 355–370.

Bayliss, K., Waeyenberge, E. V., 2017. "Unpacking the Public-Private Partnership Revival", *The Journal of Development Studies*, 54(4), pp. 577–593.

Becker, J., Jäger, J., Leubolt, B., Weissenbacher, R., 2010. "Peripheral Financialization and Vulnerability to Crisis: A Regulationist Perspective". *Competition & Change*, 14, 225–247.

Beckfield, J., Olafsdottir, S., Sosnaud, B., 2013. "Healthcare Systems in Comparative Perspective: Classification, Convergence, Institutions, Inequalities, and Five Missed Turns". *Annual Review of Sociology*, 39, pp. 127–146.

Bértola, L., Ocampo, J. A., 2012. *The Economic Development of Latin America since Independence*. Oxford: Oxford University Press.

Beswick, J., Penny, J., 2018. "Demolishing the Present to Sell off the Future? The Emergence of 'Financialized Municipal Entrepreneurialism' in London". *International Journal of Urban and Regional Research*, 42, pp. 612–632.

Bhalotra, S. R., Rocha, R., Soares, R. R., 2019. Does Universalization of Health Work? Evidence from Health Systems Restructuring and Expansion in Brazil. *LACEA Working Paper Series,* 22.

Birch, K., Muniesa, K., 2020. "Introduction: Assetization and Technoscientific Capitalism", in: Birch, K., Muniesa, F. (Eds.), *Assetization: Turning Things into Assets in Technoscientific Capitalism*. Massachusetts: The MIT Press. pp. 1–44.

Blakeley, G., 2020. *The Corona Crash: How the Pandemic Will Change Capitalism*. London and New York: Verso.

Bloomberg, 2019. "Investors Cash in on Ebola Bonds That Haven't Paid Out". *Bloomberg.com*. Available at: https://www.bloomberg.com/news/articles/2019-08 -14/ebola-bond-pays-investors-millions-while-congo-battles-outbreak (Accessed 20 January 2021).

Bodie, Z., Merton, R. C., 1995. "A Conceptual Framework for Analyzing the Financial Environment". *Harvard Business School Working Papers*, 95–062.

Böhm, K., 2017. *The Transformation of the Social Right to Healthcare: Evidence from England and Germany*. Abingdon and New York: Routledge.

Böhm, K., Schmid, A., Götze, R., Landwehr, C., Rothgang, H., 2012. "Classifying OECD Healthcare Systems: A Deductive Approach", *TranState Working Papers*, 165.

Bolzan, L. C., 2010. *Ajuste Fiscal e o Sistema Único de Saúde na Gestão Estadual do Rio Grande do Sul: A Política de Saúde Esvaziada Pela Ideologia Neoliberal*. Master Dissertation. Centro de Pesquisas Aggeu Magalhães, Fundação Oswaldo Cruz.

Bonizzi, B., 2013. "Financialization in Developing and Emerging Countries". *International Journal of Political Economy*, 42, pp. 83–107.

Bonizzi, B., Kaltenbrunner, A., Powell, J., 2020. "Subordinate Financialization in Emerging Capitalist Economies", in: Mader, P., Mertens, D., Zwan, N. van der (Eds.), *The Routledge International Handbook of Financialization*. Abingdon and New York: Routledge. pp. 177–187.

Bortz, P. G., Kaltenbrunner, A., 2018. "The International Dimension of Financialization in Developing and Emerging Economies". *Development and Change*, 49, pp. 375–393.

Boyer, R., 2000. "Is a Finance-Led Growth Regime a Viable Alternative to Fordism? A Preliminary Analysis". *Economy and Society*, 29, pp. 111–145.

Boyer, R., 2003. "Les Institutions Dans la Théorie de la Régulation". *Cahiers d'Économie Politique*, 44, pp. 79–101.

Braga, J. C., 1985. *Temporalidade da Riqueza: Uma Contribuição à Teoria da Dinâmica Capitalista*. Doctoral Thesis. Instituto de Economia, Universidade Estadual de Campinas.

Branco, I. K. C., 2010. *Financeirização e Acumulação de Capital no Brasil: 1995–2007*, Doctoral Thesis. Programa de Pós-Graduação em Economia do Desenvolvimento, Pontifícia Universidade Católica do Rio Grande do Sul.

Brazil, 1964. *Lei 4.320 de 17 de março 1964*.

Brazil, 1969. *Decreto-Lei 119, de 04 de julho de 1969*.

Brazil, 1988. *Constituição Federal de 1988*.

Brazil, 1990a. *Lei 8.080, de 19 de setembro 1990*.

Brazil, 1990b. *Lei 8.142, de 28 de dezembro 1990*.

Brazil, 1993. *Exposição de Motivos do Programa de Estabilização, EM 395, de 7 de dezembro de 1993*.

Brazil, 1998. *Letter of Intent of the Government of Brazil to the International Monetary Fund*. Available at: https://www.imf.org/external/np/loi/111398.htm (Accessed: 5 May 2020).

Brazil, 2000. *Emenda Constitucional 29, de 13 de setembro de 2000*.

Brazil, 2012. *Lei Complementar 141, de 13 de janeiro de 2012*.

Brazil, 2014. Ministério da Saúde. *Portaria 244, de 14 de fevereiro 2014*.

Brazil, 2015a. *Emenda Constitucional 86, de 17 de março de 2015.*

Brazil, 2015b. Ministério da Saúde. *Portaria 2.182, de 24 de dezemro de 2015.*

Brazil, 2016a. *Emenda Constitucional 95, de 15 de dezembro de 2016.*

Brazil, 2016b. *Exposição de Motivos da Proposta de Emenda à Constituição que visa criar o Novo Regime Fiscal no Âmbito da União, EMI 00083/2016 MF/MPDG.*

Brazil, 2017a. Ministério da Saúde. *Portaria 3.992, de 28 de dezembro de 2017.*

Brazil, 2017b. *Lei 13.479, de 5 de setembro de 2017.*

Bressan, L., 2020. "Financeirização na Educação Superior Privada: Uma Análise do Fenômeno nos Governos Lula e Dilma". *Revista da Sociedade Brasileira de Economia Política*, 56, pp. 142–175.

Bresser-Pereira, L. C., 2010. "A Descoberta da Inflação Inercial". *Revista de Economia Contemporânea*, 14, pp. 167–192.

Bresser-Pereira, L. C., Paula, L. F. de, Bruno, M., 2020. "Financialization, Coalition of Interests and Interest Rate in Brazil". *Revue de la Régulation* [online], 27.

Brígida, E. H. S., 2012. *Percepção da Gestão nos Hospitais Filantrópicos Privados Vinculados ao Sistema Único de Saúde (SUS) na Cidade de Belém e Região Metropolitana, Pará.* Master Dissertation. Universidade Lusófona de Humanidades e Tecnologias, Faculdade de Economia e Gestão.

Brito, M. B. de, 2021. *Dívida Pública: a Base da Financeirização no Brasil.* Master Dissertation. Faculdade de Ciências Econômicas Programa de Pós-Graduação em Economia, Universidade Federal do Rio Grande do Sul.

Bruno, M., Caffe, R., 2014. Crescimento, *Distribuição e Acumulação de Capital numa Economia Financeirizada: Uma Análise dos Limites Estruturais ao Desenvolvimento Brasileiro.* Presented at the 38º Encontro Anual da Anpocs, October 27–31, Caxambu.

Bruno, M., Diawara, H., Araújo, E., Reis, A. C., Rubens, M., 2011. "Finance-Led Growth Regime no Brasil: Estatuto Teórico, Evidências Empíricas e Consequências Macroeconômicas". *Revista de Economia Política*, 31.

Bruno, M., Paulani, L., 2019. *Developmentalist Policies in Financialized Economies: Contradictions and Impasses of the Brazilian Case.* Presented at the 4th Workshop on New Developmentalism: Theory and Policy for Developing Countries, July 25–26, São Paulo.

Bryan, D., Harvie, D., Rafferty, M., Tinel, B., 2020. "The Financialized State", in: Borch, C., Wosnitzer, R. (Eds.), *The Routledge Handbook of Critical Finance Studies.* Routledge, pp. 261–277.

Bryan, D., Rafferty, M., 2014. "Financial Derivatives as Social Policy beyond Crisis". *Sociology*, 48, pp. 887–903.

Bryant, J. H., Rhodes, P., 2020. "Public Health". *Encyclopedia Britannica.* Available at: www.britannica.com/topic/public-health/National-developments-in-the-18th-and-19th-centuries (Accessed: 20 May 2020).

Caisse d'Amortissement de la Dette Sociale (CADES), 1996–2018. *États Financiers*. Available at: www.cades.fr/index.php?option=com_content&view=article&id=31 &Itemid=128&lang=fr (Accessed: 5 December 2020).

Caisse d'Amortissement de la Dette Sociale (CADES), 2004. "La CADES lance une émission obligataire d'un montant de 3 milliards d'euros". *Communiqué de presse June 9*. Available at: www.cades.fr/index.php?option=com_content&view=article&id=98 &Itemid=134&lang=fr (Accessed: 14 July 2020).

Caisse d'Amortissement de la Dette Sociale (CADES), 2015. "CADES Successfully Launches France's First RMB Bond". *Press release January 28*. Available at: https: //www.cades.fr/pdf/communiques/uk/2015/CP_28janv2015_VA.pdf (Accessed: 14 July 2020).

Caisse d'Amortissement de la Dette Sociale (CADES), 2016. *Conférence de Presse, December 13*. Available at: https://www.cades.fr/index.php?option=com_content&view=article &id=36&Itemid=133&lang=fr (Accessed: 5 December 2020).

Caisse d'Amortissement de la Dette Sociale (CADES), 2017a. États Financiers – Comptes du Vingt Deuxième Exercice (2017). Available at: www.cades.fr/index.php?opt ion=com_content&view=article&id=362&lang=fr&Itemid=128 (Accessed: 5 December 2020).

Caisse d'Amortissement de la Dette Sociale (CADES), 2017b. *Conférence de Presse, December 12*. Available at: https://www.cades.fr/index.php?option=com_cont ent&view=article&id=36&Itemid=133&lang=fr (Accessed: 5 December 2020).

Caisse d'Amortissement de la Dette Sociale (CADES), 2018a. *Conférence de Presse, December 11*. Available at: https://www.cades.fr/index.php?option=com_content&view=article &id=36&Itemid=133&lang=fr (Accessed: 5 December 2020).

Caisse d'Amortissement de la Dette Sociale (CADES), 2018b. *Programme d'Émission €65,000,000,000 Global Medium Term Note Program*. Available at: www.cades.fr/pdf /docref/fr/CADES_GMTN_Update_2018.pdf (Accessed: 14 July 2020).

Caixa, 2005. *Fundo de Garantia do Tempo de Serviço: Ações e resultados 2005. Caixa Econômica Federal*. Available at: www.caixa.gov.br/Downloads/fgts-relatorios-acoes -resultados-fgts/FGTS_AcoesResultados2005.pdf (Accessed: 1 October 2020).

Çalışkan, K., Callon, M., 2009. "Economization, Part 1: Shifting Attention from the Economy towards Processes of Economization". *Economy and Society*, 38, pp. 369–398.

Câmara dos Deputados, 2016. "Deputados e Debatedores Buscam Soluções Para Crise Financeira de Santas Casas". *Portal da Câmara dos Deputados, Notícias*, June 21. Available at: www.camara.leg.br/noticias/491193-deputados-e-debatedores -buscam-solucoes-para-crise-financeira-de-santas-casas/ (Accessed 19 September 2020).

Campello, M. R., Fontana, B., 2020. "Neoliberalismo e Desdemocratização no Brasil (1990 – 2016): Uma Leitura a Partir dos Estudos de Wolfgang Streeck". *Conjuntura Global*, 9(2).

Chambost, I., Lenglet, M., Tadjeddine, Y., 2018. "Introduction: Finance as Social Science", in: Chambost, I., Lenglet, M., Tadjeddine, Y. (Eds.), *The Making of Finance: Perspectives from the Social Sciences*. Abingdon and New York: Routledge. pp. 1–14.

Chambre Régionale des Comptes, 2016. *Assistance Publique – Hôpitaux de Paris, Exercices 2010 et suivants, observations définitives*. Noisiel: Chambre Régionale des Comptes. Available at: www.ccomptes.fr/fr/documents/33274 (Accessed: 12 June 2020).

Chesnais, F., 2016. *Finance Capital Today: Corporations and Banks in the Lasting Global Slump*. Leiden and Boston: Brill.

Chiapello, È., 2017. "La Financiarisation des Politiques Publiques". *Mondes en Développement*, 178, pp. 23–40.

Chiapello, È., 2019. "The Work of Financialisation", in: Chambost, I., Lenglet, M., Tadjeddine, Y. (Eds.), *The Making of Finance: Perspectives from the Social Sciences*. Abingdon and New York: Routledge. pp. 192–200.

Chiapello, È., 2020. "Financialization as a Socio-Technical Process", in: Mader, P., Mertens, D., Zwan, N. van der (Eds.), *The Routledge International Handbook of Financialization*. Abingdon and New York: Routledge. pp. 81–91.

Christophers, B., 2015. "The Limits to Financialization". *Dialogues in Human Geography*, 5(2), pp. 183–200.

Clarke, L., Chalkidou, K., Nemzoff, C., 2019. "Development Impact Bonds Targeting Health Outcomes", *CGD Policy Papers*, 133.

Clevenot, M., 2006. *"Financiarisation, Régime d'Accumulation et Mode de Régulation. Peut-on Appliquer le 'Modèle' Américain à l'Économie Française?"*. Doctoral Thesis. Université Paris 13.

Commission des Comptes de la Sécurité Sociale (CCSS), 1993. *Les Comptes de la Sécurité Sociale*. Paris: CCSS. Available at: www.securite-sociale.fr/files/live/sites/SSFR/files/medias/CCSS/1993/RAPPORT/CCSS-RAPPORT-DECEMBRE_1993.pdf (Accessed 4 June 2020).

Commission des Comptes de la Sécurité Sociale (CCSS), 1994. *Les Comptes de la Sécurité Sociale*. Paris: CCSS. Available at: www.securite-sociale.fr/files/live/sites/SSFR/files/medias/CCSS/1994/RAPPORT/CCSS-RAPPORT-JUILLET_1994.pdf (Accessed 4 June 2020).

Commission des Comptes de la Sécurité Sociale (CCSS), 1995. *Les Comptes de la Sécurité Sociale*. Paris: CCSS. Available at: www.securite-sociale.fr/files/live/sites/SSFR/files/medias/CCSS/1995/RAPPORT/CCSS-RAPPORT-OCTOBRE_1995.pdf (Accessed 4 June 2020).

Commission des Comptes de la Sécurité Sociale (CCSS), 1996. *Les Comptes de la Sécurité Sociale.* Paris: CCSS. Available at: www.securite-sociale.fr/files/live/sites/SSFR /files/medias/CCSS/1996/RAPPORT/CCSS-RAPPORT-JUIN_1996.pdf (Accessed 4 June 2020).

Commission des Comptes de la Sécurité Sociale (CCSS), 2000–2018. *Les Comptes de la Sécurité Sociale.* Paris: CCSS. Available at: www.securite-sociale.fr/la-secu-en -detail/comptes-de-la-securite-sociale/rapports-de-la-commission (Acessed 4 June 2020).

Commission des Comptes de la Sécurité Sociale (CCSS), 2003. *Les Comptes de la Sécurité Sociale.* Paris: CCSS. Available at www.vie-publique.fr/sites/default/files /rapport/pdf/034000579.pdf (Accessed 4 June 2020).

Commission des Comptes de la Sécurité Sociale (CCSS), 2004. *Rapport du Court des Comptes: la Sécurité Sociale.* Paris: CCSS. Available at: www.ccomptes.fr/sites/defa ult/files/EzPublish/Rapport-securite-sociale-2004.pdf (Accessed 4 June 2020).

Commission des Comptes de la Sécurité Sociale (CCSS), 2005. *Les Comptes de la Sécurité Sociale.* Paris: CCSS. Available at: bdsp-ehesp.inist.fr/vibad/controllers /getNoticePDF.php?path=Ministere/Publications/2005/ccss0506_rapport.pdf (Accessed 4 June 2020).

Commission des Comptes de la Sécurité Sociale (CCSS), 2006. *Les Comptes de la Sécurité Sociale.* Paris: CCSS. Available at: www.securite-sociale.fr/files/live/sites/SSFR/files /medias/CCSS/2006/RAPPORT/CCSS-RAPPORT-SEPTEMBRE_2006-PARTIE_1.pdf (Accessed 4 June 2020).

Commission des Comptes de la Sécurité Sociale (CCSS), 2018. *Les Comptes de la Sécurité Sociale.* Paris: CCSS. Available at: https://www.securite-sociale.fr/files/live /sites/SSFR/files/medias/CCSS/2018/CCSS_RAPPORT-SEPTEMBRE%202018.pdf (Accessed 4 June 2020).

Companhia de Planejamento do Distrito Federal (CODEPLAN), 2019. *Produto Interno Bruto do Distrito Federal – 2017.* Brasília: CODEPLAN.

Confederação das Santas Casas de Misericórdia, Hospitais e Entidades Filantrópicas (CMB), 2019. Circular CMB-001/19. Assunto: Linhas de Crédito com Recursos do FGTS. Brasília: CMB.

Confederação das Santas Casas de Misericórdia, Hospitais e Entidades Filantrópicas (CMB), 2016. *A História de Misericórdia das Santas Casas.* Available at: www.cmb.org .br/cmb/index.php/institucional/quem-somos/historico (Accessed: 5 August 2019).

Confederação das Santas Casas de Misericórdia, Hospitais e Entidades Filantrópicas (CMB), 2015. *Presidente Dilma Recebe Pleito do Setor Filantrópico de Saúde.* CMB Notícias, August 4. Available at: cmb.org.br/cmb/index.php/noticias/1111-presidente-dilma-recebe-pleito-do-setor-filantropico-de-saude (Accessed: 5 August 2019).

Confederação das Santas Casas de Misericórdia, Hospitais e Entidades Filantrópicas (CMB), 2013. *Tributação na Área da Saúde.* Presented on November 5, Brasília.

Available at: legis.senado.leg.br/sdleg-getter/documento/download/8c6of4fe-4104 -49c7-b113-af5b32c775c1 (Accessed: 5 August 2019).

Conselho Regional de Medicina do Estado do Rio de Janeiro (CREMERJ), 2017. "Entidades Decretam Estado de Calamidade Técnica na Saúde". *Informes, December 12*. Available at: www.cremerj.org.br/informes/exibe/3710 (Accessed: 3 April 2020).

Controladoria-Geral da União (CGU), 2019. *Relatório de Avaliação, Fundo de Saúde do Distrito Federal, Exercício 2018. Ordem de Serviço 201900159*. Brasília: Controladoria-Geral da União, Secretaria Fiscal de Controle Interno.

Cordilha, A. C., 2015. *Desoneração da Folha de Pagamentos: Impactos na Competitividade e Política Social*. Master Dissertation. Instituto de Economia, Universidade Federal do Rio de Janeiro.

Cordilha, A. C., Lavinas, L., 2018. "Transformações dos Sistemas de Saúde na Era da Financeirização: Lições da França e do Brasil". *Ciência & Saúde Coletiva*, 23(7), pp. 2147–2158.

Coriat, B., 2006. "Moves Towards Finance-Led Capitalism: The French Case", in: Coriat, B., Petit, P., Schméder, G. (Eds.), *The Hardship of Nations: Exploring The Paths of Modern Capitalism*. Cheltenham and Northampton: Edward Elgar. pp. 69–96.

Coriat, B., 2008. "L'Installation de la Finance en France". *Revue de la Régulation* [online], 3/4.

Cour des Comptes, 2014. "La Dette des Établissements Publics de Santé". *Communication à la Commission des Affaires Sociales et à la Mission d'Évaluation et de Contrôle des Lois de Financement de la Sécurité Sociale de l'Assemblée Nationale du Avril 2014*. Paris: Cour des Comptes.

Cour des Comptes, 2017. "L'Avenir de l'Assurance Maladie". *Rapport Public Thématique*. Paris: Cour des Comptes.

Cour des Comptes, 2018. "La Dette des Hôpitaux: Des Améliorations Fragiles, Une Vigilance à Maintenir", *Rapport Public Annuel, Tome 11*. Paris: Cour des Comptes.

Cour des Comptes, 2019. "La Dette des Entités Publiques: Périmètre et Risques". *Communication à la Commission des Finances du Sénat du Janvier 2019*. Paris, Cour des Comptes.

Crane, D. B., Froot, K. A., Mason, S. P., Perold, A., Merton, R. C., Bodie, Z., Sirri, E. R., Tufano, P., 1995. *The Global Financial System: A Functional Perspective*. Boston: Harvard Business School Press.

Crepin, J., 2017. "Transmettre la Gestion de la Dette Sociale à France Trésor". *Fondation pour la Recherche sur les Administrations et les Politiques Publiques* (iFRAP). Available at: www.ifrap.org/budget-et-fiscalite/transmettre-la-gestion-de-la-dette -sociale-france-tresor (Accessed: 6 March 2019).

Cresswell, J. (Ed.), 2010. *Oxford Dictionary of Word Origins*. Oxford and New York: Oxford University Press.

Cusseddu, V., 2011. *Capire la Finanza: La Cartolarizzazione e l'Esplosione Della Crisi Finanziaria.* Florence: Fondazione Culturale Responsabilità Etica Onlus.

Damon, J., Ferras, B., 2015. *La Sécurité Sociale, Que Sais-Je ?* Paris: Presses Universitaires de France.

Dao, A., Mulligan, J., 2016. "Toward an Anthropology of Insurance and Health Reform: An Introduction to the Special Issue". *Medical Anthropology Quarterly*, 30(1), pp. 5–17.

Dao, A., Nichter, M., 2016. "The Social Life of Health Insurance in Low- to Middle-Income Countries: An Anthropological Research Agenda". *Medical Anthropology Quarterly*, 30(1), pp. 122–143.

Davis, A., Walsh, C., 2017. "Distinguishing Financialization from Neoliberalism". *Theory, Culture & Society*, 34 (5–6), pp. 27–51.

Davis, G. F., Kim, S., 2015. "Financialization of the Economy". *Annual Review of Sociology*, 41(1), pp. 203–221.

Debeaupuis, J., 2004. "Le Financement des Hôpitaux: Une Maîtrise Générale Rénovée Mais des Enjeux de Formation et de Recherche Non Résolus". *Les Tribunes de la Santé*, 3, pp. 47–55.

Deloitte, 2014. 2015 Health Care Outlook – Brazil. Available at: https://www2.deloitte.com/content/dam/Deloitte/global/Documents/Life-Sciences-Health-Care/gx-lshc-2015-health-care-outlook-brazil.pdf (Accessed: 03 March 2020).

Dempsey, J., 2017. "The Financialization of Nature Conservation?", in: Christophers, B., Leyshon. A., and Mann, G. (eds), *Money and Finance After the Crisis*. Hoboken: Wiley, 2017. pp. 191–216.

Dentico, N., 2019. "Making Health a Global Bankable Project", in: Citizens for Financial Justice (Ed.), *Spotlight on Financial Justice: Understanding Global Inequalities to Overcome Financial Injustice.* Available at: https://citizensforfinancialjustice.org/resource/spotlight-on-financial-justice-understanding-global-inequalities-to-overcome-financial-injustice/ (Accessed: 15 December 2020).

Deruytter, L., Möller, S., 2020. "Cultures of Debt Management Enter City Hall", in: Mader, P., Mertens, D., Zwan, N. van der (Eds.), *The Routledge International Handbook of Financialization.* Abingdon and New York: Routledge. pp. 400–410.

Dias, F., 2008. "Desvinculação de Receitas da União, Gastos Sociais e Ajuste Fiscal". *Consultoria Legislativa do Senado Federal, Texto para Discussão*, 38.

Direction de la Recherche, des Études, de l'Évaluation et des Statistiques (DREES), 2020. *Data Drees.* Available at: www.data.drees.sante.gouv.fr/ReportFolders/reportFolders.aspx (Accessed: 9 April 2020).

Direction de la Recherche, des Études, de l'Évaluation et des Statistiques (DREES), 2019a. *Les Établissements de Santé.* Collection Panoramas de la DRESS. Available at: drees.solidarites-sante.gouv.fr/publications/panoramas-de-la-drees/les-etablissements-de-sante-edition-2019 (Accessed: 9 April 2020).

Direction de la Recherche, des Études, de l'Évaluation et des Statistiques (DREES), 2019b. *La Complémentaire Santé: Acteurs, Bénéficiaires, Garanties*. Collection Panoramas de la DRESS. Available at: drees.solidarites-sante.gouv.fr/publications -documents-de-reference/panoramas-de-la-drees/la-complementaire-sante -acteurs (Accessed: 9 April 2020).

Direction de la Recherche, des Études, de l'Évaluation et des Statistiques (DREES), 2019c. *Les Comptes de la Santé, Tableaux de Données, CNS Édition 2018*. Available at: data.drees.solidarites-sante.gouv.fr (Accessed: 9 April 2020).

Direction de la Recherche, des Études, de l'Évaluation et des Statistiques (DREES), 2018a. *La Situation Financière des Organismes Complémentaires Assurant Une Couverture Santé*. Collection Rapports DREES. Available at: drees.solidarites -sante.gouv.fr/publications/rapports/rapport-2018-la-situation-financiere-des -organismes-complementaires-assurant (Accessed: 9 April 2020).

Direction de la Recherche, des Études, de l'Évaluation et des Statistiques (DREES), 2018b. *Les Etablissements de Santé*. Collection Panoramas de la DRESS. Available at:drees.solidarites-sante.gouv.fr/publications/panoramas-de-la-drees/les-etablisse ments-de-sante-edition-2018 (Accessed: 9 April 2020).

Direction de la Recherche, des Études, de l'Évaluation et des Statistiques (DREES), 2017. *La Situation Financière des Organismes Complémentaires Assurant Une Couverture Santé*. Collection Rapports DREES. Available at: drees.solidarites-sante.gouv .fr/publications/rapports/rapport-2016-la-situation-financiere-des-organismes -complementaires-assurant (Accessed: 9 April 2020).

Direction de la Recherche, des Études, de l'Évaluation et des Statistiques (DREES), 2008. "Vingt-Cinq Ans de Comptes de la Protection Sociale : Une Rétropolation de 1981 à 2006". *DREES Études et Résultats*, 647.

Direction de la Recherche, des Études, de l'Évaluation et des Statistiques (DREES), 2010–2014. *Les Comptes de la Santé*. Available at: drees.solidarites-sante.gouv.fr /publications-documents-de-reference/panoramas-de-la-drees/les-depenses-de -sante-en-2019-resultats#toc--historique-(Accessed: 9 April 2020).

Direction de la Recherche, des Études, de l'Évaluation et des Statistiques (DREES), 2015–2019. *Les Depenses de Santé*. Available at: drees.solidarites-sante.gouv.fr /publications-documents-de-reference/panoramas-de-la-drees/les-depenses-de -sante-en-2019-resultats#toc--historique-(Accessed: 9 April 2020).

Direction de la Sécurité Sociale (DSS), 2018. *Les Chiffres Clés 2017 de la Sécurité Sociale (Édition 2018)*. Available at: https://www.securite-sociale.fr/la-secu-cest-quoi/chiff res-cles (Accessed: 9 April 2020).

Distrito Federal, 1996. *Lei Complementar 11 de 12/07/1996*.

Distrito Federal, 2015. *Decreto 36.279, de 19/01/2015*.

Dixon, A. D., 2020. "The Strategic Logics of State Investment Funds in Asia: Beyond Financialisation". *Journal of Contemporary Asia* [online], pp. 1–25.

Dodd, R., 2010. "Municipal Bombs". *Finance and Development*, 47(2), pp. 33–35.

Duarte, C., 2019. *Unconventional Monetary Policies: Past, Present, and Future*. Doctoral Thesis. Université Sorbonne Paris Cité and Universidade Federal do Rio de Janeiro.

Ducastel, A., 2019. "Une Banque Comme les Autres? Les Mutations de Proparco et de la Finance Administrée". *Actes de la Recherche en Sciences Sociales*, 229, pp. 34–45.

Dudouet, F.-X., Grémont, E., 2009. *Les Grands Patrons en France: Du Capitalisme d'État à la Financiarisation*. Paris: Lignes de Repères.

Duménil, G., Lévy, D., 2004. *Capital Resurgent: Roots of the Neoliberal Revolution*. Cambridge and London: Harvard University Press.

Durand, C., 2017. Fictitious Capital: How Finance Is Appropriating Our Future. London and New York: Verso.

Economic Commission for Latin America and the Caribbean – ECLAC, 2018. *The Inefficiency of Inequality* (LC/SES.37/3-P). Santiago: ECLAC.

Epstein, G., 2001. "Financialization, Rentier Interests, and Central Bank Policy". Manuscript, Department of Economics, University of Massachusetts, Amherst.

Epstein, G., 2005. "Introduction: Financialization and the World Economy", in: Epstein, G. (Ed.): *Financialization and the World Economy*. Cheltenham and Northampton: Edward Elgar. pp. 3–16.

Epstein, G., 2018. "On the Social Efficiency of Finance". *Development and Change*, 49(2), pp. 330–352.

Epstein, G., 2019. "The Asset Management Industry in the United States". *Financing for Development series*, 271 (LC/TS.2019/81). Santiago: Economic Commission for Latin America and the Caribbean (ECLAC).

Epstein, G., Yeldan, E., 2008. "Inflation Targeting, Employment Creation and Economic Development: Assessing the Impacts and Policy Alternatives". *International Review of Applied Economics*, 22(2), pp. 131–144.

Erikson, S., 2015. "The Financialization of Ebola". *Somatosphere*, November 11. Available at: somatosphere.net/2015/the-financialization-of-ebola.html (Accessed 14 August 21).

Erturk, I., 2020. "Shareholder Primacy and Corporate Financialization", in: Mader, P., Mertens, D., Zwan, N. van der (Eds.), *The Routledge International Handbook of Financialization*. Abingdon and New York: Routledge. pp. 43–55.

Esping-Andersen, G., 1990. The Three Worlds of Welfare Capitalism. Princeton: Princeton University Press.

Euromoney Institutional Investor. "Financing Supranationals and Agencies: New Borrowing Strategies in a Post-Crisis World", *Euroweek*, April 2011.

Eurostat, 2021. *Taux d'Endettement Brut Des ménages – Produits Données*. Available at: ec.europa.eu/eurostat/fr/web/products-datasets/-/TEC00104 (Accessed 19 June 2021).

Evangelista, D. R., 2017. *Gerenciamento de Meta Fiscal ou de Resultado Fiscal: Uma Avaliação da Meta e do Resultado Primário do Governo Federal.* Master Dissertation. Faculdade de Economia, Administração e Contabilidade, Universidade de Brasília.

Ewert, B., 2009. "Economization and Marketization in the German Healthcare System: How Do Users Respond?" *German Policy Studies* 5(1), pp. 21–44.

Fascina, L. P., 2009. *Filantropia como Estratégia em Cinco Organizações Hospitalares Privadas no Município de São Paulo.* Doctoral Thesis. Escola de Administração de Empresas de São Paulo, Fundação Getulio Vargas.

Fastenrath, F., Schwan, M., Trampusch, C., 2017. "Where States and Markets Meet: the Financialisation of Sovereign Debt Management". *New Political Economy*, 22(3), pp. 273–293.

Fattorelli, M. L., 2017. *Exame Específico Preliminar sobre as Operações com Debêntures Realizadas pela Empresa Estatal PBH ATIVOS S/A (...).* Relatório Preliminar Específico de Auditoria Cidadã da Dívida 2/2017. Brasília: Auditoria Cidadã da Dívida.

Fattorelli, M. L., Ávila, R., 2017. "A Auditoria da Dívida e o Necessário Aumento dos Gastos com Saúde". *Futuros do Brasil: Textos para Debate*, 3, pp. 1–39.

Federação Brasileira de Hospitais – FBH, 2019. *Cenário dos Hospitais no Brasil 2019.* FBH and CNSaúde.

Federação das Indústrias do Estado do Rio de Janeiro (FIRJAN), 2017. "A Situação Fiscal dos Estados Brasileiros". *Publicações de Economia, Conjuntura Econômica.* April 2014. Available at: www.firjan.com.br/lumis/portal/file/fileDownload.jsp?fileId =2C908A8F5B87A9E3015BA6AEE3DD5828 (Accessed: 2 May 2020).

Feijó, C., Lamonica, M. T., Lima, S. S., 2016. "Financial Liberalization and Structural Change: The Brazilian Case in the 2000s". *Center for Studies on Inequality and Development (CEDE) Discussion Papers*, 118.

Fellows, F., 2019. *Financeirização das Firmas Não-Financeiras no Brasil: Um Modelo Dinâmico de Dados em Painel.* Doctoral Thesis. Instituto de Economia, Universidade Federal do Rio de Janeiro.

Ferlazzo, E., 2018. "La Financiarisation des Gouvernements Locaux". *Actes de la Recherche en Sciences Sociales*, 221–222, pp. 100–119.

Filippon, J., Giovanella, L., Konder, M., Pollock, A. M., 2016. "'Liberalizing' the English National Health Service: Background and Risks to Healthcare Entitlement". *Cadernos de Saúde Pública*, 32(8).

Finance Active, 2016. Observatoire Finance Active 2016. Établissements de Santé. Paris: Finance Active.

Financial Stability Board, 2018. *Global Shadow Banking Monitoring Report 2017.* Basel: Financial Stability Board.

Financial Times, 2013. *France's Losses on Dexia Bailout Hit €6.6bn.* July 18. Available at: https://www.ft.com/content/ff693d70-efb5-11e2-8229-00144feabdco (Accessed: 21 June 2020).

Financial Times, 2018. *Spire Shares Tumble after NHS Cuts Warning.* August 6. Available at: https://www.ft.com/content/ff96337a-9947-11e8-ab77-f854c65a4465 (Accessed: 21 June 2020).

Fine, B., 1999. "Privatization: Theory with Lessons from the United Kingdom", in: Vlachou, A. (Ed.), *Contemporary Economic Theory: Radical Critiques of Neoliberalism.* Hampshire and London: Macmillan. pp. 41–71.

Fine, B., 2008. "Privatization's Shaky Theoretical Foundations", in: Bayliss, K., Fine, B. (Eds.), *Privatization and Alternative Public Sector Reform in Sub-Saharan Africa: Delivering on Electricity and Water.* Basingstoke and New York: Palgrave Macmillan. pp. 13–30.

Fine, B., 2009. *Financialisation and Social Policy.* Presented at the UNRISD Conference Social and Political Dimensions of the Global Crisis, November 12–13, Geneva.

Fine, B., 2013. "Financialization from a Marxist Perspective". *International Journal of Political Economy* 42(4), pp. 47–66.

Fine, B., 2014. "The Continuing Enigmas of Social Policy". *UNRISD Working Papers,* 2014–10.

Fine, B., 2020. "Situating PPPs", in: J. Gideon, E. Unterhalter (Eds.), *Critical Reflections on Public-Private Partnerships.* London and New York: Routledge. pp. 26–38.

Fine, B., Bayliss, K., 2016. "Paper on Theoretical Framework for Assessing the Impact of Finance on Public Provision". *FESSUD Working Paper Series,* 192.

Fine, B., Hall, D., 2012. "Terrains of Neoliberalism: Constraints and Opportunities for Alternative Models of Service Delivery", in: *Alternatives to Privatization: Public Options for Essential Services in the Global South.* Routledge Studies in Development and Society. New York and Abingdon: Routledge. pp. 45–70.

Fine, B., Saad-Filho, A., 2017. "Thirteen Things You Need to Know About Neoliberalism". *Critical Sociology,* 43(4–5), pp. 685–706.

Firmin, C., 2008. *Financiarisation, Répartition et Croissance. Quelques Faits Stylisés à l'épreuve d'un Modèle Stock-Flux.* Doctoral Thesis. Université Panthéon-Sorbonne – Paris I.

Fitch Ratings, 2017. *Agence Centrale des Organismes de Sécurité Sociale (ACOSS) Credit Report.* Available at: https://www.fitchratings.com/entity/agence-centrale-des-org anismes-de-securite-sociale-acoss-84359470 (Accessed: 08 August 2020).

Fleury, S., 2017. "The Welfare State in Latin America: Reform, Innovation and Fatigue". *Cadernos de Saúde Pública,* 33 (sup 2). pp. 1–10.

Fonds CMU, 2016. *Rapport d'Activité 2015.* Collection Les Rapports d'Activité du Fonds CMU. Available at: https://www.complementaire-sante-solidaire.gouv.fr/rapports_a ctivite.php (Accessed: 8 January 2020).

Fortes, L., 2010. "Remédio por Juros". *Carta Capital,* February 26.

Foster, J. B., 2007. "The Financialization of Capitalism". *Monthly Review,* 58 (11), pp. 1–12.

Foureault, F., 2018. "L'organisation de la Financiarisation. Structure et Développement du Champ des Fonds d'Investissement en France". *Revue Française de Sociologie,* 59(1), pp 37–69.

France, 1946. *Constitution de 1946, IVe République.*

France, 1967. *Ordonnance n° 67–706 du 21 août 1967.*

France, 1980. *Loi 80–539 du 16 juillet 1980.*

France, 1996. *Ordonnance n° 96–50 du 24 janvier 1996.*

France, 2003. *Ordonnance 2003–850 du 4 septembre 2003.*

France, 2004. *Loi 2004–810 du 13 août 2004.*

France, 2005. *Ordonnance 2005–406 du 2 mai 2005.*

France, 2007. Ministère de la Santé, de la Jeunesse et des Sports. *Circulaire DHOS/F2 n° 2007–248 du 15 juin 2007.*

France, 2008. *Loi 2008–1330 du 17 décembre 2008.*

France, 2014. Ministère des Affaires Sociales, de la Santé et des Droits des Femmes, Ministère des Finances et des Comptes Publics. *Instruction Interministerielle DGOS/PF1/DGFiP/CL1C/CL2A/2014/363* du 24 decémbre.

France, 2018. Loi 2018–1203 du 22 Décembre 2018 de Financement de la Sécurité Sociale pour 2019, Rapport du Programme de Qualité et d'Efficience (PQE), Financement. Available at: www.securite-sociale.fr/files/live/sites/SSFR/files/medias/PLFSS /2019/ANNEXE_1/PLFSS-2019-ANNEXE_1-PQE-FINANCEMENT.pdf (Accessed: 2 March 2020).

France, n.d. Social Security Code (*Code de la Sécurité Sociale*).

Franchet, P., 2015. *Que faire de la dette sociale?* Liège: CADTM.

François, P., Lemercier, C., 2016. "Une Financiarisation à la Française (1979–2009). Mutations des Grandes Entreprises et Conversion des Elites". *Revue Française de Sociologie,* 57(2), pp. 269–320.

François, P., Lemercier, C., 2017. "The Second Financialization in France", in: Boussard, V. (Ed.), *Finance at Work.* London and New York: Routledge. pp. 142–155.

Frangakis, M., Huffschmid, Jörg, 2009. "Privatisation in Western Europe", in: Frangakis, M., Hermann, C., Huffschmid, J., Lorant, K. (Eds.), *Privatisation against the European Social Model.* Basingstoke and New York: Palgrave Macmillan. pp. 9–29.

Fraser, A., Tan, S., Kruithof, K., Sim, M., Disley, E., Giacomantonio, C., Lagarde, M., Mays, N., 2018. "Evaluation of the Social Impact Bond Trailblazers in Health and Social Care (Final Report)". *Policy Innovation Research Unit (PIRU) publication,* 2018–23.

Fraser, N., 2016. "Contradictions of Capital and Care". *New Left Review,* 100, pp. 99–117.

Freeman, R., Frisina, L., 2010. "Health Care Systems and the Problem of Classification". *Journal of Comparative Policy Analysis* 12(1–2), pp. 163–178.

Freitas, M. C. P., Prates, D. M., 2001. "A Abertura Financeira no Governo FHC: Impactos e Conseqüências". *Economia e Sociedade*, 10(2), pp. 81–111.

Frenkel, R., 2006. "An Alternative to Inflation Targeting in Latin America: Macroeconomic Policies Focused on Employment". *Journal of Post Keynesian Economics*, 28(4), pp. 573–591.

Frisina, L. D., Schmid, A., de Carvalho, G., Rothgang, H., 2021. "Comparing Apples to Oranges? Minimizing Typological Biases to Better Classify Healthcare Systems Globally". *Health Policy OPEN*, 2. pp. 1–8.

Froud, J., Haslam, C., Johal, S., Williams, K., 2000. "Shareholder Value and Financialization: Consultancy Promises, Management Moves". *Economy and Society*, 29(1), pp. 80–110.

Fullman, N., Yearwood, J., Abbafati, C., Solomon, A., et al., 2018. "Measuring Performance on the Healthcare Access and Quality Index for 195 Countries and Territories and Selected Subnational Locations". *The Lancet*, 391(10136), pp. 2236–2271.

Funcia, F. R., 2019. "Underfunding and Federal Budget of SUS: Preliminary References for Additional Resource Allocation". *Ciência & Saúde Coletiva*, 24(12), pp. 4405–4415.

Funcia, F., 2015. "Empréstimo Consignado SUS: É o Setor Financeiro Ganhando com o Processo de Subfinanciamento do SUS". *Instituto de Direito Sanitário Aplicado (IDISA), Domingueira da Saúde* [online], 27/2015.

Funcia, F., 2021. "Empréstimo Consignado SUS: Apropriação de Recursos Públicos pelo Setor Privado com Redução de Financiamento Governamental para o Atendimento das Necessidades de Saúde da População". *Observatório de Políticas Públicas, Empreendedorismo e Conjuntura da UCS, 17ª Carta de Conjuntura da UCS*, pp. 154–158.

Funcia, F., Santos, N. R. dos, 2016. "Empréstimo Consignado SUS: o Sistema Financeiro se Aproveita Tanto das Dificuldades de Fluxo de Caixa, como das Boas Intenções dos Gestores". *Instituto de Direito Sanitário Aplicado (IDISA), Domingueira da Saúde* [online], 12/2016.

Fundo Nacional de Saúde (FNS), 2019. *Resposta à Requerimento de Informação, Protocolo e-SIC 25820006773201995*. Central de Atendimento do Fundo Nacional.

Fundo Nacional de Saúde (FNS), 2020. *Consulta FNS*. Available at: consultafns.saude.gov.br (Accessed 20 September 2020).

Gabor, D., 2018. *Understanding the Financialisation of International Development through 11 FAQs*. Washington D.C.: Heinrich Böll Stiftung North America.

Garnier, D., 2015. "Les Hôpitaux Français Intoxiqués". *Club de Mediapart*. Available at: blogs.mediapart.fr/denis-garnier/blog/010315/les-hopitaux-francais-intoxiques (Accessed 3 June 2019).

Gentil, D. L., 2019. *A Política Fiscal e a Falsa Crise da Seguridade Social Brasileira: Uma História de Desconstrução e de Saques*. Rio de Janeiro: Mauad.

Gentil, D. L., Hermann, J., 2017. "A Política Fiscal do Primeiro Governo Dilma Rousseff: Ortodoxia e Retrocesso". *Economia e Sociedade*, 26(3), pp. 793–816.

Giovanella, L., Faria, M., 2015. "Health Policy Reform in South America", in: Kuhlmann, E., Blank, R., Bourgeault, I., Wendt, C. (Eds.), *The Palgrave International Handbook of Healthcare Policy and Governance*. Basingstoke and New York: Palgrave Macmillan, pp. 204–221.

Giovanella, L., Mendoza-Ruiz, A., Pilar, A. de C. A., Rosa, M. C. da, Martins, G. B., Santos, I. S., Silva, D.B., Vieira, J. M. de L., Castro, V. C. G. de, Silva, P. O. da, Machado, C. V., 2018. "Universal Health System and Universal Health Coverage: Assumptions and Strategies". *Ciência & Saúde Coletiva*, 23(6), 1763–1776.

Global Health Watch, 2014. *Global Health Watch 4: An Alternative World Health Report.* The People's Health Movement. Available at: phmovement.org/global-health -watch-4/ (Accessed: 29 April 2020).

Goldsteen, R. L., Goldsteen, K., Graham, D., 2010. *Introduction to Public Health.* New York: Springer.

Golka, P., 2019. *Financialization as Welfare: Social Impact Investing and British Social Policy, 1997–2016*. Cham: Springer.

González, F., 2020. "Micro-credit and the Financialization of Low-income Households", in: Mader, P., Mertens, D., Zwan, N. van der (Eds.), *The Routledge International Handbook of Financialization*. Abingdon and New York: Routledge. pp. 301–311.

Gorsky, M., 2011. "Health Systems and Welfare States in the West", in: Berridge, V., Gorsky, M., Mold, A. (Eds.), *Public Health in History*. Berkshire and New York: Open University Press. pp. 23–41.

Graeber, D., 2011. *Debt: The First 5,000 Years*. New York: Melville House.

Guillen, A., 2014. "Financialization and Financial Profit". *Brazilian Journal of Political Economy* 34(3), pp. 451–470.

Guttmann, R., 2008. "A Primer on Finance-Led Capitalism and its Crisis". *Revue de la Régulation* [online], 3/4.

Guttmann, R., 2016. *Finance-led Capitalism: Shadow Banking, Re-regulation, and the Future of Global Markets*. Basingstoke and New York: Palgrave Macmillan.

Hager, S. B., 2016. "The Making of the Modern 'Debt State'". *Sheffield Political Economy Research Institute (SPERI) blog.* Available at: speri.dept.shef.ac.uk/2016/03/10/the -making-of-the-modern-debt-state/ (Accessed: 24 June 2021).

Hansen, M. B., Lindholst, A. C., 2016. "Marketization Revisited". *International Journal of Public Sector Management*, 29(5), pp. 398–408.

Hassenteufel, P., Palier, B., 2007. "Towards Neo-Bismarckian Health Care States? Comparing Health Insurance Reforms in Bismarckian Welfare Systems". *Social Policy & Administration*, 41(6), pp. 574–596.

Hein, E., 2012. *The Macroeconomics of Finance-Dominated Capitalism and Its Crisis.* Cheltenham and Northampton: Edward Elgar.

Hein, E., Dodig, N., Budyldina, N., 2015. "The Transition Towards Finance-Dominated Capitalism: French Regulation School, Social Structures of Accumulation and

Post-Keynesian Approaches Compared", in: Hein, E., Detzer, D., Dodig, N. (Eds.), *The Demise of Finance-Dominated Capitalism: Explaining the Financial and Economic Crises.* Cheltenham and Northampton: Edward Elgar. pp. 7–53.

Hein, E., Treeck, T. V., 2010. "Financialisation and Rising Shareholder Power in Kaleckian/Post-Kaleckian Models of Distribution and Growth". *Review of Political Economy,* 22(2), pp. 205–233.

Hermann, C., 2010. "The Marketisation of Health Care in Europe", in: Panitch, L. Leys, C. (Eds.), *Socialist Register 46.* pp. 125–144.

Hermann, C., Verhoest, K., 2012. "The Process of Liberalisation, Privatisation and Marketisation", in: Hermann, C., Flecker, J. (Eds.), *Privatization of Public Services.* New York and Abingdon: Routledge. pp. 6–32.

Hirakuta, C., Rocha, M. C., Sarti, F., 2016. "Financeirização e Internacionalização no Setor de Serviços de Saúde: Impactos sobre o Brasil". *Blucher Engineering Proceedings,* 3(4), pp. 575–600.

Hooda, S., 2016. "Health in the Era of Neoliberalism: Journey from State Provisioning to Financialization". *Institute for Studies in Industrial Development Working Papers,* 196.

Horton, A., 2017. *Financialisation of Care: Investment and Organising in the UK and US.* Doctoral Thesis. Queen Mary University of London.

Huffschmid, J., 2009. "Finance as a Driver of Privatisation", in: Frangakis, M., Hermann, C., Huffschmid, J., Lorant, K. (Eds.), *Privatisation against the European Social Model.* Basingstoke and New York: Palgrave Macmillan. pp. 49–60.

Hunter, B. M., Murray, S. F., 2019. "Deconstructing the Financialization of Healthcare". Development and Change 50(5), pp. 1263–1287.

Iahn, J. F., Missio, F. J., 2009. "Uma Revisão da Macroeconomia Brasileira dos Anos 90: O Mix da Política Fiscal, Monetária e Cambial". *Pesquisa & Debate,* 20, 1(35), pp. 1–29.

Immergut, E. M., 1992. *Health Politics: Interests and Institutions in Western Europe.* New York: Cambridge University Press.

Inspection Générale des Affaires Sociales (IGAS), 2018. "La Gestion de Trésorerie de l'Agence Centrale des Organismes de Sécurité Sociale". *Rapport IGAS 2017–099R.* Paris: IGAS.

Institut de Recherche et Documentation en Economie de la Santé (IRDES), 2017. "Les Réformes Hospitalières en France : Aspects Historiques et Réglementaires". *Synthèse Documentaire IRDES, Septembre 2017.* Available at: www.irdes.fr/docume ntation/syntheses-et-dossiers-bibliographiques.html (Accessed 3 October 2020).

Institut de Recherche et Documentation en Economie de la Santé (IRDES), 2015. "Plans de réforme de l'Assurance Maladie en France". *Synthèse Documentaire IRDES, Septembre 2015.* Available at: www.irdes.fr/documentation/syntheses/la-reforme-du -systeme-de-sante-en-france.pdf (Accessed 3 October 2020).

Instituto Brasileiro de Geografia e Estatistica (IBGE), 2020a. Projeções da População 2018. Rio de Janeiro: IBGE.

Instituto Brasileiro de Geografia e Estatística (IBGE), 2020b. *Produto Interno Bruto – PIB*. Available at: www.ibge.gov.br/explica/pib.php (Accessed: 1 June 2020).

Instituto Brasileiro de Geografia e Estatística (IBGE), 2020c. Sistema de contas regionais 2018. Rio de Janeiro: IBGE.

Instituto Filantropia, 2019. *Mais Fôlego para a Saúde*. August 23. Available at: https://www.filantropia.org/informacao/mais-folego-para-a-saude (Accessed: 4 May 2020).

International Monetary Fund (IMF), 2017. *Global Financial Stability Report October 2017: Is Growth at Risk?*. World Economic and Financial Surveys. Washington D.C.: International Monetary Fund.

Iriart, C., Merhy, E. E., Waitzkin, H., 2001. "Managed Care in Latin America: Transnationalization of the Health Sector in a Context of Reform". *Social Science & Medicine*, 52, pp. 1243–1253.

Jansen, M., 2016. *Tendências e Contratendências de Mercantilização: As Reformas dos Sistemas de Saúde Alemão, Francês e Britânico*. Doctoral Thesis. Faculdade de Saúde Pública, Universidade de São Paulo.

Jarvis, T., Scott, F., El-Jardali, F., Alvarez, E., 2020. "Defining and Classifying Public Health Systems: A Critical Interpretive Synthesis". *Health Research Policy and Systems*, 18, 68.

Jomo, K. S., Chowdhury, A., 2019. "World Bank Financializing Development". *Development*, 62, pp. 147–153.

Junior, A. C. R. de O., Rosendo, A. B., Silva, E. F. da, Silva, J. C. da, Sato, S. Y., 2013. *Gestão dos Recursos da Saúde: Fundo de Saúde*. Instituto de Direito Sanitário Aplicado (IDISA). Available at: http://idisa.org.br/img/File/REFERENCIA%20PARA%20FUNDOS%20MUNICIPAIS%20DE%20SAUDE%20v2.pdf (Accessed 3 May 2020).

Junior, A. P., Mendes, A., 2015. "O Fundo Nacional de Saúde e a Prioridade da Média e Alta Complexidade". *Argumentum*, 7, pp. 161–177.

Kaltenbrunner, A., Painceira, J. P., 2018. "Subordinated Financial Integration and Financialisation in Emerging Capitalist Economies: The Brazilian Experience". *New Political Economy*, 23(3), pp. 290–313.

Karpov, K., 2015. "SES-DF: Secretaria de Saúde faz aplicação financeira com dinheiro que deveria ser usado para pagar fornecedores?" *Portal Política Distrital*, May 20. Available at: www.politicadistrital.com.br/2015/05/20/ses-df-secretaria-de-saude-faz-aplicacao-financeira-com-dinheiro-que-deveria-ser-usado-para-pagar-fornecedores/ (Accessed: 2 January 2020).

Karwowski, E., 2019. "Towards (De-)Financialisation: The Role of the State". *Cambridge Journal of Economics*, 43(4), pp. 1001–1027.

Karwowski, E., 2020. "Economic Development and Variegated Financialization in Emerging Economies", in: Mader, P., Mertens, D., Zwan, N. van der (Eds.),

The Routledge International Handbook of Financialization. Abingdon and New York: Routledge. pp. 162–176.

Karwowski, E., Shabani, M., Stockhammer, E., 2020. "Dimensions and Determinants of Financialisation: Comparing OECD Countries since 1997". *New Political Economy*, 25(6), pp. 957–977.

Karwowski, E., Stockhammer, E., 2017. "Financialisation in Emerging Economies: A Systematic Overview and Comparison with Anglo-Saxon Economies". *Economic and Political Studies*, 5(1), pp. 60–86.

Keynes, J. M., 1936. *The General Theory of Employment, Interest and Money*. London: Macmillan.

Klinge, T. J., Fernandez, R., Aalbers, M. B., 2020. "La Financiarización de las Grandes Empresas Farmacéuticas". *Revista Internacional de Sociología*, 78(4), e174.

Krippner, G., 2005. "The Financialization of the American Economy". *Socio-Economic Review*, 3(2), pp. 173–208.

La Finance pour Tous, 2019. Fiche Repères Endettement des Ménages, Édition avril 2019. Available at: www.lafinancepourtous.com/wp-content/uploads/2019/04/fiche_repere_endettement_menages.pdf (Accessed: 2 September 2020).

La Tribune, 2018. "Comment l'Assurance Maladie Compte Faire 2 Milliards d'Économies en 2019". June 29. Available at: www.latribune.fr/economie/france/comment-l-assurance-maladie-compte-faire-2-milliards-d-economies-en-2019-783571.html (Accessed: 1 June 2020).

Lagna, A., 2016. "Derivatives and the Financialization of the Italian State". *New Political Economy*, 21(2), pp. 167–186.

Lapavitsas, C., 2011. "Theorizing Financialization". *Work, Employment and Society*, 25(4), pp. 611–626.

Lapavitsas, C., 2013. *Profiting Without Producing: How Finance Exploits Us All*. London and New York: Verso.

Lapavitsas, C., Soydan, A., 2020. "Financialisation in Developing Countries: Approaches, Concepts, and Metrics". *SOAS Department of Economics Working Papers*, 240.

Laurell, A. C., 2016. "Las Reformas de Salud en América Latina: Procesos y Resultados". *Cuadernos de Relaciones Laborales*, 34(2), pp. 293–314.

Laurell, A. C., Giovanella, L., 2018. "Health Policies and Systems in Latin America". *Oxford Research Encyclopedia of Global Public Health* [online]. Available at: oxfordre.com/publichealth/view/10.1093/acrefore/9780190632366.001.0001/acrefore-9780190632366-e-60 (Accessed 20 October 2020).

Lavinas, L., 2013. "Latin America: Anti-Poverty Schemes Instead of Social Protection". *DesiguALdades.net Working Paper Series*, 51.

Lavinas, L., 2015a. "A Financeirização da Política Social: O Caso Brasileiro". *Politika*, 2, pp. 35–51.

Lavinas, L., 2015b. "New Trends in Inequality: The Financialisation of Social Policies", in: Gallas, A., Herr, H., Hoffer, F., Scherrer, C. (Eds.), *Combating Inequality: The Global North and South*. Abingdon and New York: Routledge. pp. 212–225.

Lavinas, L., 2016. "How Social Developmentalism Reframed Social Policy in Brazil". *Desigualdades Working Papers*, 94.

Lavinas, L., 2017. *The Takeover of Social Policy by Financialization: The Brazilian Paradox*. New York: Palgrave Macmillan.

Lavinas, L., 2018a. "How Financialization Challenges Social Protection Systems", in: Rodrigues, P. H. A., Santos, I. S. (Eds.), *Social Risks and Policies in Brazil and Europe: Convergences and Divergences*. Rio de Janeiro and São Paulo: Cebes and Hucitec. pp. 175–199.

Lavinas, L., 2018b. "The Collateralization of Social Policy under Financialized Capitalism". *Development and Change* 49(2), pp. 502–517.

Lavinas, L., 2020. "The Collateralization of Social Policy by Financial Markets in the Global South", in: Mader, P., Mertens, D., Zwan, N. van der (Eds.), The Routledge International Handbook of Financialization. Abingdon and New York: Routledge. pp. 312–323.

Lavinas, L., 2021. "The Anatomy of the Social Question and the Evolution of the Brazilian Social Security System, 1919–2020", in: Leisering, L. (Ed.), *One Hundred Years of Social Protection*. Cham: Palgrave Macmillan. pp. 303–341.

Lavinas, L., Araújo, E., Bruno, M., 2019. "Brazil: from Eliticized-to Mass-Based Financialization". *Revue de la Régulation* [online], 25.

Lavinas, L., Araújo, E., Gentil, D., 2020. "Revisiting Financialization Drives in Brazil: The Rise of Stock Markets". *IE-UFRJ Discussion Papers*, 029/2020.

Lavinas, L., Gentil, D., 2018. "Brasil Anos 2000: A Política Social Sob Regência da Financeirização". *Novos Estudos CEBRAP*, 37(2), pp. 191–211.

Lavinas, L., Simões, A., 2015. "Social Policy and Structural Heterogeneity in Latin America: The Turning Point of the 21st Century", in: Fritz, B., Lavinas, L. (Eds.) *A Moment of Equality for Latin America? Challenges for Redistribution*. Abingdon and New York: Routledge. pp. 77–102.

Lavoie, M., 2014. *Post-Keynesian Economics: New Foundations*. Cheltenham and Northampton: Edward Elgar.

Lazarus, J., 2017. "About the Universality of a Concept: Is There a Financialization of Daily Life in France?" *Civitas – Revista de Ciências Sociais* [online], 17(1), pp. 26–42.

Lazarus, J., Lacan, L., 2020. "Toward a Relational Sociology of Credit: An Exploration of the French Literature", *Socio-Economic Review*, 18(2), pp. 575–597.

Lazonick, W., Hopkins, M., Jacobson, K., Sakinç, M. E., Tulum, Ö., 2017. "US Pharma's Financialized Business Model". *Institute for New Economic Thinking Working Papers*, 60.

Lazzarato, M., 2012. The Making of the Indebted Man: An Essay on the Neoliberal Condition. Los Angeles: Semiotext(e).

Le Journal du Dimanche, 2017. Agnès Buzyn, Ministre de la Santé : 'Il Faut une Révolution Douce'. *Le Journal du Dimanche*, October 21.

Leis, S. V. G. de, Barbosa, P. R., Lima, S. M. L., Ugá, A. D., Portela, M. C., de Vasconcellos, M. M., 2003. "O Setor Hospitalar Filantrópico e Alguns Desafios Para as Políticas Públicas em Saúde". *Revista de Administração Pública* 37, pp. 265–284.

Lemoine, B., 2015. Les Finances Publiques à l'Épreuve de la Dette, in: Monnier, J.-M. (Ed.), *Finances Publiques*. Paris: La Documentation Française. pp. 27–41.

Lemoine, B., 2016. *L'Ordre de la Dette*. Paris: La Découverte.

Lemoine, B., 2017. "The Politics of Public Debt Financialisation: (Re)Inventing the Market for French Sovereign Bonds and Shaping the Public Debt Problem (1966–2012)", in: Buggeln, M., Daunton, M., Nützenadel, A., (Eds.), *The Political Economy of Public Finance: Taxation, State Spending and Debt since the 1970s*. Cambridge: Cambridge University Press. pp. 240–261.

Lemoine, B., 2018. "Dettes et Devoirs d'État: Les Obligations d'État entre Crédit Financier, Ordre Social et Morale Politique", in: Karsenti, B., Linhardt, D. (Eds.), *État et Société Politique: Approches Sociologiques et Philosophiques*. Paris: Editions de l'EHESS.

Lemoine, B., 2019. "Le 'Garrot d'Or' de la Dette et de la Finance se Resserre sur l'État Social". *Hypotheses – Sociologie Politique de l'Économie* [online]. Available at: spe.hypotheses.org/1159 (Accessed: 11 December 2020).

Lemoine, B., Ravelli, Q., 2017. Financiarisation et Classes Sociales : Introduction au Dossier. *Revue de la Régulation* [online], 22.

Lewalle, H., 2006. "A Look at Private Health Care Insurance in the European Union". *Revue Française des Affaires Sociales*, 6–7, pp. 133–157.

Leyshon, A., Thrift, N., 2007. "The Capitalization of Almost Everything: The Future of Finance and Capitalism". *Theory, Culture & Society*, 24(7–8), pp. 97–115.

Lima, J. B. de, 2018. "A Contrarreforma do Sistema Único de Saúde: o Caso das Organizações Sociais". *Argumentum*, 10(1), pp. 88–101.

Lima, S. M. L., Portela, M. C., Ugá, M. A. D., Barbosa, P. R., Gerschman, S., Vasconcellos, M. M., 2007. "Hospitais Filantrópicos e a Operação de Planos de Saúde Próprios no Brasil". *Revista de Saúde Pública*, 41(1), pp. 116–123.

Lo Vuolo, R., 2012. Introduction, in: Lo Vuolo, R. (Ed.), *Citizen's Income and Welfare Regimes in Latin America: From Cash Transfers to Rights*. New York: Palgrave MacMillan.

Lo Vuolo, R., 2016. *Finance, State and Social Protection Systems*. Presented at the INCT-PPED and MINDS International Conference, December 7–9, Rio de Janeiro.

Lobato, L. de V. C., Giovanella, L., 2012. "Sistemas de Saúde", in: Giovanella, L., Escorel, S., Lobato, L. de V. C., Noronha, J. C. de, Carvalho, A. I. de (Eds.), *Políticas e Sistema de Saúde no Brasil*. Rio de Janeiro: Editora FIOCRUZ. pp. 89–120.

Løding, T. H., 2018. "The Financialization of Local Governments: The Case of Financial Rationality in the Management of Norwegian Hydroelectric Utilities". *Socio-Economic Review*, 18(3), pp. 725–743.

Loxley, J., Hajer, J., 2019. "Public-Private Partnerships, Social Impact Bonds, and the Erosion of the State in Canada". *Studies in Political Economy*, 100(1), pp. 18–40.

Lustig, Y., 2014. *The Investment Assets Handbook: A Definitive Practical Guide to Asset Classes*. Hampshire: The Harriman House.

Maarse, H., 2006. "The Privatization of Health Care in Europe: An Eight-Country Analysis". *Journal of Health Politics, Policy and Law*, 31(5), pp. 981–1014.

Mackintosh, M., Koivusalo, M., 2005, "Health Systems and Commercialization: In Search of Good Sense", in: Mackintosh, M., Koivusalo, M. (Eds.), *Commercialization of Health Care: Global and Local Dynamics and Policy Responses*. Basingstoke and New York: Palgrave Macmillan. pp. 3–21.

MacMillan Dictionary, 2021. Dictionary entry for "Company". Available at: https://www.macmillandictionary.com/dictionary/british/company?q=companies (Accessed: 8 January 2021).

Macquarie Research, 2017. "The World's Largest Industry: Capital Manufacturing Capital". *Macquarie Research Reports*, May 22.

Mader, P., 2015. *The Political Economy of Microfinance: Financializing Poverty*. Basingstoke and New York: Palgrave Macmillan.

Mader, P., Mertens, D., Zwan, N. van der, 2020. "Financialization: An Introduction", in: Mader, P., Mertens, D., Zwan, N. van der (Eds.), *The Routledge International Handbook of Financialization*. Abingdon and New York: Routledge. pp. 1–16.

Martins, N., Carlos Ocké-Reis, Daniel Brach, 2021. "Financeirização dos Planos de Saúde: O Caso das Operadoras Líderes no Brasil (2007–2019)". *IE-UFRJ Discussion Papers*, 01/2021.

Marx, K., 1894. *Capital: A Critique of Political Economy, Volume 3, The Process of Capitalist Production as a Whole*. New York: International Publishers, 1967.

Massó, M., Davis, M., Abalde, N., 2020. "The Problematic Conceptualization of Financialisation: Differentiating Causes, Consequences and Socio Economic Actors' Financialised Behaviour". *Revista Internacional de Sociología*, 78(4), e169.

McDonald, D. A., Ruiters, G., 2006. "Rethinking Privatisation: Towards a Critical Theoretical Perspective". *Public Services Yearbook* 2005/2006, pp. 9–20.

Mckinley, T., 2008. Foreword, in: Bayliss, K., Fine, B. (Eds.), *Privatization and Alternative Public Sector Reform in Sub-Saharan Africa: Delivering on Electricity and Water*. Basingstoke and New York: Palgrave Macmillan. pp. XVIII–XX.

McKinsey, 2005. "$118 Trillion and Counting: Taking Stock of the World's Capital Markets". *McKinsey Global Institute Report*. Available at: www.mckinsey.com/ind ustries/private-equity-and-principal-investors/our-insights/118-trillion-and-count ing (Accessed: 30 January 2020).

Medeiros, M., Castro, F. Á. de, 2018. "A Composição da Renda no Topo da Distribuição: Evolução no Brasil entre 2006 e 2012, A Partir de Informações do Imposto de Renda". *Economia e Sociedade*, 27(2), pp. 577–605.

Mendes, A. N., 2012. *Tempos Turbulentos na Saúde Pública Brasileira: Os Impasses do Financiamento no Capitalismo Financeirizado*. Associate Professorship Thesis. Faculdade de Saúde Pública, Universidade de São Paulo.

Mendes, Á., 2019. *Do Subfinanciamento ao Desfinanciamento do SUS: A Gestão Orçamentária e Financeira*. Presented at the 33° congresso do COSEMS-SP, March 27–29, Águas de Lindoia.

Mendes, Á., Funcia, F., 2016. "O SUS e Seu Financiamento", in: Marques, R. M., Piola, S. F., Roa, A. C. (Eds.), *Sistema de Saúde No Brasil: Organização e Financiamento*. Rio de Janeiro and Brasília: ABRES, Ministério da Saúde, and OPAS/OMS. pp. 139–168.

Mendes, Á., Marques, R. M., 2009. "O Financiamento do SUS Sob os 'Ventos' da Financeirização". *Ciência & Saúde Coletiva* 14(3), pp. 841–850.

Mendez, R., Ragot, L., 2010. "Quel Avenir pour le Fonds de Réserve pour les Retraites ?". *Économie & Prévision*, 194(3), pp. 57–78.

Mercille, J., Murphy, E., 2017. "What is Privatization? A Political Economy Framework". *Environment and Planning*, 49(5), pp. 1040–1059.

Merriam-Webster Dictionary, 2021. *Finance*. Available at: www.merriam-webster.com /dictionary/finance (Accessed: 31 October 2020).

Mertens, D., 2017. "Borrowing for Social Security? Credit, Asset-Based Welfare and the Decline of the German Savings Regime". *Journal of European Social Policy*, 27(5), pp. 474–490.

Merton, R. C., 1995. "A Functional Perspective of Financial Intermediation". *Financial Management*, 24(2), pp. 23–41.

Messina, P. (Ed.), 2010. *Investments in Health Care Receivables. Legal Aspects*. Rome: Orrick, Herrington & Sutcliffe.

Messina, P., Denaro, A., 2006. *Transactions on "Raw" Healthcare Receivables in the Italian Market Practice*. Rome and Milan: Orrick's Italian Finance Group.

Ministério da Saúde, 2018. *Boas Práticas na Gestão em Parceria com o Terceiro Setor na Saúde*. Presentation from Francisco de A. Figueiredo, Secretary of Health Care. Available at: portal.tcu.gov.br/data/files/30/37/B5/6E/2BC75610C3630256E18818A8 /Requisitos%20-%20Francisco%20de%20Assis%20Figueiredo.pdf (Accessed: 1 July 2020).

Ministério da Saúde, 2019. *Relatório Anual de Gestão 2018*. Brasília: Ministério da Saúde.

Ministério Público do Estado do Rio de Janeiro (MPRJ), 2018. "Avaliação de Impactos e Abertura de Dados no Planejamento e Gestão Financeira da Saúde". Public Policy Monitoring and Supervision Report, 3rd Prosecutor's Office for Collective Health Protection of the Capital. Rio de Janeiro: MPRJ.

Modenesi, A., 2011. "Conservadorismo e Rigidez na Política Monetária: Uma Estimativa da Função de Reação do BCB (2000–2007)". *Revista de Economia Política*, 31(3), pp. 415–434.

Montalban, M., 2011. La Financiarisation des Big Pharma. *Savoir/Agir*, 16(2), pp. 13–21.

Montgomerie, J., 2006. "Giving Credit Where it's Due: Public Policy and Household Debt in the United States, the United Kingdom and Canada". *Policy and Society* 25(3), pp. 109–141.

Montgomerie, J., 2020. "Indebtedness and Financialization in Everyday Life", in: Mader, P., Mertens, D., Zwan, N. van der (Eds.), *The Routledge International Handbook of Financialization*. Abingdon and New York: Routledge. pp. 380–389.

Morais, H. M. M. de, Albuquerque, M. do S. V. de, Oliveira, R. S. de, Cazuzu, A. K. I., Silva, N. A. F. da, 2018. "Organizações Sociais da Saúde: Uma Expressão Fenomênica da Privatização da Saúde no Brasil". *Cadernos de Saúde Pública*, 34(1).

Moran, M., 2000. "Understanding the Welfare State: The Case of Health Care". *The British Journal of Politics and International Relations*, 2(2), pp. 135–160.

Morgan, M., 2015. *Income Concentration in a Context of Late Development: An Investigation of Top Incomes in Brazil Using Tax Records, 1933–2013*. Master Dissertation. Paris School of Economics.

Morgan, M., 2017. "Extreme and Persistent Inequality: New Evidence for Brazil Combining National Accounts, Surveys and Fiscal Data, 2001–2015". *WID.World Working Papers*, 2017/12.

Mulligan, J., 2016. "Insurance Accounts: The Cultural Logics of Health Care Financing". *Medical Anthropology Quarterly*, 30(1), pp. 37–61.

Nay, O., Béjean, S., Benamouzig, D., Bergeron, H., Castel, P., Ventelou, B., 2016. "Achieving Universal Health Coverage in France: Policy Reforms and the Challenge of Inequalities". *The Lancet*, 387(10034), pp. 2236–2249.

Negrão, C., Sousa, F. de O., 2018. "Medida provisória 848, de 2018". *Consultoria Legislativa da Câmara dos Deputados, Nota Descritiva*.

Nemi, A., 2020. "Charity and Philanthropy in the History of Brazilian Hospitals", in: Gorsky, M., Vilar-Rodríguez M., Pons-Pons J., *The Political Economy of the Hospital in History*. Huddersfield: University of Huddersfield Press. pp. 61–94.

Nery, N., 2005. "Auditoria do Ministério Encontra R$ 30 Milhões do Fundo de Saúde do Rio em Aplicações Financeiras". *Agência Brasil*, March 13. Available at: http://memo ria.ebc.com.br/agenciabrasil/noticia/2005-03-13/auditoria-do-ministerio-encon tra-r-30-milhoes-do-fundo-de-saude-do-rio-em-aplicacoes-financeiras (Accessed: 1 March 2020).

Neto, E. R., 1997. A Via do Parlamento, in: Fleury, S. (Ed.), *Saúde e Democracia: A Luta do Cebes*. São Paulo: Lemos Editorial. pp. 63–91.

Nugem, R. de C., Bordin, R., Schott-Pethelaz, A.-M., Michel, P., Piriou, V., 2019. "National Health Systems of Brazil and France: A Comparative Analysis", *World Journal of Advance Healthcare Research*, 3(6), pp. 50–61.

O Globo, 2015. "Santas Casas e Hospitais Filantrópicos do País têm Dívidas de pelo Menos R$17 Bilhões". *O Globo*, January 5.

Ocké-Reis, C., 2018. "Sustentabilidade do SUS e Renúncia de Arrecadação Fiscal em Saúde". *Ciência & Saúde Coletiva* 23(6), pp. 2035–2042.

Ocké-Reis, C., Santos, F. P. dos, 2011. "Mensuração dos Gastos Tributários em Saúde: 2003–2006". *Textos para Discussão IPEA*, 1637.

Oliveira, G. C., 2010. "Moeda Indexada, Indexação Financeira e as Peculiaridades da Estabilidade Monetária no Brasil". *Revista Economia Ensaios*, 24(2), p. 7–26.

Oliver, J. R., Robison, L. J., 2017. "Rationalizing Inconsistent Definitions of Commodification: A Social Exchange Perspective". *Modern Economy*, 8(11), pp. 1314–1327.

Oreiro, J. L., 2015. "Do Tripé Macroeconômico ao Fracasso da Nova Matriz: A Evolução do Regime de Política Macroeconômica no Brasil (1999–2014)". *Revista Politika*, 2, pp. 16–33.

Oreiro, J. L., Passos, M., 2005. "A Governança da Política Monetária Brasileira: Análise e Proposta de Mudança". *Indicadores Econômicos FEE*, 33(1), pp. 157–168.

Organization for Economic Co-operation and Development (OECD), 2020. Global Outlook on Financing for Sustainable Development 2021. Paris: OECD Publishing.

Organization for Economic Co-operation and Development (OECD), 2017. *Health at a Glance 2017*. Paris: OECD Publishing.

Organization for Economic Co-operation and Development (OECD), 2004. *Proposal for a Taxonomy of Health Insurance*. OECD Health Project.

Ortiz, I., Cummins, M., Capaldo, J., Karunanethy, K., 2015. "The Decade of Adjustment: A Review of Austerity Trends 2010–2020 in 187 Countries". *International Labor Organization, Extension of Social Security Working Paper Series*, 53.

Oxford University Press, 2006. *A Dictionary of Finance and Banking*. Oxford and New York: Oxford University Press.

Pagliari, S., Young, K. L., 2020. "How Financialization is Reproduced Politically", in: Mader, P., Mertens, D., Zwan, N. van der (Eds.), *The Routledge International Handbook of Financialization*. Abingdon and New York: Routledge. pp. 113–124.

Paim, J., Travassos, C., Almeida, C., Bahia, L., Macinko, J., 2011. "The Brazilian Health System: History, Advances, and Challenges". *The Lancet*, 377(9779), pp. 1778–1797.

Paiva, W. S. de, Lima, A. J. de, 2014. "A Financeirização da Saúde Pública no Brasil: Uma Análise do Subfinanciamento da Área da Saúde e da Priorização do Campo Privado na Saúde Brasileira". *Revista FSA* (*Centro Universitário Santo Agostinho*), 11(2), pp. 350–365.

Palier, B. (Ed.), 2010c. *A Long Goodbye to Bismarck? The Politics of Welfare Reforms in Continental Europe*. Amsterdam: Amsterdam University Press.

Palier, B., 2010a. "The Dualizations of the French Welfare System", in: Palier, B. (Ed.), *A Long Goodbye to Bismarck? The Politics of Welfare Reform in Continental Europe*. Amsterdam: Amsterdam University Press, pp. 73–100.

Palier, B., 2010b. "Ordering Change: Understanding the 'Bismarckian' Welfare Reform Trajectory", in: Palier, B. (Ed.), *A Long Goodbye to Bismarck? The Politics of Welfare Reforms in Continental Europe*. Amsterdam: Amsterdam University Press, pp. 19–44.

Palier, B., Hay, C., 2017. "The Reconfiguration of the Welfare State in Europe: Paying its Way in an Age of Austerity", in: Desmond, K., Le Galès, P., *Reconfiguring European States in Crisis*. Oxford University Press. pp. 331–352.

Palley, T., 1997. "The Institutionalization of Deflationary Monetary Policy", in: Cohen, A., Hagemann, H., Smithin, J. (Eds.), *Money, Financial Institutions and Macroeconomics, Recent Economic Thought Series*. Dordrecht: Springer, pp. 157–173.

Papanicolas, I., 2013. "International Frameworks for Health System Comparison", in: Papanicolas, I., Smith, P. *Health System Performance Comparison: An Agenda for Policy, Information and Research*. Berkshire and New York: Open University Press, Maidenhead, England, pp. 31–74.

Paulani, L. M., 2010. *Brazil in the Crisis of the Finance-Led Regime of Accumulation*. Review of Radical Political Economics, 42(3), pp. 363–372.

Pedras, G., 2009. "História da Dívida Pública no Brasil: de 1964 Até os Dias Atuais", in: Silva, A.C., Carvalho, L. O. de, Medeiros, O. L. de (Eds.), *Dívida Pública: A Experiência Brasileira*. Brasília: Secretaria do Tesouro Nacional.

Pereira, B. L. S., 2013. *Os Fundos Municipais de Saúde: Uma Análise dos Municípios das Capitais Brasileiras*. Master Dissertation. Faculdade de Ciências da Saúde, Universidade de Brasília.

Petit, P., 2020. "Understanding the Endogenous Nature of This Health Crisis". *Open Democracy*. Available at: www.opendemocracy.net/en/can-europe-make-it/understanding-endogenous-nature-health-crisis (Accessed 5 August 2020).

Pinto, É., 2008. "Seis Vezes DRU: Flexibilidade Orçamentária ou Esvaziamento de Direitos Sociais?" *De Jure – Revista Jurídica do Ministério Público do Estado de Minas Gerais*, 11, pp. 511–537.

Piola, S. F., Ribeiro, J. A. C., Reis, C.O.O., 2000. Financiamento das políticas sociais: o caso do Ministério da Saúde. Revista do Serviço Público 51, 74–98.

Piola, S. F., Benevides, R., Vieira, F., 2018. "Consolidação do Gasto com Ações e Serviços Públicos de Saúde: Trajetória e Percalços no Período de 2003 a 2017". *Textos para discussão IPEA*, 2439.

Piola, S. F., Barros, M. E., 2016. "O Financiamento dos Serviços de Saúde no Brasil", in: Marques, R. M., Piola, S. F., Roa, A. C. (Eds.), *Sistema de Saúde No Brasil: Organização e Financiamento*. Rio de Janeiro and Brasília: ABRES, Ministério da Saúde, and OPAS/OMS. pp. 101–138.

Pires, M., de Oliveira, R., de Alcantara, C., Abbas, K., 2017. "A Relação Entre a Remuneração do Sistema Único de Saúde, os Custos dos Procedimentos Hospitalares e o Resultado: Estudo nas Santas Casas de Misericórdia do Estado de São Paulo". *RAHIS – Revista de Administração Hospitalar e Inovação em Saúde*, 14(3), pp. 16–33.

Pitombo, M. A., 2015. *A Eficácia da Desvinculação de Receitas da União na Centralização de Receitas Tributárias*. Undergraduate Dissertation. Instituto de Economia, Universidade Federal do Rio de Janeiro.

Plihon, D., 2003. "Les Mutations du Capitalisme en France : Le Rôle de la Finance". *Les Notes De L'IFRI*, 50.

Plihon, D., 2019. "Les Dangers de la Financiarisation", in: Fondation Copernic, *Manuel Indocile de Sciences Sociales*. Paris: La Découverte.

Pollock, A., Shaoul, J., Vickers, N., 2002. "Private Finance and 'Value for Money' in NHS Hospitals: A Policy in Search of a Rationale?" *The British Medical Journal*, 324, pp. 1205–1209.

Ponciano, J., Hansen, S., 2019. "The World's Largest Public Companies 2019: Global 2000 By the Numbers". *Forbes Website*. Available at: www.forbes.com/sites/jonat hanponciano/2019/05/15/worlds-largest-companies-2019-global-2000/#7b5385614 ada (Accessed: 20 December19).

Popic, T., 2020. "European Health Systems and COVID-19: Some Early Lessons". *LSE European Politics and Policy (EUROPP) blog*. Available at: blogs.lse.ac.uk/europ-pblog/2020/03/20/european-health-systems-and-covid-19-some-early-lessons/ (Accessed: 3 January 2021).

Portal da Transparência, 2021. Despesa Pública. Available at: www.portaltransparen cia.gov.br/despesas (Accessed: 3 March 2021).

Porter, D., 1999. *Health, Civilization and the State: A History of Public Health from Ancient to Modern Times*. London and New York: Routledge.

Powell, J., 2013. *Subordinate Financialisation: a Study of Mexico and its Non-Financial Corporations*. Doctoral Thesis. SOAS, University of London.

Powell, J., 2018. "Towards a Marxist theory of Financialised Capitalism". *Greenwich Papers in Political Economy*, GPERC62.

Prainsack, B., 2020. The Value of Healthcare Data: To Nudge, or Not? *Policy Studies*, 41(5), pp. 547–562.

Prante, F., Bramucci, A., Truger, A., 2020. Decades of Tight Fiscal Policy Have Left the Health Care System in Italy Ill-Prepared to Fight the COVID-19 Outbreak. *Intereconomics*, 55(3), pp. 147–152.

Preker, A., Harding, A., 2003. "The Economics of Hospital Reform: From Hierarchical to Market-Based Incentives". *World Hospitals and Health Services Journal*, 39(3), p. 3–10.

Preunkert, J., 2017. "Financialization of Government Debt? European Government Debt Management Approaches 1980–2007". *Competition & Change*, 21(1), pp. 27–44.

Previdência Social, 2000. "O Perfil dos Não-Contribuintes da Previdência Social". *Informe de Previdência Social*, 12.

Quinn, S., 2017. "'The Miracles of Bookkeeping': How Budget Politics Link Fiscal Policies and Financial Markets". *American Journal of Sociology* 123(1), pp. 48–85.

Rabinovich, J., Artica, R., 2020. "Cash Holdings and the Financialisation of Latin American Nonfinancial Corporations". *SSRN Eletronic Journal*, ID 3535445.

Receita Federal, 2009–2017. *Demonstrativos dos Gastos Tributários 2010–2018 – Previsões PLOA*. Brasília: Secretaria da Receita Federal do Brasil.

Receita Federal, 2016. *Demonstrativos dos Gastos Tributários 2017 – Previsões PLOA*. Brasília: Secretaria da Receita Federal do Brasil.

Reibling, N., Ariaans, M., Wendt, C., 2019. "Worlds of Healthcare: A Healthcare System Typology of OECD Countries". *Health Policy*, 123(7), pp. 611–620.

Reis, T. B., 2018. "Why Are Policy Real Interest Rates So High In Brazil? An Analysis of the Determinants of the Central Bank of Brazil's Real Interest Rate". *International Journal of Political Economy* 47(2), pp. 178–198.

Rio de Janeiro, 1989. *Lei 1.512, de 25 agosto de 1989*.

Rio de Janeiro, 2016. *Decreto 45.692, de 17 de junho de 2016*.

Rio de Janeiro, 2020. *Portal Transparência Fiscal*. Governo do Estado do Rio de Janeiro. Available at: www.transparencia.rj.gov.br/transparencia/ (Accessed: 3 March 2020).

Roberts, A., 2016. "Household Debt and the Financialization of Social reproduction: Theorizing the UK Housing and Hunger Crises", in: Soederberg, S. (Ed.), *Risking Capitalism, Research in Political Economy, Volume 31*. Bingley: Emerald Group Publishing. pp. 135–164.

Roemer, M., 1993. "National Health Systems throughout the World". *Annual Review of Public Health*, 14(1), pp. 335–353.

Romero, M., Vervynckt, M., 2017. "Unpacking the Dangerous Illusions of PPPs", in: Kishimoto, S., Petitjean, O. (Eds.), *Reclaiming Public Services: How Cities and Citizens Are Turning Back Privatization*. Amsterdam and Paris: Transnational Institute, pp. 104–116.

Rothgang, H., 2010a. "Conceptual Framework of the Study", in: Rothgang, H., Cacace, M., Frisina, L., Grimmeisen, S., Schmid, A., Wendt, C. (Eds.), *The State and Healthcare*. Basingstoke and New York: Palgrave Macmillan. pp. 10–22.

Rothgang, H., 2010b. "Introduction to the Book", in: Rothgang, H., Cacace, M., Frisina, L., Grimmeisen, S., Schmid, A., Wendt, C. (Eds.), The State and Healthcare. Basingstoke and New York: Palgrave Macmillan. pp. 3–10.

Rothgang, H., Cacace, M., Grimmeisen, S., Wendt, C., 2005. "The Changing Role of the State in Healthcare Systems". *European Review* 13(S1), pp. 187–212.

Rowden, R., 2019. *From the Washington Consensus to the Wall Street Consensus: The Financialization Initiative of the World Bank and Multilateral Development Banks.* Washington D.C.: Heinrich Böll Stiftung North America.

Ruckert, A., Labonté, R., Parker, R., 2015. Global Healthcare Policy and the Austerity Agenda, in: Kuhlmann, E., Blank, R., Bourgeault, I., Wendt, C. (Eds.), *The Palgrave International Handbook of Healthcare Policy and Governance.* Basingstoke and New York: Palgrave Macmillan. pp. 37–53.

Ruckert, I., Borsatto, M., 1999. "Política Fiscal: FMI Pressiona para o Ajuste". *Indicadores Econômicos FEE*, 26, pp. 80–96.

Ryan, S., Young, M., 2018. "Social Impact Bonds: The Next Horizon of Privatization". *Studies in Political Economy*, 99(1), pp. 42–58.

Salvador, E., 2010. *Fundo público e Seguridade Social no Brasil.* São Paulo: Cortez Editora.

Salvador, E., 2015. "As Consequências das Renúncias Tributárias no Financiamento da Seguridade Social no Brasil". *Revista Política Social e Desenvolvimento*, 19, 8–23.

Salvador, E., 2017. "O Desmonte do Financiamento da Seguridade Social em Contexto de Ajuste Fiscal". *Serviço Social & Sociedade*, 130, pp. 426–446.

Salvador, E., 2020. "Disputa do Fundo Público em Tempos de Pandemia no Brasil". *Textos & Contextos (Porto Alegre)*, 19(2), e39326.

Sanches, O., 2002. "Fundos Federais: Origens, Evolução e Situação Atual na Administração Federal". *Revista de Informação Legislativa*, 39(154), pp. 269–299.

Sarlat, G., 2009. "Marchés Financiers, Protection Sociale et Assurance Maladie", in: *Traité d'Économie et de Gestion de la Santé.* Paris: Presses de Sciences Po. pp. 543–550.

Sarlat, G., 2012. "Marchés Financiers et Protection Sociale". *Les Tribunes de la Santé*, 36(3), 41–46.

Savas, E.S., 2000. *Privatization and Public-Private Partnerships.* New York: Chatham House.

Sawyer, M., 2009. "Theoretical Approaches to Explaining and Understanding Privatisation", in: Frangakis, M., Hermann, C., Huffschmid, J., Lorant, K. (Eds.), *Privatisation against the European Social Model.* Basingstoke and New York: Palgrave Macmillan. pp. 61–76.

Schick, A., 2013. "Reflections on Two Decades of Public Financial Management Reforms", in: Cangiano, M., Curristine, T. R., Lazare, M. (Eds.), *Public Financial Management and Its Emerging Architecture.* Washington D.C.: International Monetary Fund. pp. 21–78.

Schrecker, T., 2020. "Globalization and Health: Political Grand Challenges". *Review of International Political Economy*, 27(1), 26–47.

Schwan, M., Trampusch, C., Fastenrath, F., 2020. "Financialization of, Not by the State. Exploring Changes in the Management of Public Debt and Assets across Europe". *Review of International Political Economy*, 28(4), pp. 820–842.

Sciré, C. D. de O., 2011. "Financeirização da Pobreza: Crédito e Endividamento no Âmbito das Práticas Populares de Consumo". *Teoria & Pesquisa: Revista de Ciência Política*, 20(1), pp. 65–78.

Secretaria de Estado de Fazenda – RJ (SEF-RJ), 2015. *Contas de Governo, Exercício 2014*. Available at:www.fazenda.rj.gov.br/contabilidade/faces/menu-contabilidade /prestacao-contas/prestacao-contas-anuais (Accessed on: 2 January 2020). Rio de Janeiro: SEF.

Secretaria de Estado de Fazenda – RJ (SEF-RJ), 2017. *Contas de Governo, Exercício 2016*. Available at: www.fazenda.rj.gov.br/contabilidade/faces/menu-contabilid ade/prestacao-contas/prestacao-contas-anuais (Accessed on: 2 January 2020). Rio de Janeiro: SEF.

Secretaria de Estado de Fazenda – RJ (SEF-RJ), 2018. *Contas de Governo, Exercício 2017*. Available at:www.fazenda.rj.gov.br/contabilidade/faces/menu-contabilidade /prestacao-contas/prestacao-contas-anuais (Accessed on: 2 January 2020). Rio de Janeiro: SEF.

Secretaria do Tesouro Nacional (STN), 2017. *Aspectos Fiscais da Seguridade Social no Brasil*. Brasília: STN.

Secretaria Fiscal de Controle (SFC), 2014. *Relatório de Auditoria Anual de Contas nº 201406322*. Coordenação-Geral de Auditoria da Área de Saúde. Unidade Auditada: Diretoria Executiva do Fundo Nacional de Saúde Brasília – DF. Exercício de 2013. Brasília SFC.

Secretaria Fiscal de Controle (SFC), 2017. *Relatório de Avaliação dos Resultados da Gestão nº 201702011*. Coordenação-Geral de Auditoria da Área de Saúde. Unidade Auditada: Secretaria Executiva do Ministério da Saúde, Exercício de 2016. Brasília SFC.

Seddon, J., Currie, W., 2017. "Healthcare Financialisation and the Digital Divide in the European Union: Narrative and Numbers". *Information & Management*, 54(8), pp. 1084–1096.

Sell, S., 2019. "21st-Century Capitalism: Structural Challenges for Universal Health Care". Globalization and Health, 15(1), pp. 1–9.

Sen, A., 1992. *Inequality Reexamined*. New York: Oxford University Press.

Sen, A., 2004. "Why Health equity?", in: Anand, S., Peter, F., Sen, A. (Eds.), *Public Health, Ethics, and Equity*. New York: Oxford University Press. pp. 21–33.

Senado Federal, 2015. *Projeto de Lei 623, de 2015*.

Senado Federal, 2018. *Comissão de Assuntos Sociais. Parecer 60/2018: Avaliação da Política de Atenção Hospitalar e da Contratualização dos Hospitais Filantrópicos no*

Sistema Único de Saúde. SF/18687.17508-02. Available at: legis.senado.leg.br/sdleg -getter/documento?dm=7892130&ts=1553268734420&disposition=inline (Accessed 3 March 2020).

Senado Federal, 2020. Pronunciamento de Marcelo Crivella em 24 de março durante a 23ª Sessão Deliberativa Ordinária no Senado Federal. *Diário do Senado Federal, 43/ 2004.* Available at: https://www25.senado.leg.br/web/atividade/pronunciamentos /-/p/pronunciamento/344926 (Accessed: 3 March 2020).

Senado Notícias, 2020. *Entenda o Assunto: DRU.* Available at: www12.senado.leg.br /noticias/entenda-o-assunto/dru (Accessed: 14 September 2020).

Sénat, 2020. *Comptes Rendus de la Commission des Affaires Sociales du Mardi 23 juin 2020.* Paris: Sénat.

Sengupta, A., 2013. "Universal Health Coverage: Beyond Rhetoric". *Municipal Services Project Occasional Papers, 20.*

Serapioni, M., Tesser, C., 2020. "O Sistema de Saúde Brasileiro Ante a Tipologia Internacional: Uma Discussão Prospectiva e Inevitável". *Saúde Debate,* 43(spe5), pp. 44–57.

Serra, J., 2018. "A Saúde na Emergência". *Estadão,* April 12.

Serrano, F., Summa, R., 2011. "Política Macroeconômica, Crescimento e Distribuição de Renda na Economia Brasileira dos Anos 2000". *Observatório da Economia Global,* 6.

Sestelo, J., 2017a. *Planos e Seguros de Saúde do Brasil de 2000 a 2015 e a Dominância financeira.* Doctoral Thesis. Instituto de Estudos de Saúde Coletiva, Universidade Federal do Rio de Janeiro.

Sestelo, J., 2017b. "Fica uma Sensação de Déjà-Vu, Volta e Meia tem lá um Programa de Socorro às Santas Casas". Interview by Maíra Mathias (EPSJV/Fiocruz) on September 15. Available at: https://www.epsjv.fiocruz.br/noticias/entrevista/fica -uma-sensacao-de-deja-vu-volta-e-meia-tem-la-um-programa-de-socorro-santas (Accessed: 15 October 2015).

Sestelo, J., 2018. "Dominância Financeira na Assistência à Saúde: a Ação Política do Capital Sem Limites no Século XXI". *Ciência & Saúde Coletiva,* 23(6), pp. 2027–2034.

Sestelo, J., Cardoso, A.M., Braga, I.F., Mattos, L.V., Andrietta, L.S., 2017. "A Financeirização das Políticas Sociais e da Saúde no Brasil do Século XXI: Elementos para uma Aproximação Inicial". *Economia e Sociedade,* 26(spe), pp. 1097–1126.

Sharon, T., 2018. "When Digital Health Meets Digital Capitalism, How Many Common Goods are at Stake?" *Big Data & Society,* 5(2).

Sharon, T., 2020. "Blind-Sided by Privacy? Digital Contact Tracing, the Apple/ Google API and Big Tech's Newfound Role as Global Health Policy Makers". *Ethics and Information Technology.* Available at: https://link.springer.com/article/10 .1007%2Fs10676-020-09547-x (Accessed: 3 May 2020).

Silva, E. F., 2017. "Evolução da Economia do Estado do Rio de Janeiro na Segunda Década do Século XXI". *Câmara dos Deputados, Estudos Técnicos*, 12/2017.

Silvestre, S. R., 2020. "Cessão de Direitos Creditórios do SUS: Perspectiva Regulatória de Utilização como Garantia em Contrato de Mútuo Bancário". *Portal Migalhas*, March 18. Available at: https://www.migalhas.com.br/depeso/321960/cessao-de-direitos -creditorios-do-sus--perspectiva-regulatoria-de-utilizacao-como-garantia-em -contrato-de-mutuo-bancario (Accessed 30 January 2021).

Simonet, D., 2011. "The New Public Management Theory and the Reform of European Health Care Systems: An International Comparative Perspective". *International Journal of Public Administration*, 34(12), pp. 815–826.

Sistema de Informações sobre Orçamentos Públicos em Saúde (SIOPS), 2019. *Demonstrativos/Dados informados*. Available at: https://antigo.saude.gov.br /repasses-financeiros/siops/demonstrativos-dados-informados (Accessed: 30 January 2020).

Sistema Nacional de Auditoria (SNA), 2012. *Departamento Nacional de Auditoria do SUS, Auditoria 8079*. Brasília: Sistema Nacional de Auditoria.

Soederberg, S., 2014. *Debtfare States and the Poverty Industry: Money, Discipline and the Surplus Population*. Abingdon and New York: Routledge.

Sokol, M., 2017. Financialisation, Financial Chains and Uneven Geographical Development: Towards a Research Agenda. *Research in International Business and Finance*, 39, pp. 678–685.

Solla, J., Chioro, A., 2012. "Atenção Ambulatorial Especializada", in: Giovanella, L., Escorel, S., Lobato, L. de V. C., Noronha, J. C. de, Carvalho, A. I. de (Eds.), *Políticas e Sistema de Saúde no Brasil*. Rio de Janeiro: Editora FIOCRUZ. pp. 547–576.

Souza, L., Paim, J. S., Teixeira, C. F., Bahia, L., Guimarães, R., Almeida-Filho, N. de, Machado, C. V., Campos, G. W., Azevedo-e-Silva, G., 2019. "The Current Challenges of the Fight for a Universal Right to Health in Brazil". *Ciência & Saúde Coletiva*, 24(8), 2783–2792.

Starr, P., 1988. "The Meaning of Privatization". *Yale Law & Policy Review*, 6(1), pp. 6–41.

Stein, F., Sridhar, D., 2018. The Financialisation of Global Health. Wellcome Open Research 3.

Stockhammer, E., 2004. "Financialisation and the Slowdown of Accumulation". *Cambridge Journal of Economics*, 28(5), pp. 719–741.

Stockhammer, E., 2008. "Some Stylized Facts on the Finance-Dominated Accumulation Regime". *Competition & Change*, 12(2), pp. 189–207.

Storm, S., 2018. "Financialization and Economic Development: A Debate on the Social Efficiency of Modern Finance". *Development and Change*, 49(2), pp. 302–329.

Streeck, W., 2013. "The Politics of Public Debt: Neoliberalism, Capitalist Development, and the Restructuring of the State". *MPIfG (Max Planck Institute for the Study of Societies) Discussion Papers*, 13/7.

Streeck, W., 2014. *Buying Time: The Delayed Crisis of Democratic Capitalism*. London and Brooklyn: Verso.

Stuckler, D., Feigl, A. B., Basu, S., McKee, M., 2010. *The Political Economy of Universal Health Coverage*. Background Paper for the Global Symposium on Health Systems Research, November 16–19, Montreux.

Swedish International Development Cooperation Agency (SIDA), 2004. *Financial Sector Development*. Stockholm: SIDA.

Swyngedouw, E., Kaika, M., Castro, E., 2002. "Urban Water: A Political-Ecology Perspective". *Built Environment*, 28(2), pp. 124–137.

Szendy, P., 2020. "Infinance, or Narration and Solvency". *differences* 31(3), pp. 1–11.

Tadjeddine, Y., 2018. "Financial Services: A Collection of Arrangements", in: Chambost, I., Lenglet, M., Tadjeddine, Y. (Eds.), *The Making of Finance: Perspectives from the Social Sciences*. Abingdon and New York: Routledge. pp. 17–23.

Tansey, R., 2017. "The Creeping Privatisation of Healthcare". *Corporate Europe Observatory*, June 2. Available at: https://corporateeurope.org/en/power-lobb ies/2017/06/creeping-privatisation-healthcare (Accessed: 7 January 2020).

Tansey, R., Hoedeman, O., Ainger, K., Haar, K., 2021. *When The Market Becomes Deadly: How Pressures Towards Privatisation of Health and Long-Term Care Put Europe on a Poor Footing for a Pandemic*. Brussels: Corporate Europe Observatory.

Tchiombiano, S., 2019. "Public Health, Private Approach: The Global Fund and the Involvement of Private Actors in Global Health". *Face à Face*, 15.

Tesouro Nacional, 2018. *Despesas por Função do Governo Central, Classificação COFOG, 2015–2017*. Brasília: STN.

Tesouro Nacional, 2019a. *Histórico das Instituições Financeiras Credenciadas para Atuar como Dealers da CODIP/STN*. Available at: https://cdn.tesouro.gov.br/sistemas-inter nos///apex//desenv//sistemas//thot//arquivos//publicacoes/33849_1135461/ane xos/9120_1114578/Dealers%20-%20Hist%C3%B3rico%20-%20ago20.pdf?v=4523 (Accessed: 15 December 2020).

Tesouro Nacional, 2019b. *Dívida Pública Federal: Relatório Anual 2018*. Brasília: STN.

Tesouro Nacional, 2020. *Despesas da União, Séries Históricas, Despesa por Função*. Available at: www.tesourotransparente.gov.br/publicacoes/despesas-da-uniao-ser ies-historicas/2019/11 (Accessed: 15 December 2020).

Thomas, C., 2019. "The 'Make Do and Mend' Health Service: Solving the NHS' Capital Crisis". *Institute for Public Policy Research Publications*, September 2019.

Thomson, F., Dutta, S., 2015. Financialisation: A Primer. Amsterdam: Transnational Institute.

Titmuss, R., 1956. *The Social Division of Welfare*. Liverpool: Liverpool University Press.

Toth, F., 2016. "Classification of Healthcare Systems: Can We Go Further?", *Health Policy*, 120(5), pp. 535–543.

Tribunal de Contas da União (TCU), 2007. *Relatório e Pareceres Prévios Sobre as Contas do Governo da República, Exercício de 2006*. Brasília: TCU.

Tribunal de Contas da União (TCU), 2010. *Orientações para Conselheiros de Saúde*. Brasília: TCU.

Tribunal de Contas do Distrito Federal (TCDF), 2019. *Relatório Analítico e Parecer Prévio sobre as Contas do Governo do Distrito Federal, Exercício 2018*. Brasília: TCDF.

Tulchinsky, T., Varavikova, E., 2014. *The New Public Health*. San Diego: Elsevier, Academic Press.

Ugá, M., Lima, S., Portela, M., Vasconcellos, M., Barbosa, P., Gerschman, S., 2008. "Uma Análise das Operadoras de Planos Próprios de Saúde dos Hospitais Filantrópicos no Brasil". *Cadernos de Saúde Pública*, 24(1), pp. 157–168.

United Nations (UN), 2009. System of National Accounts 2008. New York: European Communities, International Monetary Fund, Organisation for Economic Co-operation and Development, United Nations and World Bank.

United Nations (UN), 2018. *Extreme Poverty and Human Rights*. Note by the Secretary-General. UN General Assembly, Seventy-Third Session, Agenda Item 74 (b). Available at: https://undocs.org/A/74/493 (Accessed: 15 July 2020).

United Nations (UN), 2018. *Promoting Inclusion through Social Protection: Report on the World Social Situation 2018*. New York: United Nations.

United Nations Children's Fund (UNICEF), 2019. *30 Anos da Convenção Sobre os Direitos da Criança: Avanços e Desafios para Meninas e Meninos no Brasil*. São Paulo: UNICEF.

Vahabi, M., Batifoulier, P., Silva, N. da, 2020. "A Theory of Predatory Welfare State and Citizen Welfare: the French Case", *Public Choice*, 182(3), pp. 233–242.

Vaittinen, T., Hoppania, H.-K., Karsio, O., 2018. "Marketization, Commodification and Privatization of Care Services", in: Elias, J., Roberts, A., *Handbook on the International Political Economy of Gender*. Cheltenham and Northampton: Edward Elgar.

Vallin, J., Meslé, F., 2006. "Origine des Politiques de Santé", in: Caselli, G., Vallin, J., Wunsch, G. (Eds). *Démographie : Analyse et Synthèse VII, Histoire des Idées et Politiques de Population*. Paris : Institut National d'Études Démographiques.

Valor Econômico, 2018. "Temer Libera Uso do FGTS por Santas Casas e Hospitais Filantrópicos". *Valor Econômico*, August 16.

Valor Econômico, 2019. "Saúde Intensifica Busca de Recursos no Mercado de Capitais". *Valor Econômico*, September 27.

Van der Zwan, N. van der, 2014. "Making Sense of Financialization". *Socio-Economic Review*, 12(1), pp. 99–129.

Vural, I. E., 2017. "Financialisation in Health Care: An Analysis of Private Equity Fund Investments in Turkey". *Social Science & Medicine*, 187, pp. 276–286.

Wang, Y., 2015. "The Rise of the 'Shareholding State': Financialization of Economic Management in China". *Socio-Economic Review*, 13(3), pp. 603–625.

Wang, Y., 2020. "Financialization and State Transformations", in: Mader, P., Mertens, D., Zwan, N. van der (Eds.), *The Routledge International Handbook of Financialization*. Abingdon and New York: Routledge. pp. 188–199.

Weber, B., 2020. "Reforming Money to Fix Financialization?", in: Mader, P., Mertens, D., Zwan, N. van der (Eds.), *The Routledge International Handbook of Financialization*. Abingdon and New York: Routledge. pp. 458–467.

Weisbrot, M., Johnston, J., Carrillo, J. V., 2017. "Brazil's Enormous Interest Rate Tax: Can Brazilians Afford It?". *Center for Economic and Policy Research (CEPR) Reports*, April 2017.

Wendt, C., 2009. "Mapping European Healthcare Systems: A Comparative Analysis of financing, Service Provision and Access to Healthcare". *Journal of European Social Policy*, 19(5), pp. 432–445.

Wendt, C., Frisina, L., Rothgang, H., 2009. "Healthcare System Types: A Conceptual Framework for Comparison". *Social Policy & Administration*, 43(1), pp. 70–90.

Whitfield, D., 2006. "A Typology of Privatisation and Marketisation". *European Services Strategy Unit (ESSU) Research Reports*, 1.

Whitfield, D., 2015. "Alternative to Private Finance of the Welfare State: A Global Analysis of Social Impact Bond, Pay-for-Success and Development Impact Bond Project". *Australian Workplace Innovation and Social Research Centre (WISeR) reports*, catalogue 2015.24.

Wijburg, G., Waldron, R., 2020. Financialised Privatisation, Affordable Housing and Institutional Investment: The Case of England. *Critical Housing Analysis*, 7(1), pp. 114–129.

World Health Organization (WHO), 2000. *The World Health Report*. Geneva: WHO.

World Health Organization (WHO), 2005. Sustainable Health Financing, Universal Coverage and Social Health Insurance. World Health Assembly Resolution 58, 139–140.

World Health Organization (WHO), 2010a. *Monitoring the Building Blocks of Health Systems: A Handbook of Indicators and Their Measurement Strategies*. Geneva: World Health Organization.

World Health Organization (WHO), 2010b. *Health Systems Financing: The Path to Universal Coverage (The World Health Report 2010)*. Geneva: World Health Organization.

World Health Organization (WHO), 2015. *Tracking Universal Health Coverage: First Global Monitoring Report*. Geneva: WHO.

World Health Organization (WHO), 2017. *Tracking Universal Health Coverage: 2017 Global Monitoring Report.* Geneva: WHO.

World Health Organization (WHO), 2020. Global Health Observatory Data Repository. Available at: www.who.int/data/gho (Accessed: 17 February 2021).

World Health Organization (WHO), 2022. *WHO Coronavirus (COVID-19) Dashboard.* Available at: covid19.who.int/info (Accessed 29 August 2022).

Yi, I., Koechlein, E., Filho, A. de N. "Introduction: The Universalization of Health Care in Emerging Economies", in: Yi, I. (Ed.), 2017. *Towards Universal Health Care in Emerging Economies. Social Policy in a Development Context.* London: Palgrave Macmillan. pp. 1–26.

Yilmaz, V., 2017. *The Politics of Healthcare Reform in Turkey.* Cham: Palgrave Macmillan.

Zatta, F. N., Freire, V. de L., H., de Castro, M. L., Coser, M. B., Sgarbi, A. D., Lopes, A. B., 2003. *Filantropia: Um Estudo de caso numa Instituição Hospitalar Brasileira.* Presented at the VIII Congreso Del Instituto Internacional de Costos, November 26–28, Punta del Este.

Index